William Cobbett, Pitt Cobbett

Rural rides during the Years 1821 to 1832

With economical and political Observations.

William Cobbett, Pitt Cobbett

Rural rides during the Years 1821 to 1832
With economical and political Observations.

ISBN/EAN: 9783337079499

Printed in Europe, USA, Canada, Australia, Japan

Cover: Foto ©ninafisch / pixelio.de

More available books at **www.hansebooks.com**

RURAL RIDES

In the Counties of

SURREY, KENT, SUSSEX, HANTS, BERKS, OXFORD,
BUCKS, WILTS, SOMERSET, GLOUCESTER, HEREFORD,
SALOP, WORCESTER, STAFFORD, LEICESTER,
HERTFORD, ESSEX, SUFFOLK, NORFOLK,
CAMBRIDGE, HUNTINGDON, NOTTINGHAM, LINCOLN,
YORK, LANCASTER, DURHAM, AND
NORTHUMBERLAND,

DURING THE YEARS 1821 TO 1832;

With Economical and Political Observations.

BY THE LATE

WILLIAM COBBETT,
M.P. FOR OLDHAM.

A NEW EDITION, WITH NOTES,

BY

PITT COBBETT,
VICAR OF CROFTON, HANTS.

VOL. II.

LONDON
REEVES AND TURNER
1908

[All rights reserved]

RURAL RIDES, &c.

—o—

RIDE, FROM BURGHCLERE TO PETERSFIELD.

Hurstbourne Tarrant (or Uphusband),
Monday, 7th November, 1825.

We came off from Burghclere yesterday afternoon, crossing Lord Carnarvon's park, going out of it on the west side of Beacon Hill, and sloping away to our right over the downs towards Woodcote. The afternoon was singularly beautiful. The downs (even the poorest of them) are perfectly green : the sheep on the downs look, this year, like fatting sheep ; we came through a fine flock of ewes, and, looking round us, we saw, all at once, seven flocks, on different parts of the downs, each flock on an average, containing at least 500 sheep.

It is about six miles from Burghclere to this place ; and, we made it about twelve ; not in order to avoid the turnpike-road ; but, because we do not ride about to *see* turnpike-roads ; and, moreover, because I had seen this most monstrously hilly turnpike-road before. We came through a village called Woodcote, and another, called Binley. I never saw any inhabited places more recluse than these. Yet into these, the all-searching eye of the taxing Thing reaches. Its Exciseman can tell it, what is doing even in the little odd corner of Binley ; for even there I saw, over the door of a place, not half so good as the place in which my fowls roost, " *Licensed to deal in tea and tobacco.*" Poor, half-starved wretches of Binley ! The hand of taxation, the collection for the sinecures and pensions, must fix its nails even in them, who really appeared too miserable to be called by the name of *people.* Yet there was one whom the taxing Thing had licensed (good God! *licensed!*) to serve out cat-lap to these wretched creatures![1] And, our impudent and ignorant newspaper scribes, talk of the *degraded state of the people of Spain!* Impudent impostors! Can they show a group so wretched, so miserable, so truly enslaved as this, in all Spain? No: and those of them who are not sheer fools know it well. But, there would have been misery equal to this in Spain, if the Jews and Jobbers could have carried the Bond-scheme into effect. The people of Spain were, through the instrumentality of patriot-loan makers, within an inch of being made as "enlightened" as the poor, starving things of Binley. They would soon have had people "licensed" to make them pay the Jews for permission to chew tobacco, or to have a light in their dreary abodes. The people of Spain were preserved from this by the French army, for which the Jews cursed the French army; and the same army put an end to those "bonds," by means of which *pious* Protestants hoped to be able to get at the convents in Spain, and thereby put down "idolatry" in that country. These bonds seem now not to

---

[1] Tea is supposed to have been first introduced into Europe by the Dutch A.D. 1610. It was rarely used in England until 1657, at which time it was sold for £6, and even £10, per lb. From 1660 to 1689, a duty was levied on the drink made with tea, at the rate of 8d. per gallon; but at the latter date a duty of 5s. per lb. (together with 5 per cent. *ad valorem*) was levied. For many years the duties, although continually changed, were always very high, and were levied both by the Customs and the Excise. In 1836 one uniform rate of 2s. 1d. per lb was levied. In 1865 the duty was reduced to 6d. per lb., at which it still remains. Licences to sell tea were abolished in 1869.

The consumption of tea in 1881 was as follows :—

	Millions lbs.	Oz. per inhabitant.
Great Britain	167	73
United States	72	21
Australia	14	81
Russia	37	7
Various	114	...
Total,	404	

be worth a farthing; and so, after all, the Spanish people will have no one " licensed " by the Jews to make them pay for turning the fat of their sheep into candles and soap. These poor creatures that I behold here, *pass their lives amidst flocks of sheep ;* but, never does a morsel of mutton enter their lips. A labouring man told me, at Binley, that he had not tasted meat since harvest; and his looks vouched for the statement. Let the Spaniards come and look at this poor, shotten-herring of a creature: and then let them estimate what is due to a set of "enlightening" and loan-making "patriots." Old Fortescue says that " the English are clothed in good woollens " throughout," and that they have " plenty of flesh of all sorts "to eat." Yes; but at this time, the nation was not mortgaged. The " enlightening " Patriots would have made Spain what England now is. The people must never more, after a few years, have tasted mutton, though living surrounded with flocks of sheep.

Easton, near Winchester,
Wednesday Evening, 9th Nov.

I intended to go from Uphusband to Stonehenge, thence to Old Sarum, and thence through the New Forest, to Southampton and Botley, and thence across into Sussex, to see Up-Park and Cowdry House. But, then, there must be no loss of time: I must adhere to a certain route as strictly as a regiment on a march. I had written the route: and Laverstock, after seeing Stonehenge and Old Sarum, was to be the resting-place of yesterday (Tuesday): but when it came, it brought rain with it after a white frost on Monday. It was likely to rain again to-day. It became necessary to change the route, as I must get to London by a certain day; and so the first day, on the new route, brought us here.

I had been three times at Uphusband before, and had, as my readers will, perhaps, recollect, described the bourn here, or the *brook*. It has, in general, no water at all in it, from August to March. There is the bed of a little river; but no water. In March, or thereabouts, the water begins to boil up, in thousands upon thousands of places, in the little narrow meadows, just above the village ; that is to say a little higher up the valley. When the chalk hills are full; when the chalk will hold no more water; then it comes out at the lowest spots near these immense hills and becomes a rivulet first, and then a river. But, until this visit to Uphusband (or Hurstbourn Tarrant, as the map calls it), little did I imagine, that this rivulet, dry half the year, was the head of the river Teste, which, after passing through Stockbridge and Romsey, falls into the sea near Southampton.

We had to follow the bed of this river to Bourne ; but there the water begins to appear; and it runs all the year long about a mile lower down. Here it crosses Lord Portsmouth's out-park, and our road took us the same way to the village called Down-Husband, the scene (as the broad-sheet tells us) of so many of that Noble Lord's ringing and cart-driving exploits. Here we crossed the London and Andover road, and leaving Andover to our right and Whitchurch to our left, we came on to Long Parish, where, crossing the water, we came up again to that high country, which continues all across to Winchester. After passing Bullington, Sutton, and Wonston, we veered away from Stoke-Charity, and came across the fields to the high down, whence you see Winchester, or rather the Cathedral; for, at this distance, you can distinguish nothing else clearly.

As we had to come to this place, which is three miles *up* the river Itchen from Winchester, we crossed the Winchester and Basingstoke road at King's Worthy. This brought us, before we crossed the river, along through Martyr's Worthy, so long the seat of the Ogles, and now, as I observed in my last Register, sold to a general, or colonel. These Ogles had been deans, I believe ; or prebends, or something of that sort, and the one that used to live here had been, and was when he died, an "admiral." However, this last one, "Sir Charles," the loyal address mover, is my man for the present. We saw, down by the water-side, opposite to "Sir Charles's" *late* family mansion, a beautiful strawberry garden, capable of being watered by a branch of the Itchen which comes close by it, and which is, I suppose, brought there on purpose. Just by, on the greensward, under the shade of very fine trees, is an alcove, wherein to sit to eat the strawberries, coming from the little garden just mentioned, and met by bowls of cream coming from a little milk-house, shaded by another clump a little lower down the stream. What delight! What a terrestrial paradise! "Sir Charles" might be very frequently in this paradise, while that Sidmouth, whose Bill he so applauded, had many men shut up in loathsome dungeons! Ah, well! "Sir Charles," those very men may, perhaps, at this very moment, envy neither you nor Sidmouth; no, nor Sidmouth's son and heir, even though Clerk of the Pells. At any rate, it is not likely that "Sir Charles" will sit again in this paradise, contemplating another *loyal address*, to carry to a county meeting ready engrossed on parchment, to be presented by Fleming and supported by Lockhart and the "Hampshire Parsons."

I think I saw, as I came along, the new owner of the estate. It seems that he bought it "stock and fluke" as the sailors call it; that is to say, that he bought movables and the whole. He appeared to me to be a keen man. I can't find out where he comes from, or what he, or his father, has been. I like to see the revolution going on; but I like to be able to trace the parties a little more *closely*. "Sir Charles," the royal address gentleman, lives in London, I hear. I will, I think, call upon him (if I can find him out) when I get back, and ask how he does now? There is one Hollest, a George Hollest, who figured pretty bigly on that same loyal address day. This man is become quite an inoffensive harmless creature. If we were to have another county meeting, he would not, I think, threaten to put the sash down upon any body's head! Oh! Peel, Peel, Peel! Thy bill, oh, Peel, did sicken them so! Let us, oh, thou offspring of the great Spinning Jenny promoter, who subscribed ten thousand pounds towards the late "glorious" war; who was, after that, made a Baronet, and whose biographers (in the Baronetage) tell the world, that he had a "presentiment that he should be the founder of a family." Oh, thou, thou great Peel, do thou let us have only two more years of thy Bill! Or, oh, great Peel, Minister of the interior, do thou let us have repeal of Corn Bill! Either will do, great Peel. We shall then see such *modest* 'squires, and parsons looking so queer! However, if thou wilt not listen to us, great Peel, we must, perhaps, (and only perhaps) wait a little longer. It is sure to come *at last*, and to come, too, in the most efficient way.[1]

The water in the Itchen is, they say, famed for its clearness. As I was crossing the river the other day, at Avington, I told Richard to look at it, and I asked him if he did not think it very clear. I now find, that this has been remarked by very ancient writers. I see, in a newspaper just received, an account of dreadful fires in New Brunswick. It is curious, that, in my Register of the 29th October (dated from Chilworth in Surrey,) I should have put a question, relative to

---

[1] It may be interesting to note the effects of the repeal of the Corn Laws, by the prodigious increase in the imports of grain from 1828 to the present time. The average grain imports into the United Kingdom for the

10 years ending 1830 were	5 million bushels.
,, ,, 1840 ,,	8 ,,
,, ,, 1850 ,,	31 ,,
,, ,, 1860 ,,	78 ,,
,, ,, 1870 ,,	127 ,,
,, ,, 1880 ,,	229 ,,
In 1881 ,,	256 ,,

The average price of wheat at intervals of 10 years throughout the above period was as follows :—

	s.	d.
In 1830	64	3
,, 1840	66	4
,, 1850	49	3
,, 1860	53	3
,, 1870	46	11
,, 1880	44	4
,, 1882	45	1

While, at the present time (November 1884), at a Conference just held in London, to "consider the present agricultural crisis," the chairman (Mr. G. Judd) stated that after the late splendid season, with fine corn weighing 65 lbs. to the bushel, it only fetched 32s. per quarter.

the White-Clover, the Huckleberries, or the Raspberries, which start up after the burning down of woods in America. These fires have been at two places which I saw when there were hardly any people in the whole country; and, if there never had been any people there to this day, it would have been a good thing for England. Those colonies are a dead expense without a possibility of their ever being of any use. There are, I see, a church and a barrack destroyed. And, why a barrack? What! were there bayonets wanted already to keep the people in order? For, as to an *enemy*, where was he to come from? And, if there really be an enemy any where there about, would it not be a wise way to leave the worthless country to him, to use it after his own way? I was at that very Fredericton, where they say thirty houses and thirty-nine barns have now been burnt. I can remember, when there was no more thought of there ever being a barn there, than there is now thought of there being economy in our Government. The English money used to be spent prettily in that country. What do *we* want with armies, and barracks and chaplains in those woods? What does any body want with them; but *we*, above all the rest of the world? There is nothing there, no house, no barrack, no wharf, nothing, but what is bought with taxes raised on the half-starving people of England. What do *we* want with these wildernesses? Ah! but, they are wanted by creatures who will not work in England, and whom this fine system of ours, sends out into those woods to live in idleness upon the fruit of English labour. The soldier, the commissary, the barrack-master, all the whole tribe, no matter under what *name;* what keeps them? They are paid "by Government;" and I wish, that we constantly bore in mind, that the "Government" pays *our* money. It is, to be sure, sorrowful to hear of such fires and such dreadful effects proceeding from them ; but to me, it is beyond all measure *more sorrowful* to see *the labourers of England worse fed than the convicts in the gaols;* and, I know very well, that these worthless and jobbing colonies have assisted to bring England into this horrible state. The honest labouring man is allowed (aye, by the magistrates) less food than the felon in the goal; and the felon is clothed and has fuel; and the labouring man has nothing allowed for these. These worthless colonies, which find places for people that the Thing provides for, have helped to produce this dreadful state in England. Therefore, any *assistance* the sufferers should never have from me, while I could find an honest and industrious English labourer (unloaded with a family too) fed worse than a felon in the gaols; and this I can find in every part of the country.

Petersfield, Friday Evening,
11*th November.*

We lost another day at Easton; the whole of yesterday, it having rained the whole day; so that we could not have come an inch but in the wet. We started, therefore, this morning, coming through the Duke of Buckingham's Park, at Avington, which is close by Easten, and on the same side of the Itchen. This is a very beautiful place. The house is close down at the edge of the meadow land; there is a lawn before it, and a pond, supplied by the Itchen, at the end of the lawn, and bounded by the park on the other side. The high road, through the park, goes very near to this water; and we saw thousands of wild-ducks in the pond, or sitting round on the green edges of it, while, on one side of the pond, the hares and pheasants were moving about upon a gravel walk on the side of a very fine plantation. We looked down upon all this from a rising ground, and the water, like a looking-glass, showed us the trees, and even the animals. This is certainly one of the very prettiest spots in the world. The wild water-fowl seem to take particular delight in this place. There are a great many at Lord Carnarvon's; but, there the water is much larger, and the ground about it comparatively rude and coarse. Here, at Avington, every thing is in such beautiful order; the lawn, before the house, is of the finest green, and most neatly kept; and, the edge of the pond (which is of several acres) is as smooth as if it formed part of a bowling-green. To see so many *wild*-fowl, in a situation where every thing is in the *parterre*-order, has a most pleasant effect on the mind; and Richard and I, like Pope's cock in the farm-yard, could not help *thanking* the Duke and Duchess for having generously made such ample provision for our pleasure, and that, too, merely to please us as we were passing along. Now, this is the advantage of going about on *horseback*. On foot, the fatigue is too great, and you go too slowly. In any sort of carriage, you cannot get into the *real country places*. To travel in stage coaches is to be hurried along by force, in a box, with an air-hole in it, and constantly exposed to broken limbs, the *danger* being much greater than that of ship-board, and the *noise* much more disagreeable, while the *company* is frequently not a great deal more to one's liking.

From this beautiful spot we had to mount gradually the downs to the southward; but, it is impossible to quit the vale of the Itchen without one more look back at it. To form a just estimate of its real value, and that of the lands near it, it is only necessary to know, that, from its source, at Bishop's Sutton, this river has, on its two banks, in the distance of nine miles (before it reaches Winchester) thirteen parish churches. There must have been some *people* to erect these churches. It is not true, then, that Pitt and George III. *created the English nation*, notwithstanding all that the Scotch *fœlosofers* are ready to swear about the matter. In short, there can be no doubt in the mind of any rational man, that in the time of the Plantagenets, England was, out of all comparison, more populous than it is now.

When we began to get up towards the Downs, we, to our great surprise, saw them covered with *Snow*. "Sad times coming on for poor Sir Glory,"[1] said I to Richard. "Why?" said Dick. It was too cold to talk much; and, besides, a great sluggishness in his horse made us both rather serious.

---

[1] Alluding to Sir Francis Burdett, M.P. for Westminster, who was called, by his admirers, the "Pride of Westminster," and hence nicknamed by the Author "Sir Glory."

The horse had been too hard ridden at Burghclere, and had got cold. This made us change our route again, and instead of going over the downs towards Hambledon, in our way to see the park and the innumerable hares and pheasants of Sir Harry Featherstone, we pulled away more to the left, to go through Bramdean, and so on to Petersfield, contracting greatly our intended circuit. And, besides, I had never seen Bramdean, the spot on which, it is said, Alfred fought his last great and glorious battle with the Danes. A fine country for a battle sure enough! We stopped at the village to bait our horses; and, while we were in the public-house, an Exciseman came and rummaged it all over, taking an account of the various sorts of liquor in it, having the air of a complete master of the premises, while a very pretty and modest girl waited on him to produce the divers bottles, jars, and kegs. I wonder whether Alfred had a thought of anything like this, when he was clearing England from her oppressors?

A little to our right, as we came along, we left the village of Kimston, where 'Squire Græme once lived, as was before related. Here, too, lived a 'Squire Ridge, a famous fox-hunter, at a great mansion, now used as a farm-house; and it is curious enough, that this 'Squire's son-in-law, one Gunner, an attorney at Bishop's Waltham, is steward to the man who now owns the estate.

Before we got to Petersfield, we called at an old friend's and got some bread and cheese and small beer, which we preferred to strong. In approaching Petersfield we began to descend from the high chalk-country, which (with the exception of the valleys of the Itchen and the Teste) had lasted us from Uphusband (almost the north-west point of the county) to this place, which is not far from the south-east point of it. Here we quit flint and chalk and downs, and take to sand, clay, hedges, and coppices; and here, on the verge of Hampshire, we begin again to see those endless little bubble-formed hills that we before saw round the foot of Hindhead. We have got in in very good time, and got, at the Dolphin, good stabling for our horses. The waiters and people at inns *look so hard at us* to see us so liberal as to horse-feed, fire, candle, beds, and room, while we are so very very sparing in the article of *drink!* They seem to pity our taste. I hear people complain of the "exorbitant charges" at inns; but, my wonder always is, how the people can live with charging so little. Except in one single instance, I have uniformly, since I have been from home, thought the charges too low for people to live by.

This long evening has given me time to look at the *Star* newspaper of last night; and I see, that, with all possible desire to disguise the fact, there is a great "*panic*" brewing. It is impossible that this thing can go on, in its present way, for any length of time. The talk about "speculations;" that is to say, "adventurous dealings," or rather, commercial gamblings; the talk about *these* having been the cause of the breakings and the other symptoms of approaching convulsion, is the most miserable nonsense that ever was conceived in the heads of idiots. These are *effect;* not *cause.* The cause is the *Small-note Bill,* that last brilliant effort of the joint mind of Van and Castlereagh. That Bill was, as I always called it, a *respite;* and it was, and could be, nothing more. It could only put off the evil hour; it could not prevent the final arrival of that hour. To have proceeded with Peel's Bill was, indeed, to produce total convulsion. The land must have been surrendered to the overseers for the use of the poor. That is to say, without an "Equitable Adjustment." But that adjustment, as prayed for by Kent, Norfolk, Hereford, and Surrey, might have taken place; it *ought* to have taken place; and it must, at last, take place, or convulsion must come. As to the *nature* of this "adjustment," is it not most distinctly described in the Norfolk Petition? Is not that memorable petition now in the Journals of the House of Commons? What more is wanted than to act on the prayer of that very petition? Had I to draw up a petition again, I would not change a single word of that. It pleased Mr. Brougham's "best public instructor" to abuse that petition, and it pleased Daddy Coke and the Hickory Quaker, Gurney,

and the wise barn-orator, to calumniate its author[1] They
succeeded; but, their success was but shame to them; and
that author is yet destined to triumph over them. I have seen
no London paper for ten days, until to-day; and I should not
have seen this, if the waiter had not forced it upon me. I
know *very nearly* what will happen by *next May*, or thereabouts; and, as to the manner in which things will work in
the meanwhile, it is of far less consequence to the nation,
than it is what sort of weather I shall have to ride in to-
morrow. One thing, however, I wish to observe, and that is,
that, if any attempt be made to repeal the *Corn-Bill*, the main
body of the farmers will be crushed into total ruin. I come
into *contact* with few, who are not gentlemen, or very substantial farmers: but, I know the state of the *whole;* and I
know, that, even with present prices, and with *honest labourers
fed worse than felons*, it is *rub-and-go* with nineteen twentieths
of the farmers; and of this fact I beseech the ministers to be
well aware. And with this fact staring them in the face!
with that other horrid fact, that, by the regulations of the
magistrates, (who cannot avoid it, mind,) the honest labourer
is fed worse than the convicted felon; with the breakings of
merchants, so ruinous to confiding foreigners, so disgraceful
to the name of England; with the thousands of industrious
and care-taking creatures reduced to beggary by bank-paper;
with panic upon panic, plunging thousands upon thousands
into despair: with all this notorious as the sun at noon-day,
will they again advise their Royal Master to tell the Parliament and the world, that this country is "in a state of un-
equalled prosperity," and that this prosperity "must be
permanent, because *all* the great interests are *flourishing?*"
Let them! That will not alter the *result*. I had been, for
several weeks, saying, that the *seeming prosperity* was *fal-
lacious;* that the cause of it must lead to *ultimate* and shock-

---

[1] This term the Author applied to Mr. Edmund Wodehouse, one of
the members for Norfolk, and from whom Mr. Cobbett adopted the phrase
"equitable adjustment."

ing ruin; that it could not last, because it arose from causes so manifestly *fictitious;* that, in short, it was the fair-looking, but poisonous, fruit of a miserable expedient. I had been saying this for several weeks, when, out came the King's Speech, and gave me and my doctrines the *lie direct*, as to every point. Well: now, then, we shall *soon see*.

RURAL RIDE: FROM PETERSFIELD TO KENSINGTON.

Petworth, Saturday, 12th Nov. 1825.

I was at this town in the summer of 1823, when I crossed Sussex from Worth to Huntingdon, in my way to Titchfield in Hampshire. We came this morning from Petersfield, with an intention to cross to Horsham, and go thence to Worth, and then into Kent; but Richard's horse seemed not to be fit for so strong a bout, and therefore we resolved to bend our course homewards, and first of all, to fall back upon our resources at Thursley, which we intend to reach to-morrow, going through North Chapel, Chiddingfold, and Brook.

At about four miles from Petersfield, we passed through a village, called Rogate. Just before we came to it, I asked a man who was hedging on the side of the road, how much he got a day. He said, 1*s.* 6*d.*: and he told me that the *allowed* wages was 7*d.* a day for the man *and a gallon loaf a week for the rest of his family;* that is to say, one pound and two and a quarter ounces of bread for each of them; and nothing more! And this, observe, is one-third short of the bread allowance of gaols, to say nothing of the meat and clothing and lodging of the inhabitants of gaols. If the man have full work; if he get his eighteen-pence a day, the whole nine shillings does not purchase a gallon loaf each for a wife and three children, and two gallon loaves for himself. In the gaols, the convicted felons have a pound and a half each of bread a day to begin with: they have some meat generally, and it has been found absolutely necessary to allow them meat when they work at the tread-mill. It is impossible to make them work at the tread-mill without it. However, let us take the bare allowance of bread allowed in the gaols. This allowance is, for five people, fifty-two pounds and a half in the week; whereas, the man's nine shillings will buy but fifty-two pounds of bread; and this, observe, is a vast deal better than the state of things in the north of Hampshire, where the day-labourer gets but eight shillings a week. I asked this man how much a day they gave to a young able man who had no family, and who was compelled to come to the parish-officers for work. Observe, that there are a great many young men in this situation, because the farmers will not employ single men *at full wages*, these full wages being wanted for the married man's family, just to keep them alive according to the calculation that we have just seen. About the borders of the north of Hampshire, they give to these single men two gallon loaves a week, or, in money, two shillings and eight-pence, and nothing more. Here, in this part of Sussex, they give the single man seven-pence a day, that is to say, enough to buy two pounds and a quarter of bread for six days in the week, and as he does not work on the Sunday, there is no seven-pence allowed for the Sunday, and of course nothing to eat: and this is the allowance, settled by the magistrates, for a young, hearty, labouring man; and that, too, in the part of England where, I believe, they live better than in any other part of it. The poor creature here has seven-pence a day for six days in the week to find him food, clothes, washing, and lodging! It is just seven-pence, less than one half of what the meanest foot soldier in the standing army receives; besides that the latter has clothing, candle, fire, and lodging into the bargain! Well may we call our happy state of things the "envy of surrounding nations, and the admiration of the world!" We hear of the efforts of Mrs. Fry, Mr. Buxton, and numerous other persons, to improve the situation of felons in the gaols; but never, no never, do we catch them ejaculating one single pious sigh for these innumerable sufferers, who are doomed to become felons or to waste away their bodies by hunger.

When we came into the village of Rogate, I saw a little group of persons standing before a blacksmith's shop. The church-yard was on the other side of the road, surrounded by a low wall. The earth of the church-yard was about four feet and a half higher than the common level of the ground round about it; and you may see, by the nearness of the church windows to the ground, that this bed of earth has been made by the innumerable burials that have taken place in it. The group, consisting of the blacksmith, the wheelwright, perhaps, and three or four others, appeared to me to be in a deliberative mood. So I said, looking significantly at the church-yard, "It has taken a pretty many thousands of your fore-"fathers to raise that ground up so high." "Yes, Sir," said one of them. "And," said I, "for about nine hundred years "those who built that church thought about religion very "differently from what we do." "Yes," said another. "And," said I, "do you think that all those who made that heap there "are gone to the devil?" I got no answer to this. "At any "rate," added I, "they never worked for a pound and a half "of bread a day." They looked hard at me, and then looked hard at one another; and I, having trotted off, looked round at the first turning, and saw them looking after us still. I should suppose that the church was built about seven or eight hundred years ago, that is to say, the present church; for the first church built upon this spot was, I daresay, erected more than a thousand years ago. If I had had time, I should have told this group, that, before the Protestant Reformation, the labourers of Rogate received four-pence a day from Michaelmas to Lady-day; five-pence a day from Lady-day to Michaelmas, except in harvest and grass-mowing time, when able labourers had seven-pence a day; and that, at this time, bacon was *not so much as a halfpenny a pound:* and, moreover, that the parson of the parish maintained out of the tithes all those persons in the parish that were reduced to indigence by means of old age or other cause of inability to labour. I should have told them this, and, in all probability a great deal more, but I had not time; and, besides, they will have an opportunity of reading all about it in my little book called the *History of the Protestant Reformation*.

From Rogate we came on to Trotten, where a Mr. Twyford is the squire, and where there is a very fine and ancient church close by the squire's house. I saw the squire looking at some poor devils who were making "wauste improvements, ma'am," on the road which passes by the squire's door. He looked uncommonly hard at me. It was a scrutinising sort of look, mixed, as I thought, with a little surprise, if not of jealousy, as much as to say, "I wonder who the devil you can be?" My look at the squire was with the head a little on one side, and with the cheek drawn up from the left corner of the mouth, expressive of anything rather than a sense of inferiority to the squire, of whom, however, I had never heard speak before. Seeing the good and commodious and capacious church, I could not help reflecting on the intolerable baseness of this description of men, who have remained mute as fishes, while they have been taxed to build churches for the convenience of the Cotton-Lords and the Stock-Jobbers. First, their estates have been taxed to pay interest of debts contracted with these Stock-Jobbers, and to make wars for the sale of the goods of the Cotton-Lords. This drain upon their estates has collected the people into great masses, and now the same estates are taxed to build churches for them in these masses. And yet the tame fellows remain as silent as if they had been born deaf and dumb and blind. As towards the labourers, they are sharp and vigorous and brave as heart could wish; here they are bold as Hector. They pare down the wretched souls to what is below gaol allowance. But, as towards the taxers, they are gentle as doves. With regard, however, to this Squire Twyford, he is not, as I afterwards found, without some little consolation; for, one of his sons, I understand, is, like Squire Rawlinson of Hampshire, *a police justice in London!* I hear, that Squire Twyford was always a distinguished champion of loyalty; what we call a staunch friend of Government; and, it is therefore natural that the Government should be a staunch friend to him. By the taxing of his estate, and paying the Stock-Jobbers out of the proceeds, the people have been got together in great masses, and, as there are Justices wanted to keep them in order in those masses, it seems but reasonable that the squire should, in one way or another, enjoy some portion of the profits of keeping them in order. However, this cannot be the case with every loyal squire; and there are many of them, who, for want of a share in the distribution, have been totally extinguished. I should suppose Squire Twyford to be in the second rank upwards (dividing the whole of the proprietors of land into five ranks.) It appears to me, that pretty nearly the whole of this second rank is gone; that the Stock-Jobbers have eaten them clean up, having less mercy than the cannibals, who usually leave the hands and the feet; so that this squire has had pretty good luck.

From Trotten we came to Midhurst, and, having baited our horses, went into Cowdry Park to see the ruins of that once noble mansion, from which the Countess of Salisbury (the last of the Plantagenets) was brought by the tyrant Henry the Eighth to be cruelly murdered, in revenge for the integrity and the other great virtues of her son, Cardinal Pole, as we have seen in Number Four, paragraph 115, of the "History of the Protestant Reformation." This noble estate, one of the finest in the whole kingdom, was seized on by the king, after the possessor had been murdered on his scaffold. She had committed no crime. No crime was proved against her. The miscreant Thomas Cromwell, finding that no form of trial would answer his purpose, invented a new mode of bringing people to their death; namely, a Bill brought into Parliament, condemning her to death. The estate was then granted to a Sir Anthony Brown, who was physician to the king. By the descendants of this Brown, one of whom was afterwards created Lord Montague, the estate has been held to this day; and Mr. Poyntz, who married the sole remaining heiress of this family, a Miss Brown, is now the proprietor of the estate, comprising I believe, *forty or fifty manors*, the greater part of which are in this neighbourhood, some of them, however, extending more than twenty miles from the mansion. We entered the park through a great iron-gateway, part of which being wanting, the gap was stopped up by a hurdle. We rode down to the house and all round about and in amongst the ruins, now in part covered with ivy, and inhabited by innumerable starlings and jackdaws. The last possessor, was, I believe, that Lord Montague who was put an end to by the celebrated *nautical adventure* on the Rhine along with the brother of Sir Glory. These two sensible worthies took it into their heads to go down a place something resembling the waterfall of an overshot mill. They were drowned just as two young kittens or two young puppies would have been. And, as an instance of the truth that it is an ill wind that blows nobody good, had it not been for this sensible enterprize, never would there have been a Westminster Rump to celebrate the talents and virtues of Westminster's Pride and England's glory. It was this Lord Montague, I believe, who had this ancient and noble mansion completely repaired, and fitted up as a place of residence: and a few days, or a very few weeks at any rate, after the work was completed, the house was set on fire (by accident, I suppose), and left nearly in the state in which it now stands, except that the ivy has grown up about it, and partly hidden the stones from our sight. You may see, however, the hour of the day or night at which the fire took place; for there still remains the brass of the face of the clock, and the hand pointing to the hour. Close by this mansion, there runs a little river which runs winding away through the valleys, and at last falls into the Arun. After viewing the ruins, we had to return into the turnpike road, and then enter another part of the park, which we crossed, in order to go to Petworth. When you are in a part of this road through the park, you look down and see the house in the middle of a very fine valley, the distant boundary of which, to the south and south-west, is the South down Hills. Some of the trees here are very fine, particularly some most magnificent rows of the Spanish chestnuts. I asked the people at Midhurst where Mr. Poyntz himself lived; and they told me at the *lodge* in the park, which lodge was formerly the residence of the head keeper. The land is very good about here. It is fine rich loam at top, with clay further down. It is good for all sorts of trees, and they seem to grow here very fast.

We got to Petworth pretty early in the day. On entering it you see the house of Lord Egremont, which is close up against the park-wall, and which wall bounds this little vale on two sides. There is a sort of a town hall here, and on one side of it there is the bust of Charles the Second, I should have thought; but they tell me it is that of Sir William Wyndham, from whom Lord Egremont is descended. But there is *another building* much more capacious and magnificent than the town hall; namely, the Bridewell, which from the modernness of its structure, appears to be one of those "wauste improvements, Ma'am," which distinguish this *enlightened* age. This structure vies, in point of magnitude, with the house of Lord Egremont itself, though that is one of the largest mansions in the whole kingdom. The Bridewell has a wall round it that I should suppose to be twenty feet high. This place was not wanted, when the labourer got twice as much, instead of half as much as the common standing soldier. Here you see the true cause why the young labouring man is "*content,*" to exist upon 7*d.* a day, for six days in the week, and nothing for Sunday. Oh! we are a most free and enlightened people; our happy constitution in Church and state has supplanted Popery and slavery; but we go to a Bridewell unless we quietly exist and work upon 7*d.* a day!

Thursley,
Sunday, 13th Nov.

To our great delight we found Richard's horse quite well this morning, and off we set for this place. The first part of our road, for about three miles and a half, was through Lord Egremont's Park. The morning was very fine; the sun shining; a sharp frost after a foggy evening; the grass all white, the twigs of the trees white, the ponds frozen over;

and everything looking exceedingly beautiful. The spot itself being one of the very finest in the world, not excepting, I daresay, that of the father of Saxe Cobourg itself, who has, doubtless, many such fine places.

In a very fine pond not far from the house and close by the road, there are some little artificial islands, upon one of which I observed an arbutus loaded with its beautiful fruit (quite ripe) even more thickly than any one I ever saw even in America. There were, on the side of the pond, a most numerous and beautiful collection of water-fowl, foreign as well as domestic. I never saw so great a variety of water-fowl collected together in my life. They had been ejected from the water by the frost, and were sitting apparently in a state of great dejection: but this circumstance had brought them into a comparatively small compass; and we, facing our horses about, sat and looked at them, at the pond, at the grass, at the house, till we were tired of admiring. Everything here is in the neatest and most beautiful state. Endless herds of deer, of all the varieties of colours; and, what adds greatly to your pleasure in such a case, you see comfortable retreats prepared for them in different parts of the woods. When we came to what we thought the end of the park, the gate-keeper told us that we should find other walls to pass through. We now entered upon woods, we then came to another wall, and there we entered upon farms to our right and to our left. At last we came to a third wall, and the gate in that let us out into the turnpike road. The gate-keeper here told us, that the whole enclosure was *nine miles round;* and this, after all, forms, probably, not a quarter part of what this nobleman possesses. And, is it wrong that one man should possess so much? By no means; but in my opinion it is wrong that a system should exist which compels this man to have his estate taken away from him unless he throw the junior branches of his family for maintenance upon the public.

Lord Egremont bears an excellent character. Every thing that I have ever heard of him makes me believe that he is worthy of this princely estate. But, I cannot forget that his two brothers, who are now very old men, have had, from their infancy, enormous revenues in sinecure places in the West Indies, while the general property and labour of England is taxed to maintain those West Indies in their state of dependence upon England ; and I cannot forget that the burden of these sinecures are amongst the grievances of which the West Indians justly complain. True, the taxing system has taken from the family of Wyndham, during the lives of these two gentlemen, as much, and even more, than what that family has gained by those sinecures ; but then let it be recollected, that it is not the helpless people of England who have been the cause of this system. It is not the fault of those who receive 7$d.$ a day. It is the fault of the family of Wyndham and of such persons ; and, if they have chosen to suffer the Jews and jobbers to take away so large a part of their income, it is not fair for them to come to the people at large to make up for the loss.

Thus it has gone on. The great masses of property have, in general, been able to take care of themselves : but the little masses have melted away, like butter before the sun. The little gentry have had not even any disposition to resist. They merit their fate most justly. They have vied with each other in endeavours to ingratiate themselves with power, and to obtain compensation for their losses. The big fishes have had no feeling for them ; have seen them sink with a sneer, rather than with compassion ; but, at last, the cormorant threatens even themselves ; and they are struggling with might and main for their own preservation. They every where "most liberally" take the Stock-jobber or the Jew by the hand, though they hate him mortally at the same time for his power to outdo them on the sideboard, on the table, and in the equipage. They seem to think nothing of the extinguishment of the small fry ; they hug themselves in the thought that they escape ; and yet, at times, their minds misgive them, and they tremble for their own fate. The country people really gain by the change ; for the small gentry have been rendered, by their miseries, so niggardly and so cruel, that it is quite a blessing, in a village, to see a rich Jew or Jobber come to supplant them. They come, too, with far less cunning than the half-broken gentry. Cunning as the Stock-Jobber is in Change Alley, I defy him to be cunning enough for the country people, brought to their present state of duplicity by a series of cruelties, which no pen can adequately describe. The Stock-Jobber goes from London with the *cant of humanity* upon his lips, at any rate; whereas the half-broken Squire, takes not the least pains to disguise the hardness of his heart.

It is impossible for any just man to regret the sweeping away of this base race of Squires; but the sweeping of them away is produced by causes that have a wider extent. These causes reach the good as well as the bad: all are involved alike: like the pestilence, this horrible system is no respecter of persons: and decay and beggary mark the whole face of the *country*.

North Chapel is a little town in the Weald of Sussex, where there were formerly post-chaises kept; but where there are none kept now. And here is another complete revolution. In almost every country town the post-chaise houses have been lessened in number, and those that remain have become comparatively solitary and mean. The guests at inns are not now gentlemen, but *bumpers*, who, from being called (at the inns) "riders," became "travellers," and are now "commercial gentlemen," who go about in *gigs*, instead of on horseback, and who are in such numbers as to occupy a great part of the room in all the inns, in every part of the country. There are, probably, twenty thousand of them always out, who may perhaps have, on an average throughout the year, three or four thousand "ladies" travelling with them. The expense of this can be little short of fifteen millions a year, all to be paid by the country-people who consume the goods, and a large part of it to be drawn up to the Wen.

From North Chapel we came to Chiddingfold, which is in the Weald of Surrey; that is to say, the country of oak-timber. Between these two places, there are a couple of pieces of that famous commodity, called "Government property." It seems, that these places, which have extensive buildings on them, were for the purpose of making gunpowder. Like most other of these enterprises, they have been given up, after a time, and so the ground and all the buildings, and the monstrous fences, erected at enormous expense, have been sold. They were sold, it seems, some time ago, in lots, with the intention of being pulled down and carried away, though they are now nearly new, and built in the most solid, substantial, and expensive manner; brick walls eighteen inches through, and the buildings covered with lead and slate. It appears that they have been purchased by a Mr. Stovell, a Sussex banker; but for some reason or other, though the purchase was made long ago, " Government" still holds the possession; and, what is more, it keeps people there to take care of the premises. It would be curious to have a complete history of these pretty establishments at Chiddingfold; but, this is a sort of history that we shall never be treated with until there be somebody in Parliament to rummage things to the bottom. It would be very easy to call for a specific account of the cost of these establishments, and also of the quantity of powder made at them. I should not be at all surprised, if the concern, all taken together, brought the powder to a hundred times the price at which similar powder could have been purchased.

When we came through Chiddingfold, the people were just going to church; and we saw a carriage and pair conveying an old gentleman and some ladies to the churchyard steps. Upon inquiry, we found that this was Lord Winterton, whose name, they told us, was Turnour. I thought I had heard of all the Lords, first or last; but, if I had ever heard of this one before, I had forgotten him. He lives down in the Weald, between the gunpowder establishments and Horsham, and has the reputation of being a harmless, good sort of man, and that being the case I was sorry to see that he appeared to be greatly afflicted with the gout, being obliged to be helped up the steps by a stout man. However, it is as broad, perhaps, as it is long: a man is not to have all the enjoyments of making the gout, and the enjoyments of abstinence too: that would not be fair play; and I dare say that Lord Winterton is just enough to be content with the consequences of his enjoyments.

This Chiddingfold is a very pretty place. There is a very pretty and extensive green opposite the church; and we were at the proper time of the day to perceive that the modern system of education had by no means overlooked this little village. We saw *the schools* marching towards the church in military order. Two of them passed us on our road. The boys looked very hard at us, and I saluted them with "There's brave boys, you'll all be parsons or lawyers or doctors." Another school seemed to be in a less happy state. The scholars were too much in uniform, to have had their clothes purchased by their parents; and they looked, besides, as if a little more victuals, and a little less education, would have done as well. There were about twenty of them, without one single tinge of red in their whole twenty faces. In short, I never saw more deplorable-looking objects since I was born. And can it be of any use to expend money in this sort of way upon poor creatures that have not half a bellyful of food? We had not breakfasted when we passed them. We felt, at that moment, what hunger was. We had some bits of bread and meat in our pockets, however; and these, which were merely intended as stay-stomachs, amounted, I dare say, to the allowance of any half dozen of these poor boys for the day. I could, with all my heart, have pulled the victuals out of my pocket and given it to them; but I did not like to do that which would have interrupted the march, and might have been construed into a sort of insult. To quiet my conscience, however, I gave a poor man that I met soon afterwards six-pence, under pretence of rewarding him for telling me the way to Thursley, which I knew as well as he, and which I had determined, in my own mind, not to follow.

We had now come on the turnpike road from my Lord Egremont's Park to Chiddingfold. I had made two or three attempts to get out of it, and to bear away to the north-west, to get through the oak-woods to Thursley; but I was constantly prevented, by being told that the road, which I wished to take, would lead me to Haslemere. If you talk to ostlers, or landlords, or post-boys; or, indeed, to almost anybody else, they mean by a *road* a *turnpike road;* and they positively will not talk to you about any other. Now, just after quitting Chiddingfold, Thursley lies over fine woods and coppices, in a north-west direction, or thereabouts; and the turnpike road, which goes from Petworth to Godalming, goes in a north-north-east direction. I was resolved, be the consequences what they might, not to follow the turnpike road one single inch further; for I had not above three miles or thereabouts to get to Thursley, through the woods; and I had, perhaps, six miles at least to get to it the other way; but the great thing was to see the interior of these woods; to see the stems of the trees, as well as the tops of them. I saw a lane opening in the right direction; I saw indeed, that my horses must go up to their knees in clay; but I resolved to enter and go along that lane, and long before the end of my journey I found myself most amply compensated for the toil that I was about to encounter. But talk of toil! It was the horse that had the toil; and I had nothing to do but to sit upon his back, turn my head from side to side and admire the fine trees in every direction. Little bits of fields and meadows here and there, shaded all over, or nearly all over, by the surrounding trees. Here and there a labourer's house buried in the woods. We had drawn out our luncheons and eaten them while the horses took us through the clay; but I stopped at a little house, and asked the woman, who looked very clean and nice, whether she would let us dine with her. She said " Yes," with all her heart, but that she had no place to put our horses in, and that her dinner would not be ready for an hour, when she expected her husband home from church. She said they had a bit of bacon and a pudding and some cabbage; but that she had not much bread in the house. She had only one child, and that was not very old, so we left her, quite convinced that my old observation is true, that people in the woodland countries are best off, and that it is absolutely impossible to reduce them to that state of starvation in which they are in the corn-growing part of the kingdom.

Here is that great blessing, abundance of fuel at all times of the year, and particularly in the winter.

We came on for about a mile further in these clayey lanes, when we renewed our inquiries as to our course, as our road now seemed to point towards Godalming again. I asked a man how I should get to Thursley? He pointed to some fir-trees upon a hill, told me I must go by them, and that there was no other way. "Where then," said I, "is Thursley?" He pointed with his hand, and said, "Right over those "woods; but there is no road there, and it is impossible for "you to get through those woods." "Thank you," said I; "but through those woods we mean to go." Just at the border of the woods I saw a cottage. There must be some way to that cottage; and we soon found a gate that let us into a field, across which we went to this cottage. We there found an old man and a young one. Upon inquiry we found that it was *possible* to get through these woods. Richard gave the old man threepence to buy a pint of beer, and I gave the young one a shilling to pilot us through the woods. These were oak-woods with underwood beneath: and there was a little stream of water running down the middle of the woods, the annual and long overflowings of which have formed a meadow sometimes a rod wide, and sometimes twenty rods wide, while the bed of the stream itself was the most serpentine that can possibly be imagined, describing, in many places, nearly a complete circle, going round for many rods together, and coming within a rod or two of a point that it had passed before. I stopped the man several times, to sit and admire this beautiful spot, shaded in great part by lofty and wide-spreading oak trees. We had to cross this brook several times, over bridges that the owner had erected for the convenience of the fox-hunters. At last, we came into an ash-coppice, which had been planted in regular rows, at about four feet distances, which had been once cut, and which was now in the state of six years' growth. A road through it, made for the fox-hunters, was as straight as a line, and of so great a length, that, on entering it, the further end appeared not to be a foot wide. Upon seeing this, I asked the man whom these coppices belonged to, and he told me to Squire Leech, at Lea. My surprise ceased, but my admiration did not.

A piece of ordinary coppice ground, close adjoining this, and with no timber in it, and upon just the same soil (if there had been such a piece), would, at ten years' growth, be worth, at present prices, from five to seven pounds the acre. This coppice, at ten years' growth, will be worth twenty pounds the acre; and, at the next cutting, when the stems will send out so many more shoots, it will be worth thirty pounds the acre. I did not ask the question when I afterwards saw Mr. Leech, but, I dare say, the ground was trenched before it was planted; but, what is that expense when compared with the great, the permanent profit of such an undertaking! And, above all things, what a convenient species of property does a man here create. Here are no tenants' rack, no anxiety about crops and seasons; the rust and the mildew never come here; a man knows what he has got, and he knows that nothing short of an earthquake can take it from him, unless, indeed, by attempting to vie with the stock-jobber in the expense of living, he enable the stock-jobber to come and perform the office of the earthquake. Mr. Leech's father planted, I think it was, forty acres of such coppice in the same manner; and, at the same time, he *sowed the ground with acorns.* The acorns have become oak trees, and have begun and made great progress in diminishing the value of the ash, which have now to contend against the shade and the roots of the oak. For present profit, and, indeed, for permanent profit, it would be judicious to grub up the oak; but the owner has determined otherwise. He cannot endure the idea of destroying an oak wood.

If such be the profit of planting ash, what would be the profit of planting locust, even for poles and stakes? The locust would outgrow the ash, as we have seen in the case of Mr. Gunter's plantation, more than three to one. I am satisfied that it will do this upon any soil, if you give the trees fifteen years to grow in; and, in short, that the locusts will be trees when the ash are merely poles, if both are left to grow up in single stems. If in coppice, the locust will make as good poles; I mean as large and as long poles in six years, as the ash will in ten years: to say nothing of the superior durability of the locust. I have seen locusts, at Mr. Knowles's, at Thursley, sufficient for a hop-pole, for an ordinary hop-pole, with only five years' growth in them, and leaving the last year's growth to be cut off, leaving the top of the pole three quarters of an inch through. There is nothing that we have ever heard of, of the timber kind, equal to this in point of quickness of growth. In parts of the country where hop-poles are not wanted, espalier stakes, wood for small fencing, hedge stakes, hurdle stakes, fold-shores, as the people call them, are always wanted; and is it not better to have a thing that will last twenty years, than a thing that will last only three? I know of no English underwood which gives a hedge stake to last even *two years*. I should think that a very profitable way of employing the locust would be this. Plant a coppice, the plants two feet apart. Thus planted, the trees will protect one another against the wind. Keep the side shoots pruned off. At the end of six years, the coppice, if well planted and managed, will be, at the very least, twenty feet high to the tips of the trees. Not if the grass and weeds are suffered to grow up to draw all the moisture up out of the ground, to keep the air from the young plants, and to intercept the gentle rains and the dews; but, trenched ground, planted carefully, and kept clean; and always bearing in mind that hares and rabbits and young locust trees will never live together; for the hares and rabbits will not only bite them off; but will gnaw them down to the ground, and, when they have done that, will scratch away the ground to gnaw into the very root. A gentleman bought some locust trees of me last year, and brought me a dismal account in the summer of their being all dead; but I have since found that they were all eaten up by the hares. He saw some of my refuse; some of those which were too bad to send to him, which were a great deal higher than his head. His ground was as good as mine, according to his account; but I had no hares to fight against; or else mine would have been all dead too.

I say, then, that a locust plantation, in pretty good land, well managed, would be twenty feet high in six years; suppose it, however, to be only fifteen, there would be, at the bottom, wood to make two locust PINS for ship-building; two locust pins at the bottom of each tree. Two at the very least; and here would be twenty-two thousand locust pins to the acre, probably enough for the building of a seventy-four gun ship. These pins are about eighteen inches long, and, perhaps, an inch and half through; and there is this surprising quality in the wood of the locust, that it is just as hard and as durable at five or six years' growth as it is at fifty years' growth. Of which I can produce an abundance of instances. The *stake* which I brought home from America, and which is now at Fleet-street, had stood as a stake for about eight and twenty years, as certified to me by Judge Mitchell, of North Hampstead in Long Island, who gave me the stake, and who said to me at the time, "Now are you really going to take "that crooked miserable stick to England!" Now it is pretty well known, at least, I have been so informed, that our Government have sent to America, in consequence of my writings about the locust, to endeavour to get locust pins for the navy. I have been informed that they have been told that the American Government has bought them all up. Be this as it may, I know that a waggon-load of these pins is, in America itself, equal in value to a waggon-load of barrels of the finest flour. This being undeniable, and the fact being undeniable that we can grow locust pins here, that I can take a seed to-day, and say that it shall produce two pins in seven years' time, will it not become an article of heavy accusation against the Government if they neglect even one day to set about tearing up their infernal Scotch firs and larches in Woolmer Forest and elsewhere, and putting locust trees in their stead, in order, first to provide this excellent material for ship-building; and next to have some fine plantations in the Holt Forest, Woolmer Forest, the New Forest, the Forest of Dean, and elsewhere, the only possible argument against doing which being, that I may possibly take a ride round amongst their plantations, and that it may be everlastingly recorded, that it was I, who was the cause of the Government's adopting this wise and beneficial measure?

I am disposed to believe, however, that the Government will not be brutish enough, obstinately to reject the advice given to them on this head, it being observed, however, that I wish to have no hand in their proceedings, directly or indirectly. I can sell all the trees that I have for sale to other customers. Let them look out for themselves; and, as to any reports that their creatures may make upon the subjects I shall be able to produce proofs enough that such reports, if unfavourable, are false. I wrote, in a Register from Long Island, that I could if I would tell insolent Castlereagh, who was for making Englishmen dig holes one day and fill them up the next, how he might *profitably put something into those holes*, but that I would not tell him as long as the Borough-mongers should be in the state in which they then were. They are no longer in that state, I thank God. There has been no positive law to alter their state, but it is manifest that there must be such law before it be long. Events are working together to make the country worth living in, which, for the great body of the people, is at present hardly the case. Above all things in the world, it is the duty of every man, who has it in his power, to do what he can to promote the creation of materials for the building of ships, in the best manner; and it is now a fact of perfect notoriety, that, with regard to the building of ships, it cannot be done in the best manner, without the assistance of this sort of wood.

I have seen a specimen of the locust wood used in the making of furniture. I saw it in the posts of a bed-stead; and any thing more handsome I never saw in my life. I had used it myself in the making of rules; but I never saw it in this shape before. It admits of a polish nearly as fine as that of box. It is a bright and beautiful yellow. And in bedsteads, for instance, it would last for ever, and would not become loose at the joints, like oak and other perishable wood; because, like the live oak and the red cedar, no worm or insect ever preys upon it. There is no fear of the quantity being too great. It would take a century to make as many plantations as are absolutely wanted in England. It would be a prodigious creation of real and solid wealth. Not such a creation as that of paper money, which only takes the dinner from one man and gives it to another, which only gives an unnatural swell to a city or a watering-place by beggaring a thousand villages; but it would be a creation of money's worth things. Let any man go and look at a farm-house that was built a hundred years ago. He will find it, though very well built with stone or brick, actually falling to pieces, unless very frequently repaired, owing entirely to the rotten wood in the window-sills, the door-sills, the plates, the pins, the door frames, the window frames, and all those parts of the beams, the joists, and the rafters, that come in contact with the rain or the moisture. The two parts of a park paling which give way first, are, the parts of the post that meet the ground, and the pins which hold the rails to the post. Both these rot long before the paling rots. Now, all this is avoided by the use of locust as sills, as joists, as posts, as frames, and as pins. Many a roof has come down merely from the rotting of the pins. The best of spine oak is generally chosen for these pins. But after a time, the air gets into the pin-hole. The pin rots from the moist air, it gives way, the wind shakes the roof, and down it comes, or, it swags, the wet gets in, and the house is rotten. In ships, the pins are the first things that give way. Many a ship would last twenty years after it is broken up, if put together with locust pins. I am aware that some readers will become tired of this subject: and, nothing but my conviction of its being of the very first importance to the whole kingdom could make me thus dwell upon it.

We got to Thursley after our beautiful ride through Mr.

Leech's coppices, and the weather being pretty cold we found ourselves most happily situated here by the side of an *American fireplace*, making extremely comfortable a room which was formerly amongst the most uncomfortable in the world. This is another of what the malignant parsons call Cobbett's Quackeries. But my real opinion is that the whole body of them, all put together, have never, since they were born, conferred so much benefit upon the country, as I have conferred upon it by introducing this fire-place. Mr. Judson of Kensington, who is the manufacturer of them, tells me that he has a great demand, which gives me much pleasure; but really, coming to conscience, no man ought to sit by one of these fire-places that does not go the full length with me both in politics and religion. It is not fair for them to enjoy the warmth without subscribing to the doctrines of the giver of the warmth. However, as I have nothing to do with Mr. Judson's affair, either as to the profit or the loss, he must sell the fire-places to whomsoever he pleases.

Kensington,
Sunday, 20th Nov.

Coming to Godalming on Friday, where business kept us that night, we had to experience at the inn the want of our American fire-place. A large and long room to sit in, with a miserable thing called a screen to keep the wind from our backs, with a smoke in the room half an hour after the fire was lighted, we, consuming a full bushel of coals in order to keep us warm, were not half so well off as we should have been in the same room, and without any screen, and with two gallons of coals, if we had our American fire-place. I gave the landlord my advice upon the subject, and he said he would go and look at the fire-place at Mr. Knowles's. That was precisely one of these rooms which stand in absolute need of such a fire-place. It is, I should think, five-and-thirty, or forty feet long, and pretty nearly twenty feet wide. I could sooner dine with a labouring man upon his allowance of bread, such as I have mentioned above, than I would, in winter time, dine in that room upon turbot and sirloin of beef. An American fireplace, with a good fire in it, would make every part of that room pleasant to dine in, in the coldest day in winter. I saw a public-house drinking-room, where the owner has tortured his invention to get a little warmth for his guests, where he fetches his coals in a waggon from a distance of twenty miles or thereabouts, and where he consumes these coals by the bushel, to effect that, which he cannot effect at all, and which he might effect completely with about a fourth part of the coals.

It looked like rain on Saturday morning, we therefore sent our horses on from Godalming to Ripley, and took a post-chaise to convey us after them. Being shut up in the post-chaise did not prevent me from taking a look at a little snug house stuck under the hill on the road side, just opposite the old chapel on St. Catherine's-hill, which house was not there when I was a boy. I found that this house is now occupied by the family Molyneux, for ages the owners of Losely Park, on the out-skirts of which estate this house stands. The house at Losely is of great antiquity, and had, or perhaps has, attached to it the great manors of Godalming and Chiddingfold. I believe that Sir Thomas More lived at Losely, or, at any rate, that the Molyneuxes are, in some degree, descended from him. The estate is, I fancy, theirs yet; but here they are, in this little house, while one Gunning (an East Indian, I believe) occupies the house of their ancestors. At Send, or Sutton, where Mr. Webb Weston lived, there is a Baron somebody, with a De before his name. The name is German or Dutch, I believe. How the Baron came there I know not; but as I have read his name amongst the *Justices of the Peace* for the county of Surrey, he must have been born in England, or the law has been violated in making him a Justice of the Peace, seeing that no person not born a subject of the king, and a subject in this country too, can lawfully hold a commission under the crown, either civil or military. Nor is it lawful for any man born abroad of Scotch or Irish parents, to hold such commission under the crown, though such commissions have been held, and are held, by persons who are neither natural born subjects of the king, nor born of English parents abroad. It should also be known and borne in mind by the people, that it is unlawful to grant any pension from the crown to any foreigner whatever. And no naturalisation act can take away this disability. Yet the Whigs, as they call themselves, granted such pensions during the short time that they were in power.

When we got to Ripley, we found the day very fine, and we got upon our horses and rode home to dinner, after an absence of just one month, agreeably to our original intention, having seen a great deal of the country, having had a great deal of sport, and having, I trust, laid in a stock of health for the winter, sufficient to enable us to withstand the suffocation of this smoking and stinking Wen.

But, Richard and I have done something else, besides ride, and hunt, and course, and stare about us, during this month. He was eleven years old last March, and it was now time for him to begin to know something about letters and figures. He has learned to work in the garden, and having been a good deal in the country, knows a great deal about farming affairs. He can ride any thing of a horse, and over any thing that a horse will go over. So expert at hunting, that his first teacher, Mr. Budd, gave the hounds up to his management in the field; but now he begins to talk about nothing but *fox-hunting!* That is a dangerous thing. When he and I went from home, I had business at Reigate. It was a very wet morning, and we went off long before daylight in a post-chaise, intending to have our horses brought after us. He began to talk in anticipation of the sport he was going to have, and was very inquisitive as to the probability of our meeting with fox-hounds, which gave me occasion to address him thus: "Fox-hunting
" is a very fine thing, and very proper for people to be engaged
" in, and it is very desirable to be able to ride well and to be
" in at the death; but that is not ALL; that is not every thing.
" Any fool can ride a horse, and draw a cover; any groom
" or any stable-fellow, who is as ignorant as the horse, can

"do these things; but, all gentlemen that go a fox-hunting "[I hope God will forgive me for the lie] are scholars, Richard. "It is not the riding, nor the scarlet coats, that make them "gentlemen; it is their scholarship." What he thought I do not know; for he sat as mute as a fish, and I could not see his countenance. "So," said I, "you must now begin to learn "something; and you must begin with arithmetic." He had learned from mere play, to read, being first set to work of his own accord, to find out what was said about Thurtell, when all the world was talking and reading about Thurtell. That had induced us to give him Robinson Crusoe; and that had made him a passable reader. Then he had scrawled down letters and words upon paper, and had written letters to me, in the strangest way imaginable. His knowledge of figures he had acquired from the necessity of knowing the several numbers on the barrels of seeds brought from America, and the numbers upon the doors of houses. So that I had pretty nearly a blank sheet of paper to begin upon; and I have always held it to be stupidity in the last degree to attempt to put book-learning into children who are too young to reason with.

I began with a pretty long lecture on the utility of arithmetic; the absolute necessity of it, in order for us to make out our accounts of the trees and seeds that we should have to sell in the winter, and the utter impossibility of our getting paid for our pains unless we were able to make out our accounts, which accounts could not be made out unless we understood something about arithmetic. Having thus made him understand the utility of the thing, and given him a very strong instance in the case of our nursery affairs, I proceeded to explain to him the meaning of the word arithmetic, the power of figures, according to the place they occupied. I then, for it was still dark, taught him to add a few figures together, I naming the figures one after another, while he, at the mention of each new figure, said the amount, and if incorrectly, he was corrected by me. When we had got a sum of of about 24, I said now there is another line of figures on the left of this, and therefore you are to put down the 4 and carry 2. "What is *carrying?*" said he. I then explained to him the *why* and the *wherefore* of this, and he perfectly understood me at once. We then did several other little sums; and, by the time we got to Sutton, it becoming daylight, I took a pencil and set him a little sum upon paper, which, after making a mistake or two, he did very well. By the time we got to Reigate he had done several more, and at last, a pretty long one, with very few errors. We had business all day, and thought no more of our scholarship until we went to bed, and then we did, in our post-chaise fashion, a great many lines in arithmetic before we went to sleep. Thus we went on mixing our riding and hunting with our arithmetic, until we quitted Godalming, when he did a sum very nicely in *multiplication of money*, falling a little short of what I had laid out, which was to make him learn the four rules in whole numbers first, and then in money, before I got home.

Friends' houses are not so good as inns for executing a project like this; because you cannot very well be by yourself; and we slept but four nights at inns during our absence. So that we have actually stolen the time to accomplish this job, and Richard's Journal records that he was more than fifteen days out of the thirty-one, coursing or hunting. Nothing struck me more than the facility, the perfect readiness with which he at once performed addition of money. There is a *pence table* which boys usually learn, and during the learning of which they usually get no small number of thumps. This table I found it wholly unnecessary to set him. I had written it for him in one of the leaves of his journal book. But, upon looking at it, he said, "I don't want this, because, you know, "I have nothing to do but to *divide by twelve*." "That is right," said I, "you are a clever fellow, Dick;" and I shut up the book.

Now, when there is so much talk about education, let me ask how many pounds it generally costs parents to have a boy taught this much of arithmetic; how much time it costs also; and, which is a far more serious consideration, how much mortification, and very often how much loss of health, it costs the poor scolded broken-hearted child, who becomes dunder-headed and dull for all his life-time, merely because that has been imposed upon him as a task which he ought to regard as an object of pleasant pursuit. I never even once desired him to stay a moment from any other thing that he had a mind to go at. I just wrote the sums down upon paper, laid them upon the table, and left him to tackle them when he pleased. In the case of the multiplication-table, the learning of which is something of a job, and which it is absolutely necessary to learn perfectly, I advised him to go up into his bed-room, and read it twenty times over out loud every morning, before he went a hunting, and ten times over every night, after he came back, till it all came as pat upon his lips as the names of persons that he knew. He did this, and at the end of about a week he was ready to set on upon multiplication. It is the irksomeness of the thing which is the great bar to learning of every sort. I took care not to suffer irksomeness to seize his mind for a moment, and the consequence was that which I have described. I wish clearly to be understood as ascribing nothing to extraordinary *natural* ability. There are, as I have often said, as many *sorts* of men as there are of dogs; but, I do not pretend to be of any peculiarly excellent sort, and I have never discovered any indications of it. There are, to be sure, sorts that are naturally stupid; but, the generality of men are not so; and I believe that every boy of the same age, equally healthy, and brought up in the same manner, would (unless of one of the stupid kinds) learn in just the same sort of way; but, not if begun to be thumped at five or six years old, when the poor little things have no idea of the utility of anything; who are hardly sensible beings, and have but just understanding enough to know that it will hurt them if they jump down a chalk pit. I am sure, from thousands of instances that have come under my own eyes, that to begin to teach children book-learning before they are capable of reasoning, is the sure and certain way to enfeeble their minds for life; and, if they have natural genius, to cramp, if not totally to destroy that genius.

I think I shall be tempted to mould into a little book these lessons of arithmetic given to Richard. I think that a boy of sense, and of age equal to that of my scholar, would derive great profit from such a little book. It would not be equal to my verbal explanations, especially accompanied with the other parts of my conduct towards my scholar; but, at any rate, it would be plain; it would be what a boy could understand; it would encourage him by giving him a glimpse at the reasons for what he was doing: it would contain principles; and the difference between principles and rules is this, that the former are persuasions and the latter are commands. There is a great deal of difference between carrying 2 for such and such a reason, and carrying 2 because you *must* carry 2. You see boys that can cover reams of paper with figures, and do it with perfect correctness too; and at the same time, can give you not a single reason for any part of what they have done. Now this is really doing very little. The rule is soon forgotten, and then all is forgotten. It would be the same with a lawyer, that understood none of the principles of law. As far as he could find and remember cases exactly similar in all their parts to the case which he might have to manage, he would be as profound a lawyer as any in the world; but, if there was the slightest difference between his case and the cases he had found upon record, there would be an end of his law.

Some people will say, here is a monstrous deal of vanity and egotism; and if they will tell me, how such a story is to be told without exposing a man to this imputation, I will adopt their mode another time. I get nothing by telling the story. I should get full as much by keeping it to myself; but it may be useful to others, and therefore I tell it. Nothing is so dangerous as supposing that you have eight wonders of the world. I have no pretensions to any such possession. I look upon my boy as being like other boys in general. Their fathers can teach arithmetic as well as I; and if they have not a mind to pursue my method, they must pursue their own. Let them apply to the outside of the head and to the back, if they like; let them bargain for thumps and the birch rod; it is their affair and not mine. I never yet saw in my house a child that was *afraid;* that was in any fear whatever; that was ever for a moment under any sort of apprehension, on account of the learning of anything; and I never in my life gave a command, an order, a request, or even advice, to look into any book; and I am quite satisfied that the way to make children dunces, to make them detest books, and justify that detestation, is to tease them and bother them upon the subject.

As to the *age* at which children ought to begin to be taught, it is very curious, that, while I was at a friend's house during my ride, I looked into, by mere accident, a little child's abridgment of the History of England: a little thing about twice as big as a crown-piece. Even into this abridgment the historian had introduced the circumstance of Alfred's father, who, "through a *mistaken notion* of kindness to his son, had suffered him to live to the age of twelve years without any attempt being made to give him education." How came this writer to know that it was a *mistaken notion* ? Ought he not rather, when he looked at the result, when he considered the astonishing knowledge and great deeds of Alfred—ought he not to have hesitated before he thus criticised the notions of the father? It appears from the result that the notions of the father were perfectly correct; and I am satisfied, that if they had begun to thump the head of Alfred when he was a child, we should not at this day have heard talk of Alfred the Great.[1]

---

[1] It is a great error to suppose that because a man knows a thing, therefore he can teach it.

Teaching is one of the most difficult arts, and requires skill and experience. The necessity of special study and practical training to make a "school-master," has given rise to Normal Schools and Training Colleges.

It is to an improved system of teaching that we must look, for the solution of one of the greatest difficulties of the day, viz., how to economize the time, so as most to train the thinking faculties, without undue pressure to the health and cheerfulness of the pupil. It cannot be doubted that three

Great apologies are due to the OLD LADY from me, on account of my apparent inattention towards her, during her recent, or rather, I may say, her present, fit of that tormenting disorder which, as I observed before, comes upon her by *spells*. Dr. M'CULLOCH may say what he pleases about her being "*wi' bairn*." I say it's the wet gripes; and I saw a poor old mare down in Hampshire in just the same way; but God forbid the catastrophe should be the same, for they shot poor old Ball for the hounds. This disorder comes by spells. It sometimes seems as if it were altogether going off; the pulse rises, and the appetite returns. By-and-by a fresh grumbling begins to take place in the bowels. These are followed by acute pains; the patient becomes tremulous; the pulse begins to fall, and the most gloomy apprehensions begin again to be entertained. At every spell the pulse does not cease falling till it becomes lower than it was brought to by the preceding spell; and thus, spell after spell, finally produces the natural result.

It is useless at present to say much about the equivocating and blundering of the newspapers, relative to the cause of the fall. They are very shy, extremely cautious; become wonderfully *wary*, with regard to this subject. They do not know what to make of it. They all remember, that I told them that their prosperity was delusive; that it would soon come to an end, while they were telling me of the falsification of all my predictions. I told them the Small-note Bill had only given a *respite*. I told them that the foreign loans, and the shares, and all the astonishing enterprises, arose purely out of

---

hours of hearty spirited effort in the way of learning will do more than is accomplished in most schools in double that time. The three hours thus set free would be clear gain, for time spent in trifling or in heartless fagging is worse than lost : it is mentally demoralizing. The subject of studying the "happiness" of children while they are under instruction is seldom thought of. Sidney Smith has, however, observed, "if you make them happy now, you make them happy twenty years hence by the memory of it." It is asserted that at the present time there is an alarming amount of over-pressure in elementary schools. Probably a happier system of teaching would result by shortening the school hours and by prolonging the hours for recreation and play.

the Small-note Bill; and that a short time would see the Small-note Bill driving the gold out of the country, and bring us back to another restriction, OR, to wheat at four shillings a bushel. They remember that I told them all this; and now, some of them begin to *regard me as the principal cause of the present embarrassments!* This is pretty work indeed! What! I! The poor deluded creature, whose predictions were all falsified, who knew nothing at all about such matters, who was a perfect pedlar in political economy, who was "a con- "ceited and obstinate old dotard," as that polite and enlightened paper, the *Morning Herald*, called me: is it possible that such a poor miserable creature can have had the power to produce effects so prodigious? Yet this really appears to be the opinion of one, at least, of these Mr. Brougham's best possible public instructors. The *Public Ledger*, of the 16th of November, has the following passage:—

"It is fully ascertained that the Country Banking Establish-
" ments in England have latterly been compelled to limit
" their paper circulation, for the writings of Mr. COBBETT
" are widely circulated in the Agricultural districts, and they
" have been so successful as to induce the *Boobies* to call for
" gold in place of country paper, a circumstance which has
" *produced a greater effect on the currency than any exportation*
" *of the precious metals* to the Continent, either of Europe or
" America, could have done, although it too must have con-
" tributed to render money for a season scarce."

And, so, the "*boobies*" call for gold instead of country bank-notes! Bless the "*boobies*"! I wish they would do it to a greater extent, which they would, if they were not so dependent as they are upon the ragmen. But, does the *Public Ledger* think that those unfortunate creatures who suffered the other day at Plymouth, would have been "*boobies*," if they had gone and got sovereigns before the banks broke? This brother of the broad sheet should act justly and fairly as I do. He should ascribe these demands for gold to Mr. Jones of Bristol and not to me. Mr. Jones taught the "boobies" that they might have gold for asking for, or send the rag-men to jail. It is Mr. Jones, therefore, that they should blame, and not me. But, seriously speaking, what a mess, what a pickle, what a horrible mess, must the thing be in, if any man, or any thousand of men, or any hundred thousand of men, can change the value of money, unhinge all contracts and all engagements, and plunge the pecuniary affairs of a nation into confusion? I have been often accused of wishing to be thought the cleverest man in the country; but surely it is no vanity (for vanity means unjust pretension) for me to think myself the cleverest man in the country, if I can of my own head, and at my own pleasure, produce effects like these. Truth, however, and fair dealing with my readers, call upon me to disclaim so haughty a pretension. I have no such power as this public instructor ascribes to me. Greater causes are at work to produce such effects; causes wholly uncontrollable by me, and, what is more, wholly uncontrollable in the long run by the Government itself, though heartily co-operating with the bank directors. These united can do nothing to arrest the progress of events. Peel's bill produced the horrible distresses of 1822; the part repeal of that bill produced a respite, that respite is now about to expire; and neither Government nor bank, nor both joined together, can prevent the ultimate consequences. They may postpone them for a little; but mark, every postponement will render the catastrophe the more dreadful.

I see everlasting attempts by the "Instructor" to cast blame upon the bank. I can see no blame in the bank. The bank has issued no small notes, though it has liberty to do it. The bank pays in gold agreeably to the law. What more does any body want with the bank? The bank lends money I suppose when it chooses; and is not it to be the judge, when it shall lend and when it shall not? The bank is blamed for putting out paper and causing high prices; and blamed at the same time for not putting out paper to accommodate merchants and keep them from breaking. It cannot be to blame for both, and, indeed, it is blamable for neither. It is the fellows that put out the paper and then break, that do the mischief. However, a breaking merchant, whom the bank will no longer prop up, will naturally blame the bank, just as every insolvent blames a solvent, that will not lend him money.[1]

When the foreign loans first began to go on, Peter Macculloch, and all the Scotch were cock o' whoop. They said that

---

[1] In 1797 the Bank of England found itself likely to be obliged to suspend payments, and its notes were therefore declared (by law) a legal tender although no longer convertible into coin. There was thus no check upon the Bank as to the amount of its issues, and the currency became depreciated; that is, a £5 note would not exchange for five sovereigns, and every man to whom £5 was due, was obliged to accept payment in a £5 note not worth £5. Peel's Act in 1821, however, declared that cash payments in the current coin of the realm should be made for notes if demanded. This led to a great commercial panic, and the Bank was more than once on the verge of a suspension of payments owing to foreign drains upon its gold. The Government of the day has taken upon itself, on several occasions, the responsibility of authorising the Bank to issue notes not represented by gold. The Act of 1844 prevented the issue of notes beyond the value of fifteen millions unless an equal amount of gold was held by the Bank.

It follows therefore that the gold in hand by the Bank affects the briskness or depression of trade, because her paper issue depends upon the influx of gold. Thus, between 1851 and 1852, the Bank received an addition to her gold of seven millions, and during the same period her issue of notes increased from nineteen millions to twenty-three millions. Whenever there are signs of a foreign drain, the Bank counteracts that tendency, by raising the rate of discount and restricting its loans. The purchasing power of the public is thereby limited, and prices kept down. The solvency therefore of the Bank is undoubted. The import and export of gold between Great Britain and other great trading countries since 1861 have been as follow, according to Mulhall:—

GOLD, MILLIONS POUNDS.

	Imports.		Exports.		Net Imports.	Net Exports.
	1861-70.	1871-80.	1861-70.	1881-80.	1861-80.	1861-80.
Great Britain	171	180	112	172	67	...
France	189	151	119	90	131	...
United States	31	42	113	74	...	114
Australia	9	5	108	76	...	170
Other countries	112	126	60	92	86	...
Total	512	504	512	504	...	...

there were prodigious advantages in lending money to South America, that the interest would come home to enrich us; that the amount of the loans would go out chiefly in English manufactures; that the commercial gains would be enormous; and that this country would thus be made rich, and powerful, and happy, by employing in this way its "surplus capital," and thereby contributing at the same time to the uprooting of despotism and superstition, and the establishing of freedom and liberality in their stead. Unhappy and purblind, I could not for the life of me see the matter in this light. My perverted optics could perceive no *surplus capital* in bundles of bank-notes. I could see no gain in sending out goods which somebody in England was to pay for, without, as it appeared to me, the smallest chance of ever being paid again. I could see no chance of gain in the purchase of a bond, nominally bearing interest at six per cent., and on which, as I thought, no interest at all would ever be paid. I despised the idea of paying bits of paper by bits of paper. I knew that a bond, though said to bear six per cent. interest, was not worth a farthing, unless some interest were paid upon it. I declared, when Spanish bonds were at seventy-five, that I would not give a crown for a hundred pounds in them, if I were compelled to keep them unsold for seven years; and I now declare, as to South American bonds, I think them of less value than the Spanish bonds now are, if the owner be compelled to keep them unsold for a year. It is very true, that these opinions agree with my *wishes;* but they have not been created by those wishes. They are founded on my knowledge of the state of things, and upon my firm conviction of the folly of expecting that the interest of these things will ever come from the respective countries to which they relate.

Mr. Canning's despatch, which I shall insert below, has, doubtless, had a tendency (whether expected or not) to prop up the credit of these sublime speculations. The propping up of the credit of them can, however, do no sort of good. The keeping up the price of them for the present may assist some of the actual speculators, but it can do nothing for the speculation in the end, and this speculation, which was wholly an effect of the Small-note Bill, will finally have a most ruinous effect. How is it to be otherwise? Have we ever received any evidence, or anything whereon to build a belief, that the interest of these bonds will be paid? Never; and the man must be mad; mad with avarice or a love of gambling, that could advance his money upon any such a thing as these bonds. The fact is, however, that it was not *money:* it was paper: it was borrowed, or created, for the purpose of being advanced. Observe too, that when the loans were made, money was at a lower value than it is now; therefore, those who would have to pay the interest, would have too much to pay if they were to fulfil their engagement. Mr. Canning's State Paper clearly proves to me, that the main object of it is to make the loans to South America finally be paid, because, if they be not paid, not only is the amount of them lost to the bond-holders; but, there is an end, at once, to all that brilliant *commerce* with which that shining Minister appears to be so much enchanted. All the silver and gold, all the Mexican and Peruvian dreams vanish in an instant, and leave behind the wretched Cotton-Lords and wretched Jews and Jobbers to go to the workhouse, or to Botany-Bay. The whole of the loans are said to amount to about twenty-one or twenty-two millions. It is supposed, that twelve millions have actually been sent out in goods. These goods have perhaps been paid for here, but they have been paid for out of English money or by English promises. The money to pay with, has come from those who gave money for the South American bonds, and these bond-holders are to be repaid, if repaid at all, *by the South Americans.* If not paid at all, then England will have sent away twelve millions' worth of goods for nothing; and this would be the Scotch way of obtaining enormous advantages for the country by laying out its "*surplus capital*" in foreign loans. I shall conclude this subject by inserting a letter which I find in the *Morning Chronicle,* of the 18th instant. I perfectly agree with the writer. The Editor of the *Morning Chronicle* does not, as appears by the remark which he makes at the head of it; but I shall insert the whole, his remark and all, and add a remark or two of my own.—[See *Register*, vol. 56, p. 556.]

This is a pretty round sum—a sum, the very naming of which would make anybody but half-mad Englishmen stare. To make comparisons with *our own debt* would have little effect, that being so monstrous that every other sum shrinks into nothingness at the sight of it. But let us look at the United States, for they have *a debt*, and a debt is a debt; and this debt of the United States is often cited as an apology for ours, even the parsons having at last come to cite the United States as presenting us with a system of perfection. What, then, is this debt of the United States? Why, it was on the 1st of January, 1824, 90,177,962; that is to say dollars; that is to say, at four shillings and sixpence the dollar, just *twenty millions sterling;* that is to say, 594,000 pounds *less* than our "surplus capital" men have lent to the South Americans! But now let us see what is the net revenue of this same United States. Why, 20,500,755, that it to say, in sterling money, three millions, three hundred and thirty thousand, and some odd hundreds; that is to say, almost to a mere fraction, a *sixth part* of the whole gross amount of the debt. Observe this well, that the whole of the debt amounts to only six times as much as one single year's net revenue. Then, again, look at the exports of the United States. These exports, in one single year, amount to 74,699,030 dollars, and in pounds sterling £16,599,783. Now, what can the South American State show in this way? Have they any exports? Or, at least, have they any that any man can speak of with certainty? Have they any revenue, wherewith to pay the interest of a debt, when they are borrowing the very means of maintaining themselves now against the bare name of their king? We are often told that the Americans borrowed their money to carry on their Revolutionary war with. *Money;* Aye; a farthing is money, and a double sovereign is no more than money. But surely some regard is to be had to the *quantity;* some regard is to be had to the amount of the money; and is there any man in his senses that will put the half million, which the Americans borrowed of the Dutch, in competition, that will name on the same day, this half million, with the twenty-one millions and a half borrowed by the South Americans as above stated? In short, it is almost to insult the understandings of my readers, to seem to institute any comparison between the two things; and nothing in the world, short of this gambling, this unprincipled, this maddening paper-money system, could have made men look with patience for one single moment at loans like these, tossed into the air with the hope and expectation of re-payment. However, let the bond-owners keep their bonds. Let them feel the sweets of the Small-note Bill, and of the consequent puffing up of the English funds. The affair is theirs. They have rejected my advice; they have listened to the broad sheet; and let them take all the consequences. Let them, with all my heart, die with starvation, and as they expire, let them curse Mr. BROUGHAM's best possible public Instructor.

Uphusband (Hampshire),
Thursday, 24th Aug. 1826.

We left Burghclere last evening, in the rain; but, as our distance was only about seven miles, the consequence was little. The crops of corn, except oats, have been very fine hereabouts; and, there are never any peas, nor any beans, grown here. The sainfoin fields, though on these high lands, and though the dry weather has been of such long continuance, look as green as watered meadows, and a great deal more brilliant and beautiful. I have often described this beautiful village (which lies in a deep dell) and its very variously shaped environs, in my *Register* of November, 1822. This is one of those countries of chalk and flint and dry-top soil and hard roads and high and bare hills and deep dells, with clumps of lofty trees, here and there, which are so many rookeries: this is one of those countries, or rather, approaching towards those countries, of downs and flocks of sheep, which I like so much, which I always get to when I can, and which many people seem to flee from as naturally as men flee from pestilence. They call such countries *naked* and *barren*, though they are, in the summer months, actually covered with meat and with corn.

I saw, the other day, in the *Morning Herald*, London, "best public instructor," that all those had *deceived themselves*, who had expected to see the price of agricultural produce brought down by the lessening of the quantity of paper-money. Now, in the first place, corn is, on an average, a seventh lower in price than it was last year at this time; and, what would it have been, if the crop and the stock had now been equal to what they were last year? All in good time, therefore, good Mr. Thwaites. Let us have a little time. The "best public instructors" have, as yet, only fallen, in number sold, about a third, since this time last year. Give them a little time, good Mr. Thwaites, and you will see them come down to your heart's content. Only let us fairly see an end to small notes, and there will soon be not two daily "best "public instructors" left in all the "entire" great "British "Empire."

But, as man is not to live on bread alone, so corn is not the *only* thing that the owners and occupiers of the land have to look to. There are timber, bark, underwood, wool, hides, pigs, sheep, and cattle. All these together make, in amount, four times the corn, at the very least. I know that *all* these have greatly fallen in price since last year; but, I am in a sheep and wool country, and can speak positively as to them, which are two articles of very great importance. As to sheep; I am speaking of South Downs, which are the great stock of these counties; as to sheep, they have fallen one-third in price since last August, lambs as well as ewes. And, as to the wool, it sold, in 1824, at 40s. a tod; it sold last year, at 35s. a tod; and it now sells at 19s. a tod! A tod is 28lb. avoirdupois weight; so that the price of South Down wool now is, 8d. a pound and a fraction over; and this is, I believe, cheaper than it has ever been known within the memory of the oldest man living! The "best public instructor" may, perhaps, think, that sheep and wool are a trifling affair. There are many thousands of farmers who keep each a flock of at least a thousand sheep. An ewe yields about 3lb. of wool, a wether 4lb., a ram 7lb. Calculate, good Mr. Thwaites, what a difference it is when this wool becomes 8d. a pound instead of 17d., and instead of 30d. as it was not many years ago! In short, every middling sheep farmer receives, this year, about £250 less, as the produce of sheep and wool, than he received last year; and, on an average, £250 is more than half his rent.

There is a great falling off in the price of horses, and of all cattle except fat cattle; and, observe, when the prospect is good, it shows a rise in the price of lean cattle; not in that of the meat, which is just ready to go into the mouth. Prices will go on gradually falling, as they did from 1819 to 1822 inclusive, unless upheld by untoward seasons, or by an issue of assignats; for, mind, it would be no joke, no sham, *this time;* it would be an issue of as real, as *bona fide* assignats as ever came from the mint of any set of rascals, that ever robbed and enslaved a people in the names of "liberty and law."

East Everley (Wiltshire),
Sunday, 27th August, Evening.

We set off from Uphusband on Friday, about ten o'clock, the morning having been wet. My sons came round, in the chaise, by Andover and Weyhill, while I came right across the country towards Ludgershall, which lies in the road from Andover to this place. I never knew the *flies* so troublesome, in England, as I found them in this ride. I was obliged to carry a great bough, and to keep it in constant motion, in order to make the horse peaceable enough to enable me to keep on his back. It is a country of fields, lanes, and high hedges; so that no *wind* could come to relieve my horse; and, in spite of all I could do, a great part of him was covered with foam from the sweat. In the midst of this, I got, at one time, a little out of my road, in, or near, a place called Tangley. I rode up to the garden-wicket of a cottage, and asked the woman, who had two children, and who seemed to be about thirty years old, which was the way to Ludgershall, which I knew could not be more than about *four miles* off. She did *not know!* A very neat, smart, and pretty woman; but, she did not know the way to this rotten borough, which was, I was sure, only about four miles off! "Well, my dear good woman," said I, "but you *have been* at LUDGERSHALL?"—"No."—"Nor at Andover?" (six miles another way)—"No."—"Nor at Marlborough?" (nine miles another way)—"No."—"Pray, were you born in this house?"—"Yes."—"And, how far have you ever been from this house?"—"Oh! I have been *up in the parish* and over *to Chute*." That is to say, the utmost extent of her voyages had been about two and a half miles! Let no one laugh at her, and, above all others, let not me, who am convinced, that the *facilities*, which now exist, of *moving human bodies from place to place*, are amongst the *curses* of the country, the destroyers of industry, of morals, and, of course, of happiness. It is a great error to suppose, that people are rendered stupid by remaining always in the same place.¹ This was a very acute woman, and as well behaved as need to be. There was, in July last (last month) a Preston-man, who had never been further from home than Chorley (about eight or ten miles), and who started off, *on foot*, and went, *alone*, to Rouen, in France, and back again to London, in the space of about ten days; and that, too, without being able to speak, or to understand, a word of French. N.B. Those gentlemen, who, at

---

¹ The modern farm labourer enjoys almost a magical facility of locomotion, compared with the time alluded to by the Author. He is whirled along with a velocity, ease, and comfort, which would have excited the wonder and astonishment of the country folks in those days; and wherever he has occasion to go, he knows that, by law, he can travel, by certain parliamentary trains, at the rate of one penny per mile, and sometimes at a less rate. It may be interesting to know that the railways of the world carry every month, on an average, 145 million passengers, at an average fare of 19 pence, for an average journey of 21 miles; and that the tramways of Great Britain, France, and North America, carry every month 130 million of passengers, at an average fare of two pence.

Green-street, in Kent, were so kind to this man, *upon finding that he had voted for me*, will be pleased to accept of my best thanks. Wilding (that is the man's name) was full of expressions of gratitude towards these gentlemen. He spoke of others who were good to him on his way; and even at Calais he found friends on my account; but he was particularly loud in his praises of the gentlemen in Kent, who had been so good and so kind to him, that he seemed quite in an extacy when he talked of their conduct.

Before I got to the rotten-borough, I came out upon a Down, just on the border of the two counties, Hampshire and Wiltshire. Here I came up with my sons, and we entered the rotten-borough together. It contained some rashers of bacon and a very civil landlady; but, it is one of the most mean and beggarly places that man ever set his eyes on. The curse, attending corruption, seems to be upon it. The look of the place would make one swear, that there never was a clean shirt in it, since the first stone of it was laid. It must have been a large place once, though it now contains only 479 persons, men, women, and children. The borough is, as to all practical purposes, as much private property as this pen is my private property. Aye, aye! Let the petitioners of Manchester bawl, as long as they like, against all other evils; but, until they touch this *master-evil*, they do nothing at all.

Everley is but about three miles from Ludgershall, so that we got here in the afternoon of Friday: and, in the evening a very heavy storm came and drove away all flies, and made the air delightful. This is a real *Down*-country. Here you see miles and miles square without a tree, or hedge, or bush. It is country of green-sward. This is the most famous place in all England for *coursing*. I was here, at this very inn, with a party eighteen years ago; and the landlord, who is still the same, recognised me as soon as he saw me. There were forty brace of greyhounds taken out into the field on one of the days, and every brace had one course, and some of them two. The ground is the finest in the world; from two to three miles for the hare to run to cover, and not a stone nor a bush nor a hillock. It was here proved to me, that the hare is, by far, the swiftest of all English animals; for I saw three hares, in one day, *run away* from the dogs. To give dog and hare a fair trial, there should be but *one* dog. Then, if that dog got so close as to compel the hare *to turn*, that would be a proof that the dog ran fastest. When the dog, or dogs, never get near enough to the hare to induce her to *turn*, she is said, and very justly, to "*run away*" from them; and, as I saw three hares do this in one day, I conclude, that the hare is the swifter animal of the two.

This inn is one of the nicest, and, in summer, one of the pleasantest, in England; for, I think, that my experience in this way will justify me in speaking thus positively. The house is large, the yard and the stables good, the landlord *a farmer* also, and, therefore, no cribbing your horses in hay or straw and yourself in eggs and cream. The garden, which adjoins the south side of the house, is large, of good shape, has a terrace on one side, lies on the slope, consists of well-disposed clumps of shrubs and flowers, and of short-grass very neatly kept. In the lower part of the garden there are high trees, and, amongst these, the tulip-tree and the live-oak. Beyond the garden is a large clump of lofty sycamores, and, in these a most populous rookery, in which, of all things in the world, I delight. The village, which contains 301 souls, lies to the north of the inn, but adjoining its premises. All the rest, in every direction, is bare down or open arable. I am now sitting at one of the southern windows of this inn, looking across the garden towards the rookery. It is nearly sun-setting; the rooks are skimming and curving over the tops of the trees; while, under the branches, I see a flock of several hundred sheep, coming nibbling their way in from the Down, and going to their fold.

Now, what ill-natured devil could bring Old Nic Grimshaw into my head in company with these innocent sheep? Why, the truth is this: nothing is *so swift* as *thought:* it runs over a life-time in a moment; and, while I was writing the last sentence of the foregoing paragraph, *thought* took me up at the time when I used to wear a smock-frock and to carry a wooden bottle like that shepherd's boy; and, in an instant, it hurried me along through my no very short life of adventure, of toil, of peril, of pleasure, of ardent friendship and not less ardent enmity; and after filling me with wonder, that a heart and mind so wrapped up in everything belonging to the gardens, the fields and the woods, should have been condemned to waste themselves away amidst the stench, the noise and the strife of cities, it brought me *to the present moment*, and sent my mind back to what I have yet to perform about Nicholas Grimshaw and his *ditches !* [1]

My sons set off about three o'clock to-day, on their way to Herefordshire, where I intend to join them, when I have had a pretty good ride in this country. There is no pleasure in travelling, except on horse-back, or on foot. Carriages take your body from place to place; and, if you merely want to be *conveyed*, they are very good; but they enable you to see and to know nothing at all of the country.

East Everley, Monday Morning
5 o'clock, 28th Aug. 1826.

A very fine morning; a man, *eighty-two years of age*, just beginning to mow the short-grass, in the garden: I thought it, even when I was young, the *hardest work* that man had to do. To *look on*, this work seems nothing; but, it tries every sinew in your frame, if you go upright and do your work

---

[1] Mr. Nicholas Grimshaw was Mayor of Preston in 1826 when the Author was candidate at the election of two Members for that town. Mr. Cobbett was brought forward by Sir Thomas Beevor of Hargham, near Attleborough, Norfolk, in the agricultural interest. A famous contest took place. There was comparatively little ruffianism, but sufficient to impair fair voting. The "ditches" to which reference is made, were the passages formed in the crowds for bringing up the voters. The other candidates were the Hon. E. G. Stanley (afterwards Earl Derby), Mr. John Wood a citizen merchant, and Captain Barrie, R.N. The election commenced on June 9th, and ended on June 26th. The numbers were—Stanley, 3041; Wood, 1982; Barrie, 1657; Cobbett, 995. The former two gentlemen were consequently elected.

well. This old man never knew how to do it well, and he stoops, and he hangs his scythe wrong; but, with all this, it must be a surprising man to mow short-grass, as well as he does, at *eighty*. *I wish I* may be able to mow short-grass at eighty! That's all I have to say of the matter. I am just setting off for the source of the Avon, which runs from near Marlborough to Salisbury, and thence to the sea; and, I intend to pursue it as far as Salisbury. In the distance of thirty miles, here are, I see by the books, more than thirty churches. I wish to see, with my own eyes, what evidence there is, that those thirty churches were built without hands, without money, and without a congregation; and thus, to find matter, if I can, to justify the mad wretches, who, from Committee-Rooms and elsewhere, are bothering this half-distracted nation to death, about a "surplus popalashon, mon."

My horse is ready; and the rooks are just gone off to the stubble-fields. These rooks rob the pigs; but, they have *a right* to do it. I wonder (upon my soul I do) that there is no lawyer, Scotchman, or Parson-Justice, to propose a law, to punish the rooks for *trespass*.

RIDE DOWN THE VALLEY OF THE AVON IN WILTSHIRE.

"Thou shalt not muzzle the ox when he treadeth out the corn; and, The labourer is worthy of his reward."—Deuteronomy, ch. xxv. ver. 4; 1 Cor. ix. 9; 1 Tim. v. 18.

Milston, Monday, 28th August.

I came off this morning on the Marlborough road, about two miles, or three, and then turned off, over the downs, in a north-westerly direction, in search of the source of the Avon River, which goes down to Salisbury. I had once been at Netheravon, a village in this valley; but I had often heard this valley described, as one of the finest pieces of land in all England; I knew that there were about thirty parish churches, standing in a length of about thirty miles, and in an average width, of hardly a mile; and I was resolved to see a little into the *reasons* that could have induced our fathers to build all these churches, especially if, as the Scotch would have us believe, there were but a mere handful of people in England *until of late years.*

The first part of my ride this morning was by the side of Sir John Astley's park. This man is one of the members of the county (gallon-loaf Bennet being the other). They say that he is good to the labouring people; and he ought to be good for *something*, being a member of Parliament of the Lethbridge and Dickenson stamp. However, he has got a thumping estate; though, be it borne in mind, the working-people, and the fund-holders, and the dead-weight, have each their separate mortgage upon it; of which this Baronet has, I daresay, too much justice to complain, seeing that the amount of these mortgages, was absolutely necessary, to carry on Pitt, and Perceval, and Castlereagh Wars; to support Hanoverian soldiers in England; to fight and beat the Americans, on the Serpentine River; to give Wellington, a kingly estate; and to defray the expenses of Manchester, and other yeomanry cavalry; besides all the various charges of Power-of-Imprisonment Bills and of Six-Acts. These being the cause of the mortgages, the "worthy Baronet" has, I will engage, too much justice to complain of them.

In steering across the down, I came to a large farm, which a shepherd told me was Milston Hill Farm. This was upon the high land, and before I came to the edge of this *Valley of Avon*, which was my land of promise; or, at least, of great expectation; for I could not imagine that thirty churches had been built *for nothing*, by the side of a brook (for it is no more during the greater part of the way) thirty miles long. The shepherd showed me the way towards Milston; and at the end of about a mile, from the top of a very high part of the down, with a steep slope towards the valley, I first saw this *Valley of Avon;* and a most beautiful sight it was! Villages, hamlets, large farms, towers, steeples, fields, meadows, orchards,

and very fine timber trees, scattered all over the valley. The
shape of the thing is this: on each side *downs*, very lofty and
steep, in some places, and sloping miles back, in other places;
but the *out-sides* of the valley are downs. From the edge of
the downs begin capital *arable fields*, generally of very great
dimensions, and, in some places, running a mile or two back
into little *cross-valleys*, formed by hills of downs. After the
corn-fields come *meadows*, on each side, down to the *brook*,
or *river*. The farm-houses, mansions, villages, and hamlets,
are generally situated in that part of the arable land which
comes nearest the meadows.

Great as my expectations had been, they were more than
fulfilled. I delight in this sort of country; and I had
frequently seen the vale of the Itchen, that of the Bourn, and
also that of the Teste, in Hampshire; I had seen the vales
amongst the South Downs; but I never before saw anything to
please me like this valley of the Avon. I sat upon my horse
and looked over Milston and Easton and Pewsey for half an
hour, though I had not breakfasted. The hill was very steep.
A road, going slanting down it, was still so steep, and washed so
very deep, by the rains of ages, that I did not attempt to *ride*
down it, and I did not like to lead my horse, the path was so
narrow. So seeing a boy with a drove of pigs, going out to
the stubbles, I beckoned him to come up to me; and he
came, and led my horse down for me. But now, before I
begin to ride down this beautiful vale, let me give, as well as
my means will enable me, a plan or map of it, which I have
made in this way: a friend has lent me a very old map of
Wiltshire, describing the spots where all the churches stand,
and also all the spots where Manor-houses, or Mansion-houses,
stood. I laid a piece of very thin paper upon the map, and
thus traced the river upon my paper, putting *figures* to represent the spots where churches stand, and putting *stars* to
represent the spots where Manor-houses or Mansion-houses
formerly stood.[1] Endless is the variety in the shape of the

---

[1] The map here produced is a facsimile, on a reduced scale, of the

high lands which form this valley. Sometimes the slope is very gentle, and the arable lands go back very far. At others, the downs come out into the valley almost like piers into the sea, being very steep in their sides, as well as their ends, towards the valley. They have no slope at their other ends: indeed they have no *back ends*, but run into the main high land. There is also great variety in the width of the valley; great variety in the width of the meadows; but the land appears all to be of the very best; and it must be so, for the farmers confess it.

It seemed to me, that one way, and that not, perhaps, the least striking, of exposing the folly, the stupidity, the inanity, the presumption, the insufferable emptiness and insolence and barbarity, of those numerous wretches, who have now the audacity, to propose to *transport* the people of England, upon the principle of the monster Malthus, who has furnished the unfeeling oligarchs, and their toad-eaters, with the pretence, that *man has a natural propensity to breed faster, than food can be raised for the increase;* it seemed to me, that one way of exposing this mixture of madness and of blasphemy was, to take a look, now that the harvest is in, at the produce, the mouths, the condition, and the changes that have taken place, in a spot like this, which God has favoured with every good, that he has had to bestow upon man.

From the top of the hill I was not a little surprised to see, in every part of the valley that my eye could reach, a large portion of fields of Swedish turnips, all looking extremely well. I had found the turnips, of both sorts, by no means bad, from Salt Hill to Newbury; but from Newbury through Burghclere, Highclere, Uphusband, and Tangley, I had seen but few. At and about

---

present Ordnance map, representing the Valley of the Avon. Upon examination, it will be found fully to corroborate the opinion of the Author, respecting the former population of this valley. There are several villages in the map, which are not mentioned by Mr. Cobbett, while there are several villages, mentioned by him, which do not appear in the map; probably, however, their names have been altered. It will also be seen that several villages have duplicate names. The map, supplied in the former editions of the work, was very meagre.

Ludgershall and Everley, I had seen hardly any. But, when I came, this morning, to Milston Hill farm, I saw a very large field of what appeared to me to be fine Swedish Turnips. In the valley, however, I found them much finer, and the fields were very beautiful objects, forming, as their colour did, so great a contrast with that of the fallows, and the stubbles, which latter are, this year, singularly clean and bright.

Having got to the bottom of the hill, I proceeded on to the village of Milston, the church of which is, in the map, represented by the figure 2. I left Easton (3) away at my right, and I did not go up to Wooton Rivers (1) where the river Avon rises, and which lies just close to the south-west corner of Marlborough Forest, and at about 5 or 6 miles from the town of Marlborough. Lower down the river, as I thought, there lived a friend, who was a great farmer, and whom I intended to call on. It being my way, however, always to begin making enquiries soon enough, I asked the pig-driver where this friend lived; and, to my surprise, I found that he lived in the parish of Milston (2). After riding up to the church, as being the centre of the village, I went on towards the house of my friend, which lay on my road down the valley. I have many, many times witnessed agreeable surprise; but I do not know, that I ever in the whole course of my life, saw people so much surprised and pleased, as this farmer and his family were, at seeing me. People often *tell* you, that they are *glad to see* you; and in general they speak truth. I take pretty good care not to approach any house, with the smallest appearance of a design to eat or drink in it, unless I be *quite sure* of a cordial reception; but my friend at Fifield (it is in Milston parish) (2) and all his family, really seemed to be delighted beyond all expression.

When I set out this morning, I intended to go all the way down to the city of Salisbury (31) *to-day;* but, I soon found, that to refuse to sleep at Fifield, would cost me a great deal more trouble than a day was worth. So that I made my mind up, to stay in this farm-house, which has one of the nicest gardens, and it contains some of the finest flowers, that I ever saw, and all is disposed, with as much good taste, as I have ever witnessed. Here I am, then, just going to bed after having spent as pleasant a day, as I ever spent in my life. I have heard to-day, that Birkbeck lost his life by attempting to cross a river, on horse-back; but if what I have heard besides be true, that life must have been hardly worth preserving; for, they say, that he was reduced to a very deplorable state; and I have heard, from what I deem unquestionable authority, that his two beautiful and accomplished daughters are married to two common labourers, one a Yankee, and the other an Irishman, neither of whom has, probably, a second shirt to his back, or a single pair of shoes, to put his feet into! These poor girls owe their ruin and misery (if my information be correct), and, at any rate, hundreds besides Birkbeck himself, owe their utter ruin, the most scandalous degradation, together with great bodily suffering, to the vanity, the conceit, the presumption of Birkbeck, who, observe, richly merited all that he suffered, not excepting his death; for, he sinned with his eyes open; he rejected all advice; he persevered, after he saw his error; he dragged thousands into ruin along with him; and he most vilely calumniated the man, who, after having most disinterestedly, but in vain, endeavoured to preserve him from ruin, endeavoured to preserve those who were in danger of being deluded by him. When, in 1817, before he set out for America, I was, in Catherine Street, Strand, London, so earnestly pressing him not to go to the back countries, he had one of these daughters with him. After talking to him for some time, and describing the risks and disadvantages of the back countries, I turned towards the daughter, and, in a sort of joking way, said: "Miss Birkbeck, take my advice: don't "let anybody get *you* more than twenty miles from Boston, "New York, Philadelphia, or Baltimore." Upon which he gave me a most *dignified* look, and, observed: "Miss Birk- "beck has *a father*, Sir, whom she knows it to be her duty "to obey." This snap was enough for me. I saw, that this was a man so full of self-conceit, that it was impossible to do anything with him. He seemed to me to be bent upon his own destruction. I thought it my duty to warn *others* of their danger: some took the warning; others did not; but he and his brother adventurer, Flower, never forgave me, and they resorted to all the means in their power to do me injury. They did me no injury, no thanks to them; and I have seen them most severely, but most justly, punished.[1]

Amesbury, Tuesday, 29th August.

I set off from Fifield, near Pawsey, this morning, and got here (25) about one o'clock, with my clothes wet. While they are drying, and while a mutton chop is getting ready, I sit down to make some notes of what I have seen since I left Enford (No. 15); but, here comes my dinner: and I must put off my notes till I have dined.

Salisbury, Wednesday, 30th August.

My ride yesterday, from Milston (No. 2) to this city of Salisbury, was, without any exception, the most pleasant; it brought before me the greatest number of, to me, interesting objects, and it gave rise to more interesting reflections, than I remember ever to have had brought before my eyes, or into my mind, in any one day of my life; and therefore, this ride was, without any exception, the most pleasant I ever had

---

[1] Mr. Morris Birkbeck was a prosperous farmer at Wanborough in Surrey. He left England in 1817, for America, with the view to carry out an Emigration Scheme in the Western States. After his arrival, he sent to England, for publication, two pamphlets; one called "Notes on a Journey in America from the Coast of Virginia to the Territory of Illinois;" the other was called "Letters from Illinois." He did this, for the purpose of inducing other farmers in England to join him. Mr. Cobbett (as he tells us here) tried to dissuade him from settling in the back countries; but Birkbeck acted in opposition to this advice, and subsequently found that his highly coloured theories were but illusions; at length, he lost all his property, and, finally, was drowned in trying to cross a swollen river on horseback. Mr. Benjamin Flower also emigrated to the backwoods with Mr. Birkbeck. He was originally editor of a periodical published at Harlow, in Essex, called the "Political Review and Monthly Register" (of a moderate liberal character). How long he stayed in America we are not told; but he was associated with Birkbeck in publishing the "Letters from Illinois" in 1822.

The Valley of the Avon. 61

in my life, as far as my recollection serves me. I got a little wet in the middle of the day; but I got dry again, and I arrived here in very good time, though I went over the Accursed Hill (Old Sarum), and went across to Laverstock, before I came to Salisbury.

Let us now, then, look back over this part of Wiltshire, and see whether the inhabitants ought to be "transported" by order of the "Emigration Committee," of which we shall see and say more by-and-by. I have before described this valley, generally; let me now speak of it a little more, in detail. The farms are all large, and, generally speaking, they were always large, I daresay; because *sheep* is one of the great things here; and sheep, in a country like this, must be kept in *flocks*, to be of any profit. The sheep principally manure the land. This is to be done only by *folding;* and, to fold, you must have *a flock*. Every farm has its portion of down, arable, and meadow; and, in many places, the latter are watered meadows, which is a great resource where sheep are kept in flocks; because these meadows furnish grass for the suckling ewes, early in the spring; and, indeed, because they have always food in them for sheep and cattle of all sorts. These meadows have had no part of the suffering from the drought, this year. They fed the ewes and lambs in the spring, and they are now yielding a heavy crop of hay; for I saw men mowing in them, in several places, particularly about Netheravon (18), though it was raining at the time.

The turnips look pretty well all the way down the valley; but, I see very few, except Swedish turnips. The early common turnips very nearly all failed, I believe. But, the stubbles, are beautifully bright; and the rick-yards tell us, that the crops are good, especially of wheat. This is not a country of peas and beans, nor of oats, except for home consumption. The crops are wheat, barley, wool and lambs, and these latter, not to be sold to butchers, but to be sold, at the great fairs, to those who are going to keep them for some time, whether to breed from, or, finally to fat for the butcher. It is the pulse and the oats, that appear to have failed most

this year; and, therefore, this Valley has not suffered. I do
not perceive that they have many *potatoes;* but what they
have of this base root, seem to look well enough. It was one
of the greatest villains upon earth (Sir Walter Raleigh), who
(they say) first brought this root into England. He was
beheaded at last! What a pity, since he was to be beheaded,
the execution did not take place before he became such a
mischievous devil as he was in the latter two-thirds of his life!

The stack-yards down this valley, are beautiful to behold.
They contain from five to fifteen banging wheat-ricks, besides
barley-ricks, and hay-ricks, and also besides the contents of
the barns, many of which exceed a hundred, some two
hundred, and I saw one at Pewsey (5), and another at Figheldean (19), each of which exceeded two hundred and fifty feet
in length. At a farm, which, in the old maps, is called
Chisenbury Priory (14) I think I counted twenty-seven ricks
of one sort and another, and sixteen or eighteen of them
wheat-ricks. I could not conveniently get to the yard,
without longer delay than I wished to make; but, I could not
be much out in my counting. A very fine sight this was, and
it could not meet the eye, without making one look round
(and in vain) *to see the people who were to eat all this food;*
and without making one reflect on the horrible, the unnatural,
the base and infamous state, in which we must be, when projects are on foot, and are openly avowed, for *transporting,*
those who raise this food, because they want to eat enough of
it to keep them alive; and when no project is on foot for
transporting the idlers, who live in luxury upon this same
food; when no project is on foot for transporting pensioners,
parsons, or dead-weight people!

A little while before I came to this farm-yard, I saw, in
one piece, about four hundred acres of wheat-stubble. and I
saw a sheep-fold, which, I thought, contained an acre of
ground, and had in it, about four thousand sheep and lambs.
The fold was divided into three separate flocks; but the piece
of ground was one and the same; and I thought it contained
about an acre. At one farm, between Pewsey and Upavon,

The Valley of the Avon.

I counted more than 300 hogs in one stubble. This is certainly the most delightful farming in the world. No ditches, no water-furrows, no drains, hardly any hedges, no dirt and mire even in the wettest seasons of the year: and though the downs, are naked and cold, the valleys are snugness itself. They are, as to the downs, what *ah-ahs!* are, in parks or lawns. When you are going over the downs, you look *over* the valleys, as in the case of the *ah-ah;* and, if you be not acquainted with the country, your surprise, when you come to the edge of the hill, is very great. The shelter, in these valleys, and particularly where the downs are steep and lofty on the sides, is very complete. Then, the trees are everywhere lofty. They are generally elms, with some ashes, which delight in the soil that they find here. There are, almost always, two or three large clumps of trees in every parish, and a rookery or two (not *rag*-rookery) to every parish. By the water's edge there are willows; and to almost every farm, there is a fine orchard, the trees being, in general, very fine, and, this year, they are, in general, well loaded with fruit. So that, all taken together, it seems impossible to find a more beautiful and pleasant country than this, or to imagine any life more easy and happy than men might here lead, if they were untormented by an accursed system, that takes the food from those that raise it, and gives it to those, that do nothing that is useful to man.

Here the farmer has always an abundance of straw. His farm-yard is never without it. Cattle and horses are bedded up to their eyes. The yards are put close under the shelter of a hill, or are protected by lofty and thick-set trees. Every animal seems comfortably situated; and, in the dreariest days of winter, these are, perhaps, the happiest scenes in the world; or, rather, they would be such, if those, whose labour makes it all, trees, corn, sheep and every thing, had but *their fair share* of the produce of that labour. What share they really have of it, one cannot exactly say; but, I should suppose, that every labouring *man* in this valley raises as much food, as would suffice for fifty, or a hundred persons, fed like himself!

At a farm at Milston (2) there were, according to my calculation, 600 quarters of wheat and 1200 quarters of barley of the present year's crop. The farm keeps, on an average, 1400 sheep, it breeds and rears an usual proportion of pigs, fats the usual proportion of hogs, and, I suppose, rears and fats, the usual proportion of poultry. Upon inquiry, I found that this farm, was, in point of produce, about one-fifth of the parish. Therefore, the land of this parish produces annually, about 3000 quarters of wheat, 6000 quarters of barley, the wool of 7000 sheep, together with the pigs and poultry. Now, then, leaving green, or moist, vegetables out of the question, as being things that human creatures, and especially *labouring* human creatures ought never to use *as sustenance*, and saying nothing, at present, about milk and butter; leaving these wholly out of the question, let us see how many people the produce of this parish would keep, supposing the people to live all alike, and to have plenty of food and clothing. In order to come at the fact here, let us see what would be the consumption of one family; let it be a family of five persons; a man, wife, and three children, one child big enough to work, one big enough to eat heartily, and one a baby; and this is a pretty fair average of the state of people in the country. Such a family would want 5 lb. of bread a-day; they would want a pound of mutton a-day; they would want two pounds of bacon a-day; they would want, on an average, winter and summer, a gallon and a half of beer a-day; for I mean that they should live, without the aid of the Eastern or the Western slave-drivers. If *sweets* were absolutely necessary for the baby, there would be quite *honey* enough in the parish. Now, then, to begin with the bread, a pound of good wheat, makes a pound of good bread; for, though the offal be taken out, the water is put in; and, indeed, the fact is, that a pound of wheat will make a pound of bread, leaving the offal of the wheat to feed pigs, or other animals, and to produce other human food in this way. The family would, then, use 1825 lb. of wheat in the year, which, at 60 lb. a bushel, would be (leaving out a fraction) 30 bushels, or three quarters and six bushels, *for the year*.

Next comes the mutton, 365 lb. for the year. Next the bacon, 730 lb. As to the quantity of mutton produced; the sheep are bred here, and not fatted in general; but we may fairly suppose, that each of the sheep *kept* here, each of the *standing-stock*, makes, first, or last, half a fat sheep; so that a farm that keeps, on an average, 100 sheep, produces annually 50 fat sheep. Suppose the mutton to be 15 lb. a quarter, then the family will want, within a trifle of, seven sheep a year. Of bacon or pork, 36 score will be wanted. Hogs differ so much in their propensity to fat, that it is difficult to calculate about them; but this is a very good rule: when you see a fat hog, and know how many *score* he will weigh, set down to his account a sack (half a quarter) of barley for every score of his weight; for, let him have been *educated* (as the French call it) as he may, this will be about the real cost of him when he is fat. A sack of barley will make a score of bacon, and it will not make more. Therefore, the family would want 18 quarters of barley in the year for bacon.

As to the *beer*, 18 gallons to the bushel of malt is very good; but, as we allow of no spirits, no wine, and none of the slave produce, we will suppose that a *sixth* part of the beer is *strong* stuff. This would require two bushels of malt to the 18 gallons. The whole would, therefore, take 35 bushels of malt; and a bushel of barley makes a bushel of malt, and, by the *increase* pays the expense of malting. Here, then, the family would want, for beer, four quarters and three bushels of barley. The annual consumption of the family, in victuals and drink, would then be as follows:

	Qrs.	Bush.
Wheat	3	6
Barley	22	3
Sheep	7	

This being the case, the 3000 quarters of wheat, which the parish annually produces, would suffice for 800 families. The 6000 quarters of barley, would suffice for 207 families. The 3500 fat sheep, being half the number kept, would suffice for

500 families. So that here is, produced in the parish of Milston (2), *bread* for 800, *mutton* for 500, and *bacon and beer* for 207 families. Besides victuals and drink, there are clothes, fuel, tools, and household goods wanting; but, there are milk, butter, eggs, poultry, rabbits, hares, and partridges, which I have not noticed, and these are all eatables, and are all eaten too. And as to clothing, and, indeed, fuel and all other wants beyond eating and drinking, are there not 7000 fleeces of South-down wool, weighing, all together, 21,000 lb., and capable of being made into 8400 yards of broad cloth, at two pounds and a half of wool to the yard? Setting, therefore, the wool, the milk, butter, eggs, poultry, and game against all the wants beyond the solid food and drink, we see that the parish of Milston (2) that we have under our eye, would give bread to 800 families, mutton to 500, and bacon and beer to 207. The reason why wheat and mutton are produced in a proportion so much greater than the materials for making bacon and beer, is, that the wheat and the mutton are more loudly demanded *from a distance*, and are much more cheaply conveyed away in proportion to their value. For instance, the wheat and mutton are wanted in the infernal Wen, and some barley is wanted there in the shape of malt; but hogs are not fatted in the Wen, and a larger proportion of the barley is used where it is grown.

Here is, then, bread for 800 families, mutton for 500, and bacon and beer for 207. Let us take the average of the three, and then we have 502 families, for the keeping of whom, and in this good manner too, the parish of Milston (2) yields a sufficiency. In the wool, the milk, butter, eggs, poultry, and game, we have seen ample, and much more than ample, provision for all wants, other than those of mere food and drink. What I have allowed in food and drink, is by no means excessive. It is but a pound of bread, and a little more than half-a-pound of meat a day, to each person on an average; and the beer is not a drop too much. There are no green and moist vegetables, included in my account; but, there would be some, and they would not do any harm; but, no man can say, or, at least, none but a base usurer, who would grind money out of the bones of his own father; no other man can, or will, say, that I have been *too liberal* to this family; and yet, good God! what extravagance is here, if the labourers of England be now treated justly!

Is there a family, even amongst those who live the hardest, in the Wen, that would not shudder at the thought of living upon what I have allowed to this family? Yet what do labourers' families get, compared to this? The answer to that question, ought to make us shudder indeed. The amount of my allowance, compared with the amount of the allowance that labourers now have, is necessary to be stated here, before I proceed further. The wheat, 3 qrs. and 6 bushels, at present price (56s. the quarter) amounts to 10l. 10s. The barley (for bacon and beer) 22 qrs. 3 bushels, at present price (34s. the quarter), amounts to 37l. 16s. 9d. The seven sheep, at 40s. each, amount to 14l. The total is 62l. 6s. 9d.; and this, observe, for *bare victuals and drink;* just food and drink enough to keep people in working condition.

What then *do* the labourers get? To what fare has this wretched and most infamous system brought them! Why such a family as I have described is allowed to have, *at the utmost,* only about 9s. a week. The parish allowance is only about 7s. 6d. for the five people, including clothing, fuel, bedding and everything! Monstrous state of things! But, let us suppose it to be *nine shillings.* Even that makes only 23l. 8s. a year, for food, drink, clothing, fuel and everything, whereas I allow 62l. 6s. 8d. a year for the bare eating and drinking; and that is little enough. Monstrous, barbarous, horrible as this appears, we do not, however, see it, in half its horrors; our indignation and rage against this infernal system, is not half roused, till we see the small number of labourers who raise all the food and the drink, and, of course, the mere trifling portion of it that they are suffered to retain for their own use.[1]

---

[1] The following tables, taken from Mulhall's Statistics, show—1st. The yearly average consumption of necessaries per inhabitant in different

The parish of Milston (2) does, as we have seen, produce food, drink, clothing, and all other things, enough for 502 families, or 2510 persons upon my allowance, which is a great deal more than three times the present allowance, because the present allowance includes clothing, fuel, tools and everything. Now, then, according to the "Population Return," laid before countries; 2nd, The average rate of agricultural wages in England in the years 1800, 1850, and 1880; and 3rd, average annual cost of living of agricultural family:—

1.—YEARLY CONSUMPTION OF NECESSARIES.

	Per Inhabitant, lbs.				Value.		
	Grain.	Meat.	Butter.	Sugar.			
	lbs.	lbs.	lbs.	lbs.	£	s.	d.
United Kingdom	330	105	13	68	7	2	0
France	505	74	4	21	5	11	0
Germany	585	69	8	21	5	17	0
Russia	490	48	3	7	3	4	0
Austria	410	64	5	14	4	16	0
Italy	420	23	1	7	3	3	0
United States	392	120	16	23	6	6	0
Average	445	81	7	23	5	2	0

2.—AVERAGE RATE OF AGRICULTURAL WAGES IN ENGLAND.

	Bailiff.	Shepherd.	Labourer.	Woman.	Boy.
In year 1800	£20	£16	£12	£8	£6
,, 1850	40	25	20	10	8
,, 1880	52	36	30	15	10

3.—AVERAGE ANNUAL COST OF LIVING OF AGRICULTURAL FAMILY, (five persons).

	Bread, Meat, &c.	Groceries.	Rent.	Clothing, &c.	Total.
In year 1823	£17	£3	£3	£8	£31
,, 1883	20	5	4	8	37

Parliament, this parish contains 500 persons, or, according to my division, one hundred families. So that here are about *one hundred* families to raise food and drink enough, and to raise wool and other things to pay for all other necessaries, for *five hundred* and *two* families! Aye, and five hundred and two families fed and lodged, too, on my liberal scale. Fed and lodged according to the present scale, this one hundred families raise enough to supply more, and many more, than fifteen hundred families; or seven thousand five hundred persons! And yet those who do the work are half-starved! In the 100 families there are, we will suppose, 80 able working men, and as many boys, sometimes assisted by the women and stout girls. What a handful of people to raise such a quantity of food! What injustice, what a hellish system it must be, to make those who raise it, skin and bone and nakedness, while the food and drink and wool are almost all carried away to be heaped on the fund-holders, pensioners, soldiers, dead-weight and other swarms of tax-eaters! If such an operation do not need putting an end to, then the devil himself is a saint.

Thus it must be, or something like it, all the way down this fine and beautiful and interesting valley. There are 29 agricultural parishes, the two last (30 and 31) being in town; being Fisherton and Salisbury. Now, according to the "Population Return," the whole of these 29 parishes contain 9,116 persons; or, according to my division 1,823 families. There is no reason to believe, that the proportion that we have seen in the case of Milston (2) does not hold good all the way through; that is, there is no reason to suppose, that the produce does not exceed the consumption in every other case in the same degree, that it does in the case of Milston (2). And, indeed if I were to judge from the number of houses and the number of ricks of corn, I should suppose that the excess was still greater in several of the other parishes. But, supposing it to be no greater; supposing the same proportion to continue all the way from Wooton Rivers (1) to Stratford (29), then here are 9,116 persons raising food and raiment sufficient for 45,580 persons, fed and lodged according to my scale; and sufficient for ~36,740 persons, according to the scale on which the unhappy labourers of this fine valley are now fed and lodged!

And yet there is an "*Emigration Committee*" sitting to devise the means of getting *rid*, not of the idlers, not of the pensioners, not of the dead-weight, not of the parsons (to "relieve" whom we have seen the poor labourers taxed to the tune of a million and a half of money), not of the soldiers; but to devise means of getting rid of *these working people*, who are grudged even the miserable morsel that they get! There is in the men calling themselves "English country gentlemen" something superlatively base. They are, I sincerely believe, the most cruel, the most unfeeling, the most brutally insolent: but I know, I can prove, I can safely take my oath, that they are the most base of all the creatures, that God ever suffered to disgrace the human shape. The base wretches know well, that the *taxes* amount to more than *sixty millions* a year, and that the *poor-rates* amount to about *seven millions;* yet, while the cowardly reptiles never utter a word against the taxes, they are incessantly railing against the poor-rates, though it is, (and they know it) the taxes that make the paupers. The base wretches know well, that the sum of money given, even to the fellows that gather the taxes, is greater in amount than the poor-rates; the base wretches know well, that the money, given to the dead-weight (who ought not to have a single farthing), amounts to more than the poor receive out of the rates; the base wretches know well, that the common foot soldier now receives more pay per week (7*s*. 7*d*.) exclusive of clothing, firing, candle, and lodging; the base wretches know, that the common foot soldier receives more to go down his own single throat, than the overseers and magistrates allow to a working man, his wife and three children; the base wretches know all this well; and yet their railings are confined to the *poor*, and the *poor-rates;* and it is expected that they will, next session, urge the Parliament to pass a law to enable overseers and vestries and magistrates *to transport paupers beyond the seas!* They are base enough for this, or for anything; but the whole system will go to the d—— long before

they will get such an Act passed; long before they will see
perfected this consummation of their infamous tyranny.[1]

It is manifest enough, that the *population* of this valley was,
at one time, many times over what it is now; for, in the first
place, what were the twenty-nine churches built *for?* The
population of the 29 parishes is now but little more than one-
half of that of the single parish of Kensington; and there are
several of the churches bigger than the church at Kensington.
What, then, should all these churches have been built *for?*
And besides, where did the hands come from? And where
did the money come from? These twenty-nine churches would

---

[1] On this subject, the previous Editor remarks that at the time he was writing (1853) it was reported that the emigration from the United Kingdom was at the rate of 1000 per day; and that during eleven months of 1848 244,251 persons emigrated. Upon the same subject the *Economist* paper, a ministerial organ, in an article, dated 17th February 1849, remarked :—" Not only the Continent of Europe but the United States and all our colonies are now thrown open to the industry of the farmers of England, who are no longer limited to the land owned by the English aristocracy. It is the alteration in the relation between farmers and landlords and the substitution of considerations, purely commercial, against which the landowners of England (since the soil of the United States has been offered to the industry of our farmers) will have to provide. It will be the business of the landlords, to keep them and their capital, within the nation, by offering the land to them on the easiest terms possible." If the above comment on agricultural prospects had been dated 1884, in lieu of 1849, it could not better describe the present condition of the farming interest.

With respect to the emigration of paupers (by the 4th and 5th William IV. c. 76, s. 62), parishes in England and Wales were empowered to raise funds by a yearly rate for defraying the expenses of poor persons willing to emigrate; by the 11th and 12th Vic. c. 110, the guardians were empowered to promote the voluntary emigration of the poor (as above stated), and to charge the expenses upon the "ordinary funds for the relief of the poor."

By the 12th and 13th Vic. c. 103, s. 20, the guardians are empowered to expend a sum, not extending £10 for each person, on the emigration of paupers. By the 13th and 14th Vic. c. 101, s. 4. the guardians are empowered to expend money in the emigration of any poor orphan or deserted child under the age of sixteen years. In justice to the guardians, however, it is right to state, that they are very loth to expend any large amount for emigration purposes, as they consider that the pressure of the poor rates upon many of the rate-payers is so heavy, that it is unjust to tax those who are but little removed from paupers for the purpose of aiding paupers to secure a free and independent position in life.

now not only hold all the inhabitants, men, women, and children, but all the household goods, and tools, and implements, of the whole of them, farmers and all, if you leave out the waggons and carts. In three instances, Fifield, Milston, and Durrington (16, 22, and 23), the *church-porches* will hold all the inhabitants, even down to the bed-ridden, and the babies. What then, will any man believe, that these churches were built for such little knots of people? We are told about the *great* superstition of our fathers, and of their readiness to gratify the priests, by building altars and other religious edifices. But, we must think those priests to have been most devout creatures indeed, if we believe, that they chose to have the money laid out in *useless* churches, rather than have it put into their own pockets! At any rate, we all know that Protestant Priests have no whim of *this sort;* and that they never lay out upon churches any money, that they can, by any means, get hold of.

But, suppose that we were to believe that the Priests had, in old times, this unaccountable taste; and suppose we were to believe that a knot of people, who might be crammed into a church-porch, were seized, and very frequently too, with the desire of having a big church to go to; we must, after all this, believe that this knot of people were more than *giants*, or that they had surprising *riches*, else we cannot believe that they had *the means* of gratifying the strange wishes of their Priests, and their own not less strange *piety* and *devotion*. Even if we could believe that they thought that they were paving their way to heaven, by building churches which were a hundred times too large for the population, still we cannot believe, that the building could have been effected without bodily force; and, where was this force to come from, if the people were not more numerous than they now are? What, again, I ask, were these twenty-nine churches stuck up, not a mile from each other; what were twenty-nine churches made *for*, if the population had been no greater than it is now?

But, in fact, you plainly see all the traces of a great ancient population. The churches are almost all large, and built in the best manner. Many of them are very fine edifices; very costly in the building; and, in the cases where the body of the church has been altered in the repairing of it, so as to make it smaller, the *tower*, which every where defies the hostility of time, shows you what the church must formerly have been. This is the case in several instances; and there are two or three of these villages which must formerly have been *market-towns*, and particularly Pewsey and Upavon (5 and 13). There are now no less than nine of the parishes, out of the twenty-nine, that have either no parsonage-houses, or have such as are in such a state that a Parson will not, or cannot, live in them. Three of them are without any parsonage-houses at all, and the rest are become poor, mean, falling-down places. This latter is the case at Upavon, which was formerly a very considerable place. Nothing can more clearly show, than this, that all, as far as buildings and population are concerned, have been long upon the decline and decay. Dilapidation after dilapidation have, at last, almost effaced even the parsonage-houses, and that too in *defiance of the law*, ecclesiastical as well as civil. The land remains; and the crops and the sheep come as abundantly as ever; but they are now sent almost wholly away, instead of remaining as formerly, to be, in great part, consumed in these twenty-nine parishes.

The *stars*, in my map, mark the spots where manor-houses, or gentlemen's mansions, formerly stood, and stood, too, only about sixty years ago. Every parish had its manor-house in the first place; and then there were, down this Valley, twenty-one others; so that, in this distance of about thirty miles, there stood fifty mansion-houses. Where are they *now?* I believe there are but eight, that are at all worthy of the name of mansion houses; and even these are but poorly kept up, and, except in two or three instances, are of no benefit to the labouring people; they employ but few persons; and, in short, do not half supply the place of any eight of the old mansions. All these mansions, all these parsonages, aye, and their goods and furniture, together with the clocks, the brass kettles, the brewing-vessels, the good bedding, and good clothes, and good furniture, and the stock in pigs, or in money, of the inferior classes, in this series of once populous, and gay villages and hamlets; all these have been by the accursed system of taxing and funding and paper-money, by the well-known exactions of the state, and by the not less real, though less generally understood, extortions of the *monopolies* arising out of paper-money; all these have been, by these accursed means, conveyed away, out of this Valley, to the haunts of the tax-eaters, and the monopolizers. There are many of the *mansion houses*, the ruins of which you yet behold. At Milston (2) there are two mansion houses, the walls and the roofs of which yet remain, but which are falling gradually to pieces, and the garden walls are crumbling down. At Enford (15), Bennet the Member for the county, had a large mansion house, the stables of which are yet standing. In several places, I saw, still remaining, indubitable traces of an ancient manor house, namely a dove-cote or pigeon-house. The poor pigeons have kept possession of their heritage, from generation to generation, and so have the rooks, in their several rookeries, while the paper-system has swept away, or, rather swallowed up, the owners of the dove-cotes and of the lofty trees, about forty families of which owners have been ousted in this one Valley, and have became dead-weight creatures, tax-gatherers, barrack-fellows, thief-takers, or, perhaps, paupers or thieves.

Senator Snip[1] congratulated, some years ago, that preciously honourable "Collective *Wisdom*," of which he is a most worthy Member; Snip congratulated it on the success of the late war in creating capital! Snip is, you must know, a great *feelosofer*, and a not less great *feenanceer*. Snip cited, as a proof of the great and glorious effects of paper-money, the new and fine houses in London, the new streets and squares, the new roads, new canals and bridges. Snip was not, I dare say, aware, that this same paper-money had

---

[1] This nickname (to which reference has been already made) is supposed to refer to Mr. John Maberly, M.P., who had been engaged in Government contracts for army clothing.

destroyed forty mansion houses in this Vale of Avon, and had taken away all the goods, all the substance, of the little gentry and of the labouring class. Snip was not, I dare say, aware, that this same paper-money had, in this one Vale of only thirty miles long, dilapidated, and, in some cases, wholly demolished, nine out of twenty-nine even of the parsonage houses. I told Snip at the time, (1821), that paper money could create no valuable thing. I begged Snip to bear this in mind. I besought all my readers, and particularly Mr. Mathias Atwood (one of the members for *Lowther*town), not to believe that paper-money ever did, or ever could, *create* any thing of any value. I besought him to look well into the matter, and assured him, that he would find that though paper-money could *create* nothing of value, it was able to *transfer* every thing of value; able to strip a little gentry; able to dilapidate even parsonage houses; able to rob gentlemen of their estates, and labourers of their Sunday-coats and their barrels of beer; able to snatch the dinner from the board of the reaper or the mower, and to convey it to the barrack-table of the Hessian, or Hanoverian grenadier; able to take away the wool, that ought to give warmth to the bodies of those who rear the sheep, and put it on the backs of those who carry arms to keep the poor, half-famished shepherds in order!

I have never been able clearly to comprehend what the beastly Scotch *feelosofers* mean by their "national wealth;" but, as far as I can understand them, this is their meaning: that national wealth means, that which is *left* of the products of the country over and above what is *consumed*, or *used*, by those whose labour causes the products to be. This being the notion, it follows, of course, that the *fewer* poor devils, you can screw the products out of, the *richer* the nation is.[1]

This is, too, the notion of Burdett as expressed in his silly and most nasty, musty aristocratic speech of last session.

---

[1] One of the problems, which it is the business of political economy to solve, is how to produce the most, with the least labour. The present interchange of commerce, which exists throughout the civilised world, furnishes a ready market for the over-produce of any country.

What, then, is to be done with this *over-produce*? Who is to have it? Is it to go to pensioners, placemen, tax-gatherers, dead-weight people, soldiers, gendarmerie, police-people, and, in short, to whole millions *who do no work at all*? Is this a cause of "national wealth?" Is a nation made *rich* by taking the food and clothing from those who create them, and giving them to those who do nothing of any use? Aye, but this over-produce may be given to *manufacturers*, and to those who supply the food-raisers with what they want besides food. Oh! but this is merely an *exchange* of one valuable thing for another valuable thing; it is an exchange of labour in Wiltshire, for labour in Lancashire; and, upon the whole, here is no *over-production*. If the produce be exported, it is the same thing: it is an exchange of one sort of labour for another. But, *our case* is, that there is not an exchange; that those who labour, no matter in what way, have a large part of the fruit of their labour taken away, and receive nothing in exchange. If the over-produce of this Valley of Avon were given, by the farmers, to the weavers in Lancashire, to the iron and steel chaps of Warwickshire, and to other makers or sellers of useful things, there would come an abundance of all these useful things into this valley from Lancashire and other parts; but if, as is the case, the over-produce goes to the fund-holders, the dead-weight, the soldiers, the lord and lady and master and miss pensioners and sinecure people; if the over-produce go to them, as a very great part of it does, nothing, not even the parings of one's nails, can come back to the valley in exchange. And, can this operation, then, add to the "national wealth"? It adds to the "wealth" of those who carry on the affairs of state; it fills their pockets, those of their relatives and dependents; it fattens all tax-eaters; but it can give no wealth to the "nation," which means the whole of the people. National Wealth means the Commonwealth or Commonweal; and these mean, the general good, or happiness, of the people, and the safety and honour of the state; and these are not to be secured by robbing those who labour, in order to support a large part of the community in idleness. Devizes is the market-town to which the corn goes from the greater part of this Valley. If, when a waggon-load of wheat goes off in the morning, the waggon came back at night loaded with cloth, salt, or something or other, equal in value to the wheat, except what might be necessary to leave with the shopkeeper as his profit; then, indeed, the people might see the waggon go off without tears in their eyes. But, now, they see it go to carry away, and to bring next to nothing in return.

What a *twist* a head must have before it can come to the conclusion, that the nation gains in wealth by the Government being able to cause the work to be done by those who have hardly any share in the fruit of the labour! What a *twist* such a head must have! The Scotch *feelosofers*, who seem all to have been, by nature, formed for negro-drivers, have an insuperable objection to all those establishments and customs which occasion *holidays*. They call them a great hindrance, a great bar to industry, a great drawback from "national wealth." I wish each of these unfeeling fellows had a spade put into his hand for ten days, only ten days, and that he were compelled to dig only just as much as one of the common labourers at Fulham. The metaphysical gentleman would, I believe, soon discover the *use of holidays!* But, *why* should men, why should *any* men work *hard?* Why, I ask, should they work incessantly, if working part of the days of the week be sufficient? Why should the people at Milston (2), for instance, work incessantly, when they now raise food, and clothing, and fuel, and every necessary to maintain well five times their number? Why should they not have some holidays?[1] And, pray, say, thou conceited Scotch feelosofer, how the "national wealth" can be increased by making these people

---

[1] The establishment of Bank Holidays (Act, 25th May 1871) has been of great benefit to a certain class; but it may be doubted whether it is an unmixed good to those who are enforced to sacrifice a day's pay for the holiday. Most of the agricultural labourers, for instance, would lose a day's wage if they took advantage of the Act, and their families would consequently suffer.

work incessantly, that they may raise food and clothing, to go to feed and clothe people who do not work at all?

The state of this Valley seems to illustrate the infamous, and really diabolical assertion of Malthus, which is, that the human kind have a natural tendency *to increase beyond the means of sustenance for them*. Hence, all the schemes of this, and the other Scotch writers for what they call checking population. Now, look at this Valley of Avon. Here the people raise nearly twenty times as much food and clothing, as they consume. They raise five times as much, even according to my scale of living. They have been doing this for many, many years. They have been doing it for several generations. Where, then, is their natural tendency to increase beyond the means of sustenance for them? Beyond, indeed, the means of that sustenance which a system like this will leave them. Say that, Sawneys, and I agree with you. Far beyond the means that the taxing and monopolising system will leave in their hands: that is very true; for it leaves them nothing but the scale of the poor-book: they must cease to breed at all, or they must exceed this mark: but, the *earth*, which gives them their fair share of its products, will always give sustenance in sufficiency, to those who apply to it by skilful and diligent labour.[1]

The villages down this Valley of Avon, and, indeed, it was the same in almost every part of this county, and in the North and West of Hampshire also, used to have great employment for the women and children in the carding and spinning of wool for the making of broad-cloth. This was a very general

---

[1] Lord Brougham, in a speech in the House of Commons, April 9, 1816, said, "It might be objectionable (on many grounds) to withhold relief from the future issue of marriages *already contracted:* but why may not such relief be refused to the children born of marriages contracted after a certain period?"

The dismal doctrines on "excessive population" seem to have been carried to such an excess, that a work appeared in 1838 (entitled "On the Possibility of Limiting Populousness," by Marcus), in which a plan was gravely recommended for murdering infant children, by means of (what the author calls) "painless extinction." The book (which contained 73 8vo pages) was sold by a respectable firm of publishers, viz., Messrs. Sherwood & Co.

employment for the women and girls; but, it is now wholly gone; and this has made a vast change in the condition of the people, and in the state of property and of manners and of morals. In 1816, I wrote and published a *Letter to the Luddites*, the object of which was to combat their hostility to the use of machinery. The arguments I there made use of were general. I took the matter in the abstract. The *principles* were all correct enough; but their application cannot be universal; and, we have a case here before us, at this moment, which, in my opinion, shows, that the mechanic inventions, pushed to the extent that they have been, have been productive of great calamity to this country, and that they will be productive of still greater calamity; unless, indeed, it be their brilliant destiny, to be the immediate cause of putting an end to the present system.

The greater part of manufactures consists of *clothing* and *bedding*. Now, if by using a machine, we can get our coat with less labour than we got it before, the machine is a desirable thing. But, then, mind, we must have the machine at home, and we ourselves must have the profit of it; for, if the machine be elsewhere; if it be worked by other hands; if other persons have the profit of it; and if, in consequence of the existence of the machine, we have hands at home, who have nothing to do, and whom we must keep, then the machine is an injury to us, however advantageous it may be to those who use it, and whatever traffic it may occasion with foreign States.

Such is the case with regard to this cloth-making. The machines are at Upton-Level, Warmister, Bradford, Westbury, and Trowbridge, and here are some of the hands in the Valley of Avon. This Valley raises food and clothing; but, in order to raise them, it must have *labourers*. These are absolutely necessary; for, without them, this rich and beautiful Valley becomes worth nothing, except to wild animals and their pursuers. The labourers are *men* and *boys*. Women and girls occasionally; but the men and the boys are as necessary as the light of day, or as the air and the water. Now, if beastly Malthus, or any of his nasty disciples, can discover a mode of having men and boys without having women and girls, then, certainly, the machine must be a good thing; but, if this Valley must absolutely have the women and the girls, then the machine, by leaving them with nothing to do, is a mischievous thing; and a producer of most dreadful misery. What, with regard to the poor, is the great complaint now? Why, that the *single man* does not receive the same, or any thing like the same, wages as the *married* man. Aye, it is the wife and girls that are the burden; and to be sure a burden they must be, under a system of taxation like the present, and with no work to do. Therefore, whatever may be saved in labour by the machine is no benefit, but an injury to the mass of the people. For, in fact, all that the women and children earned was so much clear addition to what the family earns now. The greatest part of the clothing in the United States of America, is made by the farm women and girls. They do almost the whole of it; and all that they do, is done at home. To be sure, they might buy cheap; but they must buy for less than nothing, if not, it would not answer their purpose to *make* the things.[1]

---

[1] It has never been questioned that machinery has aided greatly to place the poor more nearly on a par with the rich, by enabling them to obtain, at a cheap rate, many comforts which they could not otherwise possess. A fallacy often prevails, that machinery dispenses with hand labour. But machinery must, first of all, be made with hands: moreover, machinery does not diminish the capital of a country, but it increases it, and this capital is still employed in the payment of wages. It is, however, true that there is often a shifting of the parties to whom the wages are paid. The remedy for this is, for the working man to learn the faculty of turning his hand to any new employment, when he finds it necessary to do so. In 1816 the people in the Northern and Midland Counties (being in great distress) attributed their calamity to the use of machinery, and great rioting and destruction of property followed. The rioters were called "Luddites," and have already been mentioned in this work. Mr. Cobbett was requested to issue a public address in his *Register* to these misguided people, and he did so, in a twopenny paper addressed To the Journeymen and Labourers of England, Wales, Scotland, and Ireland. The effect which this address produced was marvellous. In 1831 Lord Brougham obtained permission from the Author to republish the address; so important an influence was it supposed to possess.

The survey of this Valley is, I think, the finest answer in the world, to the "Emigration Committee" fellows, and to Jerry Curteis (one of the Members for Sussex), who has been giving "evidence" before it. I shall find out, when I can get to see the *report*, what this "Emigration Committee" would be *after*. I remember, that, last winter, a young woman, complained to one of the Police Justices, that the Overseers of some parish were going to transport her orphan brother to Canada, because he became chargeable to their parish! I remember also, that the Justice said, that the intention of the Overseers was "premature," for that "the Bill had not yet passed!" This was rather an ugly story; and I do think, that we shall find, that there have been, and are, some pretty propositions before this "Committee." We shall see all about the matter, however, by-and-by; and, when we get the transporting project fairly before us, shall we not then loudly proclaim "the envy of surrounding nations and admiration of the world!"

But, what ignorance, impudence, and insolence must those base wretches have, who propose to transport the labouring people, as being too numerous, while the produce, which is obtained by their labour, is more than sufficient for three, four, or five, or even ten times their numbers! Jerry Curteis, who has, it seems, been a famous witness on this occasion, says that the poor-rates, in many cases, amount to as much as the rent. Well: and what then, Jerry? The rent may be high enough too, and the farmer may afford to pay them both; for, a very large part of what you call *poor-rates*, ought to be called *wages*. But, at any rate, what has all this to do, with the necessity of emigration? To make out such necessity, you must make out that you have more mouths, than the produce of the parish will feed? Do then, Jerry, tell us, another time, a little about the quantity of food, annually raised in four or five adjoining parishes; for, is it not something rather damnable, Jerry, to talk of *transporting* Englishmen, on account of the *excess of their numbers*, when the fact is notorious, that their labour produces, five or ten times as much food and raiment as they and their families consume?

However, to drop Jerry, for the present, the baseness, the foul, the stinking, the carrion baseness, of the fellows that call themselves "country gentlemen," is, that the wretches, while railing against the poor and the poor-rates; while affecting to believe, that the poor are wicked and lazy; while complaining that the poor, the working people, are too numerous, and that the country villages are too populous: the carrion baseness of these wretches, is that, while they are thus *bold* with regard to the working and poor people, they never even whisper a word against pensioners, placemen, soldiers, parsons, fundholders, tax-gatherers, or tax-eaters! They say not a word against the prolific dead-weight, to whom they give a premium for breeding, while they want to check the population of labourers! They never say a word about the too great populousness of the Wen; nor about that of Liverpool, Manchester, Cheltenham, and the like! Oh! they are the most cowardly, the very basest, the most scandalously base reptiles, that ever were warmed into life by the rays of the sun!

In taking my leave of this beautiful vale, I have to express my deep shame, as an Englishman, at beholding the general *extreme poverty* of those, who cause this vale to produce such quantities of food and raiment. This is, I verily believe it, the *worst used labouring people upon the face of the earth.* Dogs, and hogs, and horses, are treated with more civility; and as to food and lodging, how gladly would the labourers change with them! This state of things never can continue many years! *By some means or other* there must be an end to it, and my firm belief is, that that end will be dreadful. In the mean while I see, and I see it with pleasure, that the common people know that they are ill used; and that they cordially, most cordially, hate those who ill-treat them.

During the day, I crossed the river about fifteen or sixteen times, and in such hot weather it was very pleasant to be so much amongst meadows and water. I had been at Nether-

The Valley of the Avon. 83

Avon (18) about eighteen years ago, where I had seen a great quantity of hares. It is a place belonging to Mr. Hicks Beach, or Beech, who was once a member of parliament. I found the place altered a good deal; out of repair; the gates rather rotten; and (a very bad sign!) the roof of the dog-kennel falling in! There is a church, at this village of Netheravon, large enough to hold a thousand or two of people, and the whole parish contains only 350 souls, men, women and children. This Netheravon was formerly a great lordship, and in the parish, there were three considerable mansion-houses, besides the one near the church. These mansions are all down now; and it is curious enough to see the former *walled gardens* become *orchards*, together with other changes, all tending to prove the gradual decay in all except what appertains merely to *the land* as a thing of production for the distant market. But, indeed, the people and the means of enjoyment must go away. They are *drawn* away by the taxes, and the paper-money. How are *twenty thousand new houses* to be, all at once, building in the Wen, without people and food and raiment going from this valley towards the Wen? It must be so; and this unnatural, this dilapidating, this ruining and debasing work must go on, until that which produces it be destroyed.

When I came down to Stratford (29) I wanted to go across to Laverstock, which lay to my left of Salisbury; but just on the side of the road here, at Stratford Dean, rises the *Accursed Hill.* It is very lofty. It was originally a hill in an irregular sort of sugar-loaf shape: but, it was so altered by the Romans, or by somebody, that the upper three-quarter parts of the hill now, when seen from a distance, somewhat resemble *three cheeses,* laid one upon another; the bottom one a great deal broader than the next, and the top one like a Stilton cheese, in proportion to a Gloucester one. I resolved to ride over this accursed Hill. As I was going up a field towards it, I met a man going home from work. I asked how he *got on?* He said, very badly. I asked him what was the cause of it? He said the *hard times.* "What *times?*" said I, "was there "ever a finer summer, a finer harvest, and is there not an "*old* wheat-rick in every farm-yard?" "Ah!" said he, "*they* "make it bad for poor people, for all that." "*They?*" said I, "who are *they?*" He was silent. "Oh, no, no! my friend," said I, "it is not *they;* it is that Accursed Hill that has "robbed you of the supper that you ought to find smoking on "the table when you get home." I gave him the price of a pot of beer, and on I went, leaving the poor dejected assemblage of skin and bone to wonder at my words.

The hill is very steep, and I dismounted and led my horse up. Being as near to the top as I could conveniently get, I stood a little while reflecting, not so much on the changes which that hill had seen, as on the changes, the terrible changes, which, in all human probability, it had *yet to see*, and which it would have greatly *helped to produce*. It was impossible to stand on this accursed spot, without swelling with indignation against the base and plundering and murderous sons of corruption. I have often wished, and I, speaking out aloud, expressed the wish now; "May that man perish for ever and ever, who, having the "power, neglects to bring to justice the perjured, the suborn-"ing, the insolent and perfidious miscreants, who openly sell "their country's rights and their own souls."

From the Accursed Hill, I went to Laverstock where "Jemmy Burrough" (as they call him here) the Judge, lives. I have not heard much about "Jemmy" since he tried and condemned the two young men who had wounded the game-keepers of Ashton Smith and Lord Palmerston. His Lord-ship (Palmerston) is, I see, making a tolerable figure in the newspapers as a *share-man!* I got into Salisbury about half-past seven o'clock, less tired than I recollect ever to have been, after so long a ride; for, including my several crossings of the river, and my deviations to look at churches and farm-yards and rick-yards, I think I must have ridden nearly forty miles.

RIDE FROM SALISBURY TO WARMINSTER, FROM WARMINSTER TO FROME, FROM FROME TO DEVIZES, AND FROM DEVIZES TO HIGHWORTH.

"Hear this, O ye that swallow up the needy, even to make the poor of "the land to fail : saying, When will the new moon be gone that we may "sell corn? And the Sabbath, that we may set forth wheat, making the "Ephah small, and the Shekel great, and falsifying the balances by "deceit; that we may buy the poor for silver, and the needy for a pair of "shoes; yea, and sell the refuse of the wheat? Shall not the land "tremble for this; and every one mourn that dwelleth therein? I will "turn your feasts into mourning, saith the Lord God, and all your songs "into lamentations."—Amos, chap. viii. ver. 4 to 10.

Heytesbury (Wilts), Thursday,
31st August, 1826.

This place, which is one of the rotten boroughs of Wiltshire, and which was formerly a considerable town, is now but a very miserable affair. Yesterday morning I went into the Cathedral at Salisbury about 7 o'clock. When I got into the nave of the church, and was looking up and admiring the columns and the roof, I heard a sort of *humming*, in some place which appeared to be in the transept of the building. I wondered what it was, and made my way towards the place whence the noise appeared to issue. As I approached it, the noise seemed to grow louder. At last, I thought, I could distinguish the sounds of the human voice. This encouraged me to proceed; and, still following the sound, I at last turned in at a doorway to my left, where I found a priest and his congregation assembled. It was a parson of some sort, with a white covering on him, and five women, and four men : when I arrived, there were five couple of us. I joined the congregation, until they came to the *litany;* and then, being monstrously hungry, I did not think myself bound to stay any longer. I wonder what the founders would say, if they could rise from the grave, and see such a congregation as this, in this most magnificent and beautiful cathedral? I wonder what they would say, if they could know *to what purpose* the endowments of this Cathedral are now applied; and above all things, I wonder what they would say, if they could see the half-starved labourers, that now minister to the luxuries of those, who wallow in the wealth of those endowments. There is one thing, at any rate, that might be abstained from, by those, that revel in the riches of those endowments; namely, to abuse and blackguard those of our forefathers, from whom the endowments came, and who erected the edifice, and carried so far towards the skies, that beautiful and matchless spire, of which the present possessors have the impudence to boast, while they represent as ignorant and benighted creatures, those who conceived the grand design, and who executed the scientific and costly work. These fellows, in big white wigs, of the size of half a bushel, have the audacity, even within the walls of the Cathedrals themselves, to rail against those who founded them; and Rennell and Sturges, while they were actually, literally, fattening on the spoils of the monastery of St. Swithin, at Winchester, were publishing abusive pamphlets against that Catholic religion which had given them their very bread.[1] For my part, I could not look up at the spire and the whole of the church at Salisbury, without *feeling* that I lived in degenerate times. Such a thing never could be made *now*. We *feel* that, as we look at the building. It really does appear that if our forefathers had not made these buildings, we should have forgotten, before now, what the Christian religion was![2]

---

[1] The Author is here referring to a "pamphlet controversy," which took place in the year 1800, between Dr. Sturges, a Prebendary of Winchester, and Dr. Milner, a Roman Catholic Bishop. The correspondence of the latter, was published under the title of Letters to a Prebendary.

[2] The Author appears here, and elsewhere, to fall into the popular error, that the property of the Church of England was acquired, when the Church was under the sway of "Roman Catholicism," and therefore that the Romanists have a sort of equitable claim to it, on the ground that it was given by people who held their doctrines, for the purpose of maintaining those doctrines. The truth is, however, that nearly all the property which the Church at present possesses, was acquired either before or within two

At Salisbury, or very near to it, four other rivers fall into the Avon. The Wyly river, the Nadder, the Born, and another little river that comes from Norrington. These all become one, at last, just below Salisbury, and then, under the name of the Avon, wind along down and fall into the sea at Christchurch. In coming from Salisbury, I came up the road which runs pretty nearly parallel with the river Wyly, which river rises at Warminster and in the neighbourhood. This river runs down a valley twenty-two miles long. It is not so pretty as the valley of the Avon; but it is very fine in its whole length from Salisbury to this place (Heytesbury). Here are watered meadows, nearest to the river on both sides; then the gardens, the houses, and the corn-fields. After the corn-fields come the downs; but, generally speaking, the downs are not so bold here as they are on the sides of the Avon. The downs do not come out in promontories so often as they do, on the sides of the Avon. The *Ah-ah!* if I may so express it, is not so deep, and the sides of it not so steep, as in the case of the Avon; but the villages are as frequent; there is more than one church in every mile, and there has been a due proportion of mansion houses, demolished and defaced. The farms are very fine up this vale, and the meadows, particularly at a place called Stapleford, are singularly fine. They had just been mowed at Stapleford, and the hay carried off. At Stapleford, there is a little cross valley, running up between two hills of the down. There is a little run of water, about a yard wide at this time, coming down this little vale across the road into the river. The little vale runs up three miles. It does not appear to be half a mile

---

centuries after the Norman Conquest, or since the Reformation. The Episcopal and Capitular Estates, the Tithes, and most of the Glebe Lands, were given (as has been already shown) by Royal grants, and by landowners, before the Norman Conquest, or within two centuries of that time. Salisbury Cathedral was begun A.D. 1220, and finished A.D. 1258. From the latter date to the Reformation the property which the Church acquired consisted mainly of monasteries and chantries, and of all these she was deprived by Henry VIII., as well as of nearly one half the Great Tithes, which thenceforth passed into lay hands.

wide; but in those three miles there are four churches; namely, Stapleford, Uppington, Berwick St. James, and Winterborne Stoke. The present population of these four villages is 769 souls, men, women, and children, the whole of whom, could very conveniently be seated in the chancel of the church, at Stapleford. Indeed, the church and parish of Uppington seem to have been united, with one of the other parishes, like the parish in Kent, which was united with North Cray, and not a single house of which now remains. What were these four churches *built for* within the distance of three miles? There are three parsonage houses still remaining; but, and it is a very curious fact, neither of them good enough for the parson to live in! Here are seven hundred and sixty souls to be taken care of, but there is no parsonage house for a soul-curer to stay in, or at least that he *will* stay in; and all the three parsonages are, in the return laid before Parliament, represented to be no better than miserable labourers' cottages, though the parish of Winterborne Stoke has a church sufficient, to contain two or three thousand people. The truth is, that the parsons have been receiving the revenues of the livings, and have been suffering the parsonage houses to fall into decay. Here were two or three mansion houses, which are also gone, even from the sides of this little run of water.

To-day has been exceedingly hot. Hotter, I think, for a short time, than I ever felt it in England before. In coming through a village called Wishford, and mounting a little hill, I thought the heat upon my back was as great as I had ever felt it in my life. There were thunder storms about, and it had rained at Wishford, a little before I came to it.

My next village was one that I had lived in, for a short time, when I was only about ten or eleven years of age. I had been sent down with a horse from Farnham, and I remember that I went by *Stone-henge*, and rode up and looked at the stones. From Stone-henge I went to the village of Steeple Langford, where I remained from the month of June till the fall of the year. I remembered the beautiful villages, up and down this valley. I also remembered, very well, that the women at Steeple Langford used to card, and spin dyed wool. I was, therefore, somewhat filled with curiosity, to see this Steeple Langford again; and, indeed, it was the recollection of this village, that made me take a ride into Wiltshire this summer. I have, I dare say, a thousand times talked about this Steeple Langford, and about the beautiful farms and meadows along this valley. I have talked of these to my children, a great many times; and I formed the design of letting two of them see this valley this year, and to go through Warminster to Stroud, and so on to Gloucester and Hereford. But, when I got to Everley, I found that they would never get along fast enough to get into Herefordshire in time for what they intended; so that I parted from them in the manner, I have before described. I was resolved, however, to see Steeple Langford myself, and I was impatient to get to it, hoping to find a public-house, and a stable to put my horse in, to protect him, for a while, against the flies, which tormented him to such a degree, that to ride him was work, as hard as threshing. When I got to Steeple Langford, I found no public-house, and I found it a much more miserable place than I had remembered it. The *Steeple*, to which it owed its distinctive appellation, was gone; and the place altogether seemed to me, to be very much altered for the worse. A little further on, however, I came to a very famous inn, called Deptford Inn, which is in the parish of Wyly. I stayed at this inn till about four o'clock in the afternoon. I remembered Wyly very well, and thought it a gay place when I was a boy. I remembered a very beautiful garden belonging to a rich farmer and miller. I went to see it; but, alas! though the statues in the water and on the grass-plat were still remaining, every thing seemed to be in a state of perfect carelessness and neglect. The living of this parish of Wyly was lately owned by Dampier (a brother of the Judge), who lived at, and I believe had the living of, Meon Stoke in Hampshire. This fellow, I believe, never saw the parish of Wyly, but once, though it must have yielded him a pretty good fleece. It is a Rectory, and the great tithes must be worth, I should think, six or seven hundred pounds a year, at the least.

It is a part of our system to have certain *families*, who have no particular merit, but who are to be maintained, without why, or wherefore, at the public expense, in some shape, or. under some name, or other, it matters not much what shape or what name. If you look through the old list of pensioners, sinecurists, parsons, and the like, you will find the same names everlastingly recurring. They seem to be a sort of creatures that have an *inheritance in the public carcass*, like the maggots, that some people have in their skins. This family of Dampier seems to be one of those. What, in God's name, should have made one of these a Bishop, and the other a Judge! I never heard of the smallest particle of talent, that either of them possessed. This Rector of Wyly was another of them. There was no harm in them that I know of, beyond that of living upon the public; but, where were their merits? They had none, to distinguish them, and to entitle them, to the great sums they received; and, under any other system than such a system as this, they would, in all human probability, have been gentlemen's servants or little shopkeepers. I dare say there is some of the *breed* left; and, if there be, I would pledge my existence, that they are, in some shape or other, feeding upon the public. However, thus it must be, until that change come, which will put an end to men paying *fourpence* in tax upon a pot of beer.

This Deptford Inn was a famous place of meeting for the *Yeomanry Cavalry*, in glorious anti-jacobin times, when wheat was twenty shillings a bushel, and when a man could be crammed into gaol for years, for only *looking* awry. This inn was a glorious place in the days of Peg Nicholson[1] and her

---

[1] Peg Nicholson made an attempt upon the life of George III. in 1787. While she presented to him a petition with one hand, she attempted to stab him, with the other. She was instantly seized, and the king (altogether forgetful of the danger which he had escaped) only exclaimed, " Don't hurt the poor woman, she must be mad." This on inquiry proved to be the case, and she was sent to Bedlam for life.

Knights. Strangely altered now. The shape of the garden shows you what revelry used to be carried on here. Peel's Bill gave this inn, and all belonging to it, a terrible souse. The unfeeling brutes, who used to brandish their swords, and swagger about, at the news of what was called "a victory," have now to lower their scale in clothing, in drink, in eating, in dress, in horseflesh, and everything else. They are now a lower sort of men than they were. They look at their rusty sword and their old dusty helmet, and their once gay regimental jacket. They do not hang these up now in the "parlour" for everybody to see them: they hang them up in their bedrooms, or in a cockloft; and when they meet their eye, they look at them as a cow does at a bastard calf, or as the bridegroom does at a girl, that the overseers are about to compel him to marry. If their children should happen to see these implements of war twenty or thirty years hence, they will certainly think that their fathers were the greatest fools that ever walked the face of the earth; and that will be a most filial and charitable way of thinking of them; for, it is not from ignorance that they have sinned, but from excessive baseness; and when any of them now complain, of those acts of the Government which strip them, (as the new Order in Council will do) [1] of a fifth part of their property in an hour, let them recollect their own base and malignant conduct towards those persecuted reformers, who, if they had not been suppressed by these very yeomen, would, long ago, have put an end to the cause of that ruin of which these yeomen now complain. When they complain of their ruin, let them remember the toasts which they drank in anti-jacobin times; let them remember their base and insulting exultations on the occasion of the 16th of August at Manchester; [2] let them

---

[1] This Order in Council (dated 1st September 1826) was made for the purpose of admitting the importation of certain grain, at low duties. This was merely a foreshadowing of the great importation Bill, of Sir Robert Peel, which passed in 1846, and which led to the total repeal of the Corn Laws, in 1869.
[2] Referring to the Peterloo massacre, as the Author styles it (in 1819), in which eleven persons were killed, and six hundred wounded, by the

remember their cowardly abuse of men, who were endeavouring to free their country from that horrible scourge, which they themselves now feel.

Just close by this Deptford Inn is the farm-house of the farm, where that Gourlay lived, who has long been making a noise in the Court of Chancery, and who is now, I believe, confined in some place or other for having assaulted Mr. Brougham. This fellow, who is confined, the newspapers tell us, on a charge of being insane, is certainly one of the most malignant devils, that I ever knew anything of, in my life. He went to Canada, about the time that I went last to the United States. He got into a quarrel with the Government there about something, I know not what. He came to see me, at my house in the neighbourhood of New York, just before I came home. He told me his Canada story. I showed him all the kindness in my power, and he went away, knowing that I was just then coming to England. I had hardly got home, before the Scotch newspapers contained communications from a person, pretending to derive his information from Gourlay, relating to what Gourlay had described, as having passed between him and me; and which description was a tissue of most abominable falsehoods, all having a direct tendency to do injury to me, who had never, either by word or deed, done anything that could possibly have a tendency, to do injury to this Gourlay. What the vile Scotch newspapers had begun, the malignant reptile himself continued after his return to England, and, in an address to Lord Bathurst, endeavoured to make his court to the Government, by the most foul, false, and detestable slanders upon me, from whom, observe, he had never received any injury, or attempt at injury, in the whole course of his life; whom he had visited; to whose house he had gone, of his own accord, and that, too, as he said, out of *respect* for me; endeavoured, I say, to make his court to the Government, by the most abominable slanders

---

military, who attempted to repress a monster Reform meeting, consisting of nearly 100,000 persons. The authorities were greatly to blame in the matter. Allusion has already been made to the subject.

against me. He is now, even now, putting forth, under the form of letters to me, a revival, of what he pretends, was a *conversation* that passed between us at my house, near New York. Even if what he says were true, none but caitiffs as base as those who conduct the English newspapers, would give circulation to his letters, containing, as they must, the substance of a conversation purely private. But, I never had any conversation with him: I never talked to him at all, about the things that he is now bringing forward : I heard the fellow's stories about Canada : I thought he told me lies; and, besides, I did not care a straw whether his stories were true or not; I looked upon him as a sort of gambling adventurer; but I treated him, as is the fashion of the country in which I was, with great civility and hospitality. There are two fellows of the name of Jacob and Johnson at Winchester, and two fellows at Salisbury of the name of Brodie and Dowding. These reptiles publish, each couple of them, a newspaper; and in these newspapers, they seem to take particular delight in calumniating me. The two Winchester fellows insert the letters of this half crazy, half cunning, Scotchman, Gourlay ; the other fellows insert, still viler slanders ; and, if I had seen one of their papers, before I left Salisbury, which I have seen since, I certainly would have given Mr. Brodie something, to make him remember me. This fellow, who was a little coal-merchant but a short while ago, is now, it seems, a paper-money maker, as well as a newspaper maker. Stop, Master Brodie, till I go to Salisbury again ; and see whether I do not give you a *check*, even such as you did not receive during the late run! Gourlay, amongst other whims, took it into his head to write against the poor laws, saying that they were a bad thing. He found, however, at last, that they were necessary to keep him from starving ; for he came down to Wyly, three or four years ago, and threw himself upon the parish. The overseers, who recollected what a swaggering blade it was, when it came here to teach the moon-rakers " hoo to farm, mon," did not see the sense of keeping him like a gentleman ; so, they set him to crack stones upon the highway; and that set him off again, pretty quickly. The farm that he rented, is a very fine farm, with a fine large farm-house to it. It is looked upon, as one of the best farms in the country: the present occupier is a farmer born in the neighbourhood; a man such as ought to occupy it; and Gourlay, who came here with his Scotch impudence, to teach others how to farm,[1] is much about where, and how, he ought to be. Jacob and Johnson, of Winchester, know perfectly well, that all the fellow says about me is lies: they know also, that their parson readers know, that it is a mass of lies: they further know, that the parsons know, that they know, that it is a mass of lies; but they know, that their paper will sell the better for that; they know, that to circulate lies about me, will get them money, and this is what they do it for, and such is the character of English newspapers, and of a great part of the readers of those newspapers. Therefore, when I hear of people "suffering;" when I hear of people being "ruined;" when I hear of "unfortunate families;" when I hear a talk of this kind, I stop, before I either express or feel compassion, to ascertain *who* and *what* the sufferers are; and whether they have or have not participated in, or approved of, acts like those of Jacob and Johnson, and Brodie and Dowding; for, if they have, if they have malignantly calumniated those who have been labouring to prevent their ruin and misery, then a crushed ear-wig, or spider, or eft, or toad, is as much entitled to the compassion of a just and sensible man. Let the reptiles perish: it would be injustice; it would be to fly in the face of morality and religion, to express sorrow for their ruin. They themselves have felt for no man, and for the wife and children of no man, if that man's public virtues thwarted their own selfish views, or even excited their groundless fears.

---

[1] The previous Editor informs us that the Author here refers to the circumstance "that Gourlay claimed for the Scotch, the credit of having introduced the swing ploughs, worked by two horses abreast, driven with reins; but that the Author had himself adopted this plan (from Suffolk) as early as 1811, and that the practice was common in Surrey in 1813, and perhaps long before."

They have signed addresses, applauding every thing tyrannical and inhuman. They have seemed to glory in the shame of their country, to rejoice in its degradation, and even to exult in the shedding of innocent blood, if these things did but tend, as they thought, to give them permanent security in the enjoyment of their unjust gains. Such has been their conduct; they are numerous: they are to be found in all parts of the kingdom: therefore again I say, when I hear of "ruin" or "misery," I must know what the conduct of the sufferers has been, before I bestow my compassion.

Warminster (Wilts), Friday, 1st Sept.

I set out from Heytesbury this morning about six o'clock. Last night, before I went to bed, I found that there were some men and boys in the house, who had come all the way from Bradford, about twelve miles, in order to get *nuts*. These people were men and boys, that had been employed in the *cloth factories* at Bradford and about Bradford. I had some talk with some of these nutters, and I am quite convinced, not that the cloth making is at *an end;* but that it *never will be again what it has been.* Before last Christmas these manufacturers had full work, at one shilling and threepence a yard at broad-cloth weaving. They have now a quarter work, at one shilling a yard! One and three-pence a yard for this weaving has been given at all times within the memory of man! Nothing can show more clearly than this, and in a stronger light, the great change which has taken place in the *remuneration for labour.* There was a turn out last winter, when the price was reduced to a shilling a yard; but it was put an end to in the usual way; the constable's staff, the bayonet, the gaol. These poor nutters were extremely ragged. I saved my supper, and I fasted instead of breakfasting. That was three shillings, which I had saved, and I added five to them, with a resolution to save them afterwards, in order to give these chaps a breakfast for once in their lives. There were eight of them, six men, and two boys; and I gave them two quartern loaves, two pounds of cheese, and eight pints of strong beer. The fellows were very thankful, but the conduct of the landlord and landlady pleased me exceedingly. When I came to pay my bill, they had said nothing about my bed, which had been a very good one; and, when I asked, why they had not put the bed into the bill, they said they would not charge any thing for the bed, since I had been so good to the poor men. Yes, said I, but I must not throw the expense upon you. I had no supper, and I have had no breakfast; and, therefore, I am not called upon, to pay for them : but *I have had* the bed. It ended by my paying for the bed, and coming off, leaving the nutters at their breakfast, and very much delighted with the landlord and his wife; and I must here observe, that I have pretty generally found a good deal of compassion for the poor people to prevail amongst publicans and their wives.

From Heytesbury to Warminster is a part of the country singularly bright and beautiful. From Salisbury up to very near Heytesbury, you have the valley, as before described by me. Meadows next the water; then arable land; then the downs; but, when you come to Heytesbury, and indeed, a little before, in looking forward you see the vale stretch out, from about three miles wide to ten miles wide, from high land to high land. From a hill before you come down to Heytesbury, you see through this wide opening into Somersetshire. You see a round hill rising in the middle of the opening; but all the rest a flat enclosed country, and apparently full of wood. In looking back down this vale, one cannot help being struck with the innumerable proofs that there are, of a decline in point of population. In the first place, there are twenty-four parishes, each of which takes a little strip across the valley, and runs up through the arable land into the down. There are twenty-four parish churches, and there ought to be as many *parsonage-houses ;* but seven of these, out of the twenty-four, that is to say, nearly one-third of them, are, in the returns laid before Parliament (and of which returns I shall speak more particularly by-and-by), stated to be such miserable dwellings, as to be unfit for a parson to reside in.;

Two of them, however, are gone. There are no parsonage houses in those two parishes: there are the sites; there are the glebes; but the houses have been suffered to fall down and to be totally carried away. The tithes remain, indeed, and the parson sacks the amount of them. A journeyman parson comes and works in three or four churches of a Sunday; but the master parson is not there. He generally carries away the produce to spend it in London, at Bath, or somewhere else, to show off his daughters; and the overseers, that is to say, the farmers, manage the poor, in their own way, instead of having, according to the ancient law, a third-part of all the tithes, to keep them with.

The falling down and the beggary of these parsonage-houses, prove beyond all question the decayed state of the population. And, indeed, the mansion-houses are gone, except in a very few instances. There are but five left, that I could perceive, all the way from Salisbury to Warminster, though the country is the most pleasant that can be imagined. Here is water, here are meadows; plenty of fresh-water fish; hares and partridges in abundance, and it is next to impossible to destroy them. Here are shooting, coursing, hunting; hills of every height, size, and form; valleys, the same; lofty trees, and rookeries in every mile; roads always solid and good; always pleasant for exercise; and the air must be of the best in the world. Yet it is manifest, that four-fifths of the mansions have been swept away. There is a parliamentary return, to prove that nearly a third of the parsonage houses have become beggarly holes or have disappeared. I have now been in nearly three score villages, and in twenty or thirty or forty hamlets of Wiltshire; and I do not know that I have been in one, however small, in which I did not see a house or two, and sometimes more, either tumbled down, or beginning to tumble down. It is impossible for the eyes of man to be fixed on a finer country than that, between the village of Codford and the town of Warminster; and it is not very easy for the eyes of man to discover labouring people more miserable. There are two villages, one called Norton

Bovant, and the other Bishopstrow, which I think form, together, one of the prettiest spots that my eyes ever beheld. The former village belongs to Bennet, the member for the county, who has a mansion there, in which two of his sisters live, I am told. There is a farm at Bishopstrow, standing at the back of the arable land, up in a vale, formed by two very lofty hills, upon each of which there was formerly a Roman Camp, in consideration of which farm, if the owner would give it me, I would almost consent to let Ottiwell Wood remain quiet in his seat, and suffer the pretty gentlemen of Whitehall to go on without note or comment, till they had fairly blown up their concern. The farm-yard is surrounded by lofty and beautiful trees. In the rick-yard, I counted twenty-two ricks of one sort and another. The hills shelter the house, and the yard and the trees, most completely, from every wind but the south. The arable land goes down before the house, and spreads along the edge of the down, going, with a gentle slope, down to the meadows. So that, going along the turnpike road, which runs between the lower fields of the arable land, you see the large and beautiful flocks of sheep upon the sides of the down, while the horned-cattle are up to their eyes in grass in the meadows. Just when I was coming along here, the sun was about half an hour high; it shined through the trees most brilliantly; and, to crown the whole, I met, just as I was entering the village, a very pretty girl, who was apparently going a gleaning in the fields. I asked her the name of the place, and when she told me it was Bishopstrow, she pointed to the situation of the church, which, she said, was on the other side of the river. She really put me in mind of the pretty girls at Preston, who spat upon the "individual" of the Derby family, and I made her a bow accordingly.

The whole of the population of the twenty-four parishes down this vale, amounts to only 11,195 souls, according to the Official return to Parliament; and, mind, I include the parish of Fisherton Anger (a suburb of the city of Salisbury), which contains 893 of the number. I include the town of

Heytesbury, with its 1,023 souls; and I further include this very good and large market town of Warminster, with its population of 5,000! So that I leave, in the other twenty-one parishes, only 4,170 souls, men, women, and children! That is to say, a hundred and ninety-eight souls to each parish; or, reckoning five to a family, thirty-nine families to each parish. Above one half of the population never could be expected to be in the church at one time; so that, here are one-and-twenty churches built for the purpose of holding two thousand and eighty people! There are several of these churches, any one of which would conveniently contain the whole of these people, the two thousand and eighty! The church of Bishopstrow would contain the whole of the two thousand and eighty very well indeed; and, it is curious enough to observe, that the churches of Fisherton Anger, Heytesbury, and Warminster, though quite sufficient to contain the people that go to church, are none of them nearly so big, as several of the village churches. All these churches are built, long and long before the reign of Richard the Second; that is to say, they were founded long before that time, and if the first churches were gone, these others were built in their stead. There is hardly one of them that is not as old as the reign of Richard the Second; and yet that impudent Scotchman, George Chalmers, would make us believe, that, in the reign of Richard the Second, the population of the country was hardly anything at all! He has the impudence, or the gross ignorance, to state the population of England and Wales at *two millions*, which, as I have shown in the last Number of the Protestant Reformation, would allow only twelve able men to every parish church throughout the kingdom. What, I ask, for about the thousandth time I ask it; what were these twenty churches built for? Some of them stand within a quarter of a mile of each other. They are pretty nearly as close to each other as the churches in London and Westminster are.

What a monstrous thing, to suppose that they were built without there being people to go to them; and built, too, without money and without hands! The whole of the population in these twenty-one parishes could stand, and without much crowding too, in the bottoms of the towers of the several churches. Nay, in three or four of the parishes, the whole of the people could stand in the church porches. Then, the *church-yards* show you how numerous the population must have been. You see, in some cases, only here and there the mark of a grave, where the church-yard contains from half an acre to an acre of land, and sometimes more. In short, everything shows, that here was once a great and opulent population; that there was an abundance to eat, to wear, and to spare; that all the land that is now under cultivation, and a great deal that is not now under cultivation, was under cultivation in former times. The Scotch beggars, would make us believe that *we* sprang from beggars. The impudent scribes would make us believe, that England was formerly nothing at all, till they came to enlighten it and fatten upon it. Let the beggars answer me this question; let the impudent, the brazen scribes, that impose upon the credulous and cowed-down English; let them tell me, *why* these twenty-one churches were built? what they were built FOR? why the large churches of the two Codfords were stuck up within a few hundred yards of each other, if the whole of the population could then, as it can now, be crammed into the chancel of either of the two churches? Let them answer me this question, or shut up their mouths upon this subject, on which they have told so many lies.

As to the produce of this valley, it must be at least ten times as great as its consumption, even if we include the three towns that belong to it. I am sure I saw produce enough, in five or six of the farm-yards, or rick-yards, to feed the whole of the population of the twenty-one parishes. But the infernal system, causes it all to be carried away. Not a bit of good beef, or mutton, or veal, and scarcely a bit of bacon is left for those, who raise all this food and wool. The labourers here *look* as if they were half-starved. They answer extremely well to the picture that Fortescue gave of the French in his day.

Talk of "liberty," indeed; "civil and religious liberty:" the Inquisition, with a belly full, is far preferable to a state of things like this. For my own part, I really am ashamed to ride a fat horse, to have a full belly, and to have a clean shirt upon my back, while I look at these wretched countrymen of mine; while I actually see them reeling with weakness; when I see their poor faces present me nothing but skin and bone, while they are toiling to get the wheat and the meat, ready to be carried away to be devoured by the tax-eaters. I am ashamed to look at these poor souls, and to reflect that they are my countrymen; and particularly to reflect, that we are descended from those, amongst whom "beef, pork, mutton, and veal, "were the food of the poorer sort of people."[1] What! and is the "Emigration Committee" sitting, to invent the means of getting rid of some part of the thirty-nine families, that are employed in raising the immense quantities of food, in each of these twenty-one parishes? Are there *schemers* to go before this conjuration Committee; Wiltshire *schemers*, to tell the Committee how they can get rid of a part of these one hundred and ninety-eight persons to every parish? Are there schemers of this sort of work still, while no man, no man at all, not a single man, says a word about getting rid of the dead-weight, or the supernumerary parsons, both of whom have actually a premium given them for breeding, and are filling the country with idlers? We are reversing the maxim of the Scripture: our laws almost say, that those that work shall not eat, and that those who do not work, shall have the food. I repeat, that the baseness of the English land-owners surpasses that, of any other men that ever lived in the world. The cowards know well, that the labourers that give value to their land, are skin and bone. They are not such brutes, as not to know that

---

[1] Quoting the words of Sir John Fortescue (Lord Chancellor in the reign of Henry VI.), in his celebrated work "De Laudibus Legum Angliæ," A.D. 1463. It is to be feared that very few of the present agricultural labourers often taste fresh meat except it be a hare or a rabbit that is snared.

this starvation, is produced by taxation. They know well, how unjust it is, to treat their labourers in this way. They know well that there goes down the common foot soldier's single throat, more food than is allowed by them to a labourer, his wife, and three children. They know well, that the present standing army in time of peace, consumes more food and raiment, than a million of the labourers consume; aye, than two millions of them consume; if you include the women and the children; they well know these things; they know that their poor labourers are taxed, to keep this army in fatness and in splendour. They know that the dead-weight, which, in the opinion of most men of sense, ought not to receive a single farthing of the public money, swallow more of good food than a third or a fourth part of the real labourers of England swallow. They know that a million and a half of pounds sterling was taken out of the taxes, partly raised upon the labourers, to enable the poor Clergy of the Church of England to marry and to breed. They know that a regulation has been recently adopted, by which an old dead-weight man is enabled to sell his dead-weight to a young man; and that, thus, this burden would, if the system were to be continued, be rendered perpetual. They know that a good slice of the dead-weight money goes *to Hanover;* and that even these Hanoverians, can sell the dead-weight claim upon us. The "country gentlemen" fellows know all this: they know that the poor labourers, including all the poor manufacturers, pay one-half of their wages in taxes to support all these things; and yet not a word about these things is ever said, or even hinted at, by these mean, these cruel, these cowardly, these carrion, these dastardly reptiles. Sir James Graham, of Netherby, who, I understand, is a young fellow instead of an old one, may invoke our pity upon these "ancient families," but he will invoke in vain. It was their duty to stand forward and prevent Power-of-Imprisonment Bills, Six Acts, Ellenborough's Act, Poaching Transportation Act, New Trespass Act, Sunday Tolls, and the hundreds of other things that could be named. On the contrary, *they were the cause of them all.*

They were the cause of all the taxes, and all the debts; and now let them take the consequences![1]

Saturday, September 2nd.

After I got to Warminster yesterday, it began to rain, which stopped me in my way to Frome in Somersetshire, which lies about seven or eight miles from this place; but, as I meant to be quite in the northern part of the county, by to-morrow noon, or there-abouts, I took a post-chaise in the afternoon of yesterday, and went to Frome, where I saw, upon my entrance into the town, between two or three hundred weavers, men and boys, cracking stones, moving earth, and doing other sorts of work, towards making a fine road into the town. I drove into the town, and through the principal streets, and then I put my chaise up a little, at one of the inns.

This appears to be a sort of little Manchester. A very small Manchester, indeed; for it does not contain above ten or twelve thousand people, but, it has all the *flash* of a Manchester, and the innkeepers and their people look and behave like the Manchester fellows. I was, I must confess, glad to find proofs of the irretrievable decay of the place. I remembered how ready the bluff manufacturers had been, to *call in the troops* of various descriptions. "Let them," said I to myself, "call the troops in now, to make their trade revive. "Let them now resort to their friends of the yeomanry and of "the army; let them now threaten their poor workmen with "the gaol, when they dare to ask for the means of preventing "starvation in their families. Let them, who have, in fact, "lived and thriven by the sword, now call upon the parson- "magistrate, to bring out the soldiers to compel me, for " instance, to give thirty shillings a yard for the superfine black " broad cloth (made at Frome), which Mr. Roe, at Kensington,

---

[1] Since the time the above was written, nearly all the taxes (of which the Author so justly complains) have been repealed, so that a "*free break-fast table*" has been provided for the agricultural labourer, although in many districts he is still most inadequately paid.

"offered me at seven shillings and sixpence a yard, just before
"I left home! Yes, these men have ground down into powder
"those, who were earning them their fortunes: let the grinders
"themselves now be ground, and, according to the usual wise
"and just course of Providence, let them be crushed by the
"system which they have delighted in, because it made others
"crouch beneath them." Their poor work-people cannot be worse off than they long have been. The parish pay, which they now get upon the roads, is 2s. 6d. a week for a man, 2s. for his wife, 1s. 3d. for each child under eight years of age, 3d. a week, in addition, for each child above eight, who can go to work: and, if the children above eight years old, whether girls or boys, do not go to work upon the road, they have *nothing!* Thus, a family of five people, have just as much, and eightpence over, as goes down the throat of one single foot soldier; but, observe, the standing soldier; that "truly English institution," has clothing, fuel, candle, soap, and house-rent, over and above, what is allowed to this miserable family! And yet the base reptiles, who, are called "country gentlemen," and whom Sir James Graham calls upon us, to commit all sorts of acts of injustice in order to *preserve*, never utter a whisper about the expenses of keeping the soldiers, while they are everlastingly railing against the working people of every description, and representing them, and them only, as the cause of the loss of their estates!

These poor creatures at Frome, have pawned all their things, or nearly all. All their best clothes, their blankets and sheets; their looms; any little piece of furniture that they had, and that was good for anything. Mothers have been compelled to pawn, all the tolerably good clothes, that their children had. In case of a man having two or three shirts, he is left with only one, and sometimes without any shirt; and, though this is a sort of manufacture, that cannot very well come to a complete end; still it has received a blow from which it cannot possibly recover. The population of this Frome, has been augmented to the degree of one-third, within the last six or seven years. There are here all the usual signs of accommodation bills, and all false paper stuff, called money: new houses, in abundance, half finished; new gingerbread "places of worship," as they are called; great swaggering inns; parcels of swaggering fellows going about, with vulgarity imprinted upon their countenances, but with good clothes upon their backs.

I found the working people at Frome very intelligent; very well informed as to the cause of their misery; not at all humbugged by the canters, whether about religion or loyalty. When I got to the inn, I sent my post-chaise boy back to the road, to tell one or two of the weavers to come to me at the inn. The landlord did not at first, like to let such ragged fellows, upstairs. I insisted, however, upon their coming up, and I had a long talk with them. They were very intelligent men; had much clearer views of what is likely to happen, than the pretty gentlemen of Whitehall seem to have; and, it is curious enough, that they, these common weavers, should tell me, that they thought that the trade, never would come back again, to what it was before; or, rather, to what it has been for some years past. This is the impression everywhere; that the *puffing is over;* that we must come back again to something like reality. The first factories that I met with were at a village called Upton Lovell, just before I came to Heytesbury. There they were doing not more than a quarter work. There is only one factory, I believe, here at Warminster, and that has been suspended, during the harvest, at any rate. At Frome, they are all upon about a quarter work. It is the same at Bradford, and Trowbridge; and, as curious a thing as ever was heard of, in the world is, that here are, through all these towns, and throughout this country, weavers from the North, singing about the towns, ballads of Distress! They had been doing it at Salisbury, just before I was there. The landlord at Heytesbury told me, that people that could afford it, generally gave them something; and I was told that they did the same at Salisbury. The landlord at Heytesbury told me, that every one of them had a *license to beg*, given them he said, "by the Government." I suppose it was some *pass* from a Magistrate; though I know of no law that allows of such passes; and a pretty thing it would be, to grant such licenses, or such passes, when the law so positively commands, that the poor of every parish, shall be maintained in, and by, every such parish.[1]

However, all law of this sort, all salutary and humane law, really seems to be drawing towards an end, in this now miserable country, where the thousands are caused to wallow in luxury, to be surfeited with food and drink, while the millions are continually on the point of famishing. In order to form an idea of the degradation of the people of this country, and of the abandonment of every English principle, what need we of more than this one disgraceful and truly horrible fact, namely, that *the common soldiers, of the standing army in time of peace, subscribe, in order to furnish the meanest of diet, to keep from starving, the industrious people who are taxed to the amount of one-half of their wages, and out of which taxes, the very pay of these soldiers comes!* Is not this one fact; this disgraceful, this damning fact; is not this enough to convince us, *there must be a change;* that there must be a complete and radical change; or, that England must become a country of the basest slavery, that ever disgraced the earth?

Devizes, (Wilts),
Sunday Morning, 3rd Sept.

I left Warminster yesterday at about one o'clock. It is contrary to my practice to set out at all, unless I can do it early in the morning; but, at Warminster I was at the South-West corner of this county, and I had made a sort of promise to be to-day at Highworth, which is at the North-East corner, and which parish, indeed, joins up to Berkshire. The distance,

---

[1] In ancient times beggars were tolerated because they were often musicians and ballad-singers. Licences to beg, were granted in the reigns of Henry VIII. and Edward VI. But in 1572, by the Act (14 Elizabeth c. 5) sturdy beggars were ordered "to be grievously whipped, and burnt through the right ear," moreover "to be punished *capitally*," for the third offence. By the Vagrant Act, 1824 (5 George IV. c. 83), all public beggars are liable to one month's imprisonment. There are about 30,000 tramps and beggars in England and Wales at the present time.

including my little intended deviations, was more than fifty miles; and, not liking to attempt it in one day, I set off in the middle of the day, and got here in the evening, just before a pretty heavy rain came on.

Before I speak of my ride from Warminster to this place, I must once more observe, that Warminster is a very nice town: every thing belonging to it is *solid* and *good*. There are no villanous gingerbread houses running up, and no nasty, shabby-genteel people; no women trapesing about with showy gowns and dirty necks; no jew-looking fellows with dandy coats, dirty shirts and half-heels to their shoes. A really nice and good town. It is a great corn-market: one of the greatest in this part of England; and here things are still conducted in the good, old, honest fashion. The corn is brought and pitched in the market before it is sold; and, when sold it is paid for on the nail; and all is over, and the farmers and millers gone home by day-light. Almost every where else the corn is sold by sample; it is sold by juggling in a corner; the parties meet and drink first; it is night work; there is no fair and open market; the mass of the people do not know what the prices are; and all this favours that *monopoly* which makes the corn change hands many times, perhaps, before it reaches the mouth, leaving a profit in each pair of hands, and which monopoly is, for the greater part, carried on by the villanous tribe of *Quakers, none of whom ever work*, and all of whom prey upon the rest of the community, as those infernal devils, the wasps, prey upon the bees. Talking of the Devil, puts one in mind of his imps; and, talking of *Quakers*, puts one in mind of Jemmy Cropper of Liverpool. I should like to know precisely (I know pretty nearly) what effect "late panic" has had, and is having, on Jemmy! Perhaps the reader will recollect that Jemmy told the public, through the columns of base Bott Smith, that "Cobbett's prophecies were falsified as soon as spawned." Jemmy, canting Jemmy, has now had time to ruminate on that! But, does the reader remember James's project for "making Ireland as happy as England?" It was simply by introducing cotton-factories, steam-engines, and power-looms! That was all; and there was Jemmy in Ireland, speech-making before such Lords and such Bishops and such 'Squires as God never suffered to exist in the world before: there was Jemmy, showing, proving, demonstrating, that to make the Irish cotton-workers, would infallibly make them *happy:* If it had been now, instead of being two years ago, he might have produced the reports of the starvation-committees of Manchester to confirm his opinions. One would think, that this instance of the folly and impudence of this canting son of the monopolizing sect, would cure this public of its proneness to listen to cant; but, nothing will cure it: the very existence of this sect, none of whom ever work, and the whole of whom live like fighting-cocks upon the labour of the rest of the community; the very *existence* of such a sect shows, that the nation is, almost in its nature, *a dupe.* There has been a great deal of railing against the King of Spain; not to becall the King of Spain is looked upon as a proof of want of "liberality," and what must it be, then, to *applaud* any of the acts of the King of Spain! This I am about to do, however, think Dr. Black of it what he may.

In the first place, the mass of the people of Spain are better off, better fed, better clothed, than the people of any other country in Europe, and much better than the people of England are. That is one thing; and that is almost enough of itself. In the next place, the King of Spain has refused to mortgage the land and labour of his people for the benefit of an infamous set of Jews and Jobbers. Next, the King of Spain has most essentially thwarted the Six-Acts people, the Manchester 16th of August, the Parson Hay, the Sidmouth's Circular, the Dungeoning, the Ogden's rupture people; he has thwarted, and most cuttingly annoyed, these people, who are also the poacher-transporting people, and the new trespass law, and the apple-felony and the horse-police (or gendarmerie) and the Sunday-toll people: the King of Spain has thwarted all these, and he has materially assisted in blowing up the brutal big fellows of Manchester; and therefore, I applaud the King of Spain.

I do not much like weasels; but I hate rats; and, therefore, I say, success to the weasels. But, there is one act of the King of Spain, which is worthy of the imitation of every King, aye, and of every republic too; his edict for taxing traffickers, which edict was published about eight months ago. It imposes a pretty heavy annual tax on every one, who is a *mere buyer and seller*, and who neither produces nor consumes, nor makes, nor changes the state of, the article, or articles, that he buys and sells. Those who bring things into the kingdom, are deemed producers, and those who send things out of the kingdom, are deemed changers of the state of things. These two classes embrace all *legitimate merchants*. Thus, then, the farmer, who produces corn and meat and wool and wood, is not taxed; nor is the coach-master, who buys the corn to give to his horses, nor the miller, who buys it to change the state of it, nor the baker, who buys the flour to change its state; nor is the manufacturer, who buys the wool to change its state; and so on: but, the Jew, or Quaker, the *mere dealer*, who buys the corn of the producer, to sell it to the miller, and to deduct *a profit*, which must, at last, fall upon the consumer; this Jew or Quaker, or self-styled Christian, who acts the part of Jew or Quaker, is taxed by the King of Spain; and for this I applaud the King of Spain.

If we had a law like this, the pestiferous sect of non-labouring, sleek and fat hypocrites could not exist in England. But, ours is, altogether, *a system of monopolies*, created by taxation and paper-money, from which monopolies are inseparable. It is notorious, that the brewer's monopoly is the master even of the Government; it is well known to all who examine and reflect, that a very large part of our bread comes to our mouths loaded with the profit of nine or ten, or more, different dealers; and, I shall, as soon as I have leisure, prove as clearly as any thing ever was proved, that the people pay two millions of pounds a year in consequence of the Monopoly in tea! that is to say, they pay two millions a year more than they would pay were it not for the monopoly; and, mind, I do not mean the monopoly of the East India Company; but, the monopoly of the Quaker, and other Tea Dealers, who buy the tea of that Company! The people of this country are eaten up by monopolies. These compel those who labour to maintain those who do not labour; and hence the success of the crafty crew of Quakers, the very *existence* of which sect is a disgrace to the country.

Besides the corn market at Warminster, I was delighted, and greatly surprised, to see the *meat*. Not only the very finest veal and lamb that I had ever seen in my life, but so exceedingly beautiful, that I could hardly believe my eyes. I am a great connoisseur in joints of meat; a great judge, if five-and-thirty years of experience can give sound judgment. I verily believe that I have bought and have roasted more whole sirloins of beef than any man in England; I know all about the matter; a very great visitor of Newgate market; in short, though a little eater, I am a very great provider. It is a fancy, I like the subject, and therefore, I understand it; and with all this knowledge of the matter, I say, I never saw veal and lamb half so fine as what I saw at Warminster. The town is famed for fine meat; and I knew it, and, therefore, I went out in the morning to look at the meat. It was, too, 2*d*. a pound cheaper than I left it at Kensington.

My road from Warminster to Devizes lay through Westbury, a nasty odious rotten-borough, a really rotten place. It has cloth factories in it, and they seem to be ready to tumble down, as well as many of the houses. God's curse seems to be upon most of these rotten-boroughs. After coming through this miserable hole, I came along, on the north side of the famous hill, called Bratton Castle, so renowned in the annals of the Romans and of Alfred the Great. Westbury is a place of great ancient grandeur; and, it is easy to perceive, that it was once ten or twenty times its present size. My road was now the line of separation between what they call South Wilts and North Wilts, the former consisting of high and broad downs, and narrow valleys, with meadows, and rivers, running down them; the latter consisting of a rather flat, enclosed country: the former having a chalk bottom; the latter a bottom of marl, clay, or flat stone: the former a country for lean sheep and corn; and the latter a country for cattle, fat sheep, cheese, and bacon: the former, by far, to my taste, the most beautiful; and I am by no means sure, that it is not, all things considered, the most rich. All my way along, till I came very near to Devizes, I had the steep and naked downs up to my right, and the flat and enclosed country to my left.

Very near to Bratton Castle (which is only a hill with deep ditches on it) is the village of Eddington, so famed for the battle fought here by Alfred and the Danes. The church, in this village, would contain several thousands of persons; and the village is reduced to a few straggling houses. The land here is very good; better than almost any I ever saw; as black, and, apparently, as rich, as the land in the market-gardens at Fulham. The turnips are very good all along here for several miles; but, this is, indeed, singularly fine and rich land. The orchards very fine; finely sheltered, and the crops of apples and pears and walnuts very abundant. Walnuts *ripe now*, a month earlier than usual. After Eddington I came to a hamlet called Earl's Stoke, the houses of which stand at a few yards from each other, on the two sides of the road; every house is white; and the front of every one is covered with some sort or other of clematis, or with rose-trees, or jasmines. It was easy to guess, that the whole belonged to one owner; and that owner I found to be a Mr. Watson Taylor, whose very pretty seat is close by the hamlet, and in whose park-pond, I saw, what I never saw before; namely some *black swans*. They are not nearly so large as the white, nor are they so stately in their movements. They are a meaner bird.

Highworth (Wilts,)
Monday, 4th Sept.

I got here yesterday, after a ride, including my deviations, of about thirty-four miles, and that, too, *without breaking my fast*. Before I got into the rotten-borough of Calne, I had two *tributes* to pay to the Aristocracy; namely, two *Sunday tolls;* and, I was resolved, that the country, in which these tolls were extorted, should have not a farthing of my money, that I could, by any means, keep from it. Therefore, I fasted, until I got into the free-quarters in which I am now. I would have made my horse fast too, if I could have done it without the risk of making him unable to carry me.

RIDE FROM HIGHWORTH TO CRICKLADE AND THENCE TO MALMSBURY.

Highworth (Wilts)
Monday, 4th Sept. 1826.

When I got to Devizes, on Saturday evening, and came to look out of the inn-window into the street, I perceived, that I had seen that place before, and, always having thought, that I should like to *see* Devizes, of which I had heard so much talk as a famous corn-market, I was very much surprised to find, that it was not new to me. Presently a stage-coach came up to the door, with "Bath and London" upon its panels; and then I recollected, that I had been at this place, on my way to Bristol, last year. Devizes is, as nearly as possible, in the centre of the county, and the *canal,* that passes close by it, is the great channel through which the produce of the country is carried away to be devoured by the idlers, the thieves, and the prostitutes, who are all tax-eaters, in the Wens of Bath and London. Pottern, which I passed through in my way from Warminster to Devizes, was once a place much larger than Devizes; and, it is now a mere ragged village, with a church large, very ancient, and of most costly structure. The whole of the people, here, might, as in most other cases, be placed in the *belfry,* or the church-porches.

All the way along, the mansion-houses are nearly all gone. There is now and then a great place, belonging to a borough-monger, or some one connected with borough-mongers; but, all the *little gentlemen* are gone; and, hence it is, that parsons are now made justices of the peace! There are few other persons left, who are at all capable of filling the office in a way to suit the system! The monopolising brewers and ragrooks are, in some places, the "magistrates;" and thus is the whole thing *changed*, and England, is no more what it was. Very near to the sides of my road from Warminster to Devizes, there were formerly (within a hundred years), 22 mansion-houses of sufficient note to be marked as such in the county-map, then made. There are now only seven of them remaining. There were five parish-churches nearly close to my road; and, in one parish out of the five, the parsonage-house is, in the parliamentary return, said to be "too small" for the parson to live in, though the church would contain two or three thousand people, and though the living is a Rectory, and a rich one too! Thus has the church-property, or rather, that public property, which is called church property, been dilapidated! The parsons have swallowed the *tithes* and the rent of the glebes; and have, successively, suffered the parsonage-houses to fall into decay. But these parsonage-houses were, indeed, not intended for large families. They were intended for a priest, a main part of whose business it was to distribute the tithes amongst the poor and the strangers! The parson, in this case, at Corsley, says, "too small for an incumbent with a family." Ah! there is the mischief. It was never intended to give men tithes, as a premium for breeding! Malthus does not seem to see any harm in *this* sort of increase of population. It is the *working* population, those who raise the food and the clothing, that he and Scarlett want to put a stop to the breeding of![1]

---

[1] William Pitt and William Cobbett seem to have been in sympathy with regard to their condemnation of the views of Malthus, for William Pitt proposed (or at all events acceded to a proposal) in 1796, to give premiums to agricultural labourers with large families. It is, however, fair to state, that at the time he did so, the condition of labourers was exceedingly disastrous, the gallon barley loaf being at 12½d., while wages were only 1s. per day. Mr. Scarlett (to whom reference is here made) was a bitter

I saw, on my way through the down-countries, hundreds of acres of ploughed land in *shelves*. What I mean is, the side of a steep hill, made into the shape of *a stairs*, only the rising parts more sloping than those of a stairs, and deeper in proportion. The side of the hill, in its original form, was too steep to be ploughed, or, even to be worked with a spade. The earth, as soon as moved, would have rolled down the hill; and, besides, the rains would have soon washed down all the surface earth, and have left nothing for plants of any sort to grow in. Therefore the sides of hills, where the land was sufficiently good, and where it was wanted for the growing of corn, were thus made into a sort of steps or shelves, and the horizontal parts (representing the parts of the stairs that we put our feet upon,) were ploughed and sowed, as they generally are, indeed, to this day. Now, no man, not even the hireling Chalmers, will have the impudence to say, that these shelves, amounting to thousands and thousands of acres in Wiltshire alone, were not made by the hand of man. It would be as impudent to contend, that the churches were formed by the flood, as to contend, that these shelves were formed by that cause. Yet, thus the Scotch scribes must contend; or, they must give up all their assertions about the ancient beggary and want of population in England; for, as in the case of the churches, what were these shelves made *for?* And could they be made at all, without a great abundance of hands? These shelves are everywhere to be seen throughout the down-countries of Sussex, Hampshire, Wiltshire, Dorsetshire, Devonshire and Cornwall; and, besides this, large tracts of land, amounting to millions of acres, perhaps, which are now downs, heaths, or woodlands, still, if you examine closely, bear the marks of the plough. The fact is, I dare say, that the country has never varied much in the gross amount of its population; but, formerly the people were

---

political opponent of the Author. He was a leading counsel at the Bar, and also an M.P., and had spoken of Cobbett in the House, "*as a contemptible scribbler.*"

pretty evenly spread over the country, instead of being, as the greater part of them now are, collected together in great masses, where, for the greater part, the idlers live on the labour of the industrious.

In quitting Devizes yesterday morning, I saw, just on the outside of the town, a monstrous building, which I took for *a barrack;* but, upon asking what it was, I found it was one of those other marks of the JUBILEE REIGN; namely *a most magnificent gaol!* It seemed to me sufficient to hold one-half of the able-bodied men in the county! And it would do it too, and do it well! Such a system must come to an end, and the end must be dreadful. As I came on the road, for the first three or four miles, I saw great numbers of labourers either digging potatoes for their Sunday's dinner, or coming home with them, or going out to dig them. The land-owners, or occupiers, let small pieces of land to the labourers, and these they cultivate with the spade for their own use. They pay, in all cases, a high rent, and, in most cases, an enormous one. The practice prevails all the way from Warminster to Devizes, and from Devizes to nearly this place (Highworth). The rent is, in some places, a shilling a rod, which is, mind, 160*s.* or 8*l.* an acre! Still the poor creatures like to have the land: they work in it at their spare hours; and on Sunday mornings early: and the overseers, sharp as they may be, cannot ascertain precisely how much they get out of their plat of ground. But, good God! what a life to live; what a life to see people live; to see this sight in our own country, and to have the base vanity to *boast* of that country, and to talk of our " constitution " and our " liberties," and to affect to *pity* the Spaniards, whose working people, live like gentlemen, compared with our miserable creatures. Again I say, give me the Inquisition and well-healed cheeks and ribs, rather than " civil and religious liberty," and skin and bone. But, the fact is, that, where honest and laborious men can be compelled to starve quietly, whether all at once or by inches, with old wheat ricks and fat cattle under their eye, it is a mockery to talk of their " liberty," of any sort; for the sum total of their state is this, they have "liberty" to choose between death by starvation (quick or slow) and death by the halter!

Between Warminster and Westbury I saw thirty or more men *digging* a great field of I dare say, twelve acres. I thought, "surely, that 'humane,' half-mad fellow, Owen, is "not got at work here; that Owen, who, the *feelosofers* tell "us, went to the Continent, to find out how to prevent the "increase of the labourers' children."[1] No: it was not Owen: it was the overseer of the parish, who had set these men to dig up this field, previously to its being sown with wheat. In short, it was a digging instead of a ploughing. The men, I found upon inquiry, got 9d. a day for their work. Plain digging, in the market gardens near London, is, I believe, 3d. or 4d. a rod. If these poor men, who were chiefly weavers or spinners from Westbury, or had come home to their parish from Bradford or Trowbridge; if they digged six rods each in a day, and *fairly* did it, they must work well. This would be 1½d. a rod, or 20s. an acre; and that is as cheap as ploughing and four times as good. But, how much better to give the men higher wages, and let them do more work? If married, how are their miserable families to live on 4s. 6d. a week? And, if single, they must and will have more, either by poaching, or by taking without leave. At any rate, this is better than the *road work:* I mean better for those who pay the rates; for here is something which they

---

[1] Mr. Robert Owen was a social theorist, but whose practical efforts, for bringing about a social reform, were one long absurdity. He set about proving that the world, in all its institutions, was in as wretched a condition as any dirty demoralised manufacturing village. In 1816 he published his new views of society, or essays on the formation of the human character, and this was followed by many other pamphlets. He started three limited communities (founded on his own principles), one at Romney in America, a second at Orbiston in Lanarkshire, and a third at Harmony Hall, near Stockbridge, Hants. They proved, of course, all failures; but Owen attributed their failures to their not being sufficiently perfected on his principles. In the French Revolution of 1848 he went to Paris, but his voice was not loud enough to be heard, in that turmoil. He died in 1858.

get for the money that they give to the poor; whereas, in the case of the roadwork, the money given in relief is generally wholly so much lost to the rate-payer. What a curious spectacle this is: the manufactories *throwing the people back again upon the land!* It is not above eighteen months ago, that the Scotch FEELOSOFERS, and especially Dr. Black, were calling upon *the farm labourers to become manufacturers!* I remonstrated with the Doctor at the time; but, he still insisted, that such a transfer of hands, was the only remedy for the distress in the farming districts. However, (and I thank God for it) the *feelosofers* have enough to do at *home* now; for the poor are crying for food in dear, cleanly, warm, fruitful Scotland herself, in spite of a' the Hamiltons, and a' the Wallaces, and a' the Maxwells, and a' the Hope Johnstones, and a' the Dundases, and a' the Edinbro' Reviewers, and a' the Broughams, and Birckbecks. In spite of all these, the poor of Scotland are now helping themselves, or about to do it, for want of the means of purchasing food.

From Devizes I came to the vile rotten borough of Calne, leaving the park and house of Lord Lansdowne to my left. This man's name is Petty, and, doubtless, his ancestors "came in with the Conqueror;" for, *Petty* is, unquestionably, a corruption of the French word *Petit;* and, in this case there appears to have been not the least degeneracy; a thing rather rare in these days. There is a man whose name was Grimstone (that is, to a certainty, *Grindstone*), who is now called Lord Verulam, and who according to his pedigree in the Peerage, is descended from "a standard-bearer of the "Conqueror!" Now, the devil a bit is there the word Grindstone, or Grimstone, in the Norman language. Well, let them have all that their French descent can give them, since they will insist upon it, that they are not of this country. So help me God, I would, if I could, *give them Normandy* to live in, and, if the people would let them, to possess.

This Petty family began, or, at least, made its first *grand push*, in poor, unfortunate Ireland! The *history* of that push would amuse the people of Wiltshire! Talking of Normans and high-blood, puts me in mind of Beckford and his "Abbey." The public knows, that the *tower* of this thing fell down some time ago. It was built of Scotch-fir and cased with stone! In it there was a place which the owner had named, "The Gallery of Edward III., the frieze of which, "(says the account,) contains the achievements of seventy-"eight Knights of the Garter, from whom the owner is "lineally descended"! Was there ever vanity and impudence equal to these! the negro-driver brag of his high-blood! I dare say, that the old powder-man Farquhar, had as good pretension; and I really should like to know whether he took out Beckford's name, and put in his own, as the lineal descendant of the seventy-eight Knights of the Garter.

I could not come through that villanous hole, Calne, without cursing Corruption at every step; and, when I was coming by an ill-looking, broken-windowed place, called the town-hall, I suppose, I poured out a double dose of execration upon it. "Out of the frying pan into the fire;" for, in about ten miles more, I came to another rotten-hole, called Wootton-Basset! This also is a mean, vile place, though the country all round it is very fine. On this side of Wootton-Basset, I went out of my way to see the church at Great Lyddiard, which, in the parliamentary return, is called Lyddiard *Tregoose*. In my old map it is called *Tregose;* and, to a certainty, the word was *Tregrosse;* that is to say, *très grosse*, or, *very big*. Here is a good old mansion-house and large walled-in garden and a park, belonging, they told me, to Lord Bolingbroke. I went quite down to the house, close to which stands the large and fine church. It appears *to have been* a noble place; the land is some of the finest in the whole country; the trees show that the land is excellent; but, all, except the church, is in a state of irrepair and apparent neglect, if not abandonment. The parish is large, the living is a rich one, it is a Rectory; but though the incumbent has the great and small tithes, he, in his return tells the Parliament, that the parsonage-house is "worn out and incapable of repair!" And, observe, that Parliament lets him continue to sack the produce of the tithes and the glebe, while they know the parsonage-house to be crumbling-down, and while he has the impudence to tell them that he does not reside in it, though the law says that he shall! And, while this is suffered to be, a *poor* man may be transported for being in pursuit of a hare! What coals, how hot, how red, is this flagitious system preparing for the backs of its supporters!

In coming from Wootton-Basset to Highworth, I left Swindon a few miles away to my left, and came by the village of Blunsdon. All along here I saw great quantities of hops in the hedges, and very fine hops, and I saw at a village called Stratton, I think it was, the finest *campanula* that I ever saw in my life. The main stalk was more than four feet high, and there were four stalks, none of which were less than three feet high. All through the country, poor, as well as rich, are very neat in their gardens, and very careful to raise a great variety of flowers. At Blunsdon I saw a clump, or, rather, a sort of orchard, of as fine walnut-trees as I ever beheld, and loaded with walnuts. Indeed I have seen great crops of walnuts all the way from London. From Blunsdon to this place, is but a short distance, and I got here about two or three o'clock. This is a *cheese country;* some corn, but, generally speaking, it is a country of dairies. The sheep here are of the large kind; a sort of Leicester sheep, and the cattle chiefly for milking. The ground is a stiff loam at top, and a yellowish stone under. The houses are almost all built of stone. It is a tolerably rich, but by no means, a gay and pretty country. Highworth has a situation corresponding with its name. On every side you go up-hill to it, and from it you see to a great distance all round, and into many counties.

Highworth, Wednesday, 6th Sept.

The great object of my visit to the Northern border of Wiltshire, will be mentioned when I get to Malmsbury, whither I intend to go to-morrow, or next day, and thence, through Gloucestershire, in my way to Herefordshire. But, an additional inducement, was to have a good long political *gossip*, with some excellent friends, who detest the borough-ruffians as cordially as I do, and who, I hope, wish as anxiously to see their fall effected, and no matter by what means. There was, however, arising incidentally, a third object, which had I known of its existence, would, of itself, have brought me from the South-West to the North-East corner of this county. One of the parishes adjoining to Highworth is that of Coleshill, which is in Berkshire, and which is the property of Lord Radnor, or Lord Folkestone, and is the seat of the latter. I was at Coleshill twenty-two or three years ago, and twice at later periods. In 1824, Lord Folkestone bought some Locust trees of me; and he has several times told me, that they were growing very finely; but, I did not know, that they had been planted at Coleshill; and, indeed, I always thought that they had been planted somewhere in the South of Wiltshire. I now found, however, that they were growing at Coleshill, and yesterday I went to see them, and was, for many reasons, more delighted with the sight, than with any that I have beheld for a long while. These trees stand in clumps of 200 trees in each, and the trees being four feet apart each way. These clumps make part of a plantation of 30 or 40 acres, perhaps 50 acres. The rest of the ground; that is to say, the ground where the clumps of Locusts do not stand, was, at the same time that the Locust clumps were, planted with chestnuts, elms, ashes, oaks, beeches, and other trees. These trees were stouter and taller than the Locust trees were, when the plantation was made. Yet, if you were now to place yourself at a mile's distance from the plantation, you would not think that there was any plantation at all, except the clumps. The fact is, that the other trees have, as they generally do, made, as yet, but very little progress; are not, I should think, upon an average, more than $4\frac{1}{2}$ feet, or 5 feet, high; while the clumps of Locusts are from 12 to 20 feet high; and, I think, that I may safely say, that the average height is sixteen feet. They are the most beautiful clumps of trees that I ever saw in my life. They were, indeed, planted by a clever and most trusty servant, who, to say all that can be said in his praise, is, that he is worthy of such a master as he has.[1]

The trees are, indeed, in good land, and have been taken good care of; but, the other trees are in the same land; and, while they have been taken the same care of, since they were planted, they had not, I am sure, worse treatment before planting, than these Locust trees had. At the time when I sold them to my Lord Folkestone, they were in a field at Worth, near Crawley, in Sussex. The history of their transport is this. A Wiltshire waggon came to Worth for the trees, on the 14th of March 1824. The waggon had been stopped on the way by the snow; and, though the snow was gone off before the trees were put upon the waggon, it was very cold, and there were sharp frosts and harsh winds. I had the trees taken up, and tied up in hundreds by withes, like so many fagots. They were then put in, and upon the waggon, we doing our best to keep the roots inwards in the loading, so as to prevent them from being exposed, but as little as possible, to the wind, sun and frost. We put some fern on the top, and, where we could, on the sides; and we tied on the load with ropes, just as we should have done with a load of fagots. In this way, they were several days upon the road; and I do not know how long it was before they got safe into the ground again. All this shows how hardy these trees are, and it ought to admonish gentlemen to make pretty strict enquiries, when they have gardeners, or bailiffs, or stewards, under whose hands Locust trees die, or do not thrive.

N.B. Dry as the late summer was, I never had my Locust trees so fine as they are this year. I have some, they write

---

[1] The American Locust tree (or Acacia) is here alluded to. It is a valuable and beautiful tree, and sometimes grows to the height of seventy or eighty feet. The wood is useful for all purposes, in which great strength, and especially toughness, is required; this latter quality makes it valuable for "trenails" used in ship-building (about fifteen or eighteen inches in length, and one inch in thickness). £5000 worth of these "trenails" are imported into Great Britain annually. Several of these trees are still to be seen in the grounds at Botley, formerly occupied by Mr. Cobbett.

me, five feet high, from seed sown just before I went to Preston the first time, that is to say, on the 13th of May. I shall advertise my trees in the next Register. I never had them so fine, though the great drought has made the number comparatively small. Lord Folkestone bought of me 13,600 trees. They are, at this moment, worth the money they cost him, and, in addition the cost of planting, and in addition to that, they are worth the fee simple of the ground (very good ground) on which they stand; and this I am able to demonstrate to any man in his senses. What a difference in the value of Wiltshire, if all its Elms were Locusts! As fuel, a foot of Locust-wood is worth four or five of any English wood. It will burn better green, than almost any other wood will dry. If men want woods, beautiful woods, and *in a hurry*, let them go and see the clumps at Coleshill. Think of a wood 16 feet high, and I may say 20 feet high, in twenty-nine months from the day of planting; and the plants, on an average, not more than two feet high, when planted! Think of that: and any one may see it at Coleshill. See what efforts gentlemen make *to get a wood!* How they look at the poor slow-growing things for years; when they might, if they would, have it at once: really almost at a wish; and, with due attention, in almost any soil; and the most valuable of woods into the bargain. Mr. Palmer, the bailiff, showed me, near the house at Colehill, a Locust tree, which was planted about 35 years ago, or perhaps 40. He had measured it before. It is eight feet and an inch round at a foot from the ground. It goes off afterwards into two principal limbs; which two soon become six limbs, and each of these limbs is three feet round. So that here are six everlasting gate-posts to begin with. This tree is worth 20 pounds at the least farthing.

I saw also at Coleshill, the most complete farm yard that I ever saw, and that I believe there is in all England, many and complete as English farm yards are. This was the contrivance of Mr. Palmer, Lord Folkestone's bailiff and steward. The master gives all the credit of plantation, and farm, to the servant; but the servant ascribes a good deal of it to the master. Between them, at any rate, here are some most admirable objects in rural affairs. And here, too, there is no misery amongst those who do the work; those without whom there could have been no Locust-plantations, and no farm-yard. Here all are comfortable; gaunt hunger here stares no man in the face. That same disposition which sent Lord Folkestone to visit John Knight in the dungeons at Reading, keeps pinching hunger away from Coleshill. It is a very pretty spot all taken together. It is chiefly grazing land; and, though the making of cheese and bacon is, I dare say, the most profitable part of the farming here, Lord Folkestone fats oxen, and has a stall for it, which ought to be shown to foreigners, instead of the spinning jennies. A fat ox is a finer thing than a cheese, however good. There is a dairy here too, and beautifully kept. When this stall is full of oxen, and they all fat, how it would make a French farmer stare! It would make even a Yankee think, that "Old England" was a respectable "mother," after all. If I had to show this village off to a Yankee, I would blindfold him all the way to, and after I got him out of, the village, lest he should see the scare-crows of paupers on the road.

For a week or ten days before I came to Highworth, I had, owing to the uncertainty as to where I should be, no newspaper sent me from London; so that, really, I began to feel, that I was in the "dark ages." Arrived here, however, the *light* came bursting in upon me, flash after flash, from the Wen, from Dublin, and from Modern Athens. I had, too, for several days, nobody to enjoy the light with. I had no shares in the "*anteelactual*" treat, and this sort of enjoyment, unlike that of some other sorts, is augmented by being divided. Oh! how happy we were, and how proud we were to find (from the "instructor") that we had a king, that we were the subjects of a sovereign, who had graciously sent twenty-five pounds to Sir Richard Birnie's poor-box, there to swell the amount of the munificence of fined delinquents! Aye, and this, too, while (as the "instructor" told us) this same sovereign had just bestowed, unasked for (oh! the dear good man!), an annuity of 500l. a year on Mrs. Fox, who, observe, and whose daughters, had already a banging pension, paid out of the taxes, raised, in part, and in the greatest part, upon a people who are half-starved and half-naked. And our admiration at the poor box affair was not at all lessened by the reflection, that more money than sufficient to pay all the poor-rates of Wiltshire and Berkshire will, this very year, have been expended on new palaces, on pulling down and altera- tions of palaces before existing, and on ornaments and decorations in, and about Hyde Park, where a bridge is building, which, I am told, must cost a hundred thousand pounds, though all the water, that has to pass under it, would go through a sugar-hogshead; and does, a little while before it comes to this bridge, go through an arch which I believe to be smaller than a sugar-hogshead! besides, there was a bridge here before, and a very good one too.

Now will Jerry Curteis, who complains so bitterly about the poor-rates, and who talks of the poor working people as if their poverty were the worst of crimes; will Jerry say any thing about this bridge, or about the enormous expenses at Hyde Park Corner and in St. James Park? Jerry knows, or he ought to know, that this bridge alone will cost more money than half the poor-rates of the county of Sussex. Jerry knows, or he ought to know, that this bridge must be paid for out of the taxes. He must know, or else he must be what I dare not suppose him, that it is the taxes that make the paupers; and yet I am afraid that Jerry will not open his lips on the subject of this bridge. What they are going at, at Hyde Park Corner, nobody that I talk with seems to know. The "great Captain of the age," as that nasty palaverer, Brougham, called him, lives close to this spot, where also the "English ladies'" naked Achilles stand, having, on the base of it, the word WELLINGTON in great staring letters, while all the other letters are very, very small; so that base tax-eaters and fund-gamblers from the country, when they go to crouch before this image, think it is the image of the Great Captain himself! The reader will recollect, that after the battle of Waterloo, when we beat Napoleon with nearly a million of foreign bayonets in our pay, pay that came out of that *borrowed money*, for which we have *now* to wince and howl; the reader will recollect, that at that "glorious" time, when the insolent wretches of tax-eaters were ready to trample us under foot; that, at that time, when the Yankees were defeated on the Serpentine River, and before they had thrashed Blue and Buff so umercifully on the ocean and on the lakes; that, at that time, when the creatures called " English ladies " were flocking, from all parts of the country, to present rings, to " Old Blucher "; that, at that time cf exultation with the corrupt, and of mourning with the virtuous, the Collective, in the hey-dey, in the delirium, of its joy, resolved to expend three millions of money on triumphal arches, or columns, or monuments of some sort or other, to commemorate the glories of the war! Soon after this, however, low prices came, and they drove triumphal arches out of the heads of the Ministers, until "prosperity, unparalleled prosperity" came! This set them to work upon palaces and streets; and, I am told, that the triumphal-arch project is now going on at Hyde Park Corner! Good God! If this should be true, how apt will every thing be! Just about the time that the arch, or arches, will be completed; just about the time that the scaffolding will be knocked away, down will come the whole of the horrid borough-mongering system, for the upholding of which the vile tax-eating crew called for the war! All these palaces and other expensive projects were hatched two years ago; they were hatched in the days of "prosperity," the plans and contracts were made, I dare say, two or three years ago! However, they will be completed much about in the nick of time! They will help to exhibit the system in its true light.

The "best possible public instructor"[1] tells us, that Can-

---

[1] The journal, so satirically styled (the best possible public instructor) was the *Morning Chronicle*. Its editor, Dr. Black, a Scotchman, though not in direct antagonism to the Author, was only a half-hearted Reformer, for the *Chronicle* was essentially a Government organ. On the occasion of the Author's abrupt departure for America (in 1817), the *Morning*

ning is going to Paris. For what, I wonder? His brother Huskisson, was there last year; and he did nothing. It is supposed, that the "revered and ruptured Ogden" orator is going to try the force of his oratory, in order to induce France and her allies to let Portugal alone. He would do better to arm some ships of war! Oh! no: never will that be done again; or, at least, there never will again be war for three months as long as this borough and paper system shall last! This system has run itself out. It has lasted a good while, and has done tremendous mischief to the people of England; but, it is over: it is done for; it will live for a while, but it will go about drooping its wings, and half shutting its eyes, like a cock that has got the pip; it will never crow again; and for that I most humbly and fervently thank God! It has crowed over us long enough: it has pecked us, and spurred us, and slapped us about quite long enough. The nasty, insolent creatures, that it has sheltered under its wings, have triumphed long enough: they are now going to the workhouse; and thither let them go.

I *know* nothing of the politics of the Bourbons; but, though I can easily conceive that they would not like to see an end of the paper system, and a consequent Reform, in England; though I can see very good reasons for believing this, I do not believe, that Canning will induce them to sacrifice their own obvious and immediate interests for the sake of preserving our funding system. He will not get them out of Cadiz, and he will not induce them to desist from interfering in the affairs of Portugal, if they find it their interest to interfere. They know, that we *cannot go to war.* They know this as well as we do; and every sane person in England seems to know it well. No war for us *without Reform!* We are come to this at last. No war with *this Debt;* and this Debt defies every power but that of *Reform.* Foreign nations were, as to our

---

Chronicle, the great bulwark of Whiggism, informed its readers "that Cobbett had gone off to America because the circulation of the *Register* had fallen so low, through the operation of Sidmouth's Acts," which, of course, was a malignant satire.

real state, a good deal enlightened by "late panic." They had hardly any notion of our state before that. That opened their eyes, and led them to conclusions, that they never before dreamed of. It made them see, that that, which they had always taken for a mountain of solid gold, was only a great heap of rubbishy, rotten paper? And they now, of course, estimate us accordingly. But, it signifies not what *they* think, or what *they* do: unless they will subscribe and pay off this *Debt* for the people at Whitehall. The foreign governments (not excepting the American) all hate the English Reformers; those of Europe, because our example would be so dangerous to despots; and that of America, because we should not suffer it to build fleets and to add to its territories at pleasure. So that, we have not only our own borough-mongers and tax-eaters against us; but also all foreign governments. Not a straw, however, do we care for them all, so long as we have for us the ever-living, ever-watchful, ever-efficient, and all-subduing *Debt!* Let our foes subscribe, I say, and pay off that *Debt;* for until they do that, we snap our fingers at them.

Highworth,
Friday, 8th Sept.

"The best public instructor" of yesterday (arrived to-day) informs us, that "A number of official gentlemen conected "with finance have waited upon Lord Liverpool"! Connected with finance! And "a number" of them too! Bless their numerous and united noddles! Good God! what a state of things it is altogether! There never was the like of it seen in this world before. Certainly never; and the end must be what the far greater part of the people anticipate. It was this very Lord Liverpool that ascribed the *sufferings* of the country to a *surplus of food;* and that, too, at the very time when he was advising the King to put forth a begging proclamation, to raise money to prevent, or, rather, put a stop to, starvation in Ireland; and when, at the same time, public money was granted for the causing of English people to emigrate to Africa! Ah! Good God! who is to record or recount the endless blessings of a Jubilee-Government! The "instructor" gives us a sad account of the state of the working classes in Scotland. I am not glad that these poor people suffer: I am very sorry for it; and, if I could relieve them, out of my own means, without doing good to and removing danger from, the insolent borough-mongers and tax-eaters of Scotland, I would share my last shilling with the poor fellows. But, I must be glad that something has happened to silence the impudent Scotch quacks, who have been, for six years past, crying up the doctrine of Malthus, and railing against the English poor-laws. Let us now see what *they* will do with their poor. Let us see whether they will have the impudence to call upon *us* to maintain their poor! Well, amidst all this suffering, there is one good thing; the Scotch political economy is blown to the devil, and the Edinburgh Review and Adam Smith along with it.

Malmsbury (Wilts),
Monday, 11th Sept.

I was detained at Highworth partly by the rain, and partly by company that I liked very much. I left it at six o'clock yesterday morning, and got to this town about three or four o'clock in the afternoon, after a ride, including my deviations, of 34 miles; and as pleasant a ride as man ever had. I got to a farm-house in the neighbourhood of Cricklade, to breakfast, at which house I was very near to the source of the river Isis, which is, they say, the first branch of the Thames. They call it the "Old Thames," and I rode through it here, it not being above four or five yards wide, and not deeper than the knees of my horse.

The land here, and all round Cricklade, is very fine. Here are some of the very finest pastures in all England, and some of the finest dairies of cows, from 40 to 60 in a dairy, grazing in them. Was not this *always* so? Was it created by the union with Scotland; or was it begotten by Pitt and his crew? Aye, it was always so; and there were formerly two churches here, where there is now only one, and five, six or ten times as many people. I saw in one single farmyard here, more food than enough for four times the inhabitants of the parish; and this yard did not contain a tenth, perhaps, of the produce of the parish; but, while the poor creatures that raise the wheat, and the barley, and cheese, and the mutton, and the beef, are living upon potatoes, an accursed *Canal* comes kindly through the parish to convey away the wheat, and all the good food to the tax-eaters and their attendants in the Wen! What, then, is this "an improvement?" is a nation *richer* for the carrying away of the food from those who raise it, and giving it to bayonet men and others, who are assembled in great masses? I could broom-stick the fellow who would look me in the face, and call this "an improvement." What! was it not better for the consumers of the food to live near to the places where it was grown? We have very nearly come to the system of Hindostan, where the farmer is allowed by the *Aumil*, or tax-contractor, only so much of the produce of his farm to eat in the year! The thing is not done in so undisguised a manner here: here are assessor, collector, exciseman, supervisor, informer, constable, justice, sheriff, jailor, judge, jury, jack-ketch, barrack-man. Here is a great deal of ceremony about it; all is done according to law; it is the *free-est* country in the world: but, some how or other, the produce is, at last, *carried away;* and it is eaten, for the main part, by those who do not work.

I observed, some pages back, that, when I got to Malmsbury, I should have to explain my main object in coming to the North of Wiltshire. In the year 1818, the Parliament, by *an Act*, ordered the bishops to cause the beneficed clergy to give in an account of their livings, which account was to contain the following particulars, relating to each parish:

1. Whether a Rectory, Vicarage, or what.
2. In what rural Deanery.
3. Population.
4. Number of Churches and Chapels.
5. *Number of persons they* (the churches and chapels) *can contain.*

In looking into this account, as it was finally made up and printed by the parliamentary officers, I saw, that it was impossible for it to be true. I have always asserted, and, indeed, I have clearly proved, that one of the two last population returns is false, barefacedly false; and, I was sure, that the account, of which I am now speaking, was equally false. The falsehood, consisted, I saw principally, in the account of the capacity of the church to contain people; that is, under the head No. 5, as above stated. I saw, that, in almost every instance, this account must of necessity be false, though coming from under the pen of a beneficed clergyman. I saw, that there was a constant desire to make it appear, that the church was now become too small! And thus to help along the opinion of a great recent increase of population, an opinion so sedulously inculcated by all the tax-eaters of every sort, and by the most brutal and best public instructor. In some cases the falsehood of this account was impudent almost beyond conception; and yet, it required going to the spot, to get unquestionable proof of the falsehood. In many of the parishes, in hundreds of them, the population is next to nothing, far fewer persons than the church porch would contain. Even in these cases, the parsons have seldom said, that the church would contain more than the population! In such cases, they have generally said, that the church can contain "the population!" So it can; but, it can contain ten times the number! And thus it was, that, in words of truth, a lie in meaning was told to the Parliament, and not one word of notice was ever taken of it. Little Langford, or Landford, for instance, between Salisbury and Warminster, is returned as having a population under twenty, and a church that "can contain the population." This church, which I went and looked at, can contain, very conveniently, two hundred people! But, there was one instance, in which the parson had been singularly impudent; for, he had stated the population at eight persons, and had stated that the church could contain eight persons! This was the account of the parish of Sharncut, in this county of Wilts. It lies on the very northernmost edge of the county, and its boundary, on one side, divides Wiltshire from Gloucestershire. To this Sharncut, therefore, I was resolved to go, and to try the fact with my own eyes. When, therefore, I got through Cricklade I was compelled to quit the Malmsbury road, and go away to my right. I had to go through a village, called Ashton Keines, with which place I was very much struck. It is now a straggling village; but, to a certainty, it has been a large market town. There is a market-cross still standing in an open place in it; and, there are such numerous lanes, crossing each other, and cutting the land up into such little bits, that it must, at one time, have been a large town. It is a very curious place, and I should have stopped in it for some time, but I was now within a few miles of the famous Sharncut, the church of which, according to the parson's account, *could* contain eight persons!

At the end of about three miles more of road, rather difficult to find, but very pleasant, I got to Sharncut, which I found to consist of a church, two farm-houses, and a parsonage-house, one part of the buildings of which had become a labourer's house. The church has no tower, but a sort of crowning-piece (very ancient) on the transept. The church is sixty feet long, and, on an average, twenty-eight feet wide; so that the area of it contains one thousand six hundred and eighty square feet; or, one hundred and eighty-eight square yards! I found in the church eleven pews that would contain, that were made to contain, eighty-two people; and, these do not occupy a third part of the area of the church; and thus, more than two hundred persons, at the least, might be accommodated, with perfect convenience, in this church, which the parson says "*can* contain *eight!*" Nay, the church porch, on its two benches, would hold twenty people, taking little and big promiscuously. I have been thus particular, in this instance, because I would leave no doubt as to the barefacedness of the lie. A strict inquiry would show, that the far greater part of the account is a most impudent lie, or, rather, string of lies. For, as to the subterfuge, that this account was true, because the church "*can* contain *eight*," it is an addition to the crime of lying. What the Parliament meant was, what "is the greatest number of persons that the church can contain "at worship;" and, therefore to put the figure of 8 against the church of Sharncut was to tell the Parliament a wilful lie. This parish is a rectory; it has great and small tithes; it has a glebe, and a good solid house, though the parson says it is unfit for him to live in! In short, he is not here; a curate that serves, perhaps, three or four other churches, comes here at five o'clock in the afternoon.

The *motive* for making out the returns in this way is clear enough. The parsons see, that they are getting what they get in a declining, and a mouldering, country. The size of the church tells them, everything tells them, that the country is a mean and miserable thing, compared with what it was in former times. They feel the facts; but they wish to disguise them, because they know that they have been one great cause of the country being in its present impoverished and dilapidated state. They know, that the people look at them with an accusing eye: and they wish to put as fair a face as they can upon the state of things. If you talk to them, they will never acknowledge that there is any misery in the country; because they well know how large a share they have had in the cause of it. They were always haughty and insolent; but, the anti-jacobin times made them ten thousand times more so than ever. The cry of Atheism, as of the French, gave these fellows of ours a fine time of it: they became identified with loyalty, and what was more, with property; and, at one time, to say, or hint, a word against a parson, do what he would, was to be an enemy of God and of all property! Those were the glorious times for them. They urged on the war: they were the loudest of all the trumpeters. They saw their tithes in danger. If they did not get the Bourbons restored, there was no chance of re-establishing tithes in France; and then the example might be fatal. But, they forgot, that, to restore the Bourbons, a debt must be contracted; and that, when the nation could not pay the interest of that debt, it would, as it now does, begin to look hard at the tithes! In short, they over-reached themselves; and those of them who have common sense, now see it: each hopes that the thing will last out his time; but, they have, unless they be half-idiots, a constant dread upon their minds: this makes them a great deal less brazen than they used to be; and, I daresay, that, if the parliamentary return had to be made out again, the parson of Sharncut would not state that the church "*can* contain *eight persons.*"

From Sharncut I came through a very long and straggling village, called Somerford, another called Ocksey, and another called Crudwell. Between Somerford and Ocksey, I saw, on the side of the road, more *goldfinches* than I had ever seen together; I think, fifty times as many as I had ever seen at one time in my life. The favourite food of the goldfinch is the seed of the *thistle.* This seed is just now dead ripe. The thistles are all cut and carried away from the fields by the harvest; but, they grow alongside the roads; and, in this place, in great quantities. So that the goldfinches were here in flocks, and, as they continued to fly along before me, for nearly half a mile, and still sticking to the road and the banks, I do believe I had, at last, a flock of ten thousand flying before me. *Birds* of every kind, including partridges and pheasants and all sorts of poultry, are most abundant this year. The fine, long summer has been singularly favourable to them; and you see the effect of it in the great broods of chickens and ducks and geese and turkeys in and about every farm-yard.

The churches of the last-mentioned villages are all large, particularly the latter, which is capable of containing, very conveniently, 3,000 or 4,000 people. It is a very large church; it has a triple roof, and is nearly 100 feet long; and master parson says, in his return, that it "*can* contain *three hundred* people!" At Ocksey the people were in church as I came by. I heard the singers singing; and, as the church-yard was close by the road-side, I got off my horse and went in, giving my horse to a boy to hold. The fellow says that his church "*can* contain *two hundred* people." I counted pews for about 450; the singing gallery would hold 40 or 50; two-thirds of the area of the church have no pews in them. On benches these two-thirds would hold 2,000 persons, taking one with another! But this is nothing rare; the same sort of statement has been made, the same kind of falsehoods, relative to the whole of the parishes, throughout the country, with here and there an exception. Everywhere you see the indubitable marks of *decay* in mansions, in parsonage-houses and in people. Nothing can so strongly depict the great decay of the villages as the state of the parsonage-houses, which are so many parcels of public property, and to prevent the dilapidation of which there are laws so strict. Since I left Devizes, I have passed close by, or very near to, thirty-two parish churches; and, in fifteen, out of these thirty-two parishes, the parsonage-houses are stated, in the parliamentary return, either as being unfit for a parson to live in, or, as being wholly tumbled down and gone! What then, are there Scotch vagabonds; are there Chalmerses and Colquhouns, to swear, "mon," that Pitt and Jubilee George *begat* all us Englishmen; and, that there were only a few stragglers of us in the world before! And that our dark and ignorant fathers, who built Winchester and Salisbury Cathedrals, had neither hands nor money!

When I got in here yesterday, I went, at first, to an inn; but I very soon changed my quarters for the house of a friend, who and whose family, though I had never seen them before, and had never heard of them until I was at Highworth, gave me a hearty reception, and precisely in *the style* that I like. This town, though it has nothing particularly engaging in itself, stands upon one of the prettiest spots that can be imagined. Besides the river Avon, which I went down in the South-East part of the country, here is another river Avon, which runs down to Bath, and two branches, or sources, of which meet here. There is a pretty ridge of ground, the base of which is a mile, or a mile and a half wide. On each side of this ridge a branch of the river runs down, through a flat of very fine meadows. The town and the beautiful remains of the famous old Abbey, stand on the rounded spot, which terminates this ridge; and, just below, nearly close to the town, the two branches of the river meet; and then they begin to be called *the Avon*. The land round about is excellent, and of a great variety of forms. The trees are lofty and fine: so that what with the water, the meadows, the fine cattle and sheep, and, as I hear, the absence of *hard*-pinching poverty, this is a very pleasant place. There remains more of the Abbey than, I believe, of any of our monastic buildings, except that of Westminster, and those that have become Cathedrals. The church-service is performed in the part of the Abbey that is left standing. The parish church has fallen down and is gone; but the tower remains, which is made use of for the bells; but the Abbey is used as the church, though the church-tower is at a considerable distance from it. It was once a most magnificent building; and there is now a *door-way*, which is the most beautiful thing I ever saw, and which was, nevertheless, built in Saxon times, in "the *dark* ages," and was built by men, who were not begotten by Pitt nor by Jubilee-George.—What *fools*, as well as ungrateful creatures, we have been and are! There is a broken arch, standing off from the sound part of the building, at which one cannot look up without feeling shame at the thought of ever having abused the men who made it. No one need *tell* any man of sense; he *feels* our inferiority to our fathers, upon merely beholding the remains of their efforts to ornament their country and elevate the minds of the people. We talk of our skill and learning, indeed! How do we know how skilful, how learned *they* were? If, in all that they have left us, we see that they surpassed us, why are we to conclude, that they did not surpass us in all other things worthy of admiration?

This famous Abbey was founded, in about the year 600, by Maidulf, a Scotch Monk, who upon the suppression of a Nunnery here at that time selected the spot for this great establishment. For the great magnificence, however, to which it was soon after brought, it was indebted to Aldhelm, a Monk educated within its first walls, by the founder himself; and to

St. Aldhelm, who by his great virtues became very famous, the Church was dedicated in the time of King Edgar. This Monastery continued flourishing during those *dark* ages, until it was sacked by the great enlightener, at which time it was found to be endowed to the amount of 16,077*l*. 11*s*. 8*d*., of the money of the present day! Amongst other, many other, great men produced by this Abbey of Malmsbury, was that famous scholar and historian, William de Malmsbury.

There is a *market-cross*, in this town, the sight of which is worth a journey of hundreds of miles. Time, with his scythe, and "enlightened Protestant piety," with its pick-axes and crow-bars; these united have done much to efface the beauties of this monument of ancient skill and taste, and proof of ancient wealth; but, in spite of all their destructive efforts, this Cross still remains a most beautiful thing, though possibly, and even probably, nearly, or quite, a thousand years old. There is a *market-cross* lately erected at Devizes, and intended to imitate the ancient ones. Compare that with this, and, then you have, pretty fairly, a view of the difference between us and our forefathers of the "dark ages."

To-morrow I start for Bollitree, near Ross, Herefordshire, my road being across the county, and through the city of Gloucester.

RIDE, FROM MALMSBURY, IN WILTSHIRE, THROUGH GLOUCESTERSHIRE, HEREFORDSHIRE, AND WORCESTERSHIRE.

Stroud (Gloucestershire),
Tuesday Forenoon, 12*th Sept.,* 1826.

I set off from Malmsbury this morning at 6 o'clock, in as sweet and bright a morning, as ever came out of the heavens, and leaving behind me as pleasant a house and as kind hosts as I ever met with in the whole course of my life, either in England or America; and that is saying a great deal indeed. This circumstance was the more pleasant, as I had never before either seen or heard of, these kind, unaffected, sensible, *sans-façons*, and most agreeable friends. From Malmsbury I first came, at the end of five miles, to Tutbury, which is in Gloucestershire, there being here, a sort of dell, or ravine, which, in this place, is the boundary line of the two counties, and over which you go on a bridge, one-half of which belongs to each county. And now, before I take my leave of Wiltshire, I must observe, that, in the whole course of my life (days of *courtship* excepted, of course), I never passed seventeen pleasanter days than those which I have just spent in Wiltshire. It is, especially in the Southern half, just the sort of country that I like; the weather has been pleasant; I have been in good houses and amongst good and beautiful gardens; and, in *every* case, I have not only been most kindly entertained, but my entertainers have been of just the stamp that I like.

I saw again, this morning, large flocks of *goldfinches*, feeding on the thistle-seed, on the roadside. The French call this bird by a name derived from the thistle, so notorious has it always been, that they live upon this seed. *Thistle* is, in French, *Chardon;* and the French call this beautiful little bird *Chardonaret*. I never could have supposed, that such flocks of these birds would ever be seen in England. But, it is a great year for all the feathered race, whether wild or tame: naturally so, indeed; for every one knows, that it is the *wet* and not the *cold*, that is injurious to the breeding of birds of all sorts, whether land-birds or water-birds. They say, that there are, this year, double the usual quantity of ducks and geese: and, really, they do seem to swarm in the farmyards, wherever I go. It is a great mistake to suppose, that ducks and geese *need* water, except to drink. There is, perhaps, no spot in the world, in proportion to its size and population, where so many of these birds are reared and fatted, as in Long Island; and, it is not in one case out of ten, that they have any ponds to go to, or, that they ever see any water other than water that is drawn up out of a well.

A little way before I got to Tutbury I saw a woman digging some potatoes, in a strip of ground, making part of a field nearly an oblong square, and which field appeared to be laid out in strips. She told me, that the field was part of a farm (to the homestead of which she pointed); that it was, by the farmer, *let out* in strips to labouring people; that each strip contained a rood (or quarter of a statute acre); that each married labourer rented one strip; and that the annual rent was *a pound* for the strip. Now, the taxes being all paid by the farmer; the fences being kept in repair by him; and, as appeared to me, the land being exceedingly good; all these things considered, the rent does not appear to be too high.— This fashion is certainly a *growing* one; it is a little step towards a coming back to the ancient small life and lease-holds and common-fields! This field of strips was, in fact, a sort of common-field; and the "agriculturists," as the conceited asses of landlords call themselves, at their clubs and meetings, might, and they would if their skulls could admit any thoughts except such as relate to high prices and low wages; they might, and they would, begin to suspect, that the "dark age" people were not so very foolish, when they had so many common-fields, and when almost every man that had a family had also a bit of land, either large or small. It is a very curious thing, that the enclosing of commons, that the shutting out of the labourers *from all share* in the land; that the prohibiting of them to look at a wild animal, almost at a lark or a frog; it is curious that this hard-hearted system should have gone on, until, at last, it has produced effects so injurious and so dangerous to the grinders themselves, that they have, of their own accord, and for their own safety, begun to make a step towards the ancient system, and have, in the manner I have observed, made the labourers sharers, in some degree, in the uses, at any rate, of the soil. The far greater part of these strips of land have potatoes growing in them; but, in some cases, they have borne wheat, and, in others, barley, this year; and these have now turnips; very young, most of them, but, in some places, very fine, and in every instance, nicely hoed out. The land that will bear 400 bushels of potatoes to the acre, will bear 40 bushels of wheat; and, the ten bushels of wheat, to the quarter of an acre, would be a crop far more valuable than a hundred bushels of potatoes, as I have proved many times, in the Register.

Just before I got into Tutbury, I was met by a good many people, in twos, threes, or fives, some running, and some walking fast, one of the first of whom asked me, if I had met an "old man" some distance back. I asked, what *sort* of a man: "A *poor* man." "I don't recollect, indeed; but, "what are you all pursuing him for?" "He has been "*stealing*." "What has he been stealing?" "Cabbages." "Where?" "Out of Mr. Glover, the hatter's, garden." "What! do you call that *stealing!* and would you punish a "man, a poor man, and, therefore, in all likelihood, a hungry "man too, and, moreover an old man; do you set up a hue- "and-cry after, and would you punish, such a man for taking a "few cabbages, when that Holy Bible, which, I dare say, you "profess to believe in, and perhaps, assist to circulate, teaches "you that the hungry man may, without committing any "offence at all, go into his neighbour's vineyard and eat his "fill of grapes, one bunch of which is worth a sack-full of "cabbages?" "Yes; but he is a very bad character." "Why, my friend, very poor and almost starved people are "apt to be 'bad characters;' but the Bible, in both Testa- "ments, commands us to be merciful to the poor, to feed the "hungry, to have compassion on the aged; and it makes no "exception as to the 'character' of the parties." Another group or two of the pursuers had come up by this time; and I, bearing in mind the fate of Don Quixote, when he inter- fered in somewhat similar cases, gave my horse the hint, and soon got away; but, though, doubtless, I made no converts, I, upon looking back, perceived, that I had slackened the pur- suit! The pursuers went more slowly; I could see that they got to talking; it was now the step of deliberation rather than that of decision; and, though I did not like to call upon Mr. Glover, I hope he was merciful. It is impossible for me to witness scenes like this; to hear a man called *a thief* for such a cause; to see him thus eagerly and vindictively pursued for having taken some cabbages in a garden : it is impossible for me to behold such a scene, without calling to mind the practice in the United States of America, where, if a man were even to talk of prosecuting another (especially if that other were poor, or old) for taking from the land, or from the trees, any part of a growing crop, for his own personal and immediate use; if any man were even to talk of prosecuting another for such an act, such talker would be held in universal abhorrence : people would hate him ; and, in short, if rich as Ricardo or Baring, he might live by himself; for no man would look upon him as a neighbour.

Tutbury is a very pretty town, and has a beautiful ancient church. The country is high along here for a mile or two toward Avening, which begins a long and deep and narrow valley, that comes all the way down to Stroud. When I got to the end of the high country, and the lower country opened to my view, I was at about three miles from Tutbury, on the road to Avening, leaving the Minching-hampton road to my right. Here I was upon the edge of the high land, looking right down upon the village of Avening, and seeing, just close to it, a large and fine mansion-house, a beautiful park, and, making part of the park, one of the finest, most magnificent woods (of 200 acres, I dare say), lying facing me, going from a valley up a gently-rising hill. While I was sitting on my horse, admiring this spot, a man came along with some tools in his hand, as if going somewhere to work as plumber. "Whose beautiful place is that?" said I. "One 'Squire Ricardo, I think they call him, but . . . . . ."—You might have "knocked me down with a feather," as the old women say, ... "but" (continued the plumber) "the Old Gentleman's dead, and" . . . . "—— the old gentleman and the young gentleman too!" said I; and, giving my horse a blow, instead of a word, on I went down the hill. Before I got to the bottom, my reflections on the present state of the "market" and on the probable results of "watching the turn of it," had made me better humoured; and, as one of the first

objects that struck my eye, in the village, was the sign of the
CROSS, and of the Red, or Bloody, Cross too, I asked the landlord
some questions, which began a series of joking and bantering
that I had with the people, from one end of the village to the
other. I set them all laughing; and, though they could not
know my name, they will remember me for a long while.—
This estate of Gatcomb belonged, I am told, to a Mr. Shepperd, and to his fathers before him. I asked where this
Shepperd was NOW? A tradesman-looking man told me, that
he did not know where he was; but, that he had heard, that
he was living somewhere near to Bath! Thus they go! Thus
they are squeezed out of existence. The little ones are gone;
and the big ones have nothing left for it, but to resort to the
bands of holy matrimony, with the turn of the market watchers
and their breed. This the big ones are now doing apace; and
there is this comfort at any rate; namely, that the connection,
cannot make them baser than they are, a boroughmonger
being, of all God's creatures, the very basest.

From Avening I came on through Nailsworth, Woodchester,
and Rodborough, tō this place. These villages lie on the
sides of a narrow and deep valley, with a narrow stream of
water running down the middle of it, and this stream turns the
wheels of a great many mills and sets of machinery for the
making of *woollen-cloth*. The factories begin at Avening, and
are scattered all the way down the valley. There are steam-
engines as well as water powers. The work and the trade is
so flat, that, in, I should think, much more than a hundred
acres of ground, which I have seen to-day, covered with rails
or racks, for the drying of cloth, I do not think that I have
seen one single acre, where the racks had cloth upon them.
The workmen do not get half wages; great numbers are thrown
on the parish; but, overseers and magistrates, in this part of
England do not presume that they are to leave anybody to
starve to death; there is law here; this is in England, and not
in "the North," where those who ought to see that the poor do
not suffer, talk of their dying with hunger as Irish 'Squires do;
aye, and applaud them for their patient resignation!

The Gloucestershire people have no notion of dying with hunger; and it is with great pleasure that I remark, that I have seen no woe-worn creature this day. The sub-soil here is a yellowish ugly stone. The houses are all built with this; and, it being ugly, the stone is made *white* by a wash of some sort or other. The land on both sides of the valley, and all down the bottom of it, has plenty of trees on it; it is chiefly pasture land, so that the green and the white colours, and the form and great variety of the ground, and the water, and altogether make this a very pretty ride. Here are a series of spots, every one of which a lover of landscapes would like to have painted. Even the buildings of the factories are not ugly. The people seem to have been constantly well off. A pig in almost every cottage sty; and that is the infallible mark of a happy people. At present, indeed, this valley suffers; and, though cloth will always be wanted, there will yet be much suffering even here, while at Uly and other places, they say that the suffering is great indeed.

Huntley, between Gloucester and Ross.

From Stroud I came up to Pitchcomb, leaving Painswick on my right. From the lofty hill at Pitchcomb, I looked down into that great flat and almost circular vale, of which the city of Gloucester is in the centre. To the left I saw the Severn, become a sort of arm of the sea; and before me I saw the hills that divide this county from Herefordshire and Worcestershire. The hill is a mile down. When down, you are amongst dairy-farms and orchards all the way to Gloucester, and, this year, the orchards, particularly those of pears, are greatly productive. I intended to sleep at Gloucester, as I had, when there, already come twenty-five miles, and, as the fourteen, which remained for me to go, in order to reach Bollitree, in Herefordshire, would make about nine more than either I or my horse had a taste for. But, when I came to Gloucester, I found, that I should run a risk of having no bed, if I did not bow very low, and pay very high; for, what should there be here; but one of those scandalous and beastly fruits of the system, called a "Music-Meeting!" Those who founded the Cathedrals, never dreamed, I dare say, that they would have been put to such uses as this! They are, upon these occasions, made use of as *Opera-Houses;* and, I am told, that the money, which is collected, goes, in some shape or another, to the Clergy of the Church, or their widows, or children, or something. These assemblages of player-folks, half-rogues and half-fools, began with the small paper-money; and with it they will go. They are amongst the profligate pranks which idleness plays, when fed by the sweat of a starving people. From this scene of prostitution and of pocket-picking, I moved off with all convenient speed, but not before the ostler made me pay 9*d.* for merely letting my horse *stand* about ten minutes, and not before he had *begun* to abuse me for declining, though in a very polite manner, to make him a present in addition to the 9*d.* How he ended I do not know; for, I soon set the noise of the shoes of my horse to answer him. I got to this village, about eight miles from Gloucester, by five o'clock: it is now half past seven, and I am going to bed with an intention of getting to Bollitree (six miles only) early enough in the morning, to catch my sons in bed, if they play the sluggard.

Bollitree, Wednesday, 13*th Sept.*

This morning was most beautiful. There has been rain here now, and the grass begins (but only begins) to grow. When I got within two hundred yards of Mr. Palmer's I had the happiness to meet my son Richard, who said that he had been up an hour. As I came along I saw one of the prettiest sights in the *flower* way that I ever saw in my life. It was a little orchard; the grass in it had just taken a start, and was beautifully fresh; and, very thickly growing amongst the grass, was the purple flowered *Colchicum*, in full bloom. They say, that the leaves of this plant which come out in the spring, and die away in the summer, are poisonous to cattle if they eat much of them in the spring. The flower, if standing by itself, would be no great beauty; but, contrasted thus, with the fresh grass, which was a little shorter than itself, it was very beautiful.[1]

Bollitree, Saturday, 23d Sept.

Upon my arrival here, which, as the reader has seen, was ten days ago, I had a parcel of *letters* to open, amongst which were a large lot from correspondents, who had been good enough to set me right with regard to that conceited and impudent plagiarist, or literary thief, "Sir James Graham, Baronet of Netherby." One correspondent says, that I have reversed the rule of the Decalogue by visiting the sins of the son upon the father. Another tells me anecdotes, about the "Magnus Apollo." I hereby do the father justice by saying that, from what I have now heard of him, I am induced to believe, that he would have been ashamed to commit flagrant acts of plagiarism, which the son has been guilty of. The whole of this plagiarist's pamphlet, is bad enough. Every part of it is contemptible; but the passage, in which he says, that there was "no man, of any authority, who did not under-"rate the distress that would arise out of Peel's Bill;" this passage merits a broom-stick, at the hands of any Englishman that chooses to lay it on, and particularly from me.[2]

---

[1] The only British species of the colchicum is commonly known as the "*meadow* saffron," and is sometimes called incorrectly the Autumn crocus. The leaves, which are large and broad, appear in spring, when the stalk, which bears the ripening fruit, arises amongst them. The flowers which appear in autumn, are pale purple, unaccompanied by any leaves. It is a valuable medicinal plant, and is administered, in small doses, for gout and rheumatism. The parts used for medicinal purposes, are the root and the seeds: the latter are round, brown, and rather larger than mustard seed; they are very poisonous. Cattle have been known to have been poisoned by having eaten colchicum leaves in the spring.

[2] Sir James Robert George Graham, to whom the Author here refers, was born in 1792. In 1818 he was returned for Hull on Whig principles; in 1826 he represented Carlisle, at which period he was a warm advocate of Roman Catholic emancipation. In 1836 he obtained a seat in the Cabinet, under Earl Grey, as the First Lord of the Admiralty, and he was appointed on the Committee to discuss and settle the provisions of the first Reform Bill. He was the author of a work on "Currency and Corn," in which he maintains "that every notion of Free Trade, is worse than visionary, unless accompanied by a large reduction of taxes and duties." Graham afterwards became a stanch Conservative under Sir Robert Peel,

As to *crops* in Herefordshire and Gloucestershire, they have been very bad. Even the wheat here has been only a two-third part crop. The barley and oats, really next to nothing. *Fed off* by cattle and sheep in many places, partly for want of grass, and partly from their worthlessness. The cattle have been nearly starved in many places; and we hear the same from Worcestershire. In some places one of these beautiful calves (last spring calves) will be given for the wintering of another. Hay at Stroud, was six pounds a ton: last year it was 3*l*. a ton: and yet meat and cheese are lower in price than they were last year. Mutton (I mean alive) was, last year at this time 7½*d*.; it is now 6*d*. There has been in North Wilts, and in Gloucestershire, half the quantity of cheese made this year, and yet the price is lower than it was last year. Wool is half the last year's price. There has, within these three weeks, or a month, been a prodigious increase in the quantity of cattle food; the grass looks like the grass late in May; and the late and stubble-turnips (of which immense quantities have been sown) have grown very much, and promise large crops generally; yet lean sheep have, at the recent fairs, fallen in price; they have been lessening in price, while the facility of keeping them has been augmenting! Aye; but the paper-money has not been augmenting, notwithstanding the Branch-Bank at Gloucester! This bank is quite ready, they say, to take deposits; that is to say, to keep people's spare money for them; but, to lend them none, without such security, as would get money, even from the claws of a miser. This trick is, then, what the French call a *coup manqué;* or a missing of the mark. In spite of everything, as to the season, calculated to cause lean sheep to rise in price, they fell, I hear, at Wilton fair (near Salisbury) on the 12th instant, from 2s. to 3s. a head. And yesterday, 22nd Sept., at Newent fair, there was a fall since the last fair in this

---

and subsequently gave a warm support to the Corn Law Repeal Bill. Thus his changes from Whiggism to Conservatism, and finally to Radicalism, exposed him to well-founded charges of political inconsistency.

neighbourhood. Mr. Palmer sold, at this fair, sheep for 23s. a head, rather better than some which he sold at the same fair last year for 34s. a head: so that here is a falling off of a third! Think of the dreadful ruin, then, which must fall upon the renting farmers, whether they rent the land, or rent the money, which enables them to call the land their own! The recent Order in Council *has* ruined many. I was, a few days after that Order reached us, in Wiltshire, in a rick yard, looking at the ricks, amongst which were two of beans. I asked the farmer how much the Order would take out of his pocket; and he said it had already taken out more than a hundred pounds! This is a pretty state of things for a man to live in! The winds are less uncertain, than this calling of a farmer is now become, though it is a calling the affairs of which, have always been deemed, as little liable to accident, as any thing human.

The "best public instructor" tells us, that the Ministers are about to give the *Militia Clothing* to the poor Manufacturers! Coats, waistcoats, trousers, shoes and stockings! Oh, what a kind as well as wise "envy of surrounding nations" this is! Dear good souls! But what are the *women* to do? No *smocks*, pretty gentlemen! No royal commission to be appointed to distribute smocks to the suffering "females" of the "*disturbed* districts!" How fine our "manufacturing population" will look all dressed in *red!* Then indeed, will the farming fellows have to repent, that they did not follow the advice of Dr. Black, and fly to the "*happy* manufacturing districts" where employment, as the Doctor affirmed, was so abundant and so permanent, and where wages were so high! Out of evil comes good; and this state of things has blown the Scotch *poleeteecal ecoonoomy* to the devil, at any rate. In spite of all their plausibility and persevering brass, the Scotch writers are now generally looked upon, as so many tricky humbugs. Mr. Sedgwick's affair is enough, one would think, to open men's eyes to the character of this greedy band of *invaders;* for invaders they are, and of the very worst sort: they come only to live on the labour of others; never to work themselves; and, while they do this, they are everlastingly publishing essays, the object of which is, to keep the Irish out of England! Dr. Black has, within these four years, published more than a hundred articles, in which he has represented the invasion of the Irish as being ruinous to England! What monstrous impudence! The Irish, come to help do the work; the Scotch, to help eat the taxes; or, to tramp "*aboot mon*" with a pack and a licence; or, in other words, to cheat upon a small scale, as their superiors do upon a large one.[1] This tricky and greedy set have, however, at last, over-reached themselves, after having so long over-reached all the rest of mankind that have had the misfortune to come in contact with them. They are now smarting under the scourge, the torments of which they have long made others feel. They have been the principal inventors and executors, of all that has been damnable to England. They are *now* bothered; and I thank God for it. It may, and it must, finally deliver us from their baleful influence.

To return to the kind and pretty gentlemen of Whitehall, and their *Militia-Clothing:* if they refuse to supply the women with smocks, perhaps they would have no objection to hand them over some petticoats; or at any rate, to give their husbands a *musket* a piece, and a little powder and ball; just to amuse themselves with, instead of the employment of "digging holes one day and filling them up the next," as suggested by "the great statesman, now no more," who was one of that "noble, honourable, and venerable body" the Privy Council (to which Sturges Bourne belongs), and who cut his own throat at North Cray, in Kent, just about three years after he had brought in the bill, which compelled me to make the Register contain two sheets and a quarter, and to

---

[1] The last Editor mentions, that in the Northern Counties, the popular name for a hawker or pedlar, is "Scotchman." Hawkers and pedlars were first licensed in 1698. Licensing Commissioners were appointed in 1810. Since January 1872, a foot hawker or pedlar (of good character) can obtain from the chief officer of the Police District where he resides, a license for a year for 5s. But if he use any beast of burden, the license is £4. (34 & 35 Vic. c. 96 & 29-30 Vic. c. 64.)

compel printers to give, before they began to print, bail to
pay any fines, that might be inflicted on them, for any thing
that they might print. Let me see: where was I? Oh! the
muskets and powder and ball ought, certainly, to go with the
red clothes; but how strange it is, that the *real relief* never
seems to occur, even for one single moment, to the minds of
these pretty gentlemen; namely, *taking off the taxes.* What a
thing it is to behold, poor people receiving rates, or alms, to prevent them from starving; and to behold one half, at least, of
what they receive, taken from them in taxes! What a sight to
behold soldiers, horse and foot, employed to prevent a distressed people from committing acts of violence, when the
cost of the horse and foot would, probably, if applied in the
way of relief to the sufferers, prevent the existence of the
distress! *A cavalry horse has, I think, ten pounds of oats a day
and twenty pounds of hay.* These at present prices, cost 16s.
a week. Then there is stable room, barracks, straw, saddle,
and all the trappings. Then there is the wear of the horse.
Then the pay of them. So that one single horseman, with
his horse, does not cost so little as 36s. a week; and that is
more than the parish allowance to five labourers' or manufacturers' families, at five to a family; so that one horseman with
his horse, costs what would feed twenty-five of the distressed
creatures. If there be ten thousand of these horsemen, they
cost as much as would keep, at the parish rate, two hundred
and fifty thousand of the distressed persons. Aye; it is even
so, parson Hay, stare at it as long as you like.[1] But, suppose
it to be, only half as much: then it would maintain a hundred
and twenty-five thousand persons. However, to get rid of all
dispute, and to state one staring and undeniable fact, let me
first observe, that it is notorious, that the poor-rates are looked
upon as enormous; that they are deemed an insupportable

---

[1] Mr. Hay was Vicar of Rochdale (one of the great manufacturing towns of Lancashire) and Chairman of the Lancashire Sessions at Salford. By the allusion here made to him, he was doubtless a "political parson" as well as a magistrate, and probably took an active part in the Preston election when Cobbett was a candidate for that town.

burden;[1] that Scarlett and Nolan have asserted, that they threaten to swallow up the land; that it is equally notorious that a large part of the poor-rates ought to be called *wages;* all this is undeniable, and now comes the damning fact, namely, that the whole amount of these poor-rates falls far short of the cost of the standing army in time of peace! So that, take away this army, which is to keep the distressed people from committing acts of violence, and you have, at once, ample means of removing all the distress, and all the danger, of acts of violence! *When* will this be done? Do not say, "*Never*" reader: if you do, you are not only a slave, but you ought to be one.

I cannot dismiss this *militia-clothing* affair, without remarking, that I do not agree with those who *blame* the Ministers for having let in the foreign corn, *out of fear.* Why not do it from that motive? "The fear of the Lord is the beginning of wisdom." And what is meaned by "fear of the Lord," but the fear of doing wrong, or of persevering in doing wrong? And whence is this fear to arise? From thinking of the *consequences*, to be sure: and, therefore if the Ministers did let in the foreign corn, for fear of popular commotion, they acted rightly, and their motive was as good and reasonable, as the act was wise and just. It would have been lucky for them if

---

[1] The Author had good reason for speaking of the poor-rates (at the time) "as an insupportable burden." The Poor Law Amendment Bill of 1834, forming Unions, effected an immense reduction in the poor-rates as shown by the following Table (see Mulhall's statistics):—

POOR-RATES IN ENGLAND AND WALES.

Period.	Rental Valuation.	Poor-rate per £.	Poor-rate per Inhabitant.
1816 to 1820 . . .	58,200,000	30d.	152d.
1830 to 1835 . . .	75,900,000	22d.	116d.
1842 to 1850 . . .	90,400,000	14½d.	74d.
1880	191,150,000	10d.	74d.

The above shows "*only the rates expended on the poor*," but the poor-rate has often risen 50 per cent. higher, as it includes police, highway, sanitary and other rates.

the same sort of motive had prevailed, when the Corn-Bill was passed; but that *game-cock* statesman, who at last, sent a spur into his own throat, was then in high feather, and he, while soldiers were drawn up round the Honourable, Honourable, Honourable House, said, that he did not, for his part, care much about the Bill; but, since the mob had clamoured against *it*, he was resolved to support it! Alas! that such a *cock* statesman, should have come to such an end! All the towns and cities in England, petitioned against that odious Bill. Their petitions were rejected, and that rejection is *amongst* the causes of the present embarrassments. Therefore I am not for blaming the Ministers for acting from *fear*. They did the same, in the case of the poor Queen. Fear taught them wisely, then, also. What! would you never have people act from *fear?* What but fear of the law, restrains many men from committing crimes? What but fear of exposure, prevents thousands upon thousands of offences, moral as well as legal? Nonsense about "acting from fear." I always hear with great suspicion your eulogists of "*vigorous*" government; I do not like your vigorous governments; your game-cock governments. We saw enough of these, and *felt* enough of them too, under Pitt, Dundas, Perceval, Gibbs, Ellenborough, Sidmouth and Castlereagh. I prefer governments like those of Edward I. of England and St. Louis of France; *cocks*, as towards their enemies and rivals, and *chickens*, as towards their own people: precisely the reverse of our modern "country gentlemen," as they call themselves; very lions, as towards their poor, robbed, famishing labourers, but more than lambs, as towards tax-eaters, and especially and towards the fierce and whiskered *dead-weight*, in the presence of any of whom, they dare not say that their souls are their own. This base race of men, called "country gentlemen" must be speedily changed by almost a miracle; or they, big as well as little, must be swept away; and if it should be desirable for posterity to have a just idea of them, let posterity take this one fact; that the tithes are now, in part, received by men, who are Rectors and Vicars, and who, at the same time receive half-pay as naval or military officers; and that not one English "country gentleman" has had the courage even to complain of this, though many gallant half-pay officers have been dismissed, and beggared, upon the ground, that the half-pay is not a reward for past services, but a retaining fee for future services; so that, put the two together, they amount to this: that the half-pay is given to church parsons, that they may be, when war comes, ready to serve as officers, in the army or navy?[1] Let the world match that if it can! And yet there are scoundrels to say, that we do not want a *radical reform!* Why there must be such a reform, in order to prevent us from becoming a mass of wretches, too corrupt and profligate, and base, even to carry on the common transactions of life.

Ryall, near Upton on Severn (Worcestershire),
Monday, 25th Sept.

I set off from Mr. Palmer's yesterday, after breakfast, having his son (about 13 years old) as my travelling companion. We came across the country, a distance of about 22 miles, and, having crossed the Severn at Upton, arrived here, at Mr. John Price's, about two o'clock. On our road we passed by the estate and park of *another Ricardo!* This is Osmond; the other is David. This one has ousted two families of Normans, the Honeywood Yateses, and the Scudamores. They suppose him to have ten thousand pounds a year in rent here! Famous "watching the turn of the market"! The Barings are at work down in this country too. They are every where indeed, depositing their eggs about, like cunning old guinea-hens, in sly places, besides the great, open showy nests that they have. The "instructor" tells us, that the Ricardos have received sixty-four thousand pounds Commission, on the "Greek Loans," or, rather, "Loans to the Greeks." Oh, brave

---

[1] A legal decision has recently been given, establishing the right of retired officers in the army and navy (who have taken Holy Orders) to receive their pensions. If, however, the Author's statement be correct, that the half-pay, is not a reward for "*past services,*" but a retaining fee for "*future services,*" it places these gentlemen in rather an anomalous position.

Greeks, to have such patriots, to aid you with their financial skill; such patriots as Mr. Galloway, to make engines of war for you, while his son, is making them for the Turks; and such patriots as Burdett, and Hobhouse, to talk of your political relations! Happy Greeks! Happy Mexicans, too, it seems; for the "best instructor" tells us, that the Barings, whose progenitors came from Dutchland about the same time as, and perhaps in company with, the Ricardos; happy Mexicans too; for, the "instructor" as good as swears, that the Barings will see, that the dividends on your loans are paid in future! Now, therefore, the riches, the loads, the shiploads of silver and gold, are now to pour in upon us! Never was there a nation so foolish as this! But, and this ought to be well understood, it is not *mere* foolishness; not mere harmless folly; it is foolishness the offspring of *greediness* and of a *gambling*, which is little short of a *roguish* disposition; and this disposition prevails to an enormous extent in the country, as I am told, more than in the monstrous Wen itself. Most delightfully, however, have the greedy, mercenary, selfish, unfeeling wretches, been bit by the *loans* and *shares!* The King of Spain gave the wretches a sharp bite, for which I always most cordially thank his Majesty. I dare say, that his sponging off of the roguish Bonds, has reduced to beggary, or caused to cut their throats, many thousands of the greedy, fund-loving, stock-jobbing devils, who, if they regard it likely to raise their "securities" one per cent., would applaud the murder of half the human race. These vermin all, without a single exception, approved of, and rejoiced at, Sidmouth's *Power-of-Imprisonment-Bill*, and they applauded his *Letter of Thanks to the Manchester Yeomanry Cavalry.* No matter what it is, that puts an end to a system which engenders and breeds up vermin like these.[1]

---

[1] The previous Editor draws attention to the calamitous losses which have attended English loans to foreign nations. The Author himself supplies us here with an instance in point. It is to be hoped that foreign loans are more secure, in the present day, than they were at the time to which reference is here made; since the amount of foreign loans (quoted on the London Stock Exchange) has increased twenty-two fold the amount quoted

Mr. Hanford, of this county, and Mr. Canning of Gloucestershire, having dined at Mr. Price's yesterday, I went, to-day, with Mr. Price to see Mr. Hanford at his house and estate at Bredon Hill, which is, I believe, one of the highest in England. The ridge, or, rather, the edge of it, divides, in this part, Worcestershire from Gloucestershire. At the very highest part of it, there are the remains of an encampment, or rather, I should think, citadel. In many instances, in Wiltshire, these marks of fortifications are called castles still; and, doubtless, there were once castles on these spots. From Bredon Hill you see into nine or ten counties; and those curious bubblings-up, the Malvern Hills, are right before you, and only at about ten miles' distance, in a straight line. As this hill looks over the counties of Worcester, Gloucester, Hereford and part of Warwick, and the rich part of Stafford; and, as it looks over the vales of Esham, Worcester, and Gloucester, having the Avon and the Severn, winding down them, you certainly see from this Bredon Hill one of the very richest spots of England, and I am fully convinced, a richer spot, than is to be seen in any other country in the world; I mean *Scotland excepted*, of course, for fear Sawney should cut my throat, or, which is much the same thing, squeeze me by the hand, from which last I pray thee to deliver me, O Lord!

The Avon (this is the *third* Avon that I have crossed in this Ride) falls into the Severn just below Tewkesbury, through which town we went in our way to Mr. Hanford's. These rivers, particularly the Severn, go through, and sometimes overflow, the finest meadows of which it is possible to form an idea. Some of them contain more than a hundred acres each; and the number of cattle and sheep, feeding in them, is prodigious. Nine-tenths of the land, in these extensive vales, appears to me to be pasture, and it is pasture of the richest kind. The sheep are chiefly of the Leicestershire breed,

---

in 1825. Thus the total amount of foreign loans in 1825 was £105,000,000 sterling. In 1881, the total amount of British capital in foreign loans and railways was £1,058,000,000 sterling.

and the cattle of the Hereford, white face and dark red body, certainly the finest and most beautiful of all horn-cattle. The grass, after the fine rains that we have had, is in its finest possible dress; but, here, as in the parts of Gloucestershire and Herefordshire that I have seen, there are no turnips, except those which have been recently sown; and, though amidst all these thousands upon thousands of acres of the the finest meadows and grass land in the world, hay is, I hear, seven pounds a ton at Worcester. However, unless we should have very early and even hard frosts, the grass will be so abundant, that the cattle and sheep will do better than people are apt to think. But, be this as it may, this summer has taught us, that our climate is the *best for produce*, after all; and that we cannot have Italian sun and English meat and cheese. We complain of the *drip;* but, it is the drip, that makes the beef and the mutton.

Mr. Hanford's house is on the side of Bredon Hill; about a third part up it, and is a very delightful place. The house is of ancient date, and it appears to have been always inhabited by and the property of Roman Catholics; for there is, in one corner of the very top of the building, up in the very roof of it, a Catholic chapel, as ancient as the roof itself. It is about twenty-five feet long and ten wide. It has arch-work, to imitate the roof of a church. At the back of the altar there is a little room, which you enter through a door going out of the chapel; and, adjoining this little room, there is a closet, in which is a trap-door made to let the priest down into one of those hiding places, which were contrived for the purpose of evading the grasp of those greedy Scotch minions, to whom that pious and tolerant Protestant, James I., delivered over those English gentlemen, who remained faithful to the religion of their fathers, and, to set his country free, from which greedy and cruel grasp, that honest Englishman, Guy Fawkes, wished, as he bravely told the King and his Scotch council, "*to blow the Scotch beggars back to their mountains again.*" Even this King has, in his works (for James was an author), had the justice to call him "the English Scævola;" and we

Englishmen, fools set on by knaves, have the folly, or the baseness, to burn him in effigy on the 5th November, the anniversary of his intended exploit! In the hall of this house, there is the portrait of Sir Thomas Winter, who was one of the accomplices of Fawkes, and who was killed in the fight with the sheriff and his party. There is also the portrait of his lady, who must have spent half her life-time in the working of some very curious sacerdotal vestments, which are preserved here with great care, and are as fresh and as beautiful as they were the day they were finished.

A parson said to me, once, by letter: "your religion, Mr. "Cobbett, seems to me to be altogether *political*." "Very "much so, indeed," answered I, "and well it may, since I have "been furnished with a creed which makes part of an Act of "Parliament." And, the fact is, I am no Doctor of Divinity, and like a religion, any religion, that tends to make men innocent and benevolent and happy, by taking the best possible means of furnishing them with plenty to eat and drink and wear. I am a Protestant of the Church of England, and, as such, blush to see, that more than half the parsonage-houses are wholly gone, or are become mere hovels. What I have written on the "Protestant Reformation," has proceeded entirely from a sense of justice towards our calumniated Catholic forefathers, to whom we owe all those of our institutions that are worthy of our admiration and gratitude. I have not written as a Catholic, but as an Englishman; yet, a sincere Catholic must feel some little gratitude towards me; and, if there was an ungrateful reptile in the neighbourhood of Preston, to give, as a toast, "success to Stanley and Wood," the conduct of those Catholics that I have seen here has, as far as I am concerned, amply compensated for his baseness.

This neighbourhood has witnessed some pretty thumping transfers from the Normans. Holland, one of Baring's partners, or clerks, has recently bought an estate of Lord Somers, called Dumbleton, for, it is said, about eighty thousand pounds. Another estate of the same Lord, called Strensham, has been bought by a Brummigeham Banker of the name of Taylor, for, it is said, seventy thousand pounds. "Eastnor Castle," just over the Malvern Hills, is still building, and Lord Eastnor lives at that pretty little warm and snug place, the priory of Reigate, in Surrey, and close by the not less snug little borough of the same name. MEMORANDUM. When we were petitioning *for reform*, in 1817, my Lord Somers wrote and published a pamphlet, under his own name, condemning our conduct and our principles, and insisting that we, if let alone, should produce "*a revolution, and endanger all property!*"[1] The Barings are adding field to field and tract to tract in Herefordshire; and, as to the Ricardos, they seem to be animated with the same laudable spirit. This Osmond Ricardo has a park at one of his estates, called Broomsborough, and that park has a new porter's lodge, upon which there is a span new cross as large as life! Aye, big enough and long enough to crucify a man upon! I had never seen such an one before; and I know not what sort of thought it was, that seized me at the moment; but, though my horse is but a clumsy goer, I verily believe I got away from it at the rate of ten or twelve miles an hour. My companion, who is always upon the look-out for cross-ditches, or pieces of timber, on the road-side, to fill up the time of which my jog-trot gives him so wearisome a surplus, seemed delighted at this my new pace; and, I daresay he has wondered ever since, what should have given me wings, just for that once, and that once only.

---

[1] The previous Editor mentions the fact that the Reformers (at the time to which the Author is here alluding) were publicly denounced as "bawling, ignorant, and mischievous quacks, whose doctrines and views were exposed to universal derision and abhorrence." To every impartial observer of the history of those times, a great National Reform was absolutely and imperatively demanded, if England were to be spared the horrors of a revolution resembling that of France in 1789. And every true English patriot must rejoice, that a great National Political Reform has taken place, even a bloodless revolution. There are political zealots in the present day who would overthrow all existing institutions, in order to establish at once a "perfect Commonwealth." But those who have watched the progress of Political Reform know that it is a plant of "*gradual growth,*" and is attended with least danger when it expands in equal ratio with the intelligence and self-respect of the community at large.

Worcester, Tuesday, 26th Sept.

Mr. Price rode with us to this city, which is one of the cleanest, neatest, and handsomest towns I ever saw: indeed, I do not recollect to have seen any one equal to it. The *cathedral* is, indeed, a poor thing, compared with any of the others, except that of Hereford; and I have seen them all, but those of Carlisle, Durham, York, Lincoln, Chester, and Peterborough; but the *town* is, I think, the very best I ever saw; and which is, indeed, the greatest of all recommendations, the *people* are, upon the whole, the most suitably dressed and most decent looking people. The town is precisely in character with the beautiful and rich country, in the midst of which it lies. Everything you see gives you the idea of real, solid wealth; aye! and thus it was, too, before, long before, Pitt, and even long before "good Queen Bess" and her military law, and her Protestant racks, were ever heard or dreamed of.

At Worcester, as everywhere else, I find a group of cordial and sensible friends, at the house of one of whom, Mr. George Brooke, I have just spent a most pleasant evening, in company with several gentlemen, whom he had had the goodness to invite to meet me. I here learned a fact, which I must put upon record before it escape my memory. Some few years ago (about seven, perhaps), at the public sale by auction of the goods of a then recently deceased Attorney of the name of Hyde, in this city, there were, amongst the goods to be sold, the portraits of *Pitt*, *Burdett*, and *Paine*, all framed and glazed. Pitt, with hard driving and very lofty praises, fetched fifteen shillings; Burdett fetched twenty-seven shillings. Paine was, in great haste, knocked down at five pounds; and my informant was convinced, that the lucky purchaser might have had fifteen pounds for it. I hear Colonel Davies spoken of here, with great approbation: he will soon have an opportunity of showing us whether he deserve it.

The hop-picking and bagging is over here. The crop, as in the other hop-countries, has been very great, and the quality as good as ever was known. The average price appears to be

about 75s. the hundred weight. The reader (if he do not
belong to a hop-country) should be told, that hop-planters,
and even all their neighbours, are, as hop-ward, *mad*, though
the most sane and reasonable people as to all other matters.
They are ten times more jealous upon this score than men
ever are of their wives; aye, and than they are of their mis-
tresses, which is going a great deal farther. I, who am a
Farnham man, was well aware of this foible; and therefore,
when a gentleman told me, that he would not brew with
Farnham hops, if he could have them as a gift, I took special
care not to ask him how it came to pass, that the Farnham
hops always sold at about double the price of the Worcester;
but, if he had said the same thing to any other Farnham man
that I ever saw, I should have preferred being absent from the
spot: the hops are bitter, but nothing is their bitterness, compared to the language that my townsman would have put
forth.

This city, or this neighbourhood, at least, being the birthplace of what I have called, the "Little-Shilling project,"[1] and
Messrs. Atwood and Spooner being the originators of the
project, and the project having been adopted by Mr. Western,
and having been by him now again recently urged upon the
Ministers, in a Letter to Lord Liverpool, and it being possible
that some worthy persons may be misled, and even ruined, by
the confident assertions and the pertinacity of the projectors;
this being the case, and I having half an hour to spare, will
here endeavour to show, in as few words as I can, that this
project, if put into execution, would produce injustice the
most crying that the world ever heard of, and would, in the
present state of things, infallibly lead to a violent revolution.
The project is to "lower the standard," as they call it; that is
to say, to make a *sovereign pass for more than* 20s. In what
degree they would reduce the standard they do not say; but, a

---

[1] This sobriquet probably refers to a new silver coinage which was
issued in 1817, in which the intrinsic value of the coin was somewhat
lessened, for the sake of guarding against all temptation to melt it down
for its value as metal.

vile pamphlet writer, whose name is Crutwell, and who is a beneficed parson, and who has most foully abused me, because I laugh at the project, says that he would reduce it one half; that is to say, that he would make a sovereign pass for two pounds. Well, then, let us, for plainness' sake, suppose that the present sovereign is, all at once, to pass for two pounds. What will the consequences be? Why, here is a parson, who receives his tithes in kind and whose tithes are, we will suppose, a thousand bushels of wheat in a year, on an average; and he owes a thousand pounds to somebody. He will pay his debt with 500 sovereigns, and he will still receive his thousand bushels of wheat a year! I let a farm for 100*l.* a year, by the year; and I have a mortgage of 2000*l.* upon it, the interest just taking away the rent. Pass the project, and then I, of course, raise my rent to 200*l.* a year, and I still pay the mortgagee 100*l.* a year! What can be plainer than this? But, the Banker's is the fine case. I deposit with a banker a thousand whole sovereigns to-day. Pass the project to-morrow, and the banker pays me my deposit with a thousand half sovereigns! If, indeed, you could double the quantity of corn and meat and all goods by the same act of Parliament, then, all would be right; but that quantity will remain what it was before you passed the project; and, of course, the money being doubled in nominal amount, the price of the goods would be doubled. There needs not another word upon the subject; and whatever may be the national inference respecting the intellects of Messrs. Atwood and Spooner, I must say, that I do most sincerely believe, that there is not one of my readers, who will not feel astonishment, that any men, having the reputation of men of sound mind, should not clearly see, that such a project must almost instantly produce a revolution, of the most dreadful character.[1]

---

[1] Among the disputed points in political economy, there is none productive of more controversy, than the proper regulation of the currency. The leading question is, how far should it be restrained, and what is the most effectual method of restraining it?

The currency can most effectually be restrained by confining it to

Stanford Park,
Wednesday, 27th Sept. (Morning).

In a letter which I received from Sir Thomas Winnington (one of the Members for this county), last year, he was good enough to request that I would call upon him, if I ever came into Worcestershire, which I told him I would do; and accordingly here we are in his house, situated, certainly, in one of the finest spots in all England. We left Worcester yesterday about ten o'clock, crossed the Severn, which runs close by the town, and came on to this place, which lies in a north-western direction from Worcester, at 14 miles' distance from that city, and at about six from the borders of Shropshire. About four miles back we passed by the park and through the estate of Lord Foley, to whom is due the praise of being a most indefatigable and successful *planter of trees.* He seems to have taken uncommon pains in the execution of this work; and he has the merit of disinterestedness, the trees being chiefly oaks, which he is *sure* he can never see grow to timber. We crossed the Teme River just before we got here. Sir Thomas was out shooting; but he soon came home, and gave us a very polite reception. I had time, yesterday, to see the place, to look at trees, and the like, and I wished to get away early this morning; but, being prevailed on to stay to breakfast, here I am, at six o'clock in the morning, in one of the best and best-stocked private libraries that I ever saw; and, what is more, the owner, from what passed yesterday, when he brought me hither, convinced me that he was acquainted with the *insides* of the books. I asked, and shall ask, no

---

the precious metals, but this of course is impracticable. Before the resumption of cash payments, 1819, the notes of the Bank of England were only worth 16s. in the pound, as compared with gold. In the silver currency of this country, a £ is worth little more than four-fifths of a sovereign, *i.e.*, if a person could pay a debt of £100 in silver, he would get off with a dividend of from 16s. to 18s. in the pound; but, by law, silver is not a legal tender for more than 40s. Banks are allowed to issue their notes, beyond a certain amount, only on condition of having bullion in their coffers to pay the additional notes issued by them.

questions about who got these books together; but the collection is such as, I am sure, I never saw before in a private house.

The house and stables and courts are such as they ought to be for the great estate that surrounds them; and the park is everything that is beautiful. On one side of the house, looking over a fine piece of water, you see a distant valley, opening between lofty hills: on another side the ground descends a little at first, then goes gently rising for a while, and then rapidly, to the distance of a mile perhaps, where it is crowned with trees in irregular patches, or groups, single and most magnificent trees being scattered all over the whole of the park; on another side, there rise up beautiful little hills, some in the form of barrows on the downs, only forty or a hundred times as large, one or two with no trees on them, and others topped with trees; but, on one of these little hills, and some yards higher than the lofty trees which are on this little hill, you see rising up the tower of the parish church, which hill is, I think, taken all together, amongst the most delightful objects that I ever beheld.

"Well then," says the devil of laziness, "and could you not "be contented to live here all the rest of your life; and never "again pester yourself with the cursed politics?" "Why, I "think I have laboured enough. Let others work now. And "such a pretty place for coursing and for hare-hunting and "woodcock shooting, I dare say; and then those pretty wild-"ducks in the water, and the flowers and the grass and the "trees and all the birds in spring and the fresh air, and never, "never again to be stifled with the smoke that from the "infernal Wen ascendeth for ever more, and that every easterly "wind brings to choke me at Kensington!" The *last word* of this soliloquy carried me back, slap, to my own study (very much unlike that which I am in), and bade me think of the GRIDIRON; bade me think of the complete triumph, that I have yet to enjoy: promised me the pleasure of seeing a million of trees of my own, and sown by my own hands this very year. Ah! but the hares and the pheasants and the wild ducks! Yes, but the delight of seeing Prosperity Robinson hang his head for shame: the delight of beholding the tormenting embarrassments of those who have so long retained crowds of base miscreants to revile me; the delight of ousting spitten-upon Stanely and bound-over Wood! Yes, but, then, the flowers and the birds and the sweet air! What, then, shall Canning never again hear of the "revered and ruptured Ogden!" Shall he go into his grave, without being again reminded of "driving at the whole herd, in order to get at "the *ignoble animal!*" Shall he never again be told of Six-Acts and of his wish "to extinguish that *accursed torch of* "*discord for ever!*" Oh! God forbid! farewell hares and dogs and birds! what, shall Sidmouth, then, never again hear of his *Power of Imprisonment Bill*, of his *Circular*, of his *Letter of Thanks to the Manchester Yeomanry!* I really jumped up when this thought came athwart my mind, and, without thinking of the breakfast, said to George who was sitting by me, "Go, George, and tell them to saddle the horses;" for, it seemed to me, that I had been meditating some crime. Upon George asking me, whether I would not stop to breakfast? I bade him not order the horses out yet; and here we are, waiting for breakfast.

Ryall, Wednesday Night, 27th Sept.

After breakfast we took our leave of Sir Thomas Winnington, and of Stanford, very much pleased with our visit. We wished to reach Ryall as early as possible in the day, and we did not, therefore, stop at Worcester. We got here about three o'clock, and we intend to set off, in another direction, early in the morning.

RIDE FROM RYALL, IN WORCESTERSHIRE, TO BURGHCLERE, IN HAMPSHIRE.

> "Alas, the country! How shall tongue or pen
> Bewail her now, *un*country gentlemen!
> The last to bid the cry of warfare cease,
> The first to make a malady of peace!
> For what were all these country patriots born?
> To hunt, and vote, and raise the price of corn,
> But corn, like ev'ry mortal thing, must fall:
> Kings, conquerors, and, *markets most of all.*"
>
> LORD BYRON.

Ryall,
Friday Morning, 29th September, 1826.

I have observed, in this country, and especially near Worcester, that the working people seem to be better off than in many other parts, one cause of which is, I dare say, that *glove manufacturing,* which cannot be carried on by fire or by wind or by water, and which is, therefore, carried on by the *hands* of human beings. It gives work to women and children, as well as to men; and that work is, by a great part of the women and children, done in their cottages, and amidst the fields and hop-gardens, where the husbands and sons must live, in order to raise the food, and the drink, and the wool. This is a great thing for the land. If this glovemaking were to cease, many of these women and children, now, not upon the parish, must instantly be upon the parish. The glove-trade is, like all others, slack, from this last change in the value of money; but, there is no horrible misery here, as at Manchester, Leeds, Glasgow, Paisley, and other Holes of 84 degrees of heat. There misery walks abroad in skin, bone and nakedness. There are no subscriptions wanted for Worcester; no militia-clothing. The working people suffer, trades'-people suffer, and who is to escape, except the monopolisers, the Jews, and the tax-eaters, when the Government chooses, to raise the value of money, and lower the price of goods? The whole of the industrious part of the country, must suffer in such a case; but, where manufacturing, is mixed with agriculture, where the wife and daughters, are at the needle, or the wheel, while the men and the boys, are at plough, and where the manufacturing, of which one or two towns are the centres, is spread over the whole country round about, and particularly where it is, in very great part, performed by females at their *own homes*, and where the earnings come *in aid of the man's wages;* in such case, the misery cannot be so great; and accordingly, while there is an absolute destruction of life going on in the holes, there is no *visible* misery at, or near, Worcester; and I cannot take my leave of this county without observing, that I do not recollect to have seen, one miserable object in it. The working people, all seem to have good large gardens, and pigs in their styes; and this last, say the *feelosofers* what they will about her "antallectual enjoyments," is the *only* security for happiness, in a labourer's family.

Then, this glove-manufacturing, is not like that of cottons, a mere gambling concern, making Baronets to-day and Bankrupts to-morrow, and making those who do the work slaves. Here are no masses of people, called together by a *bell*, and "kept to *it*" by a driver; here are no "patriots," who, while they keep Englishmen to it by fines, and almost by the scourge, in a heat of 84 degrees, are petitioning the Parliament to "give freedom" to the South Americans, who, as these "patriots" have been informed, use a great quantity of *cottons!*

The dilapidation of parsonage-houses and the depopulation of villages, appears not to have been so great just round about Worcester, as in some other parts; but, they have made great progress even here. No man appears to fat an ox, or hardly a sheep, except with a view of sending it to London, or to some other infernal resort of monopolisers and tax-eaters. Here, as in Wiltshire and Gloucestershire and Herefordshire, you find plenty of large churches, without scarcely any people. I dare say, that, even in this county, more than one half of the parishes have either no parsonage-houses at all; or, have not one, that a parson thinks fit for him to live in; and, I venture to assert, that one or the other of these, is the case in four parishes out of every five, in Herefordshire! Is not this a monstrous shame? Is this "a church?" Is this "law?" The parsons get the tithes, and the rent of the glebe-lands, and the parsonage-houses are left to tumble down, and nettles, and brambles, to hide the spot where they stood. But, the fact is, the Jew-system has swept all the little gentry, the small farmers, and the domestic manufacturers away. The land is now used to raise food and drink for the monopolisers, and the tax-eaters, and their purveyors, and lackeys, and harlots; and they get together in Wens.

Of all the mean, all the cowardly reptiles, that ever crawled on the face of the earth, the *English land-owners* are the most mean, and the most cowardly: for, while they support the churches, in their several parishes, while they see the population drawn away from their parishes, to the Wens, while they are taxed to keep the people in the Wens, and while they see their own Parsons pocket the tithes, and the glebe-rents, and suffer the parsonage-houses to fall down; while they see all this, they, without uttering a word in the way of complaint, suffer themselves and their neighbours to be taxed, to build new churches for the monopolizers and tax-eaters in those Wens! Never was there in this world, a set of reptiles so base as this. Stupid as many of them are, they must clearly see the flagrant injustice of making the depopulated parishes, pay for the aggrandizement of those who have caused the depopulation, aye, actually pay taxes, *to add to* the Wens, and, of course, to cause a further depopulation of the taxed villages; stupid beasts as many of them are, they must see the flagrant injustice of this, and mean and cowardly as many of them are, some of them would remonstrate against it; but, alas! the far greater part of them are, themselves, getting, or expecting, *loaves and fishes*, either in their own persons, or in those of their family. They smouch, or want to smouch, some of the taxes; and, therefore, they must not complain. And, thus the thing goes on. These land-owners see, too, the churches falling down, and the parsonage-houses, either tumbled down or dilapidated. But, then, mind, they have, amongst them, the giving away of the benefices! Of course, all they want is the income, and, the less the parsonage-house costs, the larger the spending income. But, in the meanwhile, here is a destruction of public property; and also, from a diversion of the income of the livings, a great injury, great injustice, to the middle and the working classes.

Is this, then, is this "church" a thing to remain untouched? Shall the widow and the orphan, whose money has been borrowed *by the land-owners* (including the Parsons) to purchase "victories" with; shall they be stripped of their interest, of their very bread, and shall the Parsons, who have let half the parsonage-houses fall down, or become unfit to live in, still keep all the tithes and the glebe-lands and the immense landed estates, called Church Lands? Oh, no! Sir James Graham "of Netherby," though you are a descendant of the Earls of Monteith, of John of the bright sword, and of the Seventh Earl of Galloway, K.T. (taking care, for God's sake, not to omit the K.T.); though you may be the *Magnus Apollo;* and, in short, be you what you may, you shall never execute your project of sponging the fund-holders and of leaving Messieurs the Parsons untouched! In many parishes, where the livings are good too, there is neither parsonage-house nor church! This is the case at Draycot Foliot, in Wiltshire. The living is a Rectory; the Parson has, of course, both great and small tithes; these tithes and the glebe-land are worth, I am told, more than three hundred pounds a year; and yet there is neither church nor parsonage-house; both have been suffered to fall down and disappear; and, when a new Parson comes to take possession of the living, there is, I am told, a temporary tent, or booth, erected, upon the spot where the church ought to be, for the performance of the *ceremony of induction!* What, then!—Ought not this church to be repealed? An Act of Parliament made this church; an Act of Parliament can unmake it;[1] and, is there any but a monster who would suffer this Parson to retain this income, while that of the widow and the orphan was taken away? Oh, no? Sir James Graham of Netherby, who, with the *gridiron before you*, say, that there was "no man, of any authority, who foresaw the effects of Peel's Bill;" oh, no! thou stupid, thou empty-headed, thou insolent aristocratic pamphleteer, the widow and the orphan *shall not* be robbed of their bread, while this Parson of Draycot Foliot keeps the income of his living!

On my return from Worcester to this place, yesterday, I noticed, at a village called Severn Stoke, a very curiously-constructed grape house; that is to say, a hot-house for the raising of grapes. Upon inquiry, I found, that it belonged to a Parson, of the name of St. John, whose parsonage-house is very near to it, and who, being *sure* of having the benefice, when the then Rector should die, bought a piece of land, and erected his grapery on it, just facing, and only about 50 yards from the windows, out of which the *old parson* had to look, until the day of his death, with a view, doubtless, of piously furnishing his aged brother with a *momento mori* (remember death), quite as significant as a death's head and cross bones, and yet done in a manner expressive, of that fellow-feeling, that delicacy, that abstinence from self-gratification, which are well known to be characteristics almost peculiar to "the cloth!" To those, if there be such, who may be disposed to suspect that the grapery arose, upon the spot where it stands, merely from the desire to have the vines in bearing state, against the time that the old parson should die, or, as I heard the Botley Parson once call it, "kick the bucket;" to such persons, I would just put this one question; did they ever

---

[1] It has already been pointed out, in a previous note, that this statement of the Author (which has been more than once repeated), viz., that the Church has been established "by Act of Parliament," is entirely erroneous. The Church never was established. It is as much a part of the original constitution of the country as the monarchy, which, in point of fact, it long preceded. "Its position is of course defined and regulated by law; but it does not owe its origin to any Act of the Legislature, or to other sovereign authority."

either from Scripture or tradition, learn that any of the Apostles or their disciples, erected graperies from motives such as this? They may, indeed, say, that they never heard of the Apostles, erecting any graperies at all, much less of their having erected them from such a motive. Nor, to say the truth, did I ever hear of any such erections on the part of those Apostles and those whom they commissioned to preach the word of God; and, Sir William Scott (now a *lord* of some sort)[1] never convinced me, by his parson-praising speech of 1802, that to give the church-clergy a due degree of influence over the minds of the people, to make the people revere them, it was necessary that the parsons and their wives should shine at *balls* and in *pump-rooms*. On the contrary, these and the like, have taken away almost the whole of their spiritual influence. They never had much; but, lately, and especially, since 1793, they have had hardly any at all; and, wherever I go, I find them much better known as *Justices of the Peace*, than as Clergymen. What they would come to, if this system could go on for only a few years longer, I know not: but go on, as it is now going, it cannot much longer; there must be *a settlement of some sort:* and that settlement never can leave that mass, that immense mass, of public property, called "church property," to be used as it now is.

I have seen, in this county, and in Herefordshire, several pieces of Mangel Wurzel; and, I hear, that it has nowhere failed, as the turnips have. Even the Lucerne has, in some places, failed to a certain extent; but, Mr. Walter Palmer, at Pencoyd, in Herefordshire, has cut a piece of Lucerne four times this last summer, and, when I saw it, on the 17th Sept. (12 days ago), it was got a foot high towards another cut. But, with one exception (too trifling to mention), Mr. Walter

---

[1] Sir William Scott, afterwards made Lord Stowell. He was the son of a shipbroker in the north. He possessed an extensive estate near Cirencester. He seems to have been a champion of the clergy at that time. It is, however, melancholy to read, here and elsewhere in these Rides, "that wherever the Author went, he found the clergy better known as Justices of the Peace, than as clergymen."

Palmer's Lucerne is on the Tullian plan, that is, it is in rows, at four feet distance from each other; so that you plough between, as often as you please, and thus, together with a little hand weeding between the plants, keep the ground, at all times, clear of weeds and grass. Mr. Palmer says, that his acre (he has no more) has kept two horses all the summer; and he seems to complain, that it has done no more. Indeed! A stout horse will eat much more than a fatting ox. This grass will fat any ox, or sheep; and would not Mr. Palmer like to have ten acres of land, that would fat a score of oxen? They would do this, if they were managed well. But, is it *nothing* to keep a team of four horses, for five months in the year, on the produce of two acres of land? If a man say that, he must, of course, be eagerly looking forward to another world; for nothing will satisfy him in this. A good crop of early cabbages, may be had between the rows of Lucerne.

Cabbages have, generally, wholly failed. Those that I see are almost all too backward to make much of heads; though it is surprising how fast they will grow and come to perfection, as soon as there is *twelve hours of night*. I am here, however, speaking of the large sorts of cabbage; for, the smaller sorts will loave in summer. Mr. Walter Palmer has now a piece of these, of which I think there are from 17 to 20 *tons* to the acre; and this, too, observe, after a season which, on the same farm, has not suffered a turnip of any sort to come. If he had had 20 acres of these, he might have almost laughed at the failure of his turnips, and at the short crop of hay. And, this is a crop of which a man may always be *sure*, if he take proper pains. These cabbages (Early Yorks, or some such sort) should, if you want them in June or July, be sown early in the previous August. If you want them in winter, sown in April, and treated as pointed out in my *Cottage Economy*. These small sorts stand the winter better than the large; they are more nutritious; and they occupy the ground little more than half the time. *Dwarf Savoys* are the finest and richest and most nutritious of cabbages. Sown early in April, and planted out early in July, they will, at 18 inches apart each way, yield a crop of 30 to 40 tons by Christmas. But, all this supposes land very good, or, very well manured, and plants of a good sort, and well raised and planted, and the ground well tilled after planting; and a crop of 30 tons is worth all these, and all the care, and all the pains, that a man can possibly take.

I am here amongst the finest of cattle, and the finest sheep of the Leicester kind, that I ever saw. My host, Mr. Price, is famed as a breeder of cattle and sheep. The cattle are of the Hereford kind, and the sheep surpassing any animals of the kind that I ever saw. The animals seem to be made for the soil, and the soil for them.

In taking leave of this county, I repeat, with great satisfaction, what I before said about the apparent comparatively happy state of the labouring people; and I have been very much pleased, with the tone and manner in which they are spoken to, and spoken of, by their superiors. I hear of no *hard* treatment of them here, such as I have but too often heard of, in some counties, and too often witnessed in others; and I quit Worcestershire, and particularly the house in which I am, with all those feelings which are naturally produced, by the kindest of receptions, from frank and sensible people.

Fairford (Gloucestershire),
Saturday Morning, 30th Sept.

Though we came about 45 miles yesterday, we are up by day-light, and just about to set off to sleep at Hayden, near Swindon, in Wiltshire.

Hayden, Saturday Night,
30th Sept.

From Ryall, in Worcestershire, we came yesterday (Friday) morning, first to Tewkesbury in Gloucestershire. This is a good, substantial town, which, for many years, sent to Parliament that sensible and honest and constant hater of Pitt and his infernal politics, James Martin, and which now sends to the same place his son, Mr. John Martin, who, when the memorable *Kentish Petition* was presented, in June 1822, proposed that it should not be received, or that, if it were received, "the House should not separate, until it had resolved, that the interest of the Debt should never be reduced!" Castlereagh abused the petition; but was for *receiving* it, in *order to fix on it a mark of the House's reprobation.* I said, in the next Register, that this fellow was *mad:* and, in six or seven weeks from that day, he cut his own throat, and was declared to have been mad, at the time when this petition was presented! The mess that "*the House,*" will be in will be bad enough as it is; but, what would have been its mess, if it had, in its strong fit of "good faith," been furious enough, to adopt Mr. Martin's "resolution!"

The Warwickshire Avon falls into the Severn here, and on the sides of both, for many miles back, there are the finest meadows that ever were seen. In looking over them, and beholding the endless flocks and herds, one wonders what can become of all the meat! By riding on about eight or nine miles farther, however, this wonder is a little diminished; for here we come to one of the devouring Wens; namely, Cheltenham, which is what they call a "watering place;" that is to say, a place, to which East India plunderers, West India floggers, English tax-gorgers, together with gluttons, drunkards, and debauchees of all descriptions, female as well as male, resort, at the suggestion of silently laughing quacks, in the hope of getting rid of the bodily consequences of their manifold sins and iniquities. When I enter a place like this, I always feel disposed to squeeze up my nose with my fingers. It is nonsense, to be sure; but I conceive that every two-legged creature, that I see coming near me, is about to cover me with the poisonous proceeds of its impurities. To places like this, come all that is knavish, and all that is foolish, and all that is base; gamesters, pickpockets, and harlots; young wife-hunters, in search of rich and ugly old women, and young husband-hunters in search of rich and wrinkled or half-rotten men, the formerly resolutely bent, be the means what they may, to give the latter, heirs to their lands and tenements. These things are notorious; and, Sir William Scott, in his speech of 1802, in favour of the non-residence of the Clergy, expressly said, that they and their families ought to appear at watering places, and that this, was amongst the means, of making them respected by their flocks! Memorandum: he was a member for Oxford, when he said this!

Before we got into Cheltenham, I learned from a coal-carter, which way we had to go, in order to see "*The New Buildings*," which are now nearly at a stand. We rode up the main street of the town, for some distance, and then turned off to the left, which soon brought us to the "desolation of abomination." I have seldom seen anything, with more heartfelt satisfaction. "Oh!" said I to myself, "the accursed THING has certainly got *a blow*, then, in every part of its corrupt and corrupting carcass!" The whole town (and it was now ten o'clock) looked delightfully dull. I did not see more than four or five carriages, and, perhaps, twenty people on horse-back; and these seemed, by their hook-noses and round eyes, and by the long, and sooty necks of the women, to be, for the greater part, *Jews*, and *Jewesses*. The place really appears to be sinking very fast; and I have been told, and believe the fact, that houses, in Cheltenham, will now sell for only just about one-third as much, as the same would have sold for, only in last October. It is curious to see the names which the vermin owners have put upon the houses here. There is a new row of most gaudy and fantastical dwelling places, called "Colombia Place," given it, doubtless, by some dealer in *Bonds*. There is what a boy told us was the "*New Spa;*" there is "*Waterloo-house!*" Oh! how I rejoice at the ruin of the base creatures! There is "*Liverpool-Cottage,*" "*Canning-Cottage,*" "*Peel-Cottage;*" and, the good of it is, that the ridiculous beasts have put this word *cottage* upon scores of houses, and some very mean and shabby houses, standing along, and making part of an unbroken street! What a figure this place will cut in another year or two! I should not wonder to see it nearly wholly deserted. It is situated in a nasty, flat, stupid spot, without anything pleasant near it. A putting down of the one-pound notes, will soon take away its *spa*-people. Those of the notes, that have already been cut off, have, it seems, lessened the quantity of ailments very considerably; another brush will cure all the complaints!

They have had some rains in the summer not far from this place; for we saw in the streets very fine turnips, for sale, as vegetables, and broccoli, with heads six or eight inches over! But, as to the meat, it was nothing to be compared with that of Warminster, in Wiltshire; that is to say, the veal and lamb. I have paid particular attention to this matter, at Worcester, and Tewkesbury, as well as at Cheltenham; and I have seen no veal, and no lamb, to be compared with those of Warminster. I have been thinking, but cannot imagine how it is, that the Wen-Devils, either at Bath or London, do not get this meat away from Warminster. I hope that my observations on it, will not set them to work: for, if it do, the people of Warminster, will never have a bit of good meat again.

After Cheltenham, we had to reach this pretty little town of Fairford, the regular turnpike road to which, lay through Cirencester; but I had from a fine map, at Sir Thomas Winnington's, traced out a line for us, along through a chain of villages, leaving Cirencester away to our right, and never coming nearer than seven or eight miles to it. We came through Dodeswell, Withington, Chedworth, Winston, and the two Colnes. At Dodeswell we came up a long and steep hill, which brought us out of the great vale of Gloucester, and up upon the Cotswold Hills, which name is tautological, I believe; for I think that *wold* meaned *high lands of great extent.* Such is the Cotswold, at any rate, for it is a tract of country stretching across, in a south-eastern direction, from Dodeswell, to near Fairford, and in a north-easterly direction, from Pitchcomb Hill, in Gloucestershire (which, remember, I descended on the 12th September) to near Witney in Oxfordshire. Here we were, then, when we got fairly up upon the Wold, with the vale of Gloucester at our back, Oxford and its vale to our left, the vale of Wiltshire to our right, and the vale of Berkshire in our front: and from one particular point, I could see a part of each of them. This Wold is, in itself, an ugly country. The soil is what is called a *stone brash* below, with a reddish earth mixed with little bits of this brash at top, and, for the greater part of the Wold, even this soil is very shallow; and, as fields are divided by walls made of this brash, and, as there are, for a mile or two together, no trees to be seen, and, as the surface is not smooth and green like the downs, this is a sort of country, having less to please the eye than any other that I have ever seen, always save and except the *heaths* like those of Bagshot and Hindhead. Yet, even this Wold has many fertile dells in it, and sends out, from its highest parts, several streams, each of which has its pretty valley and its meadows. And here has come down to us, from a distance of many centuries, a particular race of sheep, called the *Cotswold* breed, which are, of course, the best suited to the country. They are short and stocky, and appear to me to be about half way, in point of size, between the Rylands and the South Downs. When crossed with the Leicester, as they are pretty generally in the North of Wiltshire, they make very beautiful and even large sheep; quite large enough, and, people say, very profitable.[1]

A *route*, when it lies through *villages*, is one thing on a *map*,

---

[1] The Cotswold breed of sheep, has long been famous for its wool. In 1464 Edward IV. sent a present of Cotswold rams to Henry of Castile, and in 1468 a similar present was sent to John of Aragon.

As the Author tells us here, the Cotswold breed, by crossing with the Leicester, has been greatly improved in value, producing shorter wool, but better mutton. The Leicester breed was greatly improved, after the middle of the last century, by the skill and care of Mr. Bakewell; the new Leicester breed being very broad on the back, with finely arched ribs. It is large limbed and is easily rendered very fat. The Ryeland, or Hereford breed, is small, short limbed, white and hornless, and produces excellent mutton. The South Down breed is generally white, and the face and legs are dun, black, or speckled. It is hornless, the wool is short, but thick and close, and curled; the mutton is far famed.

The original Forest breed of sheep, so called from being pastured in the Royal Forests, is still to be found on the barren grounds, between the English and the Bristol Channels. It is small, with face and legs russet and quite another thing on the ground. Our line of villages, from Cheltenham, to Fairford, was very nearly straight upon the map; but, upon the ground, it took us round about a great many miles, besides now and then a little going back, to get into the right road; and, which was a great inconvenience, not a public-house was there on our road, until we got within eight miles of Fairford. Resolved, that not one single farthing of my money should be spent in the Wen of Cheltenham, we came through that place, expecting to find a public-house in the first or second of the villages; but not one was there, over the whole of the Wold; and though I had, by pocketing some slices of meat and bread at Ryall, provided against this contingency, as far as related to ourselves, I could make no such provision for our horses, and they went a great deal too far, without baiting. Plenty of farm-houses, and, if they had been in America, we need have looked for no other. Very likely (I hope it at any rate) almost any farmer on the Cotswold, would have given us what we wanted, if we had asked for it; but the fashion, the good old fashion, was, by the hellish system of funding and taxing and monopolizing, driven across the Atlantic. And is England *never* to see it return? Is the hellish system to last *for ever?*

Doctor Black, in remarking upon my Ride down the vale of the Salisbury Avon, says, that there has, doubtless, been a falling off in the population of the villages, "lying amongst the chalk-hills;" aye, and lying everywhere else too; or, how comes it, that four-fifths of the parishes of Herefordshire, abounding in rich land, in meadows, orchards, and pastures, have either no parsonage-houses at all, or have none, that a

---

brown, or grey; it is wild, restless, and difficult to fatten, but produces fine wool, and excellent mutton.

The Dorset breed is one of the best of the old English Upland breeds, and is especially valuable, because it supplies early lamb for the London market. The previous Editor mentions, that a quarter of a Cotswold sheep, weighing 63 lbs., was exhibited in January 1851, as a curiosity in the market of New York. It had been sent from Devizes, Wilts; but that some of the same breed weighed from 75 lbs. to 80 lbs. the quarter, and that the Lincolnshire breed produced still heavier sheep.

Parson thinks fit for him to live in? I vouch for the fact;
I will, whether in Parliament or not, prove the fact to the
Parliament: and, if the fact be such, the conclusion is inevitable. But how melancholy is the sight of these decayed, and
still decaying villages, in the dells of the Cotswold, where the
building materials, being stone, the ruins do not totally disappear for ages! The village of Withington (mentioned above)
has a church like a small cathedral, and the whole of the
population is now only 603 persons, men, women, and children.
So that, according to the Scotch fellows, this immense and fine
church, which is as sound as it was 7 or 800 years ago, was
built by, and for a population, containing, at most, only about
120 grown-up and able-bodied men! But here, in this once
populous village, or I think town, you see *all* the indubitable
marks of most melancholy decay. There are several lanes,
crossing each other, which *must* have been *streets* formerly.
There is a large open space where the principal streets meet.
There are, against this open place, two large, old, roomy
houses, with gateways into back parts of them, and with large
stone *upping-blocks* [1] against the walls of them in the street.
These were manifestly considerable *inns*, and, in this open
place, markets or fairs, or both used to be held. I asked two
men, who were threshing in a barn, how long it was since
their public-house was put down, or dropped? They told me
about sixteen years. One of these men, who was about fifty
years of age, could remember *three* public-houses, one of which
was what was called an *inn!* The place stands by the side of
a little brook, which here rises, or rather issues, from a high
hill, and which, when it has winded down for some miles, and
through several villages, begins to be called the River Colne,
and continues on, under this name, through Fairford and
along, I suppose, till it falls into the Thames. Withington is
very prettily situated; it was, and not very long ago, a gay

---

[1] These upping blocks, or horse blocks (but little known in some parts
of the country) were three or four steps of bricks, or stone, to assist in
mounting, on horseback.

and happy place; but it now presents a picture of dilapidation, and shabbiness, scarcely to be equalled. Here are the yet visible remains of two gentlemen's houses. Great farmers have supplied their place, as to inhabiting; and, I daresay, that some tax-eater, or some blaspheming Jew, or some still more base and wicked loan-mongering robber[1] is now the owner of the land; aye, and all these people are his *slaves* as completely, and more to their wrong, than the blacks are the slaves of the planters in Jamaica, the farmers here, acting, in fact, in a capacity corresponding with that of the negro-drivers there.

A part, and, perhaps, a considerable part, of the decay and misery of this place, is owing to the use of *machinery*, and to the *monopolizing*, in the manufacture of Blankets, of which fabric the town of Witney (above mentioned) was the centre, and from which town the wool used to be sent round to, and the yarn, or warp, come back from, all these Cotswold villages, and quite into a part of Wiltshire. This work is all now gone, and so the women, and the girls, are a "surplus *popalashon, mon,*" and are, of course, to be dealt with by the "Emigration Committee" of the "Collective Wisdom"! There were, only a few years ago, above thirty blanket-manufacturers at Witney: twenty-five of these have been swallowed up by the

---

[1] The Jews, until modern and more enlightened times, have been treated with universal hatred and cruelty, because they easily acquired wealth by money-lending. Human nature revolts at exorbitant interest. A strong prejudice, however, existed in early times against exacting interest at all, from a mistaken view of the Mosaic law on usury.* In 1262 A.D. 700 Jews were massacred in London, a Jew having forced a Christian to pay more than 2s. per week on a loan of 20s.; and every Jew lending money on interest was compelled to wear a badge, signifying that he was a usurer. If that law were in force at the present day, a vast proportion of others besides Jews would have to wear the badge. It was not until 1723 that Jews acquired the right to possess land in England. In 1835 the first Jewish Sheriff was elected in London, and an Act was passed to enable him to act. In 1837, Sir Moses Montefiore was the first Jew who was knighted. In 1858 an Act was passed to enable Jews to sit in Parliament.

---

* The Mosaic law (Exod. xxii. 25, Levit. xxv. 39) forbade usury on money *lent for the relief of distress;* but its restrictions did not apply to money borrowed for purposes of trade.

five, that now have all the manufacture in their hands! And all this has been done by that system of gambling, and of fictitious money, which has conveyed property from the hands of the many, into the hands of the few. But, wise Burdett *likes* this! He wants the land to be cultivated by few hands, and he wants machinery, and all those things, which draw money into *large masses;* that make a nation consist of a few of very rich, and of millions of very poor! Burdett must look sharp; or this system, will play him a trick, before it come to an end.

The crops on the Cotswold have been pretty good; and I was very much surprised to see a scattering of early turnips, and, in some places, decent crops. Upon this Wold I saw more early turnips in a mile or two, than I saw in all Herefordshire, and Worcestershire, and in all the rich and low part of Gloucestershire. The high lands always, during the year, and especially during the summer, receive much more of rain than the low lands. The clouds hang about the hills, and the dews, when they rise, go, most frequently, and cap the hills.

Wheat-sowing is yet going on, on the Wold; but, the greater part of it is sown, and not only sown, but up, and in some places, high enough to "hide a hare." What a difference! In some parts of England, no man thinks of sowing wheat till November, and it is often done in March. If the latter were done on this Wold, there would not be a bushel on an acre. The ploughing and other work, on the Wold, is done, in great part, by oxen, and here, are some of the finest ox-teams, that I ever saw.

All the villages down to Fairford are pretty much in the same dismal condition as that of Withington. Fairford, which is quite on the border of Gloucestershire, is a very pretty little market-town, and has one of the prettiest churches in the kingdom. It was, they say, built in the reign of Henry VII.; and one is naturally surprised to see, that its windows of beautiful stained glass had the luck to escape, not only the fangs of the ferocious "good Queen Bess;" not only the unsparing plundering minions of James I.; but, even the devastating ruffians of Cromwell.

We got in here, about four o'clock, and at the house of Mr. Iles, where we slept, passed, amongst several friends, a very pleasant evening. This morning, Mr. Iles was so good, as to ride with us, as far as the house of another friend at Kempsford, which is the last Gloucestershire parish in our route. At this friend's, Mr. Arkall, we saw a fine dairy of about 60 or 80 cows, and a cheese loft with, perhaps, more than two thousand cheeses in it; at least there were many hundreds. This village contains, what are said to be the remnants and ruins of a mansion of John of Gaunt. The church is very ancient and very capacious. What tales these churches do tell upon us! What fools, what lazy dogs, what presumptuous asses, what lying braggarts, they make us appear! No people here, "*mon, teel the Scots cam to seevelize*" us! Impudent, lying beggars! Their stinking "*kelts*" ought to be taken up, and the brazen and insolent vagabonds whipped back to their heaths and their rocks. Let them go and thrive by their "cash-credits," and let their paper-money poet, Walter Scott, immortalize their deeds. That conceited, dunderheaded fellow, George Chalmers, *estimated* the whole of the population of England and Wales at a few persons more than *two millions*, when England was just at the highest point of her power and glory, and when all these churches had long been built and were resounding with the voice of priests, who resided in their parishes, and who relieved all the poor out of their tithes! But, this same Chalmers, signed his *solemn conviction*, that Vortigern and the other Ireland-manuscripts, which were written by a lad of sixteen, were written by SHAKSPEARE.

In coming to Kempsford we got wet, and nearly to the skin. But, our friends, gave us coats to put on, while ours were dried, and while we ate our breakfast. In our way to this house, where we now are (Mr. Tucky's, at Heydon), we called at Mr. James Crowdy's, at Highworth, where I was, from the 4th, to the 9th of September inclusive; but it looked rainy, and, therefore, we did not alight. We got wet again, before we reached this place; but, our journey being short, we soon got our clothes dry again.

Burghclere (Hampshire,) Monday, 2d October.

Yesterday was a really *unfortunate day*. The morning promised fair; but, its promises were like those of Burdett! There was a little snivelling, wet, treacherous frost. We had to come through Swindon, and Mr. Tucky had the kindness to come with us, until we got three or four miles on this side (the Hungerford side) of that very neat, and plain, and solid, and respectable market town. Swindon is in Wiltshire, and is in the real fat of the land, all being wheat, beans, cheese, or fat meat. In our way to Swindon, Mr. Tucky's farm exhibited to me, what I never saw before, four score oxen, all grazing upon one farm, and all nearly fat! They were, some Devonshire and some Herefordshire. They were fatting on the grass only; and, I should suppose, that they are worth, or shortly will be, thirty pounds each. But, the great pleasure, with which the contemplation of this fine sight, was naturally calculated to inspire me, was more than counterbalanced by the thought, that these fine oxen, this primest of human food, was, aye, every mouthful of it, destined to be devoured in the Wen, and that, too, for the far greater part, by the Jews, loan-jobbers, tax-eaters, and their base and prostituted followers, dependents, purveyors, parasites and pimps, literary as well as other wretches, who, if suffered to live at all, ought to partake of nothing but the offal, and ought to come, but one cut, before the dogs and cats!

Mind you, there is, in my opinion, no land in England that surpasses this. There is, I suppose, as good in the three last counties, that I have come through; but, *better* than this is, I should think, impossible. There is a pasture-field, of about a hundred acres, close to Swindon, belonging to a Mr. Goddard, which, with its cattle and sheep, was a most beautiful sight. But, every thing is full of riches; and, as fast as skill, and care, and industry, can extract these riches from the land, the unseen grasp of taxation, loan-jobbing, and monopolizing takes them away, leaving the labourers not half a bellyfull, compelling the farmer to pinch them, or to be ruined himself, and making even the landowner, little better than a steward, or bailiff, for the tax-eaters, Jews and jobbers!

Just before we got to Swindon, we crossed a canal at a place where there is a wharf and a coal-yard, and close by these a gentleman's house, with coach-house, stables, walled-in garden, paddock *orné*, and the rest of those things, which, all together, make up *a villa*, surpassing the second, and approaching towards the first class. Seeing a man in the coal-yard, I asked him to what gentleman, the house belonged: "to the *head un* o' the canal," said he. And, when, upon further inquiry of him, I found that it was the villa of the chief manager, I could not help congratulating the proprietors of this aquatic concern; for, though I did not ask the name of the canal, I could readily suppose, that the profits must be prodigious, when the residence of the manager, would imply no disparagement of dignity, if occupied by a Secretary of State for the Home, or even for the Foreign, department. I mean an *English* Secretary of State; for as to an *American* one, his salary would be wholly inadequate, to a residence in a mansion like this.

From Swindon we came up into the *down-country;* and these downs, rise higher even than the Cotswold. We left Marlborough away to our right, and came along the turnpike road towards Hungerford, but with a view of leaving that town to our left, further on, and going away, through Ramsbury, towards the northernmost Hampshire hills, under which Burghclere (where we now are) lies. We passed some fine farms, upon these downs, the houses and homesteads of which were near the road. My companion, though he had been to London, and even to France, had never seen *downs* before; and it was amusing to me to witness his surprise, at seeing the immense flocks of sheep, which were now (ten o'clock) just going out from their several folds, to the downs for the day, each having its shepherd, and each shepherd his dog. We passed the homestead of a farmer Woodman, with *sixteen* banging wheat-ricks in the rick-yard, two of which were old ones; and rick-yard, farm-yard, waste-yard, horse-paddock, and all round about, seemed to be swarming with fowls, ducks, and turkeys, and on the whole of them, not one feather, but what was white! Turning our eyes from this sight, we saw, just going out from the folds of this same farm, three separate and numerous flocks of sheep, one of which (the *lamb*-flock) we passed close by the side of. The shepherd told us, that his flock consisted of thirteen score and five; but, apparently, he could not, if it had been to save his soul, tell us how many hundreds he had: and, if you reflect a little, you will find, that his way of counting is much the easiest and best. This was a most beautiful flock of lambs; short legged, and, in every respect, what they ought to be. George,[1] though born and bred amongst sheep-farms, had never before seen sheep with dark-coloured faces and legs; but his surprise, at this sight, was not nearly so great as the surprise of both of us, at seeing numerous and very large pieces (sometimes 50 acres together) of very good early turnips, Swedish as well as White! All the three counties of Worcester, Hereford, and Gloucester (except on the Cotswold) do not, I am convinced, contain as great a weight of turnip bulbs, as we here saw in one single *piece;* for here there are, for miles and miles, no hedges, and no fences of any sort.

Doubtless they must have had *rain* here, in the months of June and July; but, as I once before observed (though I forget *when*) a chalk bottom does not suffer the surface to burn, however shallow the top soil may be. It seems to me to absorb and to *retain* the water, and to keep it ready to be drawn up by the heat of the sun. At any rate the fact is, that the surface above it does not burn; for, there never yet

---

[1] The Author's companion throughout this Rural Ride (which commenced on 29th Sept. 1826, and terminated on the 26th Oct.) was a youth (referred to frequently by his Christian name George). He was a son of Mr. William Palmer of Bollitree, near Ross, in Hereford, who was one of Mr. Cobbett's intimate friends.

was a summer, not even this last, when the downs did not *retain their greenness to a certain degree*, while the rich pastures, and even the meadows (except actually *watered*) were burnt so as to be as brown as the bare earth.

This is a most pleasing circumstance, attending the down countries; and, there are no *downs* without a chalk bottom.

Along here, the country is rather *too bare:* here, until you come to Auborne, or Aldbourne, there are *no meadows* in the valleys, and no trees, even round the homesteads. This, therefore, is too naked to please me; but I love *the downs* so much, that, if I had to choose, I would live even here, and especially I would *farm* here rather than on the banks of the Wye in Herefordshire, in the vale of Gloucester, of Worcester, or of Evesham, or, even in what the Kentish men call their "garden of Eden." I have now seen (for I have, years back, seen the vales of Taunton, Glastonbury, Honiton, Dorchester and Sherburne) what are deemed the richest and most beautiful parts of England; and, if called upon to name the spot, which I deem the brightest and most beautiful and, of its extent, *best* of all, I should say, the villages of *North Bovant and Bishopstrow*, between Heytesbury and Warminster in Wiltshire; for there is, as appertaining to rural objects, *every thing* that *I delight* in. Smooth and verdant downs in hills and valleys of endless variety as to height and depth and shape; rich corn-land, unencumbered by fences; meadows in due proportion, and those watered at pleasure; and, lastly, the homesteads, and villages, sheltered in winter, and shaded in summer, by lofty and beautiful trees; to which may be added, roads never dirty and a stream never dry.

When we came to Auborne, we got amongst trees again. This is a *town*, and was, manifestly, once a large town. Its church is as big, as three of that of Kensington. It has a market now, I believe; but, I suppose, it is, like many others, become merely nominal, the produce being nearly all carried to Hungerford, in order to be forwarded to the Jew-devils and the tax-eaters and monopolizers in the Wen, and in small

Wens on the way. It is a *decaying place;* and, I dare say, that it would be nearly depopulated, in twenty years' time if this hellish jobbing system were to last so long.

A little after we came through Auborne, we turned off to our right to go through Ramsbury, to Shallburn, where Tull, the father of the drill-husbandry[1] began and practised that husbandry at a farm called "Prosperous." Our object was to reach this place (Burghclere) to sleep, and to stay for a day or two; and as I knew Mr. Blandy of Prosperous, I determined upon this route, which, besides, took us out of the turnpike-road. We stopped at Ramsbury, to bait our horses. It is a large, and, apparently, miserable village, or "town" as the people call it. It was in remote times a *Bishop's See*. Its church is very large and very ancient. Parts of it were evidently built, long, and long before, the Norman Conquest. Burdett owns a great many of the houses in the village (which contains nearly two thousand people), and will, if he live many years, own nearly the whole; for, as his eulogist, William Friend the Actuary, told the public, in a pamphlet, in 1817, he has resolved, that his numerous *life-holds shall run out*, and that those who were life-holders under his Aunt, from whom he got the estate, shall become *rack-renters to him*, or quit the occupations. Besides this, he is continually purchasing lands and houses round about, and in, this place. He has, now let his house to a Mr. Acres; and, as the *Morning Herald* says, is safe landed at Bordeaux, with his family, for the winter! When here, he did not occupy a square inch of his land! He let it all, park and all; and only reserved "a right of road" from the highway to his door. "He had, and has a *right*, to do all this." A *right?* Who denies that? But, is this giving us a specimen of that "liberality and generosity and hospitality" of those "English Country Gentlemen," whose praises he so loudly sang last winter? His name is Francis Burdett *Jones*, which last name, he was obliged to take by his Aunt's

---

[1] Mr. Jethro Tull, to whom reference has been already made, introduced "drill husbandry about the year 1732."

will; and he actually used it for some time, after the estate came to him! "Jones" was too common a name for him, I suppose! Sounded too much of the *vulgar!*

However, what I have principally to do with, is, his *absence from the country* at a time like this, and, if the newspapers be correct, his intended absence during the whole of next winter; and such a winter, too, as it is likely to be! He, for many years, complained, and justly, of the *sinecure placemen;* and are we to suffer him to be, thus, a sinecure Member of Parliament! This is, in my opinion, a great deal worse thàn a sinecure placemen; for this is shutting an active Member out. . It is a dog-in-manger offence; and, to the people of a place such as Westminster, it is not only an injury, but a most outrageous insult. If it be true, that he intends to stay away, during the coming session of Parliament, I trust, not only, that he never will be elected again; but, that the people of Westminster, will call upon him to resign; and this, I am sure they will do too. The next session of Parliament, *must* be a most important one, and that, he knows well. Every member will be put to the test, in the next session of Parliament. On the question of Corn-Bills every man must declare, for, or against, the people. He would declare against, if he dared; and, therefore, he gets out of the way! Or, this is what we shall have a clear right to presume, if he be absent from the next session of Parliament. He knows, that there must be something like a struggle, between the land owners, and the fund-holders. His interest lies with the former; he wishes to support the law-church, and the army, and all sources of aristocratical profit; but, he knows, that the people of Westminster would be on the other side. It is better, therefore, to hear at Bordeaux, about this struggle, than to be engaged in it! He must know of the great embarrassments, distress, and of the great bodily suffering, now experienced by a large part of the people; and has he *a right*, after having got himself returned a member for such a place as Westminster, to go out of the country, at such a time and leave his seat vacant? He must know that, during the ensuing winter, there *must* be great distress in Westminster itself; for there will be a greater mass of the working people out of employ than there ever was in any winter before; and this calamity will, too, be owing to that infernal system, which he has been supporting, to those paper-money Rooks, with whom he is closely connected, and the existence of whose destructive rags he expressed his wish to prolong: he knows all this very well: he knows that, in every quarter the distress and danger are great; and is it not, then, his duty to be here? Is he, who, at his own request, has been intrusted with the representing of a great city, to get out of the way at a time like this, and under circumstances like these? If this be so, then is this great, and *once* public-spirited city, become more contemptible, and infinitely more mischievous, than the "accursed hill" of Wiltshire: but, this is *not so:* the *people* of Westminster, are what they always were, full of good sense and public spirit: they have been cheated by a set of bribed intriguers; and *how* this has been done, I will explain to them, when I *punish* Sir Francis Burdett Jones for the sins, *committed for him*, by a hired Scotch writer. I shall dismiss him for the present, with observing, that, if I had in me, a millionth part of that malignity and vindictiveness, which he so basely showed towards me, I have learned anecdotes, sufficient to enable me to take ample vengeance on him for the stabs which he, in 1817, knew that he was sending to the hearts of the defenceless part of my family![1]

---

[1] What the particular circumstances were to which the Author here alludes, it is difficult to discover, except that they occurred during his second visit to America; but it is quite evident that the warm friendship, which previously existed between him and Sir Francis Burdett, had considerably cooled down. In the first place, Sir Francis, who had called upon the people, for years past, "to rally round the standard of reform," and "to come forward," when the critical times of 1816 and 1817 arrived, seemed half-hearted, and shrank from the battle, leaving the forefront to Cobbett, and Lord Cochrane, and Cartwright. Indeed when, at the opening of Parliament, Lord Cochrane moved an amendment to the Address, Sir Francis allowed the motion to drop, without a seconder. The Author had therefore good reason to twit him with his former *sobriquets*, "England's Glory," "Sir Glory," "Westminster Pride," &c.

While our horses were baiting at Ramsbury, it began to rain, and by the time that they had done, it rained pretty hard, with every appearance of continuing to rain for the day; and it was now about eleven o'clock, we having 18 or 19 miles to go, before we got to the intended end of our journey. Having, however, for several reasons, a very great desire to get to Burghclere that night, we set off in the rain; and, as we carry no great coats, we were wet to the skin pretty soon. Immediately upon quitting Ramsbury, we crossed the River Kennet, and, mounting a highish hill, we looked back over friend Sir Glory's park, the sight of which brought into my mind the visit of Thimble and Cowhide, as described in the "intense comedy," and, when I thought of the "baker's being starved to death," and of the "heavy fall of snow," I could not help bursting out a laughing, though it poured of rain and though I already felt the water on my skin.—MEM. To ask, when I get to London, what is become of the intense "Counsellor Bric"; and whether he have yet had the justice to put the K to the end of his name.[1] I saw a lovely female shoy-hoy, engaged in keeping the rooks from a newly-sown wheat field on the Cotswold Hills, that would be a very *suitable match* for him; and, as his manners appear to be mended; as he now praises to the skies those 40s. freeholders, whom, in my hearing, he asserted to be "*beneath brute beasts;*" as he does, in short, appear to be rather less offensive than he was, I should have no objection to promote the union; and, I am sure, the *farmer* would like it, of all things; for, if Miss *Stuffed o' straw* can, when *single*, keep the devourers at a distance, say, you who know him, whether the sight of the *husband's head* would leave a rook in the country!

Another reason for this estrangement appears to have been on account of some money transactions between them. For some purpose, Cobbett seems to have given Sir Francis a bond for £3000. After Cobbett's death, when a committee was formed for the purpose of raising a memorial to him, Sir Francis sent this bond to them, telling them to take his subscription out of that.

[1] The allusion here, is to Mr. John Bric, who was a partisan of Daniel O'Connell, and who was subsequently killed in a duel in Ireland.

Turning from viewing the scene of Thimble and Cowhide's cruel disappointment, we pushed through coppices and across fields, to a little village, called Froxfield, which we found to be on the great Bath-Road. Here, crossing the road and also a run of water, we, under the guidance of a man, who was good enough to go about a mile with us, and to whom we gave a shilling and the price of a pot of beer, mounted another hill, from which, after twisting about for awhile, I saw, and recognised the out-buildings of Prosperous farm, towards which we pushed on as fast as we could, in order to keep ourselves in motion so as to prevent our catching cold; for it rained, incessantly, every step of the way. I had been at Prosperous before; so that I knew Mr. Blandy, the owner, and his family, who received us with great hospitality. They took care of our horses, gave us what we wanted, in the eating and drinking way, and clothed us, shirts and all, while they dried all our clothes; for, not only the things on our bodies were soaked, but those also which we carried in little thin leather rolls, fastened on upon the saddles before us. Notwithstanding all that could be done in the way of dispatch, it took more than three hours to get our clothes dry. At last, about three quarters of an hour before sunset, we got on our clothes again and set off: for, as an instance of real bad luck, it ceased to rain the moment we got to Mr. Blandy's. Including the numerous angles and windings, we had nine or ten miles yet to go; but, I was so anxious to get to Burghclere, that, contrary to my practice as well as my principle, I determined to encounter the darkness for once, though in crosscountry roads, presenting us, at every mile, with ways crossing each other; or forming a Y; or kindly giving us the choice of three, forming the upper part of a Y and a half. Add to this, we were in an enclosed country, the lanes very narrow, deep-worn, and banks and hedges high. There was no moon; but, it was starlight, and, as I could see the Hampshire Hills all along to my right, and knew that I must not get above a mile or so from them, I had a guide that could not deceive me; for, as to *asking* the road, in a case like this, it is of little use, unless you meet some one at every half mile : for the answer is, *keep right on ;* aye, but in ten minutes, perhaps, you come to a Y, or a T, or to a +.

A fellow told me once, in my way from Chertsey to Guildford, "keep *right on*, you can't miss your way." I was in the perpendicular part of the T, and the top part was only a few yards from me. "*Right on*," said I, "what, over *that bank* into "the wheat?" "No, no," said he, "I mean *that road*, to be "sure," pointing to the road that went off to the *left*. In *down-countries*, the direction of shepherds and pig and bird boys, is always in precisely the same words; namely, "*right* over the down?" laying great stress upon the word *right*. "But," said I, to a boy, at the edge of the down at King's Worthy (near Winchester), who gave me this direction to Stoke Charity; "but, what do you mean by *right* over the down?" "Why," said he, "*right* on to Stoke, to be sure, Zur." "Aye," said I, "but how am I, who was never here before, to know "*what* is right, my boy?" That posed him. It set him to thinking : and, after a bit he proceeded to tell me, that, when I got up the hill, I should see *some trees;* that I should go along by them; that I should then see *a barn* right before me; that I should go down to that barn; and that I should then see a *wagon track* that would lead me all down to Stoke. "Aye!" said I, "*now* indeed you are a real clever fellow." And I gave him a shilling, being part of my savings of the morning. Whoever tries it, will find, that the *less they eat and drink*, when travelling, the better they will be. I act accordingly. Many days I have no breakfast and no dinner. I went from Devizes to Highworth without breaking my fast, a distance, including my deviations, of more than *thirty miles*. I sometimes take, from a friend's house, a little bit of meat between two bits of bread, which I eat as I ride along; but, whatever I save from this fasting work, I think I have a clear right to give away; and, accordingly, I generally put the amount, in copper, into my waistcoat pocket, and dispose of it during the day. I know well, *that I am the better* for not stuffing and blowing myself out, and with the savings I make many and many a happy boy; and, now-and-then, I give a whole family a good meal with the cost of a breakfast, or a dinner, that would have done me mischief. I do not do this, because I grudge innkeepers, what they charge; for, my surprise is, how they can live, without charging *more* than they do in general.

It was dark by the time that we got to a village, called East Woodhay. Sunday evening is the time *for courting*, in the country. It is not convenient to carry this on before faces, and, at farm-houses and cottages, there are no spare apartments; so that the pairs turn out, and pitch up, to carry on their negociations, by the side of stile, or a gate. The evening was auspicious; it was *pretty dark*, the *weather mild*, and *Old Michaelmas* (when yearly services end) was fast approaching; and accordingly, I do not recollect ever having before seen, so many negociations going on, within so short a distance. At West Woodhay my horse *cast a shoe*, and, as the road was abominably flinty, we were compelled to go at a snail's pace: and I should have gone crazy with impatience, had it not been for these ambassadors and ambassadresses of Cupid, to every pair of whom, I said something or other. I began by asking the fellow *my road;* and, from the tone and manner of his answer, I could tell pretty nearly, what prospect he had of success, and knew what to say, to draw something from him. I had some famous sport with them, saying to them, more than I should have said by daylight, and a great deal less than I should have said, if my horse had been in a condition to carry me away as swiftly as he did, from Osmond Ricardo's terrific cross! "There!" exclaims Mrs. Scrip, the stock-jobber's young wife, to her old hobbling wittol of a spouse, "You see, my love, that this mischievous man could not "let even these poor *peasants* alone." "*Peasants!* you dirty-"necked ——, and where got you that word? You, who, but a "few years ago, came, perhaps, up from the country in a waggon; "who *made* the bed you now *sleep* in; and who got the "husband, by helping him to get his wife out of the world, as "some young party-coloured blade, is to get you, and the old "rogue's money by a similar process!"

We got to Burghclere about eight o'clock, after a very disagreeable day; but we found ample compensation in the house, and all within it, that we were now arrived at.

Burghclere,
Sunday, 8th Sept.

It rained steadily this morning, or else, at the end of these six days of hunting for George, and two for me, we should have set off. The rain gives me time to give an account of Mr. Budd's crop of Tullian Wheat. It was sown in rows, and on ridges, with very wide intervals, ploughed all summer. If he reckon that ground only which the wheat grew upon, he had one hundred and thirty bushels to the acre; and even if he reckoned the whole of the ground, he had 28 bushels, all but two gallons to the acre! But, the best wheat he grew this year, was dibbled in, between rows of Swedish Turnips, in November, four rows upon a ridge, with an eighteen inch interval between each two rows, and a five feet interval between the outside rows on each ridge. It is the white cone that Mr. Budd sows. He had ears with 130 grains in each. This would be the farming for labourers in their little plots. They might grow thirty bushels of wheat to the acre, and have crops of cabbages, in the intervals, at the same time; or, of potatoes, if they liked them better.

Before my arrival here, Mr. Budd had seen my description of the state of the labourers in Wiltshire, and had, in consequence, written to my son James (not knowing where I was) as follows:—"In order to see how the labourers are now
" *screwed down*, look at the following facts: Arthur Young, in
" 1771 (55 years ago) allowed for a man, his wife and three
" children 13*s*. 1*d*. a week, according to present money-prices.
" By the Berkshire Magistrates' table, made in 1795, the allow-
" ance was, for such family, according to the present money-
" prices, 11*s*. 4*d*. Now it is, according to the same standard,
" 8*s*. According to your father's proposal, the sum would be
" (supposing there to be no malt tax) 18*s*. a week; and little
" enough too." Is not that enough to convince any one of

the hellishness of this system! Yet Sir Glory applauds it. Is it not horrible to contemplate millions in this half-starving state; and, is it not the duty of "England's Glory," who has said that his estate is "*a retaining fee* for defending the rights "of the people;" is it not his duty to stay in England and endeavour to restore the people, the millions, to what their fathers were, instead of going abroad; selling off his carriage horses, and going abroad, there to spend some part, at least, of the fruits of English labour? I do not say, that he has *no right*, generally speaking, to go and spend his money abroad: but, I do say, that having got himself elected for such a city as Westminster, he had no right, at a time like this, to be absent from Parliament. However, what cares he! His "retaining fee" indeed! He takes special care to augment that fee; but, I challenge all his shoe-lickers, all the base worshippers of twenty thousand acres, to show me one single thing, that he has ever done, or, within the last twelve years, attempted to do, for his *clients*. In short, this is a man that must now be brought to book: he must not be suffered to insult Westminster any longer: he must turn-to or turn out: he is a sore to Westminster; a set-fast on its back; a cholic in its belly; a cramp in its limbs; a gag in its mouth: he is a nuisance, a monstrous nuisance, in Westminster, and he must be abated.

RIDE FROM BURGHCLERE TO LYNDHURST, IN THE NEW FOREST.

"The reformers have yet many and powerful foes; we have to contend against a host, such as never existed before in the world. Nine-tenths of the press; all the channels of speedy communication of sentiment; all the pulpits; all the associations of rich people; all the taxing-people; all the military and naval establishments; all the yeomanry cavalry tribes. Your allies are endless in number, and mighty in influence. But, we have *one ally* worth the whole of them put together, namely, the DEBT! This is an ally, whom no honours or rewards can seduce from us. She is a steady, unrelaxing, persevering, incorruptible ally. An ally that is proof against all blandishments, all intrigues, all temptations, and all open attacks. She sets at defiance all '*military*,' all '*yeomanry cavalry*.' They may as well fire at a ghost. She cares no more for the sabres of the yeomanry, or the Life Guards, than Milton's angels did for the swords of Satan's myrmidons. This ally cares not a straw about *spies*, and *informers*. She laughs at the employment of *secret-service money*. She is always erect, day and night, and is always firmly moving on in our cause, in spite of all the terrors of gaols, dungeons, halters and axes. Therefore, Mr. JABET, be not so pert. The combat is not so unequal as you seem to imagine ; and, confident and insolent as you now are, the day of your humiliation may not be far distant."—LETTER TO Mr. JABET, of Birmingham, *Register*, v. 31, p. 477. (Nov. 1816.)

Hurstbourn Tarrant,
(*commonly called Uphusband,*)
Wednesday, 11th *October,* 1826.

WHEN quarters are good, you are apt to *lurk* in them ; but, really it was so wet, that we could not get away from Burghclere till Monday evening. Being here, there were many reasons for our going to the great fair at Weyhill, which began yesterday, and, indeed, the day before, at Appleshaw. These two days are allotted for the selling of sheep only, though the horse-fair begins on the 10th. To Appleshaw they bring nothing but those fine curled-horned and long-tailed ewes, which bring the house-lambs and the early Easter-lambs ; and these, which, to my taste, are the finest and most beautiful animals of the sheep kind, come exclusively out of Dorsetshire and out of the part of Somersetshire, bordering on that county.

To Weyhill, which is a village of half a dozen houses on a down, just above Appleshaw, they bring, from the down-farms in Wiltshire and Hampshire, where they are bred, the South Down sheep ; ewes to go away into the pasture and turnip countries, to have lambs, wethers to be fatted and killed, and lambs (nine months old) to be kept to be sheep. At both fairs, there is supposed to be about two hundred thousand sheep. It was of some consequence, to ascertain how the *price* of these had been affected by "*late* panic," which ended the "respite" of 1822; or by the "*plethora of money*" as loan-man Baring called it. I can assure this political Doctor, that there was no such "plethora" at Weyhill, yesterday, where, while I viewed the long faces of the farmers, while I saw consciousness of ruin, painted on their countenances, I could not help saying to myself, "the loan-mongers think they are *cunning*; but by " ——, they will never escape the ultimate consequences of " this horrible ruin!" The prices, take them on a fair average, were, at both fairs, just about one-half what they were last year. So that my friend Mr. Thwaites of the *Herald*, who had a lying Irish reporter at Preston, was rather hasty, about three months ago, when he told his *well-informed* readers, that "those politicians were deceived, who had supposed that prices of farm produce would fall in consequence of '*late panic*' and the subsequent measures"! There were Dorsetshire ewes that sold last year, for 50s. a head. We could hear of none this year that exceeded 25s. And only think of 25s. for one of these fine, large ewes, nearly fit to kill, and having two lambs in her, ready to be brought forth in, on an average, six weeks' time! The average is *three lambs* to *two of these ewes*. In 1812 these ewes were from 55s. to 72s. each, at this same Appleshaw fair; and in that year, I bought South Down ewes at 45s. each, just such as were, yesterday, sold for 18s. Yet, the sheep and grass and all things are the same, in *real value*. What a false, what a deceptious, what an infamous thing, this paper-money system is!

However, it is a pleasure, it is a great delight, it is boundless joy to me, to contemplate this infernal system in its hour of *wreck:* swag here: crack there: scroop this way: souse that way: and such a rattling, and such a squalling: and the parsons and their wives looking so frightened, beginning, apparently, to think that the day of *judgment* is at hand! I wonder what master parson of Sharncut, whose church *can* contain *eight persons*, and master parson of Draycot Foliot, who is, for want of a church, inducted under a *tent*, or temporary *booth;* I wonder what they think of South Down lambs (9 months old) selling for 6 or 7 shillings each! I wonder what the Barings and the Ricardos think of it. I wonder what those master parsons think of it, who are half-pay naval, military officers, as well as master parsons of the church made by *law*. I wonder what the Gaffer Gooches, with their parsonships and military offices, think of it. I wonder what Daddy Coke and Suffield think of it; and when, I wonder, do they mean to get into their holes and barns again to cry aloud against the "roguery of reducing the interest of the Debt"; when, I wonder, do these manly, these modest, these fair, these candid, these open, and, above all things, these *sensible*, fellows intend to assemble again, and to call all "the House of Quidenham" and the "House of Kilmainham," or *Kinsaleham*, or whatever it is (for I really have forgotten); to call, I say, all these about them, in the holes and the barns, and then and there, again make a formal and solemn protest against COBBETT and against his roguish proposition for reducing the interest of the Debt! Now I have these fellows on the hip; and brave sport will I have with them before I have done.

Mr. Blount, at whose house (7 miles from Weyhill) I am, went with me to the fair; and we took particular pains to ascertain the prices. We saw, and spoke to, Mr. John Herbert, of Stoke (near Uphusband) who was *asking* 20s., and who did not expect to *get* it, for South Down ewes, just such as he *sold*, last year (at this fair), for 36s. Mr. Jolliff of Crux-Easton, was *asking* 16s. for just such ewes as he sold, last year (at this fair) for 32s. Farmer Holdway had sold "for less than half" his last year's price. A farmer that I did not know, told us, that he had sold to a great sheep-dealer of the name of Smallpiece, at the latter's own price! I asked him what that "own price" was: and he said that he was ashamed to say. The horse-fair appeared to have no business at all going on; for, indeed, how were people to purchase horses, who had got only half-price for their sheep?

The sales of sheep, at this one fair (including Appleshaw), must have amounted, this year, to a hundred and twenty or thirty thousand pounds, less than last year! Stick a pin there, master "Prosperity Robinson," and turn back to it, again anon! Then came the horses; not equal in amount to the sheep, but of great amount. Then comes the cheese, a very great article; and it will have a falling off, if you take quantity into view, in a still greater proportion. The hops being a monstrous crop, their *price* is nothing to judge by. But, all is fallen. Even corn, though, in many parts, all but the wheat and rye have totally failed, is, taking a quarter of each of the *six sorts* (wheat, rye, barley, oats, peas, and beans), 11*s.* 9*d.* cheaper, upon the whole; that is to say, 11*s.* 9*d.* upon 258*s.* And, if the "*late* panic" had not come, it must, and it would have been, and according to the small bulk of the crop, it ought to have been, 150*s. dearer*, instead of 11*s.* 9*d.* cheaper. Yet, it is too dear, and far too dear, for the working people to eat! The masses, the assembled masses, must starve, if the price of bread be not reduced; that is to say, in Scotland and Ireland; for, *in England*, I hope that the people will "*demand and insist*" (to use the language of the Bill of Rights) on a just and suitable provision, agreeably to the law; and, if they do not get it, I trust that law and justice will, in due course, be done, and strictly done, upon those who refuse to make such provision. Though, in time, the price of corn will come down without any repeal of the Corn Bill; and though it would have come down now, if we had had a good crop, or an average crop; still the Corn Bill ought now to be repealed, because people must not be *starved* in waiting for the next crop; and the "landowners' monopoly," as the son of "John with the bright sword" calls it, ought to be swept away; and the sooner it is done, the better for the country. I know very well that the landowners must lose their estates, if such prices continue, and if the present taxes continue; I know this very well; and I like it well; for, the landowners *may cause the taxes to be taken off if they will.* "Ah! wicked dog!" say they, " what, then, you would have us lose the half-pay and " the pensions and sinecures which our children and other " relations, or that we ourselves, are pocketing out of the " taxes, which are squeezed, in great part, out of the labourer's "skin and bone!" Yes, upon my word, I would; but, if you prefer losing your estates, I have no great objection; for it is hard that, "in a free country," people should not have their choice of the different roads to the poor-house. Here is the *rub:* the vote-owners, the seat-owners, the big borough-mongers, have, directly and indirectly, so large a share of the loaves and fishes, that the share is, in point of clear income, equal to, and, in some cases, greater than, that from their estates; and, though this is not the case with the small fry of jolterheads, they are so linked in with, and overawed by, the big ones, that they have all the same feeling; and that is, that to cut off half-pay, pensions, sinecures, commissionerships (such as that of Hobhouse's father), army, and the rest of the "good things," would be nearly as bad as to take away the estates, which, besides, are, in fact, in many instances, nearly gone (at least from the present holder) already, by the means of mortgage, annuity, rent-charge, settlement, jointure, or something or other. Then there are the parsons, who with their keen noses, have smelled out long enough ago, that if, any serious settlement should take place, *they go* to a certainty. In short, they know well how the whole nation (the interested excepted) feel towards them. They know well, that were it not for their allies, it would soon be queer times with them.

Here, then, is the *rub.* Here are the reasons why the taxes are not taken off! Some of these jolterheaded beasts were ready to cry, and I know one that did actually cry to a farmer (his tenant) in 1822. The tenant told him, that "Mr. Cobbett "had been *right* about this matter." "What!" exclaimed he, " I hope you do not read Cobbett! He will ruin you, and " he would ruin us all. He would introduce anarchy, con- " fusion, and destruction of property!" Oh, no, Jolterhead! There is no *destruction* of property. Matter, the philosophers say, is *indestructible.* But, it is all easily *transferable,* as is well-known, to the base Jolterheads and the blaspheming Jews. The former of these will, however, soon have the faint sweat upon them again. Their tenants will be ruined *first:* and, here what a foul robbery these landowners have committed, or at least, enjoyed and pocketed the gain of! They have given their silent assent, to the one-pound note abolition Bill. They knew well that this must reduce the price of farm produce *one-half*, or thereabouts; and yet, they were prepared to take, and to insist on, and they do take and insist on, as high rents, as if that Bill had never been passed! What dreadful ruin will ensue! How many, many farmers' families are now just preparing the way for their entrance into the poor-house! How many? certainly many a score farmers did I see at Weyhill, yesterday, who came there as it were to *know their fate!* and who are gone home thoroughly convinced, that they shall, as farmers, never see Weyhill fair again!

When such a man, his mind impressed with such conviction, returns home and there beholds a family of children, half bred up, and in the notion that they were *not* to be mere working people, what must be his *feelings!* Why, if he have been a bawler against Jacobins and Radicals; if he have approved of the Power-of-Imprisonment Bill and of Six-Acts; aye, if he did not rejoice at Castlereagh's cutting his own throat; if he have been a cruel screwer down of the labourers, reducing them to skeletons; if he have been an officious detector of what are called "poachers," and have assisted in, or approved of, the hard punishments, inflicted on them; then, in either of these cases, I say, that his feelings, though they put the suicidal knife into his own hand, are short of what he deserves! I say this, and this I repeat with all the seriousness and solemnity with which a man can make a declaration; for, had it not been for these base and selfish and unfeeling wretches, the deeds of 1817 and 1819 and 1820 would never have been attempted. These hard and dastardly dogs, armed up to the teeth, were always ready to come forth to destroy, not only to revile, to decry, to belie, to calumniate in all sorts of ways, but, if necessary, absolutely to cut the throats of, those who had no object, and who could have no object, other than that of preventing a continuance in that course of measures, which have finally produced the ruin, and threaten to produce the absolute destruction, of these base, selfish, hard and dastardly dogs themselves. *Pity* them ! Let them go for pity to those whom they have applauded and abetted.[1]

The farmers, I mean the renters, will not now, as they did in 1819, stand a good long emptying out. They had, in 1822, lost nearly all. The present stock of the farms is not, in one half of the cases, the property of the farmer. It is borrowed stock; and the sweeping out will be very rapid. The notion, that the Ministers will do "something" is clung on to, by all those who are deeply in debt, and all who have leases, or other engagements for time. These *believe* (because they anxiously *wish*) that the paper-money, by means of some sort or other, will be put out again; while the Ministers *believe* (because they anxiously *wish*) that the thing can go on, that they can continue to pay the interest of the debt, and meet all the rest of their spendings, without one-pound notes, and without bank-restriction. Both parties will be deceived, and in the midst of the strife, that the dissipation of the delusion will infallibly lead to, the whole THING is very likely to go to pieces; and that, too, *mind*, tumbling into the hands and placed at the mercy of a people, the millions of whom have been fed upon less, to four persons, than what goes down the throat of one single common soldier! Please to *mind* that, Messieurs the admirers of select vestries ! You have *not done it*, Messieurs Sturges Bourne and the Hampshire Parsons ! You *thought* you had ! You meaned well; but it was a *coup-manqué*, a missing of the mark, and that, too, as is frequently the case, by over-shooting it. The attempt will, however, produce its just consequences in the end; and those consequences will be of vast importance.

From Weyhill I was shown, yesterday, the wood, in which took place the battle, in which was concerned poor Turner,

---

[1] The present agricultural depression, seems to emphasise the graphic description of the lamentable times to which reference is here made; and would make one almost desire that the powerful appeal of the Author to "The Journeymen and Labourers of England, Wales, Scotland, and Ireland" which appeared in his *Register*, No. 16, November 2, 1816, and of which 44,000 copies were sold in one month, could be again republished.

one of the young men, who was hanged at Winchester, in the year 1822. There was another young man, named Smith, who was, on account of another game-battle, hanged on the same gallows! And this for the preservation of the *game*, you will observe! This for the preservation of the *sports* of that aristocracy for whose sake, and solely for whose sake, "Sir "James Graham, of Netherby, descendant of the Earls of "Monteith and of the seventh Earl of Galloway, K.T." (being sure not to omit the K.T.); this hanging of us, is for the preservation of the sports of that aristocracy, for the sake of whom this Graham, this bare-faced plagiarist, this bungling and yet impudent pamphleteer, would *sacrifice*, would reduce to beggary, according to his pamphlet, *three hundred thousand families* (making, doubtless, *two millions* of persons), in the middle rank of life! It is for the preservation, for upholding what he insolently calls the "dignity" of this sporting aristocracy, that he proposes to rob all mortgagees, all who have claims upon land! The feudal lords in France had, as Mr. Young tells us, a right, when they came in, fatigued, from hunting or shooting, to cause the belly of one of their vassals to be ripped up, in order for the lord to soak his feet in the bowels! Sir James Graham of the bright sword does not propose to carry us back so far as this; he is willing to stop at taking away the money and the victuals of a very large part of the community; and, monstrous as it may seem, I will venture to say, that there are scores of the Lord-Charles tribe who think him moderate to a fault!

But to return to the above-mentioned hanging at Winchester (a thing never to be forgotten by me), James Turner, aged 28 years, was accused of assisting to kill Robert Baker, gamekeeper to Thomas Asheton Smith, Esq., in the parish of South Tidworth; and Charles Smith, aged 27 years, was accused of shooting at (not killing) Robert Snelgrove, assistant game-keeper to Lord Palmerston (Secretary at War), at Broad-lands in the Parish of Romsey. Poor Charles Smith had better have been hunting after *shares* than after *hares !* *Mines*, however *deep*, he would have found less perilous than the pleasure grounds of Lord Palmerston! I deem this hanging at Winchester worthy of general attention, and particularly at this time when the aristocracy near Andover, and the members for that town, (of whom this very Thomas Asheton Smith, until lately, was one,) were, if the report in the Morning Chronicle (copied into the Register of the 7th instant) be correct, endeavouring, at the late Meeting at Andover, to persuade people, that they (these aristocrats) wished to keep up the price of corn for the sake of the labourers, whom Sir John Pollen (Thomas Asheton Smith's son's present colleague as member for Andover) called "poor devils," and who, he said, had "hardly a rag to cover them!" Oh! wished to keep up the price of corn for the good of the "poor devils of labourers who have hardly a rag to cover them!" Amiable feeling, tender-hearted souls! Cared not a straw about *rents!* Did not; oh, oh! did not care even about the farmers! It was only for the sake of the poor, naked devils of labourers, that the colleague of young Thomas Asheton Smith cared; it was only for those who were in the same rank of life as James Turner and Charles Smith were, that these kind Andover aristocrats cared! This was the only reason in the world for their wanting corn to sell at a high price? We often say, "*that* beats every thing;" but really, I think, that these professions of the Andover aristocrats do "*beat everything.*" Ah! but Sir John Pollen, these professions come *too late* in the day: the people are no longer to be deceived by such stupid attempts at disguising hypocrisy. However, the attempt shall do this: it shall make me repeat here that which I published on the Winchester hanging, in the *Register* of the 6th of April 1822. It made part of a "Letter to Landlords." Many boys have, since this article was published, grown up to the age of thought. Let them now read it: and I hope, that they will *remember it well.*

I, last fall, addressed ten letters to you on the subject of the *Agricultural Report.* My object was to convince you, that you would be ruined; and, when I think of your general conduct towards the rest of the nation, and especially towards the labourers, I must say that I have great pleasure in seeing that my opinions are in a fair way of being verified to the full extent. I dislike the *Jews*; but, the Jews are not so inimical to the industrious classes of the country, as you are. We should do a great deal better with the 'Squires from 'Change Alley, who, at any rate, have nothing of the ferocious and bloody in their characters. Engrafted upon your native want of feeling, is the sort of military spirit of command, that you have acquired during the late war. You appeared, at the close of that war, to think that you had made a *conquest* of the rest of the nation for ever; and, if it had not been for the burden which the war left behind it, there would have been no such thing as air, in England, for any one but a slave to breathe. The Bey of Tunis never talked to his subjects in language more insolent than you talked to the people of England. The DEBT, the blessed Debt, stood our friend, made you soften your tone, and will finally place you, where you ought to be placed.

This is the last Letter that I shall ever take the trouble to address to you. In a short time, you will become much too insignificant to merit any particular notice; but just in the way of *farewell*, and that there may be something on record to show what care has been taken of the partridges, pheasants, and hares, while the estates themselves have been suffered to slide away, I have resolved to address this one more Letter to you, which resolution has been occasioned by the recent *putting to death*, at Winchester, of two men denominated *Poachers.* This is a thing, which, whatever you may think of it, has not been passed over, and is not to be passed over, without full notice and ample record. The account of the matter, as it appeared in the public prints, was very short, but the fact is such as never ought to be forgotten. And while you are complaining of your " distress," I will endeavour to lay before the public that which will show, that the *law* has not been unmindful of even your *sports*. The time is approaching, when the people will have an opportunity of exercising their judgment as to what are called "game-laws;" when they will look back a little, at what has been done, for the sake of insuring sport to landlords. In short, landlords as well as labourers will *pass under review*. But, I must proceed to my subject, reserving reflections for a subsequent part of my letter.

The account, to which I have alluded, is this:

"HAMPSHIRE. The Lent Assizes for this county concluded "on Saturday morning. The Criminal Calendar contained 58 "prisoners for trial, 16 of whom have been sentenced to suffer "death, but two only of that number (*poachers*) were left by "the Judges for execution, viz.: James Turner, aged 28, for "aiding and assisting in killing Robert Baker, gamekeeper to "Thomas Asheton Smith, Esq., in the parish of South Tid-"worth, and Charles Smith, aged 27, for having wilfully and "maliciously shot at Robert Snellgrove, assistant gamekeeper "to Lord Palmerston, at Broadlands, in the parish of Romsey, "with intent to do him grievous bodily harm. The Judge "(Burrough) observed, it became *necessary* in *these cases*, that "the *extreme sentence of the law should be inflicted*, to *deter* "*others, as resistance to gamekeepers*, had now arrived at an "*alarming height*, and many lives had been lost."

The first thing to observe here is, that there were *sixteen* persons sentenced to suffer death; and that, the only persons actually put to death, were those who had been endeavouring to get at the hares, pheasants or partridges of Thomas Asheton Smith, and of our Secretary at War, Lord Palmerston. Whether the Judge Burrough (who was long Chairman of the Quarter Sessions in Hampshire), uttered the words ascribed to him, or not, I cannot say; but, the words have gone forth in print, and the impression they are calculated to make is this: that it was necessary to put these two *men to death*, in order to deter others from resisting gamekeepers. The putting of these men to death has excited a very deep feeling throughout the County of Hants; a feeling, very honourable to the people of that County, and very natural to the breast of every human being.

In this case there appears to have been a killing, in which Turner *assisted;* and Turner might, by possibility, have given the fatal blow; but in the case of Smith, there was no killing at all. There was a mere *shooting at*, with intention to do him bodily harm. This latter offence was not a crime for which men were put to death, even when there was no assault, or attempt at assault, on the part of the person shot at; this was not a crime punished with death, until that terrible act, brought in by the late Lord Ellenborough, was passed, and formed a part of our matchless Code, that Code which there is such a talk about *softening;* but which softening does not appear to have in view this Act, or any portion of the Game-Laws.

In order to form a just opinion with regard to the offence of these two men that have been hanged at Winchester, we must first consider the motives by which they were actuated, in committing the acts of violence laid to their charge. For, it is the intention, and not the mere act, that constitutes the crime. To make an act murder, there must be *malice afore thought*. The question, therefore, is, did these men attack, or were they the attacked? It seems to be clear that they were the attacked parties: for they are executed, according to this publication, to deter others from *resisting* gamekeepers!

I know very well that there is Law for this; but what I shall endeavour to show is, that the Law ought to be altered; that the people of Hampshire ought to petition for such alteration; and that if you, the Landlords, were wise, you would petition also, for an alteration, if not a total annihilation of that terrible Code, called the Game-Laws, which has been growing harder and harder all the time that it ought to have been wearing away. It should never be forgotten, that, in order to make punishments efficient in the way of example, they must be thought just by the Community at large; and they will never be thought just if they aim at the protection of things belonging to one particular class of the Community, and, especially, if those very things be grudged to this class by the Community in general. When punishments of this sort take place, they are looked upon as unnecessary, the sufferers are objects of pity, the common feeling of the Community is in their favour, instead of being against them; and it is those who cause the punishment, and not those who suffer it, who become objects of abhorrence.

Upon seeing two of our countrymen hanging upon a gallows, we naturally, and instantly, run back to the cause. First we find the fighting with gamekeepers; next we find that the men would have been transported if caught in or near a cover with guns, after dark; next we find that these trespassers are exposed to transportation because they are in pursuit, or supposed to be in pursuit, of partridges, pheasants or hares; and then, we ask, where is the foundation of a law to punish a man with transportation for being in pursuit of these animals? And where, indeed, is the foundation of the Law, to take from any man, be he who he may, the right of catching and using these animals? We know very well; we are instructed by mere feeling, that we have a right to live, to see and to move. Common sense tells us that there are some things which no man can reasonably call his property; and though poachers (as they are called) do not read *Blackstone's Commentaries*, they know that such animals as are of a wild and untamable disposition, any man may seize upon and keep for his own use and pleasure. "All these things, so long as they remain "in possession, every man has a right to enjoy without dis- "turbance; but if once they escape from his custody, or he "voluntarily abandons the use of them, they return to the "common stock, and any man else has an equal right to seize "and enjoy them afterwards." (Book 2, Chapter 1.)

In the Second Book and Twenty-sixth Chapter of *Blackstone*, the poacher might read as follows: "With regard likewise to "wild animals, all mankind had by the original grant of the "Creator a right to pursue and take away any fowl or insect "of the air, any fish or inhabitant of the waters, and any beast "or reptile of the field: and this natural right still continues

"in every individual, unless where it is restrained by the civil
"laws of the country. And when a man has once so seized
"them, they become, while living, his qualified property, or, if
"dead, are absolutely his own : so that to steal them, or other-
"wise invade this property, is, according to the respective
"values, sometimes a criminal offence, sometimes only a civil
"injury."

Poachers do not read this; but that reason, which is common to all mankind, tells them, that this is true, and tells them, also, *what to think* of any positive law, that is made to restrain them, from this right granted by the Creator. Before I proceed further in commenting upon the case immediately before me, let me once more quote this English Judge, who wrote fifty years ago, when the Game Code was mild indeed, compared to the one of the present day. "Another violent
"alteration," says he, "of the English Constitution consisted
"in the depopulation of whole countries, for the purposes of
"the King's royal diversion; and subjecting both them, and
"all the ancient forests of the kingdom, to the unreasonable
"severities of forest laws imported from the continent, whereby
"the slaughter of a beast was made, almost as penal as the
"death of a man. In the Saxon times, though no man was
"allowed to kill or chase the King's deer, yet he might start
"any game, pursue and kill it upon his own estate. But the
"rigour of these new constitutions vested the sole property of
"all the game in England in the King alone; and no man
"was entitled to disturb any fowl of the air, or any beast of
"the field, of such kinds as were specially reserved for the
"royal amusement of the Sovereign, without express license
"from the King, by a grant of a chase or free warren : and
"those franchises were granted as much with a view to preserve
"the breed of animals, as to indulge the subject. From a
"similar principle to which, though the forest laws are now
"mitigated, and by degrees grown entirely obsolete, yet from
"this root has sprung up a bastard slip, known by the name
"of the game-law, now arrived to and wantoning in its highest
"vigour : both founded upon the same unreasonable notions

"of permanent property in wild creatures; and both produc-
"tive of the same tyranny to the commons: but with this
"difference; that the forest laws established only one mighty
"hunter throughout the land, the game-laws have raised a
"little Nimrod in every manor." (Book 4, Chapter 33.)

When this was written nothing was known of the present severity of the law. Judge Blackstone says that the Game Law was then wantoning in its *highest vigour;* what, then, would he have said, if any one had proposed to make it *felony* to resist a Gamekeeper? He calls it tyranny to the commons, as it existed in his time; what would he have said of the present Code; which so far from being thought a thing to be *softened*, is never so much as mentioned by those humane and gentle creatures, who are absolutely supporting a sort of reputation, and aiming at distinction in Society, in consequence of their incessant talk about softening the Criminal Code?

The law may say what it will, but the feelings of mankind will never be in favour of this Code; and whenever it produces putting to death, it will, necessarily, excite horror. It is impossible to make men believe that any particular set of individuals should have a permanent property in wild creatures. That the owner of land should have a quiet possession of it is reasonable and right and necessary; it is also necessary that he should have the power of inflicting pecuniary punishment, in a moderate degree, upon such as trespass on his lands; but, his right can go no further according to reason. If the law give him ample compensation for every damage that he sustains, in consequence of a trespass on his lands, what right has he to complain?

The law authorises the King, in case of invasion, or apprehended invasion, to call upon all his people to take up arms in defence of the country. The Militia Law compels every man, in his turn, to become a soldier. And upon what ground is this? There must be some reason for it, or else the law would be tyranny. The reason is, that every man has *rights* in the country to which he belongs; and that, therefore, it is his duty to defend the country. Some rights, too, beyond that of merely living, that of merely breathing the air. And then, I should be glad to know, what rights an Englishman has, if the pursuit of even wild animals is to be the ground of transporting him from his country? There is a sufficient punishment provided by the law of trespass; quite sufficient means to keep men off your land altogether! how can it be necessary, then, to have a law to transport them for coming upon your land? No, it is not for coming upon the land, it is for coming after the wild animals, which nature and reason tells them, are as much theirs as they are yours.

It is impossible for the people not to contrast the treatment of these two young men at Winchester with the treatment of some game-keepers that have killed or maimed the persons they call poachers; and it is equally impossible for the people when they see these two men hanging on a gallows, after being recommended to mercy, not to remember the almost instant pardon, given to the exciseman, who was not recommended to mercy, and who was found guilty of wilful murder in the County of Sussex!

It is said, and, I believe truly, that there are more persons imprisoned in England for offences against the game-laws, than there are persons imprisoned in France (with more than twice the population) for all sorts of offences put together. When there was a loud outcry against the cruelties committed on the priests and the seigneurs, by the people of France, Arthur Young bade them remember the cruelties committed on the people by the game-laws, and to bear in mind how many had been made galley-slaves for having killed, or tried to kill, partridges, pheasants, and hares!

However, I am aware that it is quite useless to address observations of this sort to you. I am quite aware of that; and yet, there are circumstances, in your present situation, which, one would think, ought to make you *not very gay* upon the hanging of the two men at Winchester. It delights me, I assure you, to see the situation that you are in; and I shall, therefore, now, once more, and for the last time, address you upon that subject. We all remember how haughty, how insolent you have been. We all bear in mind your conduct for the last thirty-five years; and the feeling of pleasure at your present state is as general as it is just. In my *ten Letters* to you, I told you that you would lose your estates. Those of you who have any capacity, except that which is necessary to enable you to kill wild animals, see this now, as clearly as I do; and yet you evince no intention to change your courses. You hang on with unrelenting grasp; and cry "pauper" and "poacher" and "radical" and "lower orders" with as much insolence as ever! It is always thus: men like you may be convinced of error, but they never change their conduct. They never become just because they are convinced that they have been unjust: they must have a great deal more than that conviction to make them just.[1]

Such was what I *then* addressed to the Landlords. How well it fits the *present* time! They are just in the same sort of *mess*, now, that they were in 1822. But, there is this most important difference, that the paper-money cannot *now* be

---

[1] Although the Game Laws, since the Author's day, have been considerably modified, they are still oppressive, as their very existence is an incentive to poaching. They have, however, been already referred to, in the notes to this work. On the one hand, the Game Laws are severe against poachers, inasmuch as the Justices, who administer them, are generally game-preservers; on the other hand, it is argued that poaching is in reality stealing, and that game is as much the fruit of the soil, as apples or turnips; and that the transition from poaching to stealing is not only easy, but inevitable. The Author, who makes the Game Laws a special point of severe criticism, addressed a letter on the subject, in 1828, to the Duke of Wellington, who was at that time First Minister of the Crown, which has already been noticed in the biography of Cobbett. Notwithstanding, however, the Author's censure of the Game Laws, he himself, while living at Botley, was a strict preserver of game. Although he was no shot, he kept sometimes from thirty to forty dogs, consisting of greyhounds, pointers, setters and spaniels. Moreover, he had a large number of live hares, brought from Berkshire, to turn down on his farms. In the year 1816, he prosecuted a poacher, at Winchester, by suing him as "for a trespass," in the Court of Pie Powder (called also the Court of Dustyfoot), which was an ancient court held in fairs and markets, to administer justice, in a rough-and-ready way, to all comers.

put out, in a quantity sufficient to save them, without producing not only a "*late* panic," worse than the last, but, in all probability, a total blowing up of the whole system, game-laws, new trespass laws, tread-mill, Sunday-tolls, six-acts, sun-set and sun-rise laws, apple-felony laws, select-vestry laws, and all the whole THING, root and trunk and branch! Aye, not sparing, perhaps, even the tent, or booth of induction, at Draycot Foliot! Good Lord! How should we be able to live without game-laws! And tread-mills, then? And Sunday-tolls? How should we get on without pensions, sinecures, tithes, and the other "glorious institutions" of this "mighty *empire?*" Let us turn, however, from the thought; but, bearing this in mind, if you please, Messieurs the game-people; that if, no matter in what shape and under what pretence; if, I tell you, paper be put out again, sufficient to raise the price of a South Down ewe to the last year's mark, the whole system goes to atoms. I tell you that; mind it; and look sharp about you, O ye fat parsons; for tithes and half-pay will, be you assured, never, from that day, again go in company into parson's pocket.

In this North of Hampshire, as every where else, the churches and all other things exhibit indubitable marks of decay. There are along under the North side of that chain of hills, which divide Hampshire from Berkshire, in this part, taking into Hampshire about two or three miles wide of the low ground under the chain, eleven churches in a string, in about fifteen miles, the chancels of which would contain a great many more than all the inhabitants, men, women, and children, sitting at their ease with plenty of room. How should this be otherwise, when, in the parish of Burghclere, one single farmer holds by lease, under Lord Carnarvon, as one farm, the lands that men, now living, can remember to have formed fourteen farms, bringing up, in a respectable way, fourteen families? In some instances these small farm-houses and homesteads are completely gone; in others, the buildings remain, but in a tumble-down state; in others the house is gone, leaving the barn for use as a barn, or as a cattle-shed; in others the out-buildings are gone, and the house, with rotten thatch, broken windows, rotten door-sills, and all threatening to fall, remains as the dwelling of a half-starved, and ragged family of labourers, the grandchildren, perhaps, of the decent family of small farmers, that formerly lived happily in this very house.

This, with few exceptions, is the case all over England; and, if we duly consider the nature and tendency of the hellish system of taxing, of funding, and of paper-money, it must be so. Then, in this very parish of Burghclere, there was, until a few months ago, a famous cock-parson, the "Honourable and Reverend" George Herbert, who had grafted the *parson* upon the *soldier* and the *justice* upon the parson; for, he died, a little while ago, a half-pay officer in the army, rector of two parishes, and chairman of the quarter sessions of the county of Hants!! Mr. HONE gave us, in his memorable "*House that Jack built*," a portrait of the "Clerical Magistrate."[1] Could not he, or somebody else, give us a portrait of the *military* and of the *naval parson?* For, such are to be found all over the kingdom. Wherever I go, I hear of them. And yet, there sits Burdett, and even Sir Bobby of the Borough, and say not a word upon the subject![2] This is the case: the King dismissed Sir Bobby from the half-pay list, scratched his name out, turned him off, stopped his pay. Sir Bobby complained, alleging that the half-pay was a reward for past services. No, no, said the Ministers: it is *a retaining fee* for *future* services. Now, the law is, and

---

[1] "The House that Jack Built" was supposed to be one of the many clever political satires which were published by Mr. William Hone. This pamphlet was an attack upon George IV., and his Ministers, at the time of Queen Caroline coming to England in 1820. No less than twenty-eight editions, and 140,000 copies, were said to have been sold in six weeks.

[2] "Sir Bobby," was General Sir Robert Wilson, who served under Sir Ralph Abercromby in Egypt. He subsequently espoused the cause of Queen Caroline, and was dismissed the army in consequence. His gallant conduct in the matter is frequently the subject of the Author's praise. In 1818 he was returned to Parliament, in the Liberal interest, for Southwark, and retained his seat until 1831.

the Parliament declared, in the case of parson Horne Tooke,[1] that once a parson always a parson, and that a parson cannot, of course, again serve as an officer under the crown. Yet these military and naval parsons have "a retaining fee for future military and naval services!" Never was so barefaced a thing before heard of in the world. And yet there sits Sir Bobby, stripped of his "retaining fee," and says not a word about the matter; and there sit the *big Whigs*, who gave Sir Bobby the subscription, having sons, brothers, and other relations, military and naval parsons, and the *big Whigs* of course, bid Sir Bobby (albeit given enough to twattle) hold his tongue upon the subject; and there sit Mr. Wetherspoon (I think it is), and the rest of Sir Bobby's Rump, toasting "the *independence* of the Borough and its member!"

"That's our case," as the lawyers say: match it if you can, D——, in all your roamings up and down throughout the earth! I have often been thinking, and, indeed, expecting, to see Sir Bobby turn parson himself, as the likeliest way to get back his half-pay. If he should have "a call," I do hope we shall have him for parson at Kensington; and, as an inducement, I promise him, that I will give him a good thumping Easter-offering.

In former RIDES, and especially in 1821 and 1822, I described very fully this part of Hampshire. The land is a chalk bottom, with a bed of reddish, stiff loam, full of flints, at

---

[1] John Horne Tooke was a celebrated etymologist and political adventurer, who, to please his father, and strongly against his own inclination, took holy orders in 1760. But the disgust which he entertained for his profession, led him to indulge in a licence of speech and life, which fatally affected his honesty of character. In 1773 he relinquished his profession, and studied law, but he was never admitted to the Bar. In 1775, he was fined and imprisoned in the King's Bench for publishing a statement accusing the King's troops of having barbarously murdered the Americans at Lexington. In 1790, and again in 1796, he stood as a candidate for Westminster, but was unsuccessful on both occasions. At length, in 1801, this great declaimer against "rotten boroughs" was returned to Parliament for the most rotten borough in England, viz., "Old Sarum," but by a vote it was declared that he could not take his seat because he was in holy orders.

top. In those parts, where the bed of loam and flints is deep, the land is arable or woods: where the bed of loam and flints is so shallow as to let the plough down to the chalk, the surface is downs. In the deep and long valleys, where there is constantly, or occasionally, a stream of water, the top soil is blackish, and the surface meadows. This has been the distribution from all antiquity, except that, in ancient times, part of that which is now downs and woods was *corn-land*, as we know from the *marks of the plough*. And yet the Scotch fellows would persuade us, that there were scarcely any inhabitants in England before it had the unspeakable happiness to be united to that fertile, warm, and hospitable country, where the people are so well off, that they are *above* having poor-rates!

The tops of the hills here, are as good corn-land as any other part; and it is all excellent corn-land, and the fields and woods singularly beautiful. Never was there what may be called a more *hilly* country, and *all in use*. Coming from Burghclere, you come up nearly a mile of steep hill, from the top of which you can see all over the country, even to the Isle of Wight; to your right, a great part of Wiltshire; into Surrey, on your left; and, turning round, you see, lying below you, the whole of Berkshire, great part of Oxfordshire, and part of Gloucestershire. This chain of lofty hills was a great favourite with Kings and rulers in ancient times. At Highclere, at Combe, and at other places, there are remains of great encampments, or fortifications; and, Kingsclere was a residence of the Saxon Kings, and continued to be a royal residence long after the Norman Kings came. KING JOHN, when residing at Kingsclere, founded one of the charities which still exists in the town of Newbury, which is but a few miles from Kingsclere.

From the top of this lofty chain, you come to Uphusband (or the Upper Hurstbourn) over two miles or more of ground, descending in the way that the body of a snake descends (when he is going fast) from the high part, near the head, down to the tail; that is to say, over a series of hill and dell, but the dell part going constantly on increasing upon the hilly part, till you come down to this village; and then you, continuing on (southward) towards Andover, go up, directly, half a mile of hill so steep, as to make it very difficult, for an ordinary team with a load, to take that load up it. So this *Up*-hurstbourn (called so because *higher up the valley* than the other Hurstbourns) the flat part of the road to which, from the north, comes in between two side-hills, is in as narrow and deep a dell, as any place that I ever saw.

The houses of the village are, in great part, scattered about, and are amongst very lofty and fine trees; and, from many, many points round about, from the hilly fields, now covered with the young wheat, or with scarcely less beautiful sainfoin, the village is a sight worth going many miles to see. The lands, too, are pretty beyond description. These chains of hills make, below them, an endless number of lower hills, of varying shapes and sizes and aspects and of relative state as to each other; while the surface presents, in the size and form of the fields, in the woods, the hedge-rows, the sainfoin, the young wheat, the turnips, the tares, the fallows, the sheep-folds and the flocks, and, at every turn of your head, a fresh and different set of these; this surface all together presents that, which I, at any rate, could look at with pleasure for ever. Not a sort of country that I like so well, as when there are *downs*, and a *broader valley*, and *more of meadow;* but, a sort of country that I like next to that; for, here, as there, there are no ditches, no water-furrows, no dirt, and never any drought to cause inconvenience. The chalk is at bottom, and it takes care of all. The crops of wheat have been very good here this year, and those of barley not very bad. The sainfoin has given a fine crop of the finest sort of hay in the world, and, this year, without a drop of wet.

I wish, that, in speaking of this pretty village (which I always return to with additional pleasure), I could give *a good account* of the state of *those, without whose labour, there would be neither corn, nor sainfoin, nor sheep.* I regret to say, that my account of this matter, if I gave it truly, must be a dismal account indeed! For, I have, in no part of England, seen the labouring people so badly off as they are here. This has made so much impression on me, that I shall enter fully into the matter, with names, dates, and all the particulars in the IVth Number of the "POOR MAN'S FRIEND." This is one of the great purposes for which I take these "Rides." I am persuaded, that, before the day shall come when my labours must cease, *I shall have mended the meals of millions.* I may over-rate the effects of my endeavours; but, this being my persuasion, I should be guilty of a great neglect of duty, were I not to use those endeavours.

Andover, Sunday, 15th October.

I went to Weyhill, yesterday, to see the close of the hop and of the cheese fair; for, after the sheep, these are the principal articles. The crop of hops has been, in parts where they are grown, unusually large, and of super-excellent quality. The average price of the Farnham *hops* has been, as nearly as I can ascertain, seven pounds for a hundred weight; that of Kentish hops, five pounds, and that of the Hampshire and Surrey hops (other than those of Farnham), about five pounds also. The prices are, considering the great weight of the crop, very good; but, if it had not been for the effects of "*late panic*" (proceeding, as Baring said, from a "plethora of money,") these prices would have been a full third, if not nearly one half, higher; for, though the crop has been so large and so good, there was hardly any stock on hand; the country was almost wholly without hops.

As to cheese, the price, considering the quantity, has been not one half so high, as it was last year. The fall in the positive price has been about 20 per cent., and the quantity made in 1826 has not been above two-thirds as great as that made in 1825. So that, here is a fall of *one-half* in real relative price; that is to say, the farmer, while he has the same rent to pay that he paid last year, has only half as much money to receive for cheese, as he received for cheese last year; and observe, on some farms, cheese is almost the only saleable produce.

After the fair was over, yesterday, I came down from the Hill (3 miles) to this town of Andover; which has, within the last 20 days, been more talked of, in other parts of the kingdom, than it ever was before from the creation of the world to the beginning of those 20 days. The Thomas Asheton Smiths and the Sir John Pollens, famous as they have been under the banners of the Old Navy Purser, George Rose, and his successors, have never, ever since the death of poor Turner, been half so famous, they and this Corporation, whom they represent, as they have been since the Meeting which they held here, which ended in their defeat and confusion, pointing them out, as worthy of that appellation of "Poor Devils," which Pollen thought proper to give to those labourers, without whose toil, his estate would not be worth a single farthing.

Having laid my plan to sleep at Andover last night, I went with two Farnham friends, Messrs. Knowles and West, to dine at the ordinary at the George Inn, which is kept by one Sutton, a rich old fellow, who wore a round-skirted sleeved fustian waistcoat, with a dirty white apron tied round his middle, and with no coat on; having a look the *eagerest* and the *sharpest*, that I ever saw in any set of features, in my whole life-time; having an air of authority and of mastership, which, to a stranger, as I was, seemed quite incompatible with the meanness of his dress and the vulgarity of his manners: and there being, visible to every beholder, constantly going on in him, a pretty even contest between the servility of avarice, and the insolence of wealth. A great part of the farmers, and other fair-people having gone off home, we found preparations made for dining only about ten people. But, after we sat down, and it was seen that we designed to dine, guests came in apace, the preparations were augmented, and as many as could dine, came and dined with us.

After the dinner was over, the room became fuller and fuller; guests came in from the other inns, where they had been dining, till, at last, the room became as full as possible in every part, the door being opened, the door-way blocked

up, and the stairs, leading to the room, crammed from bottom
to top. In this state of things, Mr. Knowles, who was our
chairman, gave *my health*, which, of course, was followed by
a *speech;* and, as the reader will readily suppose, to have an
opportunity of making a speech was the main motive for my
going to dine at *an inn*, at any hour, and especially at *seven
o'clock* at night. In this speech, I, after descanting on the
present devastating ruin, and on those successive acts of the
Ministers and the parliament by which such ruin had been
produced; after remarking on the shuffling, the tricks, the
contrivances from 1797 up to last March, I proceeded to offer
to the company *my reasons* for believing, that no attempt would
be made to relieve the farmers and others, by putting out the
paper-money again, as in 1822, or by a bank-restriction. Just
as I was stating these my reasons, on a prospective matter
of such deep interest to my hearers, amongst whom were
land-owners, land-renters, cattle and sheep dealers, hop and
cheese producers and merchants, and even one, two or more,
country bankers; just as I was engaged in stating *my reasons*
for my opinion on a matter of such vital importance to the
parties present, who were all listening to me with the greatest
attention; just at this time, a noise was heard, and a sort of
row was taking place in the passage, the cause of which was,
upon inquiry, found to be no less a personage than our landlord, our host Sutton, who, it appeared, finding that my
speech-making had cut off, or, at least, suspended, all inter-
course between the dining, now become a drinking, room
and the *bar;* who, finding that I had been the cause of a
great "restriction in the exchange" of our money for his
"neat" "genuine" commodities down stairs, and being,
apparently, an ardent admirer of the "liberal" system of
"free trade"; who, finding, in short, or, rather, supposing,
that, if my tongue were not stopped from running, his taps
would be, had, though an old man, fought, or, at least,
forced his way up the thronged stairs and through the passage
and door-way, into the room, and was (with what breath the
struggle had left him) beginning to bawl out to me, when

some one called to him, and told him that he was causing
an interruption, to which he answered, that that was what
he had come to do! And then he went on to say, in so
many words, that my speech injured his sale of liquor!
 The disgust and abhorrence, which such conduct could not
fail to excite, produced, at first, a desire to quit the room and
the house, and even a proposition to that effect. But, after a
minute or so, to reflect, the company resolved not to quit the
room, but to turn him out of it, who had caused the interruption; and the old fellow, finding himself *tackled*, saved the
labour of shoving, or kicking, him out of the room, by retreat-
ing out of the door-way, with all the activity of which he was
master. After this, I proceeded with my speech-making; and,
this being ended, the great business of the evening, namely,
drinking, smoking, and singing, was about to be proceeded in,
by a company, who had just closed an arduous and anxious
week, who had before them a Sunday morning to sleep in,
and whose wives were, for the far greater part, at a convenient
distance. An assemblage of circumstances, more auspicious
to "free-trade" in the "neat" and "genuine," has seldom
occurred! But, now behold, the old fustian-jacketed fellow,
whose head was, I think, *powdered*, took it into that head, not
only to lay "restrictions" upon trade, but to impose an absolute embargo; cut off entirely all supplies whatever from his
bar to the room, *as long as I remained in that room*. A
message to this effect, from the old fustian man, having been,
through the waiter, communicated to Mr. Knowles, and he
having communicated it to the company, I addressed the
company in nearly these words: "Gentlemen, born and
"bred, as you know I was, on the borders of this county, and
"fond, as I am of bacon, *Hampshire hogs* have, with me,
"always been objects of admiration rather than of contempt;
"but that which has just happened here, induces me to ob-
"serve, that this feeling of mine has been confined to hogs of
"*four legs*. For my part, I like your company too well to
"quit it. I have paid this fellow *six shillings* for the wing of
"a fowl, a bit of bread, and a pint of small beer. I have a

"right to sit here; I want no drink, and those who do, being "refused it here, have a right to send to other houses for it, "and to drink it here."

However, Mammon soon got the upper hand down stairs, all the fondness for "free trade" returned, and up came the old fustian-jacketed fellow, bringing pipes, tobacco, wine, grog, sling, and seeming to be as pleased as if he had just sprung a mine of gold! Nay, he, soon after this, came into the room with two gentlemen, who had come to him to ask where I was. He actually came up to me, making me a bow, and, telling me that those gentlemen wished to be introduced to me, he, with a fawning look, laid his hand upon my knee! "Take away your *paw*," said I, and, shaking the gentlemen by the hand, I said, "I am happy to see you, gentlemen, "even though introduced by this fellow." Things now proceeded without interruption; songs, toasts, and speeches filled up the time, until half-past two o'clock this morning, though in the house of a landlord who receives the sacrament, but who, from his manifestly ardent attachment to the "liberal principles" of "free trade," would, I have no doubt, have suffered us, if we could have found money and throats and stomachs, to sit and sing and talk and drink until two o'clock of a Sunday afternoon instead of two o'clock of a Sunday morning. It was not politics; it was not *personal* dislike to me; for the fellow knew nothing of me. It was, as I told the company, just this: he looked upon their bodies as so many gutters to drain off the contents of his taps, and upon their purses, as so many small heaps from which to take the means of augmenting his great one; and, finding that I had been, no matter how, the cause of suspending this work of "reciprocity," he wanted, and no matter how, to restore the reciprocal system to motion. All that I have to add is this: that the next time this old sharp-looking fellow gets *six shillings* from me, for a dinner, he shall, if he choose, *cook me*, in any manner that he likes, and season me with hand so unsparing as to produce in the feeders thirst unquenchable.

To-morrow morning we set off for the New Forest; and,

indeed, we have lounged about here long enough. But, as some apology, I have to state, that, while I have been in a sort of waiting upon this great fair, where one hears, sees, and learns so much, I have been writing No. IV. of the "*Poor Man's Friend*," which, price twopence, is published once a month.

I see, in the London newspapers, accounts of *dispatches from Canning!* I thought, that he went solely "on a party of pleasure!" So, the "dispatches" come to tell the King how the pleasure party gets on! No: what he is gone to Paris for, is, to endeavour to prevent the "*Holy* Allies" from doing any thing which shall sink the English Government in the eyes of the world, and *thereby favour the radicals*, who are enemies of *all* "regular Government," and whose success in England would *revive republicanism* in France. This is my opinion. The subject, if I be right in my opinion, was too ticklish to be committed to paper: Granville Levison Gower (for that is the man that is now Lord Granville) was, perhaps, not thought quite a match for the French as *a talker;* and, therefore, the Captain of Eton, who, in 1817, said, that the "ever living luminary of British prosperity was only hidden behind a cloud;" and who, in 1819, said, that "Peel's Bill had set the currency question at rest for ever;" therefore the profound Captain is gone over to see what *he* can do.

But, Captain, a word in your ear: we do not care for the Bourbons any more than we do for you! My real opinion is, that there is nothing that can put England to rights, that will not shake the Bourbon Government. This is my opinion; but I defy the Bourbons to save, or to assist in saving, the present system in England, unless they and their friends will subscribe and pay off your debt for you, Captain of toad-eating and nonsensical and shoe-licking Eton! Let them pay off your debt for you, Captain; let the Bourbons and their allies do that; or they cannot save you; no, nor can they help you, even in the smallest degree.

Romsey (Hampshire),
Monday, Noon, 16th Oct.

Like a very great fool, I, out of senseless complaisance, waited, this morning, to breakfast with the friends, at whose house we slept last night, at Andover. We thus lost two hours of dry weather, and have been justly punished by about an hour's ride in the rain. I settled on Lyndhurst as the place to lodge at to-night; so we are here, feeding our horses, drying our clothes, and writing the account of our journey. We came, as much as possible, all the way through the villages, and, almost all the way, avoided the turnpike-roads. From Andover to Stockbridge (about seven or eight miles) is, for the greater part, an open corn and sheep country, a considerable portion of the lands being downs. The wheat and rye and vetch and sainfoin fields look beautiful here; and, during the whole of the way from Andover to Romsey, the early turnips of both kinds are not bad, and the stubble turnips very promising. The downs are green as meadows usually are in April. The grass is most abundant in all situations, where grass grows. From Stockbridge to Romsey we came nearly by the river side, and had to cross the river several times. This, the River Teste, which, as I described, in my Ride of last November, begins at Uphusband, by springs, bubbling up, in March, out of the bed of that deep valley. It is at first a bourn, that is to say, a stream that runs only a part of the year, and is the rest of the year as dry as a road. About 5 miles from this periodical source, it becomes a stream all the year round. After winding about between the chalk hills, for many miles, first in a general direction towards the south-east, and then in a similar direction towards the south-west and south, it is joined by the little stream that rises just above and that passes through, the town of Andover. It is, after this, joined by several other little streams, with names; and here, at Romsey, it is a large and very fine river, famous, all the way down, for trout and eels, and both of the finest quality.

Lyndhurst (New Forest),
Monday Evening, 16th October.

I have just time, before I go to bed, to observe that we arrived here, about 4 o'clock, over about 10 or 11 miles of the best road in the world, having a choice too, for the great part of the way, between these smooth roads and green sward. Just as we came out of Romsey, and crossed our River Teste once more, we saw to our left, the sort of park, called *Broad-Lands*, where poor Charles Smith, who (as mentioned above) was hanged for *shooting at* (*not killing*) one Snelgrove, an assistant game-keeper of Lord Palmerston, who was then our Secretary at War, and who is in that office, I believe, now, though he is now better known as a Director of the grand Mining Joint-Stock Company, which shows the great *industry* of this Noble and "Right Honourable person," and also the great scope and the various nature and tendency of his talents. What would our old fathers of the "dark ages" have said, if they had been told, that their descendants would, at last, become so enlightened as to enable Jews and loan-jobbers to take away noblemen's estates by mere "watching the turn of the market," and to cause members, or, at least, one Member, of that "most Honourable, Noble, and Reverend Assembly," the King's Privy Council, in which he himself sits: so *enlightened*, I say, as to cause one of this "most Honourable and Reverend body" to become a Director in a mining speculation! How one *pities* our poor, "dark-age, bigoted" ancestors, who would, I dare say, have been as ready to *hang* a man for proposing such a "liberal" system as this, as they would have been to hang him for *shooting at* (not killing) an assistant game-keeper! Poor old fellows! How much they lost by not living in our enlightened times! I am here close by the Old Purser's son George Rose's!

RIDE: FROM LYNDHURST (NEW FOREST) TO BEAULIEU ABBEY; THENCE TO SOUTHAMPTON AND WESTON; THENCE TO BOTLEY, ALLINGTON, WEST END, NEAR HAMBLEDON; AND THENCE TO PETERSFIELD, THURSLEY, GODALMING.

> But where is now the goodly audit ale?
> The purse-proud tenant, never known to fail?
> The farm which never yet was left on hand?
> The marsh reclaim'd to most improving land?
> The impatient hope of the expiring lease?
> The doubling rental? What an evil's peace!
> In vain the prize excites the ploughman's skill,
> In vain the Commons pass their patriot Bill;
> The *Landed Interest*—(you may understand
> The phrase much better leaving out the *Land*)—
> The land self-interest groans from shore to shore,
> For fear that plenty should attain the poor.
> Up, up again, ye rents! exalt your notes,
> Or else the Ministry will lose their votes,
> And patriotism, so delicately nice,
> Her loaves will lower to the market price.
>
> LORD BYRON, *Age of Bronze.*

Weston Grove, Wednesday, 18 *Oct.,* 1826.

Yesterday, from Lyndhurst to this place, was a ride, including our round-abouts, of more than forty miles; but the roads the best in the world, one half of the way green turf; and the day as fine an one as ever came out of the heavens. We took in a breakfast, calculated for a long day's work, and for no more eating till night. We had slept in a room, the access to which was only through another sleeping room, which was also occupied; and, as I had got up about *two o'clock* at Andover, we went to bed, at Lyndhurst, about *half-past seven* o'clock. I was, of course, awake by three or four; I had eaten little over night; so that here lay I, not liking (even after day-light began to glimmer) to go through a chamber, where, by possibility, there might be "a lady" actually *in bed;* here lay I, my bones aching with lying in bed, my stomach growling for victuals, imprisoned by my *modesty*. But, at last, I grew impatient; for, modesty here or modesty there, I was not to be penned up and starved : so, after having shaved and dressed and got ready to go down, I thrusted George out a little before me into the other room; and, through we pushed, previously resolving, of course, not to look towards *the bed* that was there. But, as the devil would have it, just as I was about the middle of the room, I, like Lot's wife, turned my head! All that I shall say is, first, that the consequences that befell her, did not befall me, and, second, that I advise those, who are likely to be hungry in the morning, not to sleep in *inner rooms;* or, if they do, to take some bread and cheese in their pockets. Having got safe down stairs, I lost no time in inquiry after the means of obtaining a breakfast to make up for the bad fare of the previous day; and finding my landlady rather tardy in the work, and not, seemingly, having a proper notion of the affair, I went myself, and, having found a butcher's shop, bought a loin of small, fat, wether mutton, which I saw cut out of the sheep and cut into chops. These were brought to the inn; George and I ate about 2 lb. out of the 5 lb., and, while I was writing a letter, and making up my packet, to be ready to send from Southampton, George went out and found a poor woman to come and take away the rest of the loin of mutton; for, our *fastings* of the day before enabled us to do this; and though we had about forty miles to go, to get to this place (through the route that we intended to take), I had resolved, that we would go without any more *purchase* of victuals and drink this day also. I beg leave to suggest to my *well-fed* readers; I mean, those who have at their command more victuals and drink than they can possibly swallow; I beg to suggest to such, whether this would not be a good way for them all to find the means of bestowing charity? Some poet has said, that that which is given in *charity* gives a blessing on both sides; to the giver as well as the receiver.[1] But, I really think, that, if, *in general*, the food

---

[1] The quotation is from "The Merchant of Venice," act iv., scene 1 :—Portia, addressing the Court, says,

"The quality of mercy is not strain'd;
It droppeth, as the gentle rain from heaven,

and drink given, came out of food and drink *deducted* from the usual quantity swallowed by the giver, the *blessing* would be still greater, and much more certain. I can speak for myself, at any rate. I hardly ever eat more than *twice* a day; when at home, never; and I never, if I can well avoid it, eat any meat later than about one or two o'clock in the day. I drink a little tea, or milk and water, at the usual tea-time (about 7 o'clock); I go to bed at eight, if I can; I write or read, from about four to about eight, and then, hungry as a hunter, I go to breakfast eating *as small a parcel* of cold meat and bread, as I can prevail upon my teeth to be satisfied with. I do just the same at dinner time. I very rarely taste *garden-stuff* of any sort. If any man can show me, that he has done, or can do *more work*, bodily and mentally united; I say nothing about good health, for of that, the public can know nothing; but, I refer to *the work:* the public know, they see, what I can do, and what I actually have done, and what I do; and, when any one has shown the public, that he has done, or can do more, then I will advise my readers attend to him, on the subject of diet, and not to me. As to *drink*, the less the better; and mine is milk and water, or, *not-sour* small beer, if I can get the latter; for the former I always can. I like the milk and water best; but I do not like much water; and, if I drink much milk, it loads, and stupifies, and makes me fat.

Having made all preparations for a day's ride, we set off, as our first point, for a station, in the Forest called New Park, there to see something about *plantations* and other matters connected with the affairs of our prime cocks, the Surveyors of Woods and Forests and Crown Lands and Estates. But, before I go forward any further, I must just step back again to Romsey, which we passed rather too hastily through on the 16th, as noticed in the RIDE that was published last week. This town was, in ancient times, a very grand place, though

---

Upon the place beneath; it is twice bless'd;
It blesseth him that gives, and him that takes."

it is now nothing more than a decent market-town, without any thing to entitle it to particular notice, except its church, which was the church of an Abbey Nunnery (founded more, I think, than a thousand years ago), and which church was the burial place of several of the Saxon Kings, and of Viscountess Palmerston, who, a few years ago (in 1769), "died in child-birth!" What a mixture! But, there was another personage buried here, and who was, it would seem, a native of the place; namely, Sir William Petty, the ancestor of the present Marquis of Lansdowne. He was the son of *a cloth-weaver*, and was, doubtless, himself, a weaver when young. He became a surgeon, was first in the service of Charles I.; then went into that of Cromwell, whom he served as physician-general to his army in Ireland (alas! poor Ireland), and in this capacity, he resided at Dublin till Charles II. came, when he came over to London (having become very rich), was knighted by that profligate and ungrateful King, and he died in 1687, leaving a fortune of 15,000*l.* a year! This is what his biographers say. He must have made pretty good use of his time, while physician-general to Cromwell's army, in poor Ireland! *Petty* by nature, as well as by name, he got, from Cromwell, a "patent for *double-writing*, invented by him;" and he invented a "*double-bottomed ship to sail against wind and tide*, a model "of which is still preserved in the library of the Royal "Society," of which he was a most worthy member. His great art was, however, the amassing of money, and the getting of *grants of lands in poor Ireland*, in which he was one of the most successful of the English adventurers. I had, the other day, occasion to observe, that the word *Petty* manifestly is the French word *Petit*, which means *little;* and that it is, in these days of degeneracy, pleasing to reflect that there is *one family*, at any rate, that "Old England" still boasts one family, which retains the character designated by its pristine name; a reflection that rushed with great force into my mind, when, in the year 1822, I heard the present noble head of the family say, in the House of Lords, that he thought, that a currency of paper, convertible into gold, was the best and most solid and safe, especially since *Platina* had been discovered! "Oh, God!" exclaimed I to myself, as I stood listening and admiring "below the bar;" "Oh, great God! there it is, there it "is, still running in the blood, that genius which discovered "the art of double-writing, and of making ships with double-"bottoms to sail against wind and tide!" This noble and profound descendant of Cromwell's army-physician has now seen, that "paper, convertible into gold," is not quite so "solid and safe" as he thought it was! He has now seen what a "late panic" is! And he might, if he were not so very well worthy of his family name, openly confess, that he was deceived, when, in 1819, he, as one of the Committee, who reported in favour of Peel's Bill, said that the country could pay the interest of the debt in gold! Talk of a *change of Ministry*, indeed! What is to be *gained* by putting this man in the place of any of those who are in power now?

To come back now to Lyndhurst, we had to go about three miles to New Park, which is a *farm* in the New Forest, and nearly in the centre of it. We got to this place about nine o'clock. There is a good and large mansion-house here, in which the "Commissioners" of Woods and Forests reside, when they come into the Forest. There is a garden, a farm-yard, a farm, and a nursery. The place looks like a considerable gentleman's seat; the house stands in a sort of *park*, and you can see that a great deal of expense has been incurred in levelling the ground, and making it pleasing to the eye of my lords "the Commissioners." My business here was to see, whether any thing had been done towards the making of *Locust plantations*. I went first to Lyndhurst to make inquiries, but, I was there told, that New Park was the place, and the only place, at which to get information on the subject; and I was told, further, that the Commissioners were now at New Park; that is to say those experienced tree-planters, Messrs. Arbuthnot, Dawkins, and Company. Gad! thought I, I am here coming in close contact with a branch, or at least, a twig of the great THING itself! When I heard this, I was at breakfast, and, of course, dressed for the day. I could not, out of my extremely limited wardrobe, afford a clean shirt for the occasion; and so, off we set, just as we were, hoping that their worships, the nation's tree-planters, would, if they met with us, excuse our dress, when they considered the nature of our circumstances. When we came to the house, we were stopped by a little fence and fastened gate. I got off my horse, gave him to George to hold, went up to the door, and rang the bell. Having told my business to a person, who appeared to be a foreman, or bailiff, he, with great civility, took me into a nursery which is at the back of the house; and, I soon drew from him the disappointing fact, that my lords, the tree-planters, had departed the day before! I found, as to *Locusts*, that a patch were sowed last spring, which I saw, which are from one foot to four feet high, and very fine and strong, and are, in number, about enough to plant two acres of ground, the plants at four feet apart each way. I found, that, last fall, some few Locusts had been put out into plantations of other trees already made; but that they had *not thriven*, and had been *barked* by the hares! But, a little bunch of these trees (same age), which were planted in the nursery, ought to convince my lords, the tree-planters, that if they were to do what they ought to do, the public would very soon be owners of fine plantations of Locusts, for the use of the navy. And what are the *hares* kept *for* here? *Who* eats them? What *right* have these Commissioners to keep hares here, to eat up the trees? Lord Folkestone killed his hares before he made his plantation of Locusts; and, why not kill the hares in the *people's* forest; for, the *people's* it is, and that these Commissioners ought always to remember. And, then, again, why this farm? What is it *for?* Why, the pretence for it is this: that it is necessary to give the deer *hay*, in winter, because the lopping down of limbs of trees for them to *browse*, (as used to be the practice) is injurious to the growth of timber. That will be a very good reason for having a *hay-farm*, when my lords shall have proved two things; first, that hay in quantity equal to what is raised here, could not be bought for a twentieth part of the money, that this farm and all its trappings cost; and, second, that there ought to be any deer kept! What are these deer *for?* Who are to *eat* them? Are they for the Royal Family? Why, there are more deer bred in Richmond Park alone, to say nothing of Bushy Park, Hyde Park, and Windsor Park; there are more deer bred in Richmond Park alone, than would feed all the branches of the Royal Family and all their households all the year round, if every soul of them ate as hearty as ploughmen, and if they never touched a morsel of any kind of meat but venison! For what, and *for whom*, then, are deer kept, in the New Forest; and why an expense of hay-farm, of sheds, of racks, of keepers, of lodges, and other things attending the deer and the game; an expense, amounting to more money annually than would have given relief to all the starving manufactures in the North! And, again I say, *who* is all this venison and game *for?* There is more game even in Kew Gardens than the Royal Family can want! And, in short, do they ever taste, or even hear of, any game, or any venison, from the New Forest?

What a pretty thing here is, then! Here is another deep bite into us by the long and sharp-fanged Aristocracy, who so love Old Sarum! Is there a man who will say that this is right? And that the game should be kept, too, to eat up trees, to destroy plantations, to destroy what is first paid for the planting of! And that the public should pay keepers to preserve this game! And that the *people* should be *transported* if they go out by night, to catch the game that they pay for feeding! Blessed state of an Aristocracy! It is pity that it has got a nasty, ugly, obstinate DEBT to deal with! It might possibly go on for ages, deer and all, were it not for this DEBT. This New Forest is a piece of property, as much belonging *to the public* as the Custom-House at London is. There is no man, however poor, who has not a right in it. Every man is owner of a part of the deer, the game, and of the money that goes to the keepers; and yet, any man may be *transported*, if he go out by night, to catch any part of this game! We are compelled to pay keepers for preserving game, to eat up the trees, that we are compelled to pay people to plant! Still however there is comfort; we *might* be worse off; for the Turks made the Tartars pay a tax called *tooth-money;* that is to say, they eat up the victuals of the Tartars, and then made them pay for the *use of their teeth*. No man can say that we are come quite to that yet: and, besides, the poor Tartars had no DEBT, no blessed Debt to hold out hope to them.

The same person (a very civil and intelligent man) that showed me the nursery, took me, in my way, back, through some plantations of *oaks*, which have been made amongst fir-trees. It was, indeed, a plantation of Scotch firs, about twelve years old, in rows, at six feet apart. Every third row of firs was left, and oaks were (about six years ago) planted instead of the firs that were grubbed up; and the winter shelter, that the oaks have received from the remaining firs, has made them grow very finely, though the land is poor. Other oaks planted in the *open*, *twenty years* ago, and in land deemed better, are not nearly so good. However, these oaks, between the firs, will take fifty or sixty good years to make them timber, and, until they be *timber*, they are of very little use; whereas, the same ground, planted with Locusts (and the *hares* of "my lords" kept down), would, at this moment, have been worth fifty pounds an acre. What do "my lords" care about this? *For them*, for "my lords," the New Forest would be no better than it is now; no, nor *so good*, as it is now; for there would be no hares for them.

From New Park, I was bound to Beaulieu Abbey, and I ought to have gone in a south-easterly direction, instead of going back to Lyndhurst, which lay in precisely the opposite direction. My guide through the plantations was not apprised of my intended route, and, therefore, did not instruct me. Just before we parted, he asked me *my name:* I thought it lucky that he had not asked it before! When we got nearly back to Lyndhurst, we found that we had come three miles out of our way; indeed, it made six miles altogether; for, we were, when we got to Lyndhurst, three miles further from Beaulieu Abbey than we were when we were at New Park. We wanted, very much, to go to the site of this ancient and famous Abbey, of which the people of the New Forest seemed to know very little. They call the place *Bewley*, and even in the maps, it is called *Bauley*. *Ley*, in the Saxon language, means *place*, or rather, *open place;* so that they put *ley* in place of *lieu*, thus beating the Normans out of some part of the name at any rate. I wished, besides, to see a good deal of this New Forest. I had been, before, from Southampton to Lyndhurst, from Lyndhurst to Lymington, from Lymington to Sway, I had now come in on the north of Minstead from Romsey, so that I had seen the north of the Forest and all the west side of it, down to the sea. I had now been to New Park and had got back to Lyndhurst; so that, if I rode across the Forest down to Beaulieu, I went right across the middle of it, from north-west to south-east. Then, if I turned towards Southampton, and went to Dipten, and on to Eling, I should see, in fact, the whole of this Forest, or nearly the whole of it.

We therefore started, or, rather, turned away from Lyndhurst, as soon as we got back to it, and went about six miles over a heath, even worse than Bagshot-Heath; as barren as it is possible for land to be. A little before we came to the village of Beaulieu (which, observe, the people call *Beusley*), we went through a wood, chiefly of beech, and that beech seemingly destined to grow food for pigs, of which we saw, during this day, many, many thousand. I should think that we saw at least a hundred hogs, to one deer. I stopped, at one time, and counted the hogs and pigs just round about me, and they amounted to 140, all within 50 or 60 yards of my horse. After a very pleasant ride, on land without a stone in it, we came down to the Beaulieu river, the highest branch of which rises at the foot of a hill, about a mile and a half to the north-east of Lyndhurst. For a great part of the way down to Beaulieu, it is a very insignificant stream. At last, however, augmented by springs from the different sand-hills, it becomes a little river, and has, on the sides of it, lands which were, formerly, very beautiful meadows. When it comes to the village of Beaulieu, it forms a large pond of a great many acres; and on the east side of this pond is the spot, where this famous Abbey formerly stood, and where the external walls of which, or a large part of them, are now actually standing. We went down on the western side of the river. The Abbey stood, and the ruins stand, on the eastern side.

Happening to meet a man, before I got into the village, I, pointing with my whip, across towards the Abbey, said to the man, "I suppose there is a bridge down here, to get across "to the Abbey." "That's not the Abbey, Sir," says he: "the "Abbey is about four miles further on." I was astonished to hear this; but he was very positive; said that some people, called it the Abbey; but that the Abbey was further on; and was at a farm occupied by farmer John Biel. Having chapter and verse for it, as the saying is, I believed the man; and pushed on towards farmer John Biel's, which I found, as he had told me, at the end of about four miles. When I got there (not having, observe, gone over the water to ascertain that the other was the spot where the Abbey stood) I really thought, at first, that this must have been the site of the Abbey of Beaulieu; because, the name meaning *fine place*, this was a thousand times finer place than that where the Abbey, as I afterwards found, really stood. After looking about it for some time, I was satisfied that it had not been an Abbey; but the place is one of the finest, that ever was seen in this world. It stands at about half a mile's distance from the water's edge at high-water mark, and at about the middle of the space along the coast, from Calshot castle, to Lymington haven. It stands, of course, upon a rising ground; it has a gentle slope down to the water. To the right, you see Hurst castle, and that narrow passage called the Needles, I believe; and, to the left, you see Spithead, and all the ships that are sailing, or lie anywhere opposite Portsmouth. The Isle of Wight is right before you, and you have in view, at one, and the same time, the towns of Yarmouth, Newtown,

Cowes and Newport, with all the beautiful fields of the island, lying upon the side of a great bank before, and going up the ridge of hills in the middle of the island. Here are two little streams, nearly close to the ruin, which filled ponds for fresh-water fish; while there was the Beaulieu river, at about half a mile or three quarters of a mile to the left, to bring up the salt-water fish. The ruins consist of part of the walls of a building about 200 feet long, and about 40 feet wide. It has been turned into a barn, in part, and the rest into cattle-sheds, cow-pens, and inclosures and walls to inclose a small yard. But there is another ruin, which was a church or chapel, and which stands now very near to the farm-house of Mr. John Biel, who rents the farm of the Duchess of Buccleugh, who is now the owner of the abbey-lands and of the lands belonging to this place. The little church or chapel, of which I have just been speaking, appears to have been a very beautiful building. A part only of its walls are standing; but you see, by what remains of the arches, that it was finished in a manner the most elegant and expensive of the day in which it was built. Part of the outside of the building is now surrounded by the farmer's garden; the interior is partly a pig-stye, and partly a goose-pen. Under that arch which had once seen so many rich men bow their heads, we entered into the goose-pen, which is by no means one of the *nicest* concerns in the world. Beyond the goose-pen was the pig-stye, and in it a hog, which, when fat, will weigh about 30 score, actually rubbing his shoulders, against a little sort of column which had supported the font and its holy water. The farmer told us that there was a hole, which, indeed, we saw, going down into the wall, or rather, into the column where the font had stood. And he told us that many attempts had been made to bring water to fill that hole, but that it never had been done.

Mr. Biel was very civil to us. As far as related to us, he performed the office of hospitality, which was the main business of those who formerly inhabited the spot. He asked us to dine with him, which we declined, for want of time; but being exceedingly hungry, we had some bread and cheese and some very good beer. The farmer told me that a great number of gentlemen, had come there to look at that place; but that he never could find out what the place had been, or what the place at Beuley had been. I told him that I would, when I got to London, give him an account of it; that I would write the account down, and send it down to him. He seemed surprised that I should make such a promise, and expressed his wish not to give me so much trouble. I told him not to say a word about the matter, for that his bread and cheese and beer were so good that they deserved a full history, to be written of the place, where they had been eaten and drunk. "God bless me, Sir, no, no!" I said, I will, upon my soul, farmer. I now left him, very grateful on our part for his hospitable reception, and he, I dare say, hardly being able to believe his own ears, at the generous promise that I had made him, which promise, however, I am now about to about to fulfil. I told the farmer a little, upon the spot, to begin with. I told him that the name was all wrong: that it was not *Beuley* but *Beaulieu;* and that Beaulieu meant *fine place;* and I proved this to him, in this manner. You know, said I, farmer, that when a girl has a sweet-heart, people call him her *beau?* Yes, said he, so they do. Very well. You know, also, that we say, sometimes, you shall have this in *lieu* of that; and that when we say *lieu,* we mean in *place* of that. Now the *beau* means *fine,* as applied to the young man, and the *lieu* means *place;* and thus it is, that the name of this place is *Beaulieu,* as it is so fine as you see it is. He seemed to be wonderfully pleased with the discovery; and we parted, I believe, with hearty good wishes on his part, and, I am sure, with very sincere thanks on my part.

The Abbey of Beaulieu was founded in the year 1204, by King John, for thirty monks of the reformed Benedictine Order. It was dedicated to the Blessed Virgin Mary; it flourished until the year 1540, when it was suppressed, and the lands confiscated, in the reign of Henry VIII. Its revenues were, at that time, *four hundred and twenty-eight pounds, six shillings and eight pence a year,* making in money of the present day, upwards of *eight thousand five hundred pounds* a year. The lands and the abbey, and all belonging to it, were granted by the king, to one Thomas Wriothesley, who was a court-pander of that day. From him it passed by sale, by will, by marriage or by something or another, till, at last, it has got, after passing through various hands, into the hands of the Duchess of Buccleugh. So much for the abbey; and now, as for the ruins on the farm of Mr. John Biel: they were the dwelling-place of Knights' Templars, or Knights of St. John of Jerusalem. The building they inhabited was called an Hospital, and their business was, to relieve travellers, strangers, and persons in distress: and, if called upon, to accompany the king in his wars to uphold christianity. Their estate was also confiscated by Henry VIII. It was worth at the time of being confiscated, upwards of *two thousand pounds a year*, money of the present day. This establishment was founded a little before the Abbey of Beaulieu was founded; and it was this foundation, and not the other, that gave the name of Beaulieu to both establishments. The Abbey is not situated in a very fine place. The situation is low; the lands above it rather a swamp than otherwise; pretty enough, altogether; but, by no means a fine place. The Templars had all the reason in the world to give the name of Beaulieu to their place. And it is by no means surprising, that the monks were willing to apply it to their Abbey.

Now, farmer John Biel, I dare say, that you are a very good Protestant; and I am a monstrous good Protestant too. We cannot bear the Pope, nor "they their priests that make "men confess their sins and go down upon their marrow- "bones before them." But, Master Biel, let us give the devil his due: and, let us not act worse by those Roman Catholics (who, by-the-bye, were our forefathers) than we are willing to act by the d—— himself. Now, then, here were a set of monks, and also, a set of Knights' Templars. Neither of them could marry; of course, neither of them could have wives and families. They could possess no private property;

they could bequeath nothing; they could own nothing; but
that which they owned in common with the rest of their
body. They could hoard no money; they could save nothing. Whatever they received, as rent for their lands, they
must necessarily spend upon the spot, for, they never could
quit that spot. They did spend it all upon the spot; they
kept all the poor; Beuley, and all round about Beuley, saw
no misery, and had never heard the d—— name of pauper
pronounced, as long as those monks and Templars continued!
You and I are excellent Protestants, farmer John Biel; you
and I have often assisted on the 5th of November to burn
Guy Fawkes, the Pope and the Devil. But, you and I,
farmer John Biel, would much rather be life holders under
monks and Templars, than rack-renters under Duchesses.
The monks and the knights were the *lords* of their manors;
but, the farmers under them were not rack-renters; the
farmers under them held by lease of lives, continued in the
same farms from father to son for hundreds of years; they
were real yeomen, and not miserable rack-renters, such as
now till the land of this once happy country, and who are
little better than the drivers of the labourers, for the profit of
the landlords. Farmer John Biel, what the Duchess of
Buccleugh does, you know, and I do not. She may, for
any thing that I know to the contrary, lease her farms on
lease of lives, with rent so very moderate and easy, as for
the farm, to be half as good, as the farmer's own, at any rate.
The Duchess may, for any thing that I know to the contrary,
feed all the hungry, clothe all the naked, comfort all the
sick, and prevent the hated name of *pauper* from being pronounced in the district of Beuley; her Grace may, for any
thing that I know to the contrary, make poor-rates to be
wholly unnecessary and unknown in your country; she may
receive, lodge, and feed, the stranger; she may, in short,
employ the rents of this fine estate of Beuley, to make the
whole district happy; she may not carry a farthing of the
rents away from the spot; and she may consume, by herself,
and her own family and servants, only just as much as is

necessary to the preservation of their life and health. Her Grace may do all this; I do not say or insinuate that she does not do it all; but, Protestant here or Protestant there, farmer John Biel, this I do say, that unless her Grace do all this, the monks and the Templars, were better for Beuley, than her Grace.

From the former station of the Templars, from real Beaulieu of the New Forest, we came back to the village of Beaulieu, and there crossed the water to come on towards Southampton. Here we passed close along under the old abbey walls, a great part of which are still standing. There is a mill here which appears to be turned by the fresh water, but, the fresh water falls, here, into the salt water, as at the village of Botley. We did not stop to go about the ruins of the abbey; for you seldom make much out, by minute inquiry. It is the political history of these places; or, at least, their connexion with political events, that is interesting. Just about the banks of this little river, there are some woods and coppices, and some corn-land; but, at the distance of half a mile from the water-side, we came out again upon the intolerable heath, and went on for seven or eight miles over that heath, from the village of Beaulieu to that of Marchwood. Having a list of trees and inclosed lands away to our right all the way along, which list of trees extends from the south-west side of that arm of the sea, which goes from Calshot castle to Redbridge, passing by Southampton, which lies on the north-east side. Never was a more barren tract of land than these seven or eight miles. We had come seven miles across the forest in another direction in the morning; so that a poorer spot than this New Forest, there is not in all England; nor, I believe in the whole world. It is more barren and miserable than Bagshot heath. There are less fertile spots in it, in proportion to the extent of each. Still, it is so large, it is of such great extent, being, if moulded into a circle, not so little, I believe, as 60 or 70 miles in circumference, that it must contain some good spots of land, and, if properly and honestly managed, those spots must produce a prodigious quantity of timber. It is a pretty curious thing, that, while the admirers of the paper-system are boasting of our "*waust improvements Ma'am,*" there should have been such a visible, and such an enormous dilapidation in all the solid things of the country. I have, in former parts of this ride, stated, that, in some counties, while the parsons have been pocketing the amount of the tithes and of the glebe, they have suffered the parsonage-houses either to fall down and to be lost, brick by brick, and stone by stone, or to become such miserable places as to be unfit, for any thing bearing the name of a gentleman to live in; I have stated, and I am at any time ready to prove, that, in some counties, this is the case, in more than one half of the parishes!

And, now, amidst all these "waust improvements," let us see how the account of timber, stands in the New Forest! In the year 1608, a survey of the timber, in the New Forest, was made, when there were loads of oak timber fit for the navy, 315,477. Mark that, reader. Another survey was taken in the year 1783; that is to say, in the glorious Jubilee reign. And, when there were, in this same New Forest, loads of oak timber fit for the navy, 20,830. "Waust improvements, Ma'am," under "the Pilot that weathered the storm," and in the reign of Jubilee! What the d——, some one would say, could have become of all this timber? Does the reader observe, that there were three hundred and fifteen thousand, four hundred and seventy-seven *loads?* and does he observe that a load is *fifty-two cubic feet?* Does the reader know, what is the price of this load of timber? I suppose it is now, taking in lop, top and bark, and bought upon the spot, (timber fit for the navy, mind!) ten pounds a load at the least. But, let us suppose, that it has been, upon an average, since the year 1608, just the time that the Stuarts were mounting the throne; let us suppose, that it has been, on an average, four pounds a load. Here is a pretty tough sum of money. This must have gone into the pockets of somebody. At any rate, if we had the same quantity of timber now, that we had when the Protestant Reformation took place, or even when Old Betsy turned up her toes, we should be now three millions of money richer than we are; not in *bills;* not in notes payable to bearer on demand; not in Scotch "cash credits;" not, in short, in lies, falseness, impudence, downright blackguard cheatery and mining shares and "Greek cause" and the d—— knows what.

I shall have occasion to return to this New Forest, which is, in reality, though, in general, a very barren district, a much more interesting object to Englishmen than are the services of my Lord Palmerston, and the warlike undertakings of Burdett, Galloway and Company; but, I cannot quit this spot, even for the present, without asking the Scotch population-mongers, and Malthus and his crew, and especially George Chalmers, if he should yet be creeping about upon the face of the earth, what becomes of all their notions of the scantiness of the ancient population of England; what becomes of all these notions, of all their bundles of ridiculous lies, about the fewness of the people in former times; what becomes of them all, if historians have told us one word of truth, with regard to the formation of the New Forest, by William the Conqueror. All the historians say, every one of them says, that this King destroyed several populous towns and villages in order to make this New Forest.[1]

---

[1] Some historians assert the fact—which, however, has been doubted by others—that the Conqueror, for the purpose of gratifying his love for the chase, destroyed thirty-six churches and a great number of villages, hamlets, and scattered dwellings, and laid waste upwards of 60,000 acres of land which constitute the present site of the New Forest. It now comprises 66,000 acres of crown land and about 28,000 acres of freehold land. An Act was passed (9 William III.), to enclose 6000 acres as a nursery for timber. These 6000 nursery acres are not all in one spot, but are scattered over the Forest. Deer abound in the Forest, and are often captured by poachers, who bait a hook with an apple and hang it to the bough of a tree. Charles I. introduced a breed of the wild boar from Germany. A few cross-breds still remain in a wild state. Their colour is dark brindled, or black; their ears are short, firm, and erect, and there is a fiery glare in their eyes. Many droves of ponies, almost wild, are also to be seen. They are supposed to be descended from the Spanish jennets, which

RIDE: FROM WESTON, NEAR SOUTHAMPTON, TO
KENSINGTON.

Western Grove, 18*th Oct.* 1826.

I broke off abruptly, under this same date, in my last Register, when speaking of William the Conqueror's demolishing of towns and villages to make the New Forest; and, I was about to show, that all the historians have told us lies the most abominable about this affair of the New Forest; or, that the Scotch writers on population, and particularly Chalmers, have been the greatest of fools, or the most impudent of impostors. I, therefore, now resume this matter, it being, in my opinion, a matter of great interest, at a time, when, in order to account for the present notoriously *bad living* of the people of England, it is asserted, that they are become greatly more numerous than they formerly were. This would be no defence of the Government, even if the fact were so; but, as I have over and over again, proved, the fact is false; and, to this I challenge denial, that, either churches, and great mansions, and castles, were formerly made, without hands; or, England was, seven hundred years ago, much more populous than it is now. But, what has the formation of the New Forest to do with this? A great deal; for the historians tell us, that, in order to make this Forest, William the Conqueror destroyed "many populous towns and vil-"lages, and thirty-six parish churches!" The d—— he did! How *populous*, then, must England have been at that time, which was about the year 1090; that is to say, 736 years ago! For, the Scotch will hardly contend, that the *nature of the soil* has been changed for the worse, since that time, especially as it has not been cultivated. No, no; *brassey* as they are,

---

escaped from the vessels comprising the Spanish Armada, sunk off the the coast in 1588. There are a great number of cabins of the rudest construction, inhabited by woodmen and charcoal-burners, many of whom, it it said, supplement their livelihood by poaching.

they will not do that. Come, then, let us see how this matter stands.

This forest has been crawled upon, by favourites, and is now much smaller than it used to be. A time may, and *will* come, for inquiring HOW George Rose, and others, became *owners* of some of the very best parts of this once-public property; a time for such inquiry *must* come, before the people of England will ever give their consent to *a reduction of the interest of the debt!* But this we know that the New Forest formerly extended, westward, from the Southampton Water and the River Oux, to the River Avon, and northward, from Lymington Haven to the borders of Wiltshire. We know, that this was its utmost extent; and we know, also, that the towns of Christchurch, Lymington, Ringwood, and Fordingbridge, and the villages of Bolder, Fawley, Lyndhurst, Dipden, Eling, Minsted, and all the other villages that now have churches; we know, I say (and, pray mark it), that all these towns, and villages, existed before the Norman Conquest: because the *Roman names* of several of them (all the towns) are in print, and because an account of them all, is to be found in *Domesday Book*, which was made, by this very William the Conqueror. Well, then, now Scotch population-liars, and you Malthusian blasphemers, who contend that God has implanted in man a *principle*, that *leads him to starvation;* come, now, and face this history of the New Forest. Cooke, in his geography of Hampshire, says, that the Conqueror destroyed here "many populous towns and villages " and thirty-six parish churches." The same writer says, that, in the time of Edward the Confessor (*just* before the Conqueror came), "two-thirds of the Forest was inhabited and " cultivated." Guthrie says nearly the same thing. But, let us hear the two historians, who are now pitted against each other, Hume and Lingard. The former (vol. II. p. 277) says " There was one pleasure to which William, as well as all " the Normans, and ancient Saxons, was extremely addicted, " and that was hunting; but this pleasure he indulged more " at the expense of his unhappy subjects, whose interests he "always disregarded, than to the loss or diminution of his "own revenue. Not content with those large forests, which "former Kings possessed, in all parts of England, he resolved "to make a new Forest, near Winchester, the usual place "of his residence: and, for that purpose he *laid waste* "the county of Hampshire, *for an extent of thirty miles, ex-* "*pelled the inhabitants* from their houses, seized their pro- "perty, even *demolished churches and convents*, and made the "sufferers no compensation for the injury." Pretty well for a pensioned Scotchman: and, now let us hear Dr. Lingard, to prevent his Society from *presenting whose work to me*, the sincere and pious Samuel Butler was ready to go down upon his *marrow bones;* let us hear the good Doctor upon this subject. He says (vol. I. p. 452 and 453), "Though the "King possessed sixty-eight forests, besides parks and "chases, in different parts of England, he was not yet satis- "fied, but for the occasional accommodation of his court, "afforested an *extensive tract of country* lying between the "city of Winchester and the sea coast. The *inhabitants were* "*expelled:* the cottages and the *churches were burnt:* and "more than *thirty square miles*, of a *rich and populous* district "were *withdrawn from cultivation* and converted into a *wil-* "*derness*, to afford sufficient range for the deer, and ample "space for the royal diversion. The memory of this act of "despotism, has been perpetuated in the name of the New "Forest, which it retains at the present day, after the lapse "of seven hundred and fifty years."

"*Historians*" should be careful how they make statements relative to *places*, which are within the scope of the reader's *inspection*. It is next to impossible not to believe, that the Doctor has, in this case (a very interesting one), merely *copied* from HUME. Hume says, that the King "*expelled* the in- "habitants;" and Lingard says "the inhabitants were *ex-* "*pelled:*" Hume says, that the King "*demolished* the "churches;" and Lingard says that "the churches were "*burnt;*" but, Hume says, churches "and *convents*," and Lingard *knew* that to be a lie. The Doctor was too learned upon the subject of "*convents*," to follow the Scotchman here. Hume says, that the King laid "*waste* the country "for an *extent of thirty miles.*" The Doctor says, "that a "district of *thirty square miles* was withdrawn from cultiva- "tion, and converted into a *wilderness.*" Now, what HUME meaned by the loose phrase, "an *extent* of *thirty miles*," I cannot say; but this I know, that Dr. Lingard's "thirty "square miles," is a piece of ground only five and a half miles each way! So that the Doctor has got here a curious "*dis- "trict*," and a not less curious "*wilderness;*" and, what number of *churches* could WILLIAM find to *burn* in a space five miles and a half each way? If the doctor meaned thirty *miles square*, instead of *square miles*, the falsehood is so monstrous as to destroy his credit for ever; for here we have Nine Hundred Square Miles, containing *five hundred and seventy-six thousand acres of land;* that is to say, 56,960 acres more than are contained in the whole of the county of Surrey, and 99,840 acres more than are contained in the whole of the county of Berks! This is "*history*," is it! And these are "*historians.*"

The true statement is this: the New Forest, according to its ancient state, was bounded thus: by the line, going from the River Oux, to the River Avon, and which line there separates Wiltshire from Hampshire; by the river Avon; by the sea from Christchurch to Calshot Castle: by the Southampton Water; and by the River Oux. These are the boundaries; and (as any one may, by scale and compass, ascertain), there are, within these boundaries, about 224 square miles, containing 143,360 acres of land. Within these limits there are now remaining eleven parish churches, all of which were in existence before the time of William the Conqueror; so that if he destroyed thirty-six parish churches, what a populous country this must have been! There must have been forty-seven parish churches; so that there was, over this whole district, one parish church to every four and three quarters square miles! Thus, then, the churches must have stood, on an average, at within one mile and about two hundred yards of each other! And observe, the parishes could, on an average, contain no more, each, than 2,966 acres of land! Not a very large farm; so that here was a parish church to every large farm, unless these historians are all fools and liars.

I defy any one to say that I make hazardous assertions: I have plainly described the ancient boundaries: there are *the maps:* any one can, with scale and compass, measure the area as well as I can. I have taken the statements of historians, as they call themselves: I have shown that their histories, as they call them, are fabulous; OR (and mind this *or*) that England was, at one time, and that too, eight hundred years ago, *beyond all measure, more populous than it is now.* For, observe, notwithstanding what Dr. Lingard asserts; notwithstanding that he describes this district as "*rich*," it is the very poorest in the whole kingdom. Dr. Lingard was, I believe, born and bred at Winchester; and how, then, could he be so careless; or, indeed, so regardless of truth (and I do not see why I am to mince the matter with him), as to describe this as a *rich district?* Innumerable persons have seen *Bagshot-Heath;* great numbers have seen the barren heaths between London and Brighton; great numbers, also, have seen that wide sweep of barrenness which exhibits itself between the Golden Farmer Hill, and Black-water. Nine-tenths of each of these are less barren than four-fifths of the land in the New Forest. Supposing it to be credible, that a man so prudent and so wise as William the Conqueror; supposing that such a man should have pitched upon a *rich* and *populous* district, wherewith to make a chase; supposing, in short, these historians to have spoken the truth, and supposing this barren land to have been all inhabited and cultivated, and the people so numerous and so rich, as to be able to build and endow a parish church, upon every four and three quarters square miles upon this extensive district; supposing them to have been so rich in the produce of the soil as to want a priest to be stationed at every mile, and 200 yards, in order to help them to eat it; supposing, in a word, these historians not to be the most farcical liars that ever put pen upon paper, this country must, at the time of the Norman conquest, have literally *swarmed* with people; for, *there is the land now*, and all the land, too: neither Hume nor Dr. Lingard can change the nature of that. There it is, an acre of it not having, upon an average, so much of productive capacity in it as one single square rod, taking the average, of Worcestershire; and, if I were to say, one single *square yard*, I should be right; there is the land; and if that land were, as these historians say it was, covered with people and with churches, what the d—— must Worcestershire have been! To this, then, we come at last: having made out, what I undertook to show; namely, that the historians, as they call themselves, are either the greatest fools or the greatest liars that ever existed, or that England was beyond all measure, more populous eight hundred years ago than it is now.[1]

Poor, however, as this district is, and culled about as it has been, for the best spots of land, by those favourites who have got grants of land, or leases, or something or other, still there are some spots, here and there, which would grow trees; but, never will it grow trees, or anything else *to the profit of this nation*, until it become *private property*. Public property must, in some cases, be in the hands of public officers; but, this is not an affair of that nature. This is too loose a con-

---

[1] I am afraid that the Author's well-argued theory respecting the decrease of the population of the United Kingdom, since the time of the Conquest, is not borne out by the opinions of trustworthy statisticians. Mr. Mulhall, for instance, supplies us with the following table:—

	THOUSANDS OMITTED.			INHABITANTS PER SQ. MILE.		
	England.	Scotland.	Ireland.	England.	Scotland.	Ireland.
1066 . . .	2,150	350	1,000	37	11	32
1381 . . .	2,360	400	1,100	41	13	35
1672 . . .	5,500	900	1,320	96	29	41
1754 . . .	7,020	1,265	2,373	120	40	74
1821 . . .	12,090	2,092	6,802	207	68	212
1841 . . .	16,038	2,620	8,195	275	86	256
1861 . . .	20,202	3,062	5,800	347	100	181
1881 . . .	26,110	3,734	5,160	443	122	161

cern; too little controllable by superiors. It is a thing calculated for jobbing, above all others; calculated to promote the success of favouritism. Who can imagine that the persons employed about plantations and farms for the public, are employed because *they are fit* for the employment? Supposing the commissioners to hold in abhorrence, the idea of paying for services to themselves, under the name of paying for services to the public; supposing them never to have heard of such a thing in their lives, can they imagine that nothing of this sort takes place, while they are in London eleven months out of twelve in the year? I never feel disposed to cast much censure, upon any of the persons engaged in such concerns. The temptation is too great to be resisted. The public must pay for everything *à pois d'or*. Therefore, no such thing should be in the hands of the public, or, rather, of the government; and I hope to live, to see this thing completely taken out of the hands of this government.

It was night-fall when we arrived at Eling, that is to say, at the head of the Southampton Water. Our horses were very hungry. We stopped to bait them, and set off just about dusk to come to this place (Weston Grove), stopping at Southampton on our way, and leaving a letter to come to London. Between Southampton and this place, we cross a bridge over the Itchen river, and, coming up a hill into a common, which is called Town-hill Common, we passed, lying on our right, a little park and house, occupied by the Irish Bible-man, Lord Ashdown, I think they call him, whose real name is French, and whose family are so very *well known* in the most unfortunate sister-kingdom. Just at the back of his house, in another sort of paddock-place, lives a man, whose name I forget, who was, I believe, a coachmaker in the East Indies, and whose father, or uncle, kept a turnpike gate at Chelsea, a few years ago. See the effects of "*industry* and "*enterprise!*" But even these would be nothing, were it not for this wondrous system by which money can be snatched away from the labourer in this very parish, for instance, sent off to the East Indies, there help to make a mass, to put into the hands of an adventurer, and then the mass may be brought back in the pockets of the adventurer, and cause him to be called a 'Squire by the labourer, whose earnings were so snatched away! Wondrous system! Pity it cannot last for ever! Pity that it has got a Debt of a thousand millions to pay! Pity that it cannot turn paper into gold! Pity that it will make such fools of Prosperity Robinson and his colleagues!

The moon shone very bright by the time that we mounted the hill; and now, skirting the enclosures upon the edge of the common, we passed several of those cottages which I so well recollected, and in which I had the satisfaction to believe that the inhabitants were sitting comfortably with bellies full, by a good fire. It was eight o'clock before we arrived at Mr. Chamberlayne's, whom I had not seen since, I think, the year 1816; for, in the fall of that year I came to London, and I never returned to Botley (which is only about three miles and a half from Weston) to stay there for any length of time. To those who like water-scenes (as nineteen-twentieths of people do) it is the prettiest spot, I believe, in all England. Mr. Chamberlayne built the house about twenty years ago. He has been bringing the place to greater and greater perfection from that time to this. All round about the house is in the neatest possible order. I should think, that, altogether, there cannot be so little as *ten acres of short grass;* and, when I say *that*, those who know anything about Gardens will form a pretty correct general notion as to the *scale* on which the thing is carried on. Until of late, Mr. Chamberlayne was owner of only a small part, comparatively, of the lands hereabouts. He is now the owner, I believe, of the whole of the lands that come down to the water's edge and that lie between the ferry over the Itchen at Southampton, and the river which goes out from the Southampton Water at Hamble. And, now let me describe, as well as I can, what this land and its situation are.

The Southampton Water begins at Portsmouth, and goes up by Southampton, to Redbridge, being, upon an average,

about two miles wide, having, on the one side, the New
Forest, and on the other side, for a great part of the way,
this fine and beautiful estate of Mr. Chamberlayne. Both
sides of this water have rising lands divided into hill and
dale, and very beautifully clothed with trees, the woods
and lawns and fields being most advantageously intermixed.
It is very curious that, at the *back* of each of these tracts
of land, there are extensive heaths, on this side as well
as on the New Forest side. To stand here and look across
the water at the New Forest, you would imagine that it
was really *a country of woods;* for you can see nothing of
the heaths from here; those heaths over which we rode,
and from which we could see a windmill down among the
trees, which windmill is now to be seen just opposite this
place. So that, the views from this place are the most
beautiful that can be imagined. You see up the water and
down the water, to Redbridge one way, and out to Spithead,
the other way. Through the trees, to the right, you see the
spires of Southampton, and you have only to walk a mile,
over a beautiful lawn and through a not less beautiful wood,
to find, in a little dell, surrounded with lofty woods, the
venerable ruins of *Netley Abbey*, which make part of Mr.
Chamberlayne's estate.[1]

The woods here are chiefly of oak; the ground consists
of a series of hill and dale, as you go long-wise from one

---

[1] Netley Abbey is reckoned to be the finest monastic ruin in the south
of England. It was founded by Henry III., its first monks coming from
the neighbouring abbey of Beaulieu. In 1537, Henry VIII., having plundered its revenues, granted the site to Sir William Paulet, afterwards
Marquis of Winchester. From his family, it passed to the Seymours,
Earls of Hertford, and after many other changes, at the beginning of the
present century, it passed into the hands of the Chamberlayne family. The
ruins of the Abbey Church, from their extent and magnificence, suggest the
question which the Author so often asks with respect to other churches
which he visited, viz., Where did the population come from to require so
large an edifice? The length of the church is 200 feet, and its width 120
feet. It is situated in the parish of Hound, which also possesses an ancient
church, built about the same time as the Abbey, A.D. 1230, and yet the
whole parish of Hound, consisting of 2638 acres, had, in 1801, a population of only 274, which increased, in 1831, to 417, and in 1861, to 2039.

end of the estate to the other, *about six miles in length.* Down almost every little valley, that divides these hills or hillocks, there is more or less of water, making the underwood, in those parts, very thick, and dark to go through; and these form the most delightful contrast, with the fields, and lawns. There are innumerable vessels of various sizes continually upon the water; and, to those that delight in water-scenes, this is certainly the very prettiest place that I ever saw in my life. I had seen it many years ago; and, as I intended to come here on my way home, I told George, before we set out, that I would show him *another Weston,* before we got to London. The parish in which his father's house is, is also called Weston, and a very beautiful spot it certainly is; but I told him I questioned whether I could not show him, a still prettier Weston, than that. We let him alone for the first day. He sat in the house, and saw great multitudes of pheasants, and partridges upon the lawn before the window; he went down to the water-side by himself, and put his foot upon the ground to see the tide rise. He seemed very much delighted. The second morning, at breakfast, we put it to him, which he would rather have; this Weston, or the Weston he had left in Herefordshire; but, though I introduced the question in a way almost to extort a decision in favour of the Hampshire Weston, he decided instantly and plump for the other, in a manner very much to the delight of Mr. Chamberlayne and his sister. So true it is, that, when people are uncorrupted, they always *like home best*, be it, in itself, what it may.

Every thing that nature can do, has been done here; and money most judiciously employed, has come to her assistance. Here are a thousand things to give pleasure to any rational mind; but there is one thing, which, in my estimation, surpasses, in pleasure, to contemplate, all the lawns, and all the groves, and all the gardens, and all the game, and every thing else; and that is, the real, unaffected goodness of the owner of this estate. He is a member for Southampton; he has other fine estates; he has great talents;

he is much admired by all who know him; but, he has done more by his justice, by his just way of thinking with regard to the labouring people, than in all other ways put together. This was nothing new to me; for I was well informed of it several years ago, though I had never heard him speak of it in my life. When he came to this place, the common wages of day-labouring men were *thirteen shillings a week*, and the wages of carpenters, bricklayers, and other tradesmen, were in proportion. Those wages he *has given, from that time to this*, without any abatement whatever. With these wages, a man can live, having, at the same time, other advantages attending the working for such a man as Mr. Chamberlayne. He has got less money in his bags than he would have had, if he had ground men down in their wages; but, if his sleep be not sounder than that of the hard-fisted wretch, that can walk over grass and gravel, kept in order by a poor creature that is half-starved; if his sleep be not sounder than the sleep of such a wretch, then all that we have been taught is false, and there is no difference between the man who feeds, and the man who starves the poor: all the Scripture is a bundle of lies, and instead of being propagated it ought to be flung into the fire.[1]

It is curious enough, that those who are the least disposed to give good wages to the labouring people, should be the most disposed to discover for them *schemes for saving their*

---

[1] The present average of wages for farm labourers throughout Hampshire, is 13s. per week, frequently in addition to a comfortable cottage; but very recently a reduction of 1s. per week has been made in many parishes, in consequence of the existing agricultural depression. The previous Editor, in a note on this subject, alludes to meetings of farmers, at the time he wrote (1852-1853), at which it was resolved that it was expedient to pay their labourers better wages; he also alludes to the following pleasing incident, viz., that the oldest farmers remembered the time when their labourers were not pleased if their masters did not at Whitsuntide go to their cottages, to smoke a pipe with them, and to tell them which of them had brewed the best ale. It would be in vain to search for a farm labourer in the present day, who could afford to brew his own beer; but it would materially strengthen the bonds of society, if employers of labour were occasionally to be seen in the cottages of those whom they employ, making them feel that the labourer's welfare and the employer's interests were identical.

money! I have lately seen, I saw it at Uphusband, a prospectus, or scheme, for establishing what they call a *County Friendly Society*. This is a scheme for getting from the poor a part of the wages that they receive. Just as if a poor fellow could *put anything by* out of eight shillings a week! If, indeed, the schemers were to pay the labourers twelve or thirteen shillings a week; then these might have something to lay by at some times of the year; but, then indeed, there would be *no poor-rates wanted;* and, it is to *get rid of the poor-rates* that these schemers have invented their society. What wretched drivellers they must be: to think that they should be able to make the pauper, keep the pauper; to think that they shall be able to make the man that is half-starved, lay by part of his loaf! I know of no county, where the poor are worse treated than in many parts of this county of Hants. It is happy to know of one instance in which they are well treated; and I deem it a real honour to be under the roof of him, who has uniformly set so laudable an example in this most important concern. What are all his riches to me? They form no title to my respect. 'Tis not for me to set myself up in judgment as to his taste, his learning, his various qualities and endowments; but, of these his unequivocal works, I am a competent judge. I know how much good he must do; and there is a great satisfaction, in reflecting on the great happiness that he must feel, when, in laying his head upon his pillow of a cold and dreary winter night he reflects that there are scores, aye scores upon scores, of his country-people, of his poor neighbours, of those whom the Scripture denominates his brethren, who have been enabled, through him, to retire to a warm bed after spending a cheerful evening and taking a full meal by the side of their own fire. People may talk what they will about *happiness;* but I can figure to myself no happiness surpassing that of the man who falls to sleep with reflections like these in his mind.

Now observe, it is a duty, on my part, to relate what I have here related as to the conduct of Mr. Chamberlayne; not a duty towards *him;* for, I can do him no good by it, and I do most sincerely believe, that both he and his equally benevolent sister, would rather that their goodness remained unproclaimed; but, it is a duty towards my country, and particularly towards my readers. Here is a striking and a most valuable practical example. Here is a whole neighbourhood of labourers living as they ought to live; enjoying that happiness which is the just reward of their toil. And shall I suppress facts so honourable to those who are the cause of this happiness, facts so interesting in themselves, and so likely to be useful in the way of example; shall I do this, aye, and, besides this, *tacitly* give a *false account* of Weston Grove, and this, too, from the stupid and cowardly fear, of being accused of flattering a rich man?

Netley Abbey ought, it seems, to be called Letley Abbey, the Latin name being Lætus Locus, or Pleasant Place. *Letley* was made up of an abbreviation of the *Lætus* and of the Saxon word *ley*, which meaned *place, field*, or *piece of ground*. This Abbey was founded by Henry III. in 1239, for 12 monks of the Benedictine order; and, when suppressed, by the wife-killer, its revenues amounted to 3,200*l.* a year of our present money. The possessions of these monks were by the wife-killing founder of the Church of England, given away (though they belonged to the public) to one of his court sycophants, Sir William Paulet, a man the most famous in the whole world for sycophancy, time-serving, and for all those qualities, which usually distinguish the favourites of kings like the wife-killer. This Paulet changed from the Popish to Henry the Eighth's religion, and was a great actor in punishing the papists: when Edward VI. came to the throne, this Paulet turned protestant, and was a great actor in punishing those who adhered to Henry VIIIth's religion: when Queen Mary came to the throne, this Paulet turned back to papist, and was one of the great actors in sending protestants to be burnt in Smithfield: when Old Bess came to the throne, this Paulet turned back to protestant again, and was, until the day of his death, one of the great actors in persecuting, in fining, in mulcting, and in putting to death those who still had the virtue, and the courage, to adhere to the religion, in which they, and he, had been born and bred. The *head* of this family got, at last, to be Earl of Wiltshire, Marquis of Winchester, and Duke of Bolton. This last title is now *gone;* or, rather, it is changed to that of "Lord Bolton," which is now borne by a man of the name of Orde, who is the son of a man of that name, who died some years ago, and who married a daughter (I think it was) of the last "Duke of Bolton."

Pretty curious, and not a little interesting, to look back at the *origin* of this Dukedom of Bolton, and, then, to look at the person now bearing the title of *Bolton;* and, then, to go to Abbotston, near Winchester, and survey the ruins of the proud palace, once inhabited by the Duke of Bolton, which ruins, and the estate on which they stand, are now the property of the Loan-maker, Alexander Baring! Curious turn of things! Henry the wife-killer and his confiscating successors *granted* the estates of Netley, and of many other monasteries, to the head of these Paulets: to maintain these and other similar grants, a thing called a "Reformation" was made: to maintain the "Reformation" a "Glorious Revolution" was made: to maintain the "Glorious Revolution," a *Debt* was made: to maintain the Debt, a large part of the rents must go to the Debt-Dealers, or Loan-makers: and thus, at last, the Barings, only in this one neighbourhood, have become the successors of the Wriothesleys, the Paulets, and the Russells, who, throughout all the reigns of confiscation, were constantly *in the way*, when a distribution of good things was taking place! Curious enough all this; but, the thing will not *stop here*. The Loan-makers think that they shall out-wit the old grantee-fellows; and, so they might, and the people too, and the devil himself; but, they cannot out-wit *events*. Those events *will have a thorough rummaging;* and of this fact the "turn-of-the-market" gentlemen may be assured. Can it be *law* (I put the question to *lawyers*), can it be *law* (I leave reason and justice out of the inquiry), can it be *law*, that, if I, to-day, see dressed in good clothes, and with a full purse, a man who was notoriously pennyless yesterday; can it be law, that I (being a justice of the peace) have a right to demand of that man *how he came by his clothes and his purse?* And, can it be *law*, that I, seeing with an estate a man who was notoriously not worth a crown piece a few years ago, and who is notoriously related to nothing more than one degree above beggary; can it be *law*, that I, a magistrate, seeing this, have not a right to demand of this man how he came by his estate? No matter, however; for, if both these be law now, they will not, I trust, be law in a few years from this time.

Mr. Chamberlayne has caused the ancient *fish-ponds*, at Netley Abbey, to be "reclaimed," as they call it. What a loss, what a national loss, there has been in this way, and in the article of water fowl! I am quite satisfied, that, in these two articles and in that of *rabbits*, the nation has lost, has had annihilated (within the last 250 years) food sufficient for two days in the week, on an average, taking the year throughout. These are things, too, which cost so little labour! You can see the marks of old fish-ponds in thousands and thousands of places. I have noticed, I dare say, five hundred, since I left home. A trifling expense would, in most cases, restore them; but, now-a-days, all is looked for at shops: all is to be had by trafficking: scarcely any one thinks of providing for his own wants out of his own land and other his own domestic means. To buy the thing *ready made*, is the taste of the day; thousands, who are housekeepers, buy their dinners ready cooked: nothing is so common as to rent breasts for children to suck: a man actually advertised, in the London papers, about two months ago, to supply childless husbands with heirs. In this case, the articles were of course, to be *ready made;* for, to make them "to order" would be the d—— of a business; though, in desperate cases, even this is, I believe, sometimes resorted to.

Hambledon, Sunday,
22nd Oct. 1826.

We left Weston Grove on Friday morning, and came across to Botley, where we remained during the rest of the day, and until after breakfast yesterday. I had not seen "the "Botley Parson" for severa lyears, and I wished to have a look at him now, but could not get a sight of him, though we rode close before his house, at much about his breakfast time, and though we gave him the strongest of invitation, that could be expressed by hallooing, and by cracking of whips! The fox was too cunning for us, and, do all we could, we could not provoke him to put even his nose out of kennel. From Mr. James Warner's at Botley,[1] we went to Mr. Hallett's, at Allington, and had the very great pleasure of seeing him in excellent health. We intended to go back to Botley, and then to go to Titchfield, and, in our way to this place, over Portsdown Hill, whence I intended to show George the harbour and the fleet, and (of still more importance), the spot on which we signed the "Hampshire Petition," in 1817; that petition which foretold that which the "Norfolk Petition" confirmed; that petition which will be finally acted upon, or . . . . . . ! That petition was the very *last thing I wrote at Botley*. I came to London in November 1816; the Power-of-Imprisonment Bill was passed in February, 1817; just before it was passed, the meeting took place on Portsdown Hill; and I, in my way to the hill from London, stopped at Botley and wrote the petition. We had one meeting afterwards at Winchester, when I heard parsons swear like troopers, and saw one of them hawk up his spittle, and spit it into Lord Cochrane's poll! Ah! my bucks, we have you *now!* You are got nearly to the end of your tether; and what is more, *you know it*. Pay off the Debt, parsons! It is useless to swear and spit, and to present addresses applauding Power-of-Imprisonment Bills, unless you can pay off the Debt!

---

[1] Mr. James Warner and the Author were closely related; having married two sisters. The Warner family have been extensive proprietors of land, and lords of the manor of Botley, for many years. Mr. James Warner founded the Botley and South Hants Farmers' Club, in 1844, which is still in existence.

There is an excellent portrait of Mr. Warner in the Market House of the town of Botley.

Pay off the Debt, parsons! They say you can lay the d——. Lay *this* d——, then; or, confess that he is too many for you; aye, and for Sturges Bourne, or Bourne Sturges (I forget which), at your backs! [1]

From Allington, we, fearing that it would rain before we could get round by Titchfield, came across the country over Waltham Chase and Soberton Down. The chase was very green and fine; but the down was the very greenest thing that I have seen in the whole country. It is not a large down; perhaps not more than five or six hundred acres; but the land is good, the chalk is at a foot from the surface, or more; the mould is a hazel mould; and when I was upon the opposite hill, I could, though I knew the spot very well, hardly believe that it was a down. The green was darker than that of any pasture, or even any sainfoin or clover, that I had seen throughout the whole of my ride; and I should suppose, that there could not have been many less than a thousand sheep, in the three flocks, that were feeding upon the down when I came across it. I do not speak with anything like positiveness as to the measurement of this down; but I do not believe that it exceeds six hundred and fifty acres. They must have had more rain in this part of the country, than in most other parts of it. Indeed, no part of Hampshire seems to have suffered very much from the drought. I found the turnips pretty good, of both sorts, all the way from Andover to Rumsey. Through the New Forest, you may as well expect to find loaves of bread growing in fields as turnips, where there are any fields for them to grow in. From Redbridge to Weston, we had not light enough to see much about us; but when we came down to Botley, we there found

---

[1] It is greatly to be regretted that such apparently unceasing animosity embittered the mind of the Author against the clergy of his day. The state of religion at the time, however, was one of supreme deadness and supineness, and the clergy were, to a great extent, rather dependents of political parties than spiritual directors of their flocks. Happily such a state of reproach has long since passed away, and a political parson, in its true sense, at the present time is as much a "*rara avis*" as a hunting parson.

the turnips as good as I had ever seen them in my life, as far as I could judge from the time I had to look at them. Mr. Warner has as fine turnip fields, as I ever saw him have, swedish turnips and white also; and pretty nearly the same may be said of the whole of that neighbourhood for many miles round.

After quitting Soberton Down, we came up a hill leading to Hambledon, and turned off to our left to bring us down to Mr. Goldsmith's at West End, where we now are, at about a mile from the village of Hambledon. A village it *now* is; but it was formerly a considerable market-town, and it had three fairs in the year. There is now not even the name of market left, I believe; and the fairs amount to little more than a couple, or three gingerbread-stalls, with dolls and whistles for children. If you go through the place, you see that it has been a considerable town. The church tells the same story; it is now a tumble-down rubbishy place; it is partaking in the fate of all those places which were formerly a sort of rendezvous for persons who had things to buy and things to sell. *Wens* have devoured market-towns and villages; and *shops* have devoured *markets and fairs;* and this, too, to the infinite injury of the most numerous classes of the people. Shop-keeping, merely as shop-keeping, is injurious to any community. What are the shop and the shop-keeper for? To receive and distribute the produce of the land. There are other articles, certainly; but the main part is the produce of the land. The shop must be paid for; the shop-keeper must be kept; and the one must be paid for and the other must be kept by the consumer of the produce; or, perhaps, partly by the consumer and partly by the producer.

When fairs were very frequent, shops were not needed. A manufacturer of shoes, of stockings, of hats; of almost any thing that man wants, could manufacture at home in an obscure hamlet, with cheap house-rent, good air, and plenty of room. He need pay no heavy rent for shop; and no disadvantages from confined situation; and, then, by attending

three or four or five or six fairs in a year, he sold the work of
his hands, unloaded with a heavy expense attending the keeping of a shop. He would get more for ten shillings in a booth
at a fair or market, than he would get in a shop for ten or
twenty pounds. Of course he could afford to sell the work of
his hands for less; and thus a greater portion of their earnings,
remained with those who raised the food, and the clothing
from the land. I had an instance of this in what occurred to
myself at Weyhill fair. When I was at Salisbury, in September,
I wanted to buy a whip. It was a common hunting-whip,
with a hook to it, to pull open gates with, and I could not get
it for less than seven shillings and sixpence. This was more
than I had made up my mind to give, and I went on with my
switch. When we got to Weyhill fair, George had made shift
to lose his whip some time before, and I had made him go
without one, by way of punishment. But now, having come
to the fair, and seeing plenty of whips, I bought him one, just
such a one as had been offered me at Salisbury for seven and
sixpence, for four and sixpence; and, seeing the man with his
whips afterwards, I thought I would have one myself; and he
let me have it for three shillings. So that, here were two
whips, precisely of the same kind and quality as the whip at
Salisbury, bought for the money which the man at Salisbury
asked me for one whip. And yet, far be it from me to accuse
the man at Salisbury of an attempt at extortion: he had an
expensive shop, and a family in a town to support, while my
Weyhill fellow had been making his whips in some house in
the country, which he rented, probably for five or six pounds
a year, with a good garden to it. Does not every one see,
in a minute, how this exchanging of fairs, and markets for
shops creates *idlers and traffickers;* creates those locusts,
called middle-men, who create nothing, who add to the value
of nothing, who improve nothing, but who live in idleness, and
who live well, too, out of the labour of the producer and the
consumer. The fair and the market, those wise institutions
of our forefathers, and with regard to the management of
which they were so scrupulously careful; the fair, and the

market, bring the producer, and the consumer, in contact with each other. Whatever is gained is, at any rate, gained by one or the other of these. The fair and the market bring them together, and enable them to act for their mutual interest and convenience. The shop and the trafficker keep them apart; the shop hides from both producer and consumer, the real state of matters. The fair and the market lay every thing open: going to either, you see the state of things at once; and the transactions are fair and just, not disfigured, too, by falsehood, and by those attempts at deception, which disgrace traffickings in general.

Very wise, too, and very just, were the laws against *forestalling* and *regrating*. They were laws to prevent the producer and the consumer from being cheated by the trafficker. There are whole bodies of men; indeed, a very large part of the community, who live in idleness in this country, in consequence of the whole current of the laws now running in favour of the trafficking monopoly. It has been a great object with all wise governments, in all ages, from the days of Moses to the present day, to confine trafficking, mere trafficking, to as few hands as possible. It seems to be the main object of this government to give all possible encouragement to traffickers of every description, and to make them swarm like the lice of Egypt. There is that numerous sect, the Quakers. This sect arose in England: they were engendered by the Jewish system of usury. Till *excises* and *loanmongering* began, these vermin were never heard of in England. They seem to have been hatched by that fraudulent system, as maggots are bred by putrid meat, or as the flounders come in the livers of rotten sheep. The base vermin do not pretend to work: all they talk about is dealing; and the government, in place of making laws that would put them in the stocks, or cause them to be whipped at the cart's tail, really seem anxious to encourage them and to increase their numbers; nay, it is not long since Mr. Brougham had the effrontery to move for leave to bring in a bill to make men liable to be hanged upon the bare word of these vagabonds.¹ This is, with me, something never to be forgotten. But, every thing tends the same way: all the regulations, all the laws that have been adopted of late years, have a tendency to give encouragement to the trickster and the trafficker, and to take from the labouring classes, all the honour and a great part of the food, that fairly belonged to them.

In coming along yesterday, from Waltham Chase to Soberton Down, we passed by a big white house upon a hill that was, when I lived at Botley, occupied by one Goodlad, who was a cock justice of the peace, and who had been a chap, of some sort or other, in *India*. There was a man of the name of Singleton, who lived in Waltham Chase, and who was deemed to be a great poacher. This man, having been forcibly ousted by the order of this Goodlad, and some others, from an encroachment that he had made in the forest, threatened revenge. Soon after this, a horse (I forget to whom it belonged) was stabbed or shot in the night-time in a field. Singleton was taken up, tried at Winchester, convicted and *transported*. I cannot relate exactly what took place. I remember that there were some curious circumstances attending the conviction of this man. The people in that neighbourhood were deeply impressed with these circumstances. Singleton was transported; but Goodlad and his wife, were both dead and buried, in less, I believe, than three months after the departure of poor Singleton. I do not know that any injustice really was done; but I do know that a great

---

¹ Reference is here made to the enactments which enabled Quakers to make an "affirmation," instead of taking an oath, in a court of justice. The Author is always very severe upon the Quakers, but he distinguishes, as has been already noted, between Quakers engaged in trade, and Quakers engaged in farming pursuits. He had some Quaker friends in Philadelphia who were farmers, and whom he highly respected. It was Justice Bennett of Derby who gave the Society of Friends the name of Quakers *in* 1650; because George Fox, their founder, admonished him, "to quake at the word of the Lord." The Quakers, in times past, have suffered terrible persecutions. It was not until 1833 that a Quaker was admitted to Parliament on his affirmation.

impression was produced, and a very sorrowful impression, too, on the minds of the people in that neighbourhood.

I cannot quit Waltham Chase without observing, that I heard, last year, that a Bill was about to be petitioned for, to enclose that Chase! Never was so monstrous a proposition in this world. The Bishop of Winchester, is Lord of the Manor over this Chase. If the Chase be enclosed, the timber must be cut down, young and old; and here are a couple of hundred acres of land, worth ten thousand acres of land in the New Forest. This is as fine timber land as any in the wealds of Surrey, Sussex or Kent. There are two enclosures of about 40 acres each, perhaps, that were simply surrounded by a bank being thrown up about twenty years ago, only twenty years ago, and on the poorest part of the Chase, too; and these are now as beautiful plantations of young oak trees as man ever set his eyes on; many of them as big or bigger round than my thigh! Therefore, besides the sweeping away of two or three hundred cottages; besides plunging into ruin and misery all these numerous families, here is one of the finest pieces of timber land in the whole kingdom, going to be cut up into miserable clay fields, for no earthly purpose but that of gratifying the stupid greediness of those who think that they must gain, if they add to the breadth of their private fields. But, if a thing like this be permitted, we must be prettily furnished with Commissioners of woods and forests! I do not believe that they will sit in Parliament, and see a Bill like this passed, and hold their tongues; but if they were to do it, there is no measure of reproach which they would not merit. Let them go and look at the two plantations of oaks, of which I have just spoken; and then let them give their consent to such a Bill if they can.

Thursley, Monday Evening,
23rd October.

When I left Weston, my intention was, to go from Hambledon to Up Park, thence to Arundel, thence to Brighton, thence to East-bourne, thence to Wittersham in Kent, and then by Cranbrook, Tunbridge, Godstone and Reigate to London; but, when I got to Botley, and particularly when I got to Hambledon, I found my horse's back so much hurt by the saddle, that I was afraid to take so long a stretch, and therefore resolved to come away straight to this place, to go hence to Reigate, and so to London. Our way, therefore, this morning, was over Butser-hill to Petersfield, in the first place; then to Liphook and then to this place, in all about twenty-four miles. Butser-hill belongs to the back chain of the South-downs; and, indeed, it terminates that chain to the westward. It is the highest hill in the whole country. Some think that Hindhead, which is the famous sand-hill over which the Portsmouth road goes at sixteen miles to the north of this great chalk-hill; some think that Hindhead is the higher hill of the two. Be this as it may, Butser-hill, which is the right-hand hill of the two between which you go at three miles from Petersfield going towards Portsmouth; this Butser-hill is, I say, quite high enough; and was more than high enough for us, for it took us up amongst clouds, that wet us very nearly to the skin. In going from Mr. Goldsmith's to the hill, it is all up hill for five miles. Now and then a little stoop; not much; but regularly, with these little exceptions, up hill for these five miles. The hill appears, at a distance, to be a sharp ridge on its top. It is, however, not so. It is, in some parts, half a mile wide or more. The road lies right along the middle of it, from west to east, and, just when you are at the highest part of the hill, it is very narrow from north to south; not more, I think, than about a hundred or a hundred and thirty yards.

This is as interesting a spot, I think, as the foot of man ever was placed upon. Here are two valleys, one to your right and the other to your left, very little less than half a mile down to the bottom of them, and much steeper than a tiled roof of a house. These valleys may be, where they join the hill, three or four hundred yards broad. They get wider as they get farther from the hill. Of a clear day you see all the north of Hampshire; nay, the whole county, together with a great part of Surrey and of Sussex. You see the whole of the South-Downs to the eastward as far as your eye can carry you; and, lastly, you see over Portsdown Hill, which lies before you to the south; and there are spread open to your view the isle of Portsea, Porchester, Wimmering, Fareham, Gosport, Portsmouth, the harbour, Spithead, the Isle of Wight, and the ocean.

But something still more interesting occurred to me here in the year 1808, when I was coming on horseback over the same hill from Botley to London. It was a very beautiful day and in summer. Before I got upon the hill (on which I had never been before), a shepherd told me to keep on in the road in which I was, till I came to the London turnpike road. When I got to within a quarter of a mile of this particular point of the hill, I saw, at this point, what I thought was a cloud of dust; and, speaking to my servant about it, I found that he thought so too; but this cloud of dust disappeared all at once. Soon after, there appeared to arise another cloud of dust at the same place, and then that disappeared, and the spot was clear again. As we were trotting along, a pretty smart pace, we soon came to this narrow place, having one valley to our right and the other valley to our left, and, there, to my great astonishment, I saw the clouds come one after another, each appearing to be about as big as two or three acres of land, skimming along in the valley on the north side, a great deal below the tops of the hills; and successively, as they arrived at our end of the valley, rising up, crossing the narrow pass, and then descending down into the other valley and going off to the south; so that we who sat there upon our horses, were alternately in clouds and in sunshine. It is an universal rule, that if there be a fog in the morning, and that fog go from the valleys to the tops of the hills, there will be rain that day; and if it disappear by sinking in the valley, there will be no rain that day. The truth is, that fogs are clouds, and clouds are fogs. They are more or less, full of water; but, they are all water; sometimes a sort of steam, and sometimes water, that falls in drops. Yesterday morning the fogs had ascended to the tops of the hills; and it was raining on all the hills round about us, before it began to rain in the valleys. We, as I observed before, got pretty nearly wet to the skin upon the top of Butser-hill; but, we had the pluck to come on, and let the clothes dry upon our backs.

I must here relate something that appears very interesting to me, and something, which, though it must have been seen by every man that has lived in the country, or, at least, in any hilly country, has never been particularly mentioned by anybody as far as I can recollect. We frequently talk of clouds coming from *dews;* and we actually see the heavy fogs become clouds. We see them go up to the tops of hills, and, taking a swim round, actually come, and drop down upon us, and wet us through. But, I am now going to speak of clouds, coming out of the sides of hills in exactly the same manner that you see smoke come out of a tobacco pipe, and, rising up, with a wider and wider head, like the smoke from a tobacco-pipe, go to the top of the hill or over the hill, or very much above it, and then come over the valleys in rain. At about a mile's distance from Mr. Palmer's house at Bollitree, in Herefordshire, there is a large, long beautiful wood, covering the side of a lofty hill, winding round in the form of a crescent, the bend of the crescent being towards Mr. Palmer's house. It was here, that I first observed this mode of forming clouds. The first time I noticed it, I pointed it out to Mr. Palmer. We stood and observed cloud after cloud, come out from different parts of the side of the hill, and tower up and go over the hill out of sight. He told me that that was a certain sign that it would rain that day, for that these clouds would come back again, and would fall in rain. It rained sure enough; and I found that the country people, all round about, had this mode of the forming of the clouds as a sign of rain. The hill is called Penyard, and this forming of the clouds, they call Old Penyard's *smoking his pipe;* and it is a rule that it is sure to rain during the day, if Old Penyard smokes his pipe in the morning. These appearances take place, especially in warm and sultry weather. It was very warm yesterday morning: it had thundered violently the evening before: we felt it hot even while the rain fell upon us at Butser-hill. Petersfield lies in a pretty broad and very beautiful valley. On three sides of it are very lofty hills, partly downs and partly covered with trees: and, as we proceeded on our way from the bottom of Butser-hill to Petersfield, we saw thousands upon thousands of clouds, continually coming puffing out from different parts of these hills and towering up to the top of them. I stopped George several times to make him look at them; to see them come puffing out of the chalk downs as well as out of the woodland hills; and bade him remember to tell his father of it, when he should get home, to convince him that the hills of Hampshire, could smoke their pipes, as well as those of Herefordshire. This is a really curious matter. I have never read, in any book, anything to lead me to suppose that the observation has ever found its ways into print before. Sometimes you will see only one or two clouds during a whole morning, come out of the side of a hill; but we saw thousands upon thousands, bursting out, one after another, in all parts of these immense hills. The first time that I have leisure, when I am in the high countries again, I will have a conversation with some old shepherd about this matter: if he cannot enlighten me upon the subject, I am sure that no philosopher can.

We came through Petersfield without stopping, and baited our horses at Liphook, where we stayed about half an hour. In coming from Liphook to this place, we overtook a man who asked for relief. He told me he was a weaver, and, as his accent was northern, I was about to give him the balance that I had in hand arising from our savings in the fasting way, amounting to about three shillings and sixpence; but, unfortunately for him, I asked him what place he had lived at as a weaver; and he told me he was a Spitalfields weaver. I instantly put on my glove and returned my purse into my pocket, saying, go, then, to Sidmouth and Peel and the rest of them "and get relief; for, I have this minute, while I was "stopping at Liphook, read in the *Evening Mail* newspaper, "an address to the King from the Spitalfields' weavers, for "which address they ought to suffer death and starvation. In "that address those base wretches tell the King, that they "were loyal men: that they detested the designing men who "were guilty of seditious practices in 1817; they, in short, "express their approbation of the Power-of-imprisonment Bill, "of all the deeds committed against the Reformers in 1817 "and 1819; they, by fair inference, express their approbation "of the thanks given to the Manchester Yeomanry. You are "one of them; my name is William Cobbett, and I would "sooner relieve a dog than relieve you." Just as I was closing my harangue, we overtook a country-man and woman that were going the same way. The weaver attempted explanations. He said, that they only said it, in order to get relief; but that they did not mean it in their hearts. "Oh, base "dogs!" said I: "it is precisely by such men that ruin is "brought upon nations; it is precisely by such baseness and "insincerity, such scandalous cowardice, that ruin has been "brought upon them. I had two or three shillings to give "you; I had them in my hand: I have put them back into "my purse: I trust I shall find somebody more worthy of them: "rather than give them to you, I would fling them into that "sand-pit and bury them for ever."

How curiously things happen! It was by mere accident that I took up a newspaper to read: it was merely because I was compelled to stay a quarter of an hour in the room without doing any thing. and above all things it was miraculous that I should take up the *Evening Mail*, into which, I believe, I never before looked, in my whole life. I saw the royal arms at the top of the paper; took it for the *Old Times*, and, in a sort of a lounging mood, said to George, "Give me hold of that paper, and let us see what that foolish d—— Anna Brodie says." Seeing the word "*Spitalfields*," I read on till I got to the base and scoundrelly part of the address. I then turned over, and looked at the title of the paper and the date of it, resolving, in my mind, to have satisfaction, of some sort or other, upon these base vagabonds. Little did I think that an opportunity would so soon occur, of showing my resentment against them, and that, too, in so striking, so appropriate, and so efficient a manner. I dare say, that it was some tax-eating scoundrel who drew up this address (which I will insert in the Register, as soon as I can find it); but, that is nothing to me and my fellow-sufferers of 1817 and 1819. This infamous libel upon us, is published under the name of the Spitalfields weavers; and, if I am asked what the poor creatures were to do, being without bread as they were, I answer by asking, whether they could find no knives to cut their throats with; seeing that they ought to have cut their throats ten thousand times over, if they could have done it, rather than sanction the publication of so infamous a paper as this.

It is not thus that the weavers in the north have acted. Some scoundrel wanted to inveigle them into an applauding of the Ministers; but they, though nothing so infamous as this address was proposed to them, rejected the proposition, though they were ten times more in want, than the weavers, of Spitalfields have ever been. They were only called upon to applaud the Ministers for the recent Orders in Council; but they justly said that the Ministers had a great deal more to do, before they would merit their applause. What would these brave and sensible men have said to a tax-eating scoundrel, who should have called upon them to present an address to the King, and in that address to applaud the terrible deeds committed against the people in 1817 and 1819! I have great happiness in reflecting that this baseness of the Spitalfields weavers will not bring them one single mouthful of bread. This will be their lot; this will be the fruit of their baseness: and the nation, the working classes of the nation, will learn, from this, that the way to get redress of their grievances, the way to get food and raiment in exchange for their labour, the way to ensure good treatment from the Government, is not to crawl to that Government, to lick its hands, and seem to deem it an honour to be its slaves.

Before we got to Thursley, I saw three poor fellows getting in turf for their winter fuel, and I gave them a shilling apiece.

To a boy at the bottom of Hindhead, I gave the other sixpence, towards buying him a pair of gloves; and thus I disposed of the money which was, at one time, actually out of my purse, and going into the hand of the loyal Spitalfields' weaver.

We got to this place (Mr. Knowles's of Thursley) about 5 o'clock in the evening, very much delighted with our ride.

Kensington,
Thursday, 26th Oct.

We left Mr. Knowles's on Thursday morning, came through Godalming, stopped at Mr. Rowland's at Chilworth, and then came on through Dorking to Colley Farm, near Reigate, where we slept. I have so often described the country from Hindhead to the foot of Reigate Hill, and from the top of Reigate Hill to the Thames, that I shall not attempt to do it again here. When we got to the river Wey, we crossed it from Godalming Pismarsh, to come up to Chilworth. I desired George to look round the country, and asked him if he did not think it was very pretty. I put the same question to him, when we got into the beautiful neighbourhood of Dorking, and when we got to Reigate, and especially when we got to the tip-top of Reigate Hill, from which there is one of the finest views in the whole world; but ever after our quitting Mr. Knowles's, George insisted that, that was the prettiest country that we had seen in the course of our whole ride, and that he liked Mr. Knowles's place better, than any other place that he had seen. I reminded him of Weston Grove; and I reminded him of the beautiful ponds and grass and plantations at Mr. Leach's; but he still persisted in his judgment in favour of Mr. Knowles's place, in which decision, however, the grey hounds and the beagles, had manifestly a great deal to do.

From Thursley to Reigate inclusive, on the chalk-side as well as on the sand-side, the crops of turnips, of both kinds, were pretty nearly as good as I ever saw them in my life. On a farm of Mr. Drummond's at Aldbury, rented by a farmer

Peto, I saw a piece of cabbages, of the large kind, which will produce, I should think, not much short of five and twenty tons to the acre; and here I must mention (I do not know *why* I must, by the bye) an instance of my own skill in measuring land by the eye. The cabbages stand upon half a field, and on that part of it farthest from the road, where we were. We took the liberty to open the gate and ride into the field, in order to get closer to the cabbages to look at them. I intended to notice this piece of cabbages, and I asked George how much ground he thought there was in the piece. He said, *two acres;* and asked me how much I thought. I said there were *above four acres,* and that I should not wonder if there were *four acres and a half.* Thus divided in judgment, we turned away from the cabbages to go out of the field at another gate, which pointed towards our road. Near this gate we found a man turning a heap of manure. This man, as it happened, had hoed the cabbages by the acre, or had had a hand in it. We asked him how much ground there was in that piece of cabbages, and he told us, *four acres and a half!* I suppose it will not be difficult to convince the reader, that George looked upon me, as a sort of conjuror. At Mr. Pym's, at Colley farm, we found one of the very finest pieces of mangel wurzel that I had ever seen in my life. We calculated that there would be little short of *forty tons to the acre;* and, there being three acres to the piece, Mr. Pym calculates that this mangel wurzel, the produce of these three acres of land, will carry his ten or twelve milch-cows nearly, if not wholly, through the winter. There did not appear to be a spurious plant, and there was not one plant that had gone to seed in the whole piece. I have never seen a more beautiful mass of vegetation, and I had the satisfaction to learn, after having admired the crop, that the seed came from my own shop, and that it had been saved by myself.

Talking of the shop, I came to it in a very few hours after looking at this mangel wurzel; and I soon found that it was high time for me to get home again; for here had been pretty d—— works going on. Here I found the "Greek cause," and all its appendages, figuring away in grand style. But, I must make this matter of separate observation.[1]

I have put an end to my Ride of August, September, and October, 1826, during which I have travelled five hundred and sixty-eight miles, and have slept in thirty different beds, having written three monthly pamphlets, called the "Poor Man's Friend," and have also written (including the present one) eleven Registers. I have been, in three cities, in about twenty market towns, in perhaps five hundred villages; and I have seen the people, no where so well off as in the neighbourhood of Weston Grove, and no where so badly off, as in the dominions of the Select Vestry of Hurstbourn Tarrant, commonly called Uphusband. During the whole of this ride, I have very rarely been a-bed after day-light; I have drunk, neither wine nor spirits. I have eaten no vegetables, and only a very moderate quantity of meat; and, it may be useful to my readers to know, that the riding of twenty miles, was not so fatiguing to me at the end of my tour, as the riding of ten miles was, at the beginning of it. Some ill-natured fools will call this "*egotism.*" Why is it egotism? Getting upon a good strong horse, and riding about the country, has no merit in it; there is no conjuration in it; it requires neither talents nor virtues of any sort; but *health* is a very valuable thing; and when a man has had the experience which I have had, in this instance, it is his duty to state to the world, and to his own countrymen, and neighbours in particular, the happy effects of early rising, sobriety, abstinence, and a resolution to be active. It is his duty to do this; and it becomes imperatively his duty, when he has seen, in the course of his life, so many men; so many men of excellent hearts and of good talents, rendered prematurely old, cut off ten or twenty years

---

[1] The Kingdom of Greece had been trodden down by the tyranny, cruelty, and avarice of the Turks since A.D. 1453. In 1820, the Greeks rebelled against their conquerors; and, by the assistance of Britain, France, and Russia, Greece, in 1829, was declared an independent kingdom. In 1826, the date of the Author's remarks upon the "Greek cause," a loan of £70,000 was being raised, to assist the Greeks, who were at the time in a state of actual warfare with the Turks.

before their time, by a want of that early rising, sobriety, abstinence and activity, from which he himself has derived so much benefit, and such inexpressible pleasure. During this ride, I have been several times wet to the skin. At some times of my life, after having indulged for a long while in coddling myself up in the house, these soakings would have frightened me half out of my senses; but I care very little about them: I avoid getting wet if I can; but, it is very seldom that rain, come when it would, has prevented me from performing the day's journey that I had laid out beforehand. And, this is a very good rule : stick to your intention, whether it be attended with inconveniences or not; to look upon yourself as *bound* to do it. In the whole of this ride, I have met with no one untoward circumstance, properly so called, except the wounding of the back of my horse, which grieved me much more on his account, than on my own. I have a friend, who, when he is disappointed in accomplishing anything that he has laid out, says that he has been *beaten*, which is a very good expression for the thing. I was beaten in my intention to go through Sussex and Kent; but I will retrieve the affair in a very few months' time, or, perhaps few weeks'. The COLLECTIVE will be here now in a few days; and, as soon as I have got the Preston Petition fairly before them, and find (as I daresay I shall) that the petition will not be *tried* until February,[1] I shall take my horse and set off again to that very spot, in the London turnpike road, at the foot of

---

[1] The General Election of 1826 was a severe struggle for popular candidates. A great effort was made by Cobbett's supporters, headed by Sir Thomas Beevor, to bring him forward as a candidate for Preston. A famous contest ensued. Two members were to be elected. Four candidates appeared on the field. Mr. Cobbett was on that occasion unsuccessful. His supporters believed, that there had been sufficient impediment to fair voting to upset the election. A petition against the election was thereupon prepared ; but whether it was actually presented to the House or not, we have no means of knowing. The Author appears, however, to have taken his defeat with very good humour, for on his return from the election through Blackburn, Bolton and Manchester, he met with a perfect ovation, attended with bands of music, banners and flags, resembling those remarkable political tours in the north, recently made, by the "grand old man."

Butser-hill, whence I turned off to go to Petersfield, instead
of turning the other way to go to Up Park : I shall take my
horse and go to this spot, and, with a resolution not to be
beaten, next time, go along through the whole length of Sussex, and sweep round through Kent and Surrey till I come to
Reigate again, and then home to Kensington ; for I do not
like to be beaten by a horse's sore back, or by any thing else ;
and besides that, there are several things in Sussex and Kent
that I want to see and give an account of. For the present,
however, farewell to the country, and now for the Wen and its
villanous corruptions.

RURAL RIDE: TO TRING, IN HERTFORDSHIRE.

Barn-Elm Farm, 23rd Sept. 1829.

As if to prove the truth of all that has been said in *The
Woodlands* about the impolicy of cheap planting, as it is
called, Mr. Elliman has planted another, and larger field, with
a mixture of ash, locusts, and larches ; not upon *trenched*
ground, but upon ground moved with the plough. The larches
made great haste to *depart this life*, bequeathing to Mr. Elliman a very salutary lesson. The ash appeared to be alive,
and that is all : the locusts, though they had to share in all
the disadvantages of their neighbours, appeared, it seems, to
be doing pretty well, and had made decent shoots, when a
neighbour's sheep invaded the plantation, and, being fond of
the locust leaves and shoots, as all cattle are, reduced them to
mere stumps, as it were to put them upon a level, with the
ash. In *The Woodlands*, I have strongly pressed the necessity of effectual fences : without these, you plant and sow in
vain : you plant and sow the plants and seeds of disappointment and mortification ; and the earth, being always grateful,
is sure to reward you with a plentiful crop. One half acre of
Mr. Elliman's plantation of locusts before mentioned, time

will tell him, is worth more than the whole of the six or seven acres, of this *cheaply* planted field.

Besides the 25,000 trees which Mr. Elliman had from me, he had some (and a part of them fine plants) which he himself had raised from seed, in the manner described in *The Woodlands* under the head "Locust." This seed he bought from me; and, as I shall sell but a very few more locust plants, I recommend gentlemen to sow the seed for themselves, according to the directions given in *The Woodlands* (in paragraphs 383 to 386 inclusive). In that part of *The Woodlands* will be found the most minute directions for the sowing of this seed, and particularly in the preparing of it for sowing; for, unless the proper precautions are taken here, one seed out of one hundred will not come up; and, with the proper precautions, one seed in one hundred will not fail to come up. I beg the reader, who intends to sow locusts, to read with great care the latter part of paragraph 368 of *The Woodlands*.

At this town of Tring, which is a very pretty and respectable place, I saw what reminded me of another of my endeavours to introduce useful things into this country. At the door of a shop I saw a large *case*, with the lid taken off, containing *bundles of straw for platting*. It was straw of spring wheat, tied up in small bundles, with the ear on; just such as I myself have grown in England many times, and bleached for platting, according to the instructions so elaborately given in the last edition of my *Cottage Economy*; and which instructions I was enabled to give from the information collected, by my son in America. I asked the shopkeeper where he got this straw: he said, that it came from Tuscany; and that it was manufactured there at Tring, and other places, for, as I understood, some single individual master-manufacturer. I told the shopkeeper, that I wondered that they should send to Tuscany for the straw, seeing that it might be grown, harvested, and equally well bleached at Tring; that it was now, at this time, grown, bleached, and manufactured into bonnets in Kent; and I showed to several persons at Tring a bonnet, made in Kent, from the straw of wheat grown in

Kent, and presented by that most public-spirited, and excellent man, Mr. John Wood, of Wettersham, who died, to the great sorrow of the whole country round about him, three or four years ago. He had taken infinite pains with this matter, had brought a young woman from Suffolk at his own expense, to teach the children at Wettersham the whole of this manufacture, from beginning to end; and, before he died, he saw as handsome bonnets made, as ever came from Tuscany. At Benenden, the parish in which Mr. Hodges resides, there is now a manufactory of the same sort, begun, in the first place, under the benevolent auspices of that gentleman's daughters, who began by teaching a poor fellow who had been a cripple from his infancy, who was living with a poor widowed mother, and who is now the master of a school of this description, in the beautiful villages of Benenden and Rolvenden, in Kent. My wife, wishing to have her bonnet cleaned some time ago, applied to a person who performs such work, at Brighton, and got into a conversation with her about the *English Leghorn* bonnets. The woman told her that they looked very well at first, but that they would not retain their colour, and added, "They will not clean, ma'am, like this bonnet that you have." She was left with a request to clean that; and the result being the same as with all Leghorn bonnets, she was surprised upon being told that that was an "English Leghorn." In short, there is no difference at all in the two; and if these people at Tring choose to grow the straw, instead of importing it from Leghorn; and if they choose to make plat, and to make bonnets just as beautiful and as lasting, as those which come from Leghorn, they have nothing to do but to read my Cottage Economy (paragraph 224 to paragraph 234, inclusive), where they will find, as plain as words can make it, the whole mass of directions for taking the seed of the wheat, and converting the produce into bonnets. There they will find directions, first, as to the sort of wheat; second, as to the proper land for growing the wheat; third, season for sowing; fourth, quantity of seed to the acre, and manner of sowing; fifth, season for cutting the wheat; sixth, manner of cutting it; seventh, manner of bleaching; eighth, manner of housing the straw; ninth, platting; tenth, manner of knitting; eleventh, manner of pressing.

I request my correspondents to inform me, if any one can, where I can get some spring wheat. The botanical name of it is, *Triticum Æstivum*.[1] It is sown in the spring, at the same time that barley is; these Latin words mean *summer wheat*. It is a small-grained, bearded wheat. I know, from experience, that the little brown-grained winter wheat is just as good for the purpose: but that must be sown earlier; and there is danger of its being thinned on the ground, by worms and other enemies. I should like to sow some this next spring, in order to convince the people of Tring, and other places, that they need not go to Tuscany for the straw.

Of "*Cobbett's Corn*" there is no considerable piece in the neighbourhood of Tring; but I saw some plants, even upon the high hill where the locusts are growing, and which is very backward land, which appeared to be about as forward as my own is at this time.[2] If Mr. Elliman were to have a patch of good corn by the side of his locust trees, and a piece of spring wheat by the side of the corn, people might then go and see specimens of the three great undertakings, or rather, great additions to the wealth of the nation, introduced under the name of *Cobbett*.

I am the more desirous of introducing this manufacture at Tring on account of the very marked civility which I met

---

[1] Some botanists have attempted to distinguish species among the numerous varieties of wheat, assigning the term "Triticum æstivum," or summer wheat, to the awnless or beardless varieties, and "Triticum hibernum," or winter wheat, to the awned or bearded varieties; but the length or shortness of the awn depends upon accidental circumstances. Neither do the awnless or beardless varieties perfectly correspond with the varieties of summer wheat (preferred for sowing in spring), nor do the awned or bearded varieties correspond with the winter wheat (sown in autumn), as some of the hardy varieties of winter wheat are awnless, while some of the spring varieties are bearded.

[2] The previous Editor reminds us, in his note on "Cobbett's Indian corn," that although its utility for human food has been questioned, "it appears to be eaten by the wealthier classes" in all countries "where it grows."

with at that place. A very excellent friend of mine, who is professionally connected with that town, was, some time ago, apprised of my intention of going thither to see Mr. Elliman's plantation. He had mentioned this intention to some gentlemen of that town and neighbourhood; and I, to my great surprise, found that a *dinner had been organized*, to which I was to be invited. I never like to disappoint any body; and, therefore, to this dinner I went. The company consisted of about forty-five gentlemen of the town and neighbourhood; and, certainly, though I have been at dinners in several parts of England, I never found, even in Sussex, where I have frequently been so delighted, a more sensible, hearty, entertaining, and hospitable company, than this. From me, something in the way of speech was expected, as a matter of course; and though I was, from a cold, so hoarse as not to be capable of making myself heard in a large place, I was so pleased with the company, and with my reception, that, first and last, I dare say I addressed the company for an hour and a half. We dined at two, and separated at nine; and, as I declared at parting, for many, many years, I had not spent a happier day. There was present the editor, or some other gentleman, from the newspaper called *The Bucks Gazette and General Advertiser*, who has published in his paper the following account of what passed at the dinner. As far as the report goes, it is substantially correct; and, though this gentleman went away at a very early hour, that which he has given of my speech (which he has given very judiciously) contains matter, which can hardly fail to be useful, to great numbers of his readers.

MR. COBBETT AT TRING.

"Mr. Elliman, a draper of Tring, has lately formed a considerable plantation of the locust tree, which Mr. Cobbett claims the merit of having introduced into this country. The number he has planted is about 30,000, on five acres and a half of very indifferent land, and they have thrived so uncommonly well, that not more than 500 of the whole number have failed. The success of the plantation being made known to Mr. Cobbett, induced him to pay a visit to Tring to inspect it, and during his sojourn, it was determined upon by his friends, to give him a dinner, at the Rose and Crown Inn. Thursday was fixed for the purpose; when about forty persons, agriculturists and tradesmen of Tring and the neighbouring towns, assembled, and sat down to a dinner served up in very excellent style, by Mr. Northwood, the landlord: Mr. Faithful, solicitor, of Tring, in the chair.

"The usual routine toasts having been given,

"The Chairman said, he was sure the company would drink the toast, with which he should conclude what he was about to say, with every mark of respect. In addressing the company, he rose under feelings of no ordinary kind, for he was about to give the health of a gentleman who had the talent of communicating to his writings, an energy, and perspicuity, which he had never met with elsewhere; who conveyed knowledge in a way so clear, that all who read, could understand. He (the Chairman) had read the Political Register, from the first of them to the last, with pleasure and benefit to himself, and he would defy any man to put his finger upon a single line, which was not in direct support of a kingly government. He advocated the rights of the people, but he always expressed himself favourable to our ancient form of government; he certainly had strongly, but not too strongly, attacked the corruption of the government; but had never attacked its form or its just powers. As a public writer, he considered him the most impartial, that he knew. He well recollected—he knew not if Mr. Cobbett himself recollected it—a remarkable passage in his writings: he was speaking of the pleasure of passing from censure to praise, and thus expressed himself. 'It is turning from the frowns of a surly winter, to welcome a smiling spring come dancing over the daisied lawn, crowned with garlands, and surrounded with melody.' Nature had been bountiful to him; it had blessed him with a constitution capable of enduring the greatest fatigues; and a mind of superior order,

Brilliancy, it was said, was a mere meteor; it was so: it was the solidity, and depth of understanding, such as he possessed, that were really valuable. He had visited this place in consequence of a gentleman having been wise, and bold enough, to listen to his advice, and to plant a large number of locust trees; and he trusted he would enjoy prosperity and happiness, in duration equal to that of the never-decaying wood of those trees. He concluded by giving Mr. Cobbett's health."

"Mr. Cobbett returned thanks for the manner in which his health had been drunk, and was certain that the trees which had been the occasion of their meeting, would be a benefit to the children of the planter. Though it might appear like presumption to suppose that those who were assembled that day, came solely in compliment to him, yet it would be affectation not to believe that it was expected he should say something on the subject of politics. Every one who heard him, was convinced that there was something wrong, and that a change of some sort must take place, or ruin to the country would ensue. Though there was a diversity of opinions as to the cause of the distress, and as to the means by which a change might be effected, and though some were not so deeply affected by it as others, all now felt that a change must take place before long, whether they were manufacturers, brewers, butchers, bakers, or of any other description of persons, they had all arrived at the conviction, that there must be a change. It would be presumptuous to suppose that many of those assembled, did not understand the cause of the present distress, yet there were many who did not: and those gentlemen who did, he begged to have the goodness to excuse him, if he repeated what they already knew. Politics was a science which they ought not to have the trouble of studying; they had sufficient to do in their respective avocations without troubling themselves with such matters. For what were the ministers, and a whole tribe of persons under them, paid large sums of money from the country, but for the purpose of governing its political affairs. Their fitness for their stations was another thing. He had been told that Mr. Huskisson was so ignorant of the cause of the distress, that he had openly said, he should be glad if any practical man, would tell him what it all meant. If any man present were to profess his ignorance of the cause of the distress it would be no disgrace to him; he might be a very good butcher, a very good farmer, or a very good baker: he might well understand the business by which he gained his living; and if any one should say to him, because he did not understand politics, 'You are a very stupid fellow!' he might fairly reply, 'What is that to you?' But it was another thing in those who were so well paid to manage the affairs of the country to plead ignorance of the cause of the prevailing distress.

* * * * * *

"Mr. Goulburn, with a string of figures as long as his arm, had endeavoured to prove in the House of Commons, that the withdrawal of the one-pound notes, being altogether so small an amount, little more than two millions, would be of no injury to the country, and that its only effect would be to make bankers more liberal in discounting with their fives. He would appeal to the company, if they had found this to be the case. Mr. Goulburn had forgotten that the one-pound notes were the legs upon which the fives walked. He had heard the Duke of Wellington use the same language in the other House. Taught as they now were, by experience, it would scarcely be believed, fifty years hence, that a set of men could have been found with so little foresight as to have devised measures so fraught with injury.

"He felt convinced that if he looked to the present company, or any other, accidentally assembled, that he would find thirteen gentlemen more fit to manage the affairs of the kingdom than were those who now presided at the head of Government; not that he imputed to them any desire to do wrong, or that they were more corrupt than others; it was clear, that with the eyes of the public upon them they must wish to do right; it was owing to their sheer ignorance, their entire unfitness to carry on the Government, that they did no better. Ignorance and unfitness were, however, pleas which they had no business to make. It was nothing to him if a man was ignorant and stupid, under ordinary circumstances ; but if he entrusted a man with his money, thinking that he was intelligent, and was deceived, then it was something ; he had a right to say, 'You are not what I took you for, you are an ignorant fellow ; you have deceived me, you are an impostor.' Such was the language proper to all under such circumstances : never mind their titles !

"A friend had that morning taken him to view the beautiful vale of Aylesbury, which he had never before seen; and the first thought that struck him, on seeing the rich pasture was this, 'Good God! is a country like this to be ruined by the folly of those who govern it?' When he was a naughty boy, he used to say that if he wanted to select Members for our Houses of Parliament, he would put a string across any road leading *into* London, and that the first 1000 men that ran against his string, he would choose for Members, and he would bet a wager, that they would be better qualified, than those who now filled those Houses. That was when he was a naughty boy ; but since that time a bill has been passed, which made it banishment for life, to use language that brought the Houses of Parliament into contempt, and therefore he did not say so now. The Government, it should be recollected, had passed all these acts with the hearty concurrence of both houses of Parliament ; they were thus backed by these Houses, and they were backed by ninety-nine out of one hundred of the papers, which affected to see all their acts in rose-colour, for no one who was in the habit of reading the papers, could have anticipated, from what they there saw, the ruin which had fallen on the country. Thus we had an ignorant Government, an ignorant Parliament, and something worse than an ignorant press ; the latter being employed (some of them with considerable talent) to assail and turn into ridicule those who had the boldness and honesty to declare their dissent from the opinion of the wisdom of the measures of Government. It was no easy task to stand, unmoved, their ridicule and sarcasms, and many were thus deterred from expressing the sentiments of their minds. In this country we had all the elements of prosperity; an industrious people, such as were nowhere else to be found; a country too, which was once called the finest and greatest on the earth (for whatever might be said of the country in comparison with others, the turnips of England were worth more, this year, than all the vines of France.) It was a glorious and a great country until the government had made it otherwise; and it ought still to be what it was once, and to be capable of driving the Russians back from the country of our old and best ally,— the Turks.[1] During the time of war, we were told that it was necessary to make great sacrifices to save us from disgrace. The people made those sacrifices; they gave up their all. But had the Government done its part; had it saved us from disgrace? No: we were now the laughing-stock of all other countries. The French and all other nations derided us; and by and by it would be seen that they would make a partition of Turkey with the Russians, and make a fresh subject for laughter. Never since the time of Charles had such disgrace been brought upon the country; and why was this? When were we again to see the labourer receiving his wages from the farmer, instead of being sent on the road to break stones? Some people, under this state of things, consoled themselves

---

[1] The opinions of the Author seem to have been substantiated by recent events. At the peace which followed the memorable Crimean War (1854 to 1856), "by the Treaty of Paris," Russia renounced her claims on the Principalities of Moldavia and Wallachia, agreed to dismantle the fortifications of Sebastopol, guaranteed not to keep ships of war in the Black Sea, and ceded a portion of territory to form a new frontier. The Russian Government, however, taking the opportunity of the Franco-German War, declared, in 1871, that it felt itself no longer bound by the Paris Treaty, which forbade Russia to have a fleet in the Black Sea; and a London Conference sanctioned this stroke of Russian diplomacy. Afterwards occurred the war between Russia and Turkey (1877-1878), in which Russia was the victor. By the Treaty of Berlin, which followed the peace, the provinces of Roumania, Servia, Montenegro and Bulgaria were declared "independent." Bessarabia was added to Russia, Herzegovina and Bosnia were added to Austro-Hungary; and in Asia a portion of Armenia was also ceded to Russia. The English Government undertook to defend the Porte's dominions in Asia, and to receive in return the right to occupy the island of Cyprus.

by saying things would come about again; they had come about before, and would come about again. They deceived themselves, things did not come about; the seasons came about, it was true; but something must be *done* to bring things about. Instead of the *neuter* verb (to speak as a grammarian) they should use the *active ;* they should not say things will *come* about, but things must be *put* about. He thought that the distress would shortly become so great, perhaps, about Christmas, that the Parliamentary gentlemen, finding they received but a small part of their rents, without which they could not do, any more than the farmer, without his crops, would endeavour to bring them about; and the measures they would propose for that purpose, as far as he could judge, would be Bank restriction, and the re-issue of one-pound notes, and what the effect of that would be they would soon see. One of those persons who were so profoundly ignorant would come down to the House, prepared to propose a return to Bank restriction, and the issue of small notes, and that a bill to that effect should be passed.[1] If such a bill did pass, he would advise all persons to be cautious in their dealings; it would be perilous to make bargains under such a state of things. Money was the measure of value; but if this measure was liable to be three times as large at one time as at another, who could know what to do? how was any one to know how to purchase wheat, if the bushel was to be altered at the pleasure of the Government to three times its present size? The remedy for the evils of the country, was not to be found in palliatives; it was not to be found in strong measures. The first step must be taken in the House of Commons, but that was almost hopeless; for although many persons possessed the right of voting, it was of little use to them; whilst a few great men could render their votes of no avail. If we had possessed a House of Commons that represented the feelings and wishes of the people, they would not have submitted to

---

[1] The previous Editor alludes to the fact, that both these measures were afterwards proposed in Parliament during a similar state of depression which existed in 1847.

much of what had taken place; and until we had a reform we should never, he believed, see measures, emanating from that House, which would conduce to the glory and safety of the country. He feared that there would be no improvement, until a dreadful convulsion took place, and that was an event which he prayed God to avert from the country."

"The Chairman proposed '*Prosperity to Agriculture*,' when

"Mr. Cobbett again rose, and said the chairman had told him, he was entitled to give a sentiment. He would give prosperity to the towns of Aylesbury and Tring; but he would again advise those who calculated upon the return of prosperity, to be careful. Until there was an equitable adjustment, or Government took off part of the taxes, which was the same thing, there could be no return of prosperity."

After the reporter went away, we had a great number of toasts, most of which were followed by more or less of speech; and, before we separated, I think that the seeds of common sense, on the subject of our distresses, were pretty well planted in the lower part of Hertfordshire, and in Buckinghamshire.

The gentlemen present were men of information, well able to communicate to others that which they themselves had heard; and I endeavoured to leave no doubt in the mind of any man that heard me, that the cause of the distress was the work of the Government and House of Commons, and that it was nonsense to hope for a cure, until the people had a real voice, in the choosing of that House. I think that these truths were well implanted; and I further think that if I could go to the capital of every county in the kingdom, I should leave no doubt in the minds of any part of the people. I must not omit to mention, in conclusion, that though I am no eater or drinker, and though I tasted nothing but the breast of a little chicken, and drank nothing but water, the dinner was the best that ever I saw called a *public dinner*, and certainly unreasonably cheap. There were excellent joints of meat of the finest description, fowls and geese in abundance; and, finally, a very fine haunch of venison, with a bottle of wine for each person; and all for *seven shillings and sixpence per head.* Good waiting upon; civil landlord and landlady; and, in short, every thing at this very pretty town pleased me exceedingly. Yet, what is Tring but a fair specimen of English towns and English people? And is it right, and is it to be suffered, that such a people should be plunged into misery by the acts of those whom they pay so generously, and whom they so loyally and cheerfully obey?

As far as I had an opportunity of ascertaining the facts, the farmers feel all the pinchings of distress, and the still harsher pinchings of anxiety for the future; and the labouring people are suffering in a degree not to be described. The shutting of the male paupers up in pounds, is common through Bedfordshire and Buckinghamshire. Left at large during the day, they roam about and maraud. What are the farmers to do with them? God knows how long the peace is to be kept, if this state of things be not put a stop to. The natural course of things is, that an attempt to impound the paupers in cold weather, will produce resistance in some place; that those of one parish will be joined by those of another; that a formidable band will soon be assembled; then will ensue the rummaging of pantries and cellars; that this will spread from parish to parish; and that, finally, mobs of immense magnitude will set the law at open defiance.[1] Jails are next to useless in such a

---

[1] The subject of Pauper Relief has already been touched upon. The previous Editor reminds us, in this place, that the Poor Law Amendment Bill, which was passed August 14, 1834, was intended as a sop to the land, in its distressed condition, and to reduce those £6,000,000 or £7,000,000 of rates (mentioned in these Rides), and also to induce the rural population to migrate to the manufacturing towns. The Author asserted, in the House of Commons, when this Bill was being debated, that a document existed, showing that the projectors of the Bill, contemplated bringing the labouring people "to live on coarser food." The thirteenth Poor Law Report, 1847, states that the sums actually paid in relief, were as follows:—

In 1843	£5,208,027
„ 1844	4,976,093
„ 1845	4,039,703
„ 1846	4,962,026

For the year ending Lady-day 1883, the Poor-rates amounted to £15,238,111 —but more than one third of this amount was expended for other purposes than the relief of the poor.

case: their want of room must leave the greater part of the offenders at large: the agonizing distress of the farmers will make them comparatively indifferent with regard to these violences; and, at last, general confusion will come. This is by no means an unlikely progress, or an unlikely result. It therefore becomes those who have much at stake, to join heartily in their applications to Government, for a timely remedy for these astounding evils.

NORTHERN TOUR.

Sheffield, 31*st January*, 1830.

On the 26th instant I gave my third lecture at Leeds. I should in vain endeavour to give an adequate description of the pleasure which I felt at my reception, and at the effect which I produced in that fine and opulent capital of this great county of York; for the *capital* it is in fact, though not in name. On the first evening, the play-house, which is pretty spacious, was not completely filled in all its parts; but on the second and the third, it was filled brim full, boxes, pit and gallery; besides a dozen or two of gentlemen who were accommodated with seats on the stage. Owing to a cold which I took at Huddersfield, and which I spoke of before, I was, as the players call it, not in very good *voice;* but the audience made allowance for that, and very wisely preferred sense, to sound. I never was more delighted than with my audience at Leeds; and what I set the highest value on, is, that I find I produced a prodigious effect in that important town.

There had been a meeting at Doncaster, a few days before

Great opposition was raised to the Poor Law Bill of 1834, and especially to the separation of the sexes in the unions and to the restrictions of out-door relief; but these provisions have been fully justified; and the working of the Bill has not only reduced the poor rates, but raised the labouring class in industry and virtue.

I went to Leeds from Ripley, where one of the speakers, a Mr. Becket Denison had said, speaking of the taxes, that there must be an application of the *pruning hook* or of the *sponge*. This gentleman is a banker, I believe: he is one of the Beckets connected with the Lowthers; and he is a brother, or very near relation of that Sir John Becket who is the Judge Advocate General. So that, at last, others can talk of the pruning hook and the sponge, as well as I.

From Leeds, I proceeded on to this place, not being able to stop at either Wakefield or Barnsley, except merely to change horses. The people in those towns were apprised of the time that I should pass through them; and, at each place, great numbers assembled to see me, to shake me by the hand, and to request me to stop. I was so hoarse as not to be able to make the post-boy hear me, when I called to him; and, therefore, it would have been useless to stop; yet I promised to go back if my time and my voice would allow me. They do not; and I have written to the gentlemen of those places to inform them, that when I go to Scotland in the spring, I will not fail to stop in those towns, in order to express my gratitude to them. All the way along, from Leeds to Sheffield, it is coal and iron, and iron and coal. It was dark before we reached Sheffield; so that we saw the iron furnaces, in all the horrible splendour of their everlasting blaze. Nothing can be conceived more grand or more terrific than the yellow waves of fire, that incessantly issue from the top of these furnaces, some of which are close by the way-side. Nature has placed the beds of iron and the beds of coal alongside of each other, and art has taught man to make one, to operate upon the other so as to turn the iron-stone into liquid matter, which is drained off from the bottom of the furnace, and afterwards moulded into blocks and bars, and all sorts of things. The combustibles are put into the top of the furnace, which stands thirty, forty, or fifty feet up in the air, and the ever-blazing mouth of which is kept supplied with coal and coke and iron-stone, from little iron waggons forced up by steam, and brought down again to be re-filled. It is a surprising thing to behold;

and it is impossible to behold it without being convinced that, whatever other nations may do with cotton and with wool, they will never equal England, with regard to things made of iron and steel. This Sheffield, and the land all about it, is one bed of iron and coal. They call it Black Sheffield, and black enough it is; but from this one town and its environs go nine-tenths of the knives that are used in the whole world; there being, I understand, no knives made at Birmingham; the manufacture of which place consists of the larger sorts of implements, of locks of all sorts, and guns and swords, and of all the endless articles of hardware which go to the furnishing of a house. As to the land, viewed in the way of agriculture, it really does appear to be very little worth. I have not seen, except at Harewood and Ripley, a stack of wheat since I came into Yorkshire; and even there, the whole I saw, and all that I saw during a ride of six miles that I took into Derbyshire the day before yesterday, all put together would not make the one-half of what I have many times seen in one single rick-yard of the vales of Wiltshire. But this is all very proper: these coal-diggers, and iron-smelters, and knife-makers, compel us to send the food to them, which, indeed, we do very cheerfully, in exchange for the produce of their rocks, and the wondrous works of their hands.

The trade of Sheffield has fallen off, less in proportion than that of the other manufacturing districts. North America, and particularly the United States, where the people have so much victuals to cut, form a great branch of the custom of this town. If the people of Sheffield could only receive a tenth part of what their knives sell for by retail in America, Sheffield might pave its streets with silver. A *gross* of knives and forks is sold to the Americans, for less than three knives and forks, can be bought at retail in a country store in America.[1] No fear of

---

[1] Probably the Author had in his recollection, when he was making this statement, what had actually occurred in America, shortly after he left it for England in 1819, viz., that English goods were almost "given away" at the auction sales there. Indeed, it was the common saying, not only in America but in all the English Colonies, that commerce oscillated between

rivalship in this trade. The Americans may lay on their tariff, and double it, and triple it; but as long as they continue to *cut* their victuals, from Sheffield, they must have the things to cut it with.

The ragged hills all round about this town, are bespangled with groups of houses inhabited by the working cutlers. They have not suffered like the working weavers; for, to make knives, there must be the hand of man. Therefore, machinery cannot come to destroy the wages of the labourer. The home demand, has been very much diminished; but still the depression has here, not been what it has been, and what it is, where the machinery can be brought into play. We are here just upon the borders of Derbyshire, a nook of which runs up, and separates, Yorkshire from Nottinghamshire. I went to a village, the day before yesterday, called *Mosborough*, the whole of the people of which are employed in the making of *sickles* and *scythes;* and where, as I was told, they are very well off even in these times. A prodigious quantity of these things, go to the United States of America. In short, there are about twelve millions of people there, continually consuming these things; and the hardware merchants here, have their agents, and their stores, in the great towns of America; which country, as far as relates to this branch of business, is still a part of old England.

Upon my arriving here on Wednesday night, the 27th instant, I by no means intended to lecture, until I should have a little recovered from my cold; but to my great mortification, I found that the lecture had been advertised, and that great numbers of persons had actually assembled. To send them out again, and give back the money, was a thing not to be attempted. I, therefore, went to the Music Hall, the place which had been taken for the purpose, gave them a specimen of the state of my voice, asked them whether I should proceed,

---

scarcity and glut. Happily, at the present time the telegraphic cable, equalizes supply and demand, and prevents the ruinous losses which were previously made by shippers. Sheffield at the present time has competitors, in the cutlery and steel trade, in France, Belgium, and Canada.

and they answering in the affirmative, on I went. I then rested until yesterday, and shall conclude my labours here to-morrow, and then proceed to "*fair Nottingham*," as we used to sing when I was a boy, in celebrating the glorious exploits of "Robin Hood and Little John." By the by, as we went from Huddersfield to Dewsbury, we passed by a hill which is celebrated as being the burial-place of the famed Robin Hood, of whom the people in this country talk to this day.

At Nottingham, they have advertised for my lecturing at the play-house, for the 3rd, 4th, and 6th of February, and for a public breakfast to be given to me on the first of those days, I having declined a dinner agreeably to my original notification, and my friends insisting upon something or other in that sort of way. It is very curious that I have always had a very great desire to see Nottingham. This desire certainly originated in the great interest that I used to take, and that all country boys took, in the history of Robin Hood, in the record of whose achievements, which were so well calculated to excite admiration in the country boys, this Nottingham, with the word "*fair*" always before it, was so often mentioned. The word *fair*, as used by our forefathers, meant fine; for we frequently read in old descriptions of parts of the country of such a district or such a parish, containing a *fair* mansion, and the like; so that this town appears to have been celebrated as a very fine place, even in ancient times; but within the last thirty years, Nottingham has stood high in my estimation, from the conduct of its people; from their public spirit; from their excellent sense as to public matters; from the noble struggle, which they have made from the beginning of the French war, to the present hour; if only forty towns in England equal in size to Nottingham, had followed its bright example, there would have been no French war against liberty; the Debt would have been now nearly paid off, and we should have known nothing of those manifold miseries, which now afflict, and those greater miseries, which now menace, the country. The French would not have been in Cadiz; the Russians would not have been at Constantinople; the Americans would not have been in the Floridas; we should not have had to dread the combined fleets of America, France and Russia; and, which is the worst of all, we should not have seen the jails four times as big as they were; and should not have seen Englishmen reduced to such a state of misery, as for the honest labouring man to be fed, worse than the felons in the jails.

EASTERN TOUR.

"You permit the Jews openly to preach in their synagogues, and call "Jesus Christ an impostor; and you send women to jail (to be brought "to bed there, too), for declaring their unbelief in Christianity."—*King of Bohemia's Letter to Canning, published in the Register, 4th of January, 1823.*

Hargham, 22nd *March*, 1830.

I set off from London on the 8th of March, got to Bury St. Edmund's that evening; and, to my great mortification, saw the county-election, and the assizes both going on, at Chelmsford, where, of course, a great part of the people of Essex were met. If I had been aware of that, I should certainly have stopped at Chelmsford, in order to address a few words of *sense* to the unfortunate constituents of Mr. Western. At Bury St. Edmund's I gave a lecture on the ninth, and another on the tenth of March, in the playhouse, to very crowded audiences. I went to Norwich on the 12th, and gave a lecture there on that evening, and on the evening of the 13th. The audience here was more numerous than at Bury St. Edmund's, but not so numerous in proportion to the size of the place; and, contrary to what has happened in most other places, it consisted more of town's people than of country people.

During the 14th and 15th, I was at a friend's house at Yelverton, half way between Norwich and Bungay, which last is in Suffolk, and at which place I lectured on the 16th to an audience consisting chiefly of farmers, and was entertained there in a most hospitable and kind manner, at the house of a friend.

The next day, being the 17th, I went to Eye, and there lectured in the evening in the neat little playhouse of the place, which was crowded in every part, stage and all. The audience consisted almost entirely of farmers, who had come in from Diss, from Harleston, and from all the villages round about, in this fertile and thickly-settled neighbourhood. I staid at Eye all the day of the 18th, having appointed to be at Ipswich on the 19th. Eye is a beautiful little place, though an exceedingly rotten borough.

All was harmony and good humour: everybody appeared to be of one mind; and as these friends observed to me, so I thought, that more effect had been produced by this one lecture in that neighbourhood, than could have been produced in a whole year, if the Register had been put into the hands of every one of the hearers, during that space of time; for though I never attempt to put forth that sort of stuff which the "intense" people on the other side of St. George's Channel call "*eloquence*," I bring out strings of very interesting facts; I use pretty powerful arguments; and I hammer them down so closely upon the mind, that they seldom fail to produce a lasting impression.

On the 19th I proceeded to Ipswich, not imagining it to be the fine, populous and beautiful place that I found it to be. On that night, and on the night of the 20th, I lectured to boxes and pit, crowded principally with opulent farmers, and to a gallery filled, apparently, with journeymen tradesmen and their wives. On the Sunday before I came away, I heard, from all quarters, that my audiences had retired deeply impressed with the truths which I had endeavoured to inculcate. One thing, however, occurred towards the close of the lecture of Saturday, the 20th, that I deem worthy of particular attention. In general it would be useless for me to attempt to give anything like *a report* of these speeches of mine, consisting as they do of words uttered pretty nearly as fast as I can utter them, during a space of never less than two, and sometimes of nearly three hours. But there occurred here, something that I must notice. I was speaking of *the degrees* by which the established church had been losing its *legal influence* since the peace. First, the *Unitarian Bill*, removing the penal act which forbade an impugning of the doctrine of the Trinity; second, the repeal of the *Test Act*, which declared, in effect, that the religion of any of the Dissenters was as good as that of the Church of England; third, the repeal of the penal and excluding laws with regard to the *Catholics;* and this last act, said I, does in effect declare that the thing called "the *Reformation*" was *unnecessary.* "No," said one gentleman, in a very loud voice, and he was followed by four or five more, who said "No, No." "Then," said I, "we will, if you like, put it *to the vote.* Under-"stand, gentlemen, that *I do not say*, whatever I may think, that "the Reformation was unnecessary; but I say that *this act* "*amounts to a declaration*, that it was unnecessary; and, without "losing our good humour, we will, if that gentleman choose, "put this question to the vote." I paused a little while, receiving no answer, and perceiving that the company were with me, I proceeded with my speech, concluding with the complete demolishing blow which the church would receive, by the bill for giving civil and political power for training to the bar, and seating on the bench, for placing in the commons and amongst the peers, and for placing in the council, along with the King himself, *those who deny that there ever existed a Redeemer;* who give the name of *impostor* to Him whom *we worship as God*, and who boast of having hanged Him upon the cross. "Judge you, gentlemen," said I, "of the figure "which England will make, when its laws will seat on the "bench, from which people have been sentenced to suffer "most severely for denying the truth of Christianity; from "which bench it has been held that *Christianity is part and* "*parcel of the law of the land;* judge you of the figure which "England will make amongst Christian nations, when a Jew, "a blasphemer of Christ, a professor of the doctrines of those "who murdered him, shall be sitting upon that bench; and "judge, gentlemen, what we must think of *the clergy* of this "church of ours, *if they remain silent* while such a law shall "be passed."

We were entertained at Ipswich by a very kind and excellent friend, whom, as is generally the case, I had never seen or heard of before. The morning of the day of the last lecture, I walked about five miles, then went to his house to breakfast, and staid with him and dined. On the Sunday morning, before I came away, I walked about six miles, and repeated the good cheer at breakfast at the same place. Here I heard the first singing of the birds this year; and I here observed an instance of that *petticoat government*, which, apparently, pervades the whole of animated nature. A lark, very near to me in a ploughed field, rose from the ground, and was saluting the sun with his delightful song. He was got about as high as the dome of St. Paul's, having me for a motionless and admiring auditor, when the hen started up from nearly the same spot whence the cock had risen, flew up and passed close by him. I could not hear what she said; but supposed that she must have given him a pretty smart reprimand; for down she came upon the ground, and he, ceasing to sing, took a twirl in the air, and came down after her. Others have, I daresay, seen this a thousand times over; but I never observed it before.

About twelve o'clock, my son and I set off for this place (Hargham), coming through Needham Market, Stow-market, Bury St. Edmund's, and Thetford, at which latter place I intended to have lectured to-day and to-morrow, where the theatre was to have been the scene, but the mayor of the town thought it best not to give his permission until the assizes (which commence to-day the 22nd) should be over, lest the judge should take offence, seeing that it is the custom, while his Lordship is in the town, to give up the civil jurisdiction to him. Bless his worship! what in all the world should he think would take me to Thetford, *except it being a time for holding the assizes!* At no *other* time should I have dreamed of finding an audience in so small a place, and in a country so thinly inhabited. I was attracted, too, by the desire of meeting some of my "*learned friends*" from the Wen; for I deal in arguments, founded on the *law of the land*, and on *Acts of Parliament*. The deuce take this Mayor for disappointing me; and, now, I am afraid that I shall not fall in with this learned body during the whole of my spring tour.

Finding Thetford to be forbidden ground, I came hither to Sir Thomas Beevor's, where I had left my two daughters, having, since the 12th inclusive, travelled 120 miles, and delivered six lectures. These 120 miles have been through a fine *farming country*, and without my seeing, until I came to Thetford, but one spot of waste or common land, and that not exceeding, I should think, from fifty to eighty acres. From this place to Norwich, and through Attleborough and Wymondham, the land is all good, and the farming excellent. It is pretty nearly the same from Norwich to Bungay, where we enter Suffolk. Bungay is a large and fine town, with three churches, lying on the side of some very fine meadows. Harleston, on the road to Eye, is a very pretty market-town: of Eye, I have spoken before. From Eye to Ipswich, we pass through a series of villages, and at Ipswich, to my great surprise, we found a most beautiful town, with a population of about twelve thousand persons; and here our profound Prime Minister might have seen most abundant evidence of prosperity; for the *new houses* are, indeed, very numerous. But if our famed and profound Prime Minister, having Mr. Wilmot Horton by the arm, and standing upon one of the hills that surround this town, and which, each hill seeming to surpass the other hill in beauty, command a complete view of every house, or, at least, of the top of every house, in this opulent town; if he, thus standing, and thus accompanied, were to hold up his hands, clap them together, and bless God for the proofs of prosperity contained in the new and red bricks, and were to cast his eye southward of the town, and see the numerous little vessels, upon the little arm of the sea, which comes up from Harwich, and which here finds its termination; and were, in those vessels, to discover an additional proof of prosperity; if he were to be thus situated, and to be thus feeling, would not some doubts be awakened in his mind, if I, standing behind him, were to whisper in his ear, "Do you not think that the greater part of these new houses have been created by taxes which went to pay the, about, 20,000 *troops* that were stationed here for pretty nearly 20 years during the war, and some of which are stationed here still? Look at that immense building, my Lord Duke: it is fresh and *new* and fine and splendid, and contains indubitable marks of opulence; but it is a BARRACK; aye, and the money to build that barrack, and to maintain the 20,000 troops, has assisted to beggar, to dilapidate, to plunge into ruin and decay, hundreds upon hundreds of villages and hamlets in Wiltshire, in Dorsetshire, in Somersetshire, and in other counties who shared not in the ruthless squanderings of the war. But," leaning my arm upon the Duke's shoulder, and giving Wilmot a poke in the poll, to make him listen and look, and pointing with my fore-finger to the twelve large, lofty, and magnificent churches, each of them at least 700 years old, and saying, "Do you think Ipswich was "not larger and far more populous 700 years ago than it is at "this hour?" Putting this question to him, would it not check his exultation, and would it not make even Wilmot begin to reflect?

Even at this hour, with all the unnatural swellings of the war, there are not two thousand people, *including the bedridden and the babies*, to each of the magnificent churches. Of adults, there cannot be more than about 1400 to a church; and there is one of the churches which, being well filled, as in ancient times, would contain from four to seven thousand persons, for the nave of it appears to me to be larger than St. Andrew's Hall at Norwich, which Hall was formerly the church of the Benedictine Priory. And, perhaps, the great church here, might have belonged to some monastery; for here were three Augustine priories, one of them founded in the reign of William the Conqueror, another founded in the reign of Henry the Second, another in the reign of King John, with an Augustine friary, a Carmelite friary, an hospital founded in the reign of King John; and here, too, was the College founded by

Cardinal Wolsey, the gateway of which, though built in brick, is still preserved, being the same sort of architecture as that of Hampton Court, and St. James's Palace.

There is no doubt, but that this was a much greater place than it is now. It is the great outlet for the immense quantities of corn grown in this most productive county, and by farmers the most clever that ever lived. I am told that wheat is worth six shillings a quarter more, at some times, at Ipswich than at Norwich, the navigation to London being so much more speedy and safe. Immense quantities of flour are sent from this town. The windmills on the hills in the vicinage are so numerous that I counted, whilst standing in one place, no less than seventeen. They are all painted or washed white; the sails are black; it was a fine morning, the wind was brisk, and their twirling altogether, added greatly to the beauty of the scene, which, having the broad and beautiful arm of the sea on the one hand, and the fields and meadows, studded with farmhouses, on the other, appeared to me the most beautiful sight of the kind that I had ever beheld. The town and its churches were down in the dell before me, and the only object that came to disfigure the scene was THE BARRACK, and made me utter involuntarily the words of BLACKSTONE: "The laws of England recognise no distinction "between the citizen and the soldier; they know of no stand- "ing soldier; no inland fortresses; no barracks." "Ah!" said I to myself, but loud enough for any one to have heard me a hundred yards, "such *were* the laws of England when mass "was said in those magnificent churches, and such they con- "tinued until a *septennial* parliament came and deprived the "people of England of their rights."

I know of no town to be compared with Ipswich, except it be Nottingham; and there is this difference in the two; that Nottingham stands high, and, on one side, looks over a very fine country; whereas Ipswich is in a dell, meadows running up above it, and a beautiful arm of the sea below it. The town itself is substantially built, well paved, every thing good and solid, and no wretched dwellings to be seen on its outskirts. From the town itself, you can see nothing; but you can, in no direction, go from it a quarter of a mile without finding views, that a painter might crave, and then, the country round about it, so well cultivated; the land in such a beautiful state, the farm-houses all white, and all so much alike; the barns, and every thing about the homesteads so snug; the stocks of turnips so abundant every where; the sheep and cattle in such fine order; the wheat all drilled; the ploughman so expert; the furrows, if a quarter of a mile long, as straight as a line, and laid as truly as if with a level: in short, here is every thing to delight the eye, and to make the people proud of their country; and this is the case throughout the whole of this county. I have always found Suffolk farmers great boasters of their superiority over others; and I must say that it is not without reason.

But, observe, this has been a very *highly-favoured county:* it has had poured into it millions upon millions of money, drawn from Wiltshire, and other inland counties. I should suppose that Wiltshire alone has, within the last forty years, had two or three millions of money drawn from it, *to be given to Essex and Suffolk.* At one time there were not less than sixty thousand men kept on foot in these counties. The increase of London, too, the swellings of the immortal Wen, have assisted to heap wealth upon these counties; but, in spite of all this, the distress pervades all ranks and degrees, except those who live on the taxes. At Eye, butter used to sell for eighteen-pence a pound: it now sells for nine-pence halfpenny, though the grass has not yet begun to spring; and eggs were sold at thirty for a shilling. Fine times for me, whose principal food is eggs, and whose sole drink is milk, but very bad times for those who sell me the food and the drink.

Coming from Ipswich to Bury St. Edmund's, you pass through Needham-market and Stowmarket, two very pretty market towns; and, like all the other towns in Suffolk, free from the drawback of shabby and beggarly houses on the outskirts. I remarked that I did not see in the whole county one single instance of paper or rags supplying the place of glass in any window, and did not see one miserable hovel in which a labourer resided. The county, however, is *flat:* with the exception of the environs of Ipswich, there is none of that beautiful variety of hill and dale, and hanging woods, that you see at every town in Hampshire, Sussex, and Kent. It is curious, too, that though the people, I mean the poorer classes of people, are extremely neat in their houses, and though I found all their gardens dug up and prepared for cropping, you do not see about their cottages (and it is just the same in Norfolk) that *ornamental gardening;* the walks, and the flower borders, and the honey-suckles, and roses, trained over the doors, or over arched sticks, that you see in Hampshire, Sussex, and Kent, that I have many a time sat upon my horse to look at so long and so often, as greatly to retard me on my journey. Nor is this done for show or ostentation. If you find a cottage in those counties, by the side of a *by lane*, or in the midst of a forest, you find just the same care about the garden and the flowers. In those counties, too, there is great taste with regard *to trees* of every description, from the hazel to the oak. In Suffolk it appears to be just the contrary: here is the great disfigurement of all these three eastern counties. Almost every bank of every field is studded with *pollards*, that is to say, trees that have been *beheaded*, at from six to twelve feet from the ground, than which nothing in nature can be more ugly. They send out shoots from the head, which are lopped off once in ten or a dozen years for fuel, or other purposes. To add to the deformity, the ivy is suffered to grow on them, which, at the same time, checks the growth of the shoots. These pollards become hollow very soon, and, as timber, are fit for nothing but gate-posts, even before they are hollow. Upon a farm of a hundred acres these pollards, by root and shade, spoil at least six acres of the ground, besides being most destructive to the fences. Why not plant six acres of the ground with timber and underwood? Half an acre a year would most amply supply the farm with poles and brush, and with every thing wanted in the way of fuel; and why not plant hedges to be unbroken by these pollards? I have scarcely seen a single farm of a hundred acres without pollards, sufficient to find the farm-house in fuel, without any assistance from coals, for several years.

However, the great number of farm-houses in Suffolk, the neatness of those houses, the moderation in point of extent which you generally see, and the great store of the food in the turnips, and the admirable management of the whole, form a pretty good compensation for the want of beauties. The land is generally as clean as a garden ought to be; and, though it varies a good deal as to lightness and stiffness, they make it all bear prodigious quantities of Swedish turnips; and on them pigs, sheep, and cattle, all equally thrive. I did not observe a single poor miserable animal in the whole county.

To conclude an account of Suffolk, and not to sing the praises of Bury St. Edmund's, would offend every creature of Suffolk birth; even at Ipswich, when I was praising *that place*, the very people of that town asked me if I did not think Bury St. Edmund's the nicest town in the world. Meet them wherever you will, they have all the same boast; and indeed, as a town *in itself*, it is the neatest place that ever was seen. It is airy, it has several fine open places in it, and it has the remains of the famous abbey walls and the abbey gate entire; and it is so clean and so neat that nothing can equal it in that respect. It was a favourite spot in ancient times; greatly endowed with monasteries and hospitals. Besides the famous Benedictine Abbey, there was once a college and a friary; and as to the abbey itself, it was one of the greatest in the kingdom; and was so ancient as to have been founded only about forty years after the landing of Saint Austin in Kent. The land all round about it is good; and the soil is of that nature as not to produce much dirt at any time of the year; but the country about it is *flat*, and not of that beautiful variety that we find at Ipswich.

After all, what is the reflection now called for? It is that this fine county, for which nature has done all that she can do, soil, climate, sea-ports, people; every thing that can be done, and an internal government, civil and ecclesiastical, the most complete in the world, wanting nothing but to *be let alone*, to make every soul in it as happy as people can be upon earth; the peace provided for by the county rates; property protected by the law of the land; the poor provided for by the poor-rates; religion provided for by the tithes and the church-rates; easy and safe conveyance provided for by the highway-rates; extraordinary danger provided against by the militia-rates; a complete government in itself; *but having to pay a portion of sixty millions a year in taxes over and above all this; and that, too, on account of wars carried on, not for the defence of England;* not for the upholding of *English liberty and happiness*, but for the purpose of crushing liberty and happiness in other countries; and all this because, and only because, a septennial parliament has deprived the people of their rights.

That which we *admire* most, is not always that, which would be *our choice*. One might imagine, that after all that I have said about this fine county, I should certainly prefer it as a place of residence. I should not, however: my choice has been always very much divided between the woods of Sussex, and the downs of Wiltshire. I should not like to be compelled to decide: but if I were compelled I do believe that I should fix on some vale in Wiltshire. Water meadows at the bottom, corn-land going up towards the hills, those hills being *down land*, and a farm-house, in a clump of trees, in some little cross vale between the hills, sheltered on every side but the south. In short, if Mr. Bennet would give me a farm, the house of which lies on the right-hand side of the road going from Salisbury to Warminster, in the parish of Norton Bovant, just before you enter that village; if he would but be so good as to do that, I would freely give up all the rest of the world to the possession of whoever may get hold of it. I have hinted this to him once or twice before, but I am sorry to say that he turns a deaf ear to my hinting.

Cambridge, 28th March, 1830.

I went from Hargham to Lynn on Tuesday, the 23rd; but

owing to the disappointment at Thetford, every thing was deranged. It was market-day at Lynn, but no preparations of any sort had been made, and no notification given. I therefore resolved, after staying at Lynn on Wednesday, to make a short tour, and to come back to it again. This tour was to take in Ely, Cambridge, St. Ives, Stamford, Peterborough, Wisbeach, and was to bring me back to Lynn, after a very busy ten days. I was particularly desirous to have a little political preaching at *Ely*, the place where the flogging of the English local militia under a guard of German bayonets cost me so dear.

I got there about noon on Thursday, the 25th, being market-day; but I had been apprised even before I left Lynn that no place had been provided for my accommodation. A gentleman at Lynn gave me the name of one at Ely, who, as he thought, would be glad of an opportunity of pointing out a proper place, and of speaking about it; but just before I set off from Lynn I received a notification from this gentleman, that he could do nothing in the matter. I knew that Ely was a small place, but I was determined to go and see the spot where the militia-men were flogged, and also determined to find some opportunity or other of relating that story as publicly as I could at Ely, and of describing the *tail* of the story; of which I will speak presently. Arrived at Ely, I first walked round the beautiful cathedral, that honour to our Catholic forefathers, and that standing disgrace to our Protestant selves. It is impossible to look at that magnificent pile without *feeling* that we are a fallen race of men. The cathedral would, leaving out the palace of the bishop, and the houses of the dean, canons, and prebendaries, weigh more, if it were put into a scale, than all the houses in the town, and all the houses for a mile round the neighbourhood if you exclude the remains of the ancient monasteries. You have only to open your eyes to be convinced that England must have been a far greater, and more wealthy country, in those days than it is in these days. The hundreds of thousands of loads of stone, of which this cathedral and the monasteries in the neighbourhood were built, must all have been brought by sea from distant parts of the kingdom. These foundations were laid more than a thousand years ago; and yet there are vagabonds who have the impudence to say that it is the Protestant religion, that has made England a great country.[1]

Ely is what one may call a miserable little town: very prettily situated, but poor and mean. Everything seems to be on the decline, as, indeed, is the case every where, where the clergy are the masters. They say that this bishop has an income of £18,000 a year. He and the dean and chapter are the owners of all the land and tithes, for a great distance round about, in this beautiful and most productive part of the country; and yet this famous building, the cathedral, is in a state of disgraceful irrepair and disfigurement. The great and magnificent windows to the east have been shortened at the bottom, and the space plastered up with brick and mortar, in a very slovenly manner, for the purpose of saving the expense of keeping the glass in repair. Great numbers of the windows in the upper part of the building, have been partly closed up in the same manner, and others quite closed up. One door-way, which apparently had stood in need of repair, has been rebuilt in modern style, because it was cheaper; and the churchyard contained a flock of sheep, acting as vergers for those, who live upon the immense income, not a penny of which ought to be expended upon themselves, while any part of this beautiful building is in a state of irrepair. This cathedral was erected "to the honour of God and the Holy Church." My daughters went to the service in the afternoon, in the choir of which they

---

[1] What has already been observed, with respect to Salisbury and Winchester Cathedrals, may be repeated with respect to Ely Cathedral, viz., that it was built and endowed before England could have been called, in any sense, "a Roman Catholic country." A monastery was founded on the site of Ely Cathedral, as early as A.D. 673, by Ethelreda, wife of Oswy, king of Northumberland. The monastery was destroyed by the Danes; but it was rebuilt by Ethelwold, Bishop of Winchester, A.D. 970. In 1081, a new Church was begun. This Church was converted into a Cathedral; and the Abbey erected into a See in 1109. The possessions of the Abbey were divided between the Bishop and the town. Among the noted abbots, of which it can boast, was Abbot Thurstan, who defended the Isle of Ely, against William the Conqueror, for seven years.

saw God honoured by the presence of *two old men*, forming the whole of the congregation. I dare say, that in Catholic times, five thousand people at a time have been assembled in this church. The cathedral and town stand upon a little hill, about three miles in circumference, raised up, as it were, for the purpose, amidst the rich fen land, by which the hill is surrounded, and I dare say that the town formerly consisted of houses built over a great part of this hill, and of, probably, from fifty to a hundred thousand people. The people do not now exceed above four thousand, including the bed-ridden and the babies.

Having no place provided for lecturing, and knowing no single soul in the place, I was thrown upon my own resources. The first thing I did was to walk up through the market, which contained much more than an audience sufficient for me; but, leaving the market people to carry on their affairs, I picked up a sort of labouring man, asked him if he recollected when the local militia-men were flogged under the guard of the Germans; and, receiving an answer in the affirmative, I asked him to go and show me the spot, which he did; he showed me a little common along which the men had been marched, and into a piece of pasture-land, where he put his foot upon the identical spot, where the flogging had been executed. On that spot, I told him what I had suffered, for expressing my indignation at that flogging.[1] I told him that a large sum of English money was now every year sent abroad to furnish half-pay and allowances to the Officers of those German troops, and to maintain the widows and children of such of them as were dead; and I added, "You have to work to help to pay that money; part of the taxes which you pay on your malt, hops, beer, leather, soap, candles, tobacco, tea, sugar, and

---

[1] This disgraceful proceeding has already been commented on, viz., that in 1810, the Author was sentenced to imprisonment for two years in Newgate and fined £1000, for having, in his *Political Register*, made some deservedly severe remarks upon the Government for permitting the flogging of five militia-men at Ely for a trifling offence, under a guard of German soldiers. A more infamous instance of political tyranny, in gagging the freedom of the press, can scarcely be found in English history.

every thing else, goes abroad every year to pay these people: it has thus been going abroad ever since the peace; and it will thus go abroad for the rest of your life, if this system of managing the nation's affairs continue; and I told him that about one million seven hundred thousand pounds had been sent abroad on this account, *since the peace.*

When I opened, I found that this man was willing to open too; and he uttered sentiments that would have convinced me, if I had not before been convinced of the fact, that there are very few, even amongst the labourers, who do not clearly understand the cause of their ruin. I discovered that there were two Ely men flogged upon that occasion, and that one of them was still alive and residing near the town. I sent for this man, who came to me in the evening when he had done his work, and who told me, that he had lived seven years with the same master when he was flogged, and was bailiff or head man to his master. He has now a wife and several children, is a very nice-looking, and appears to be a hard-working, man, and to bear an excellent character.

But how was I to harangue? For I was determined not to quit Ely, without something of that sort. I told this labouring man, who showed me the flogging spot, my name, which seemed to surprise him very much, for he had heard of me before. After I had returned to my inn, I walked back again through the market among the farmers; then went to an inn that looked out upon the market-place, went into an up-stairs room, threw up the sash, and sat down at the window, and looked out upon the market. Little groups soon collected to survey me, while I sat in a very unconcerned attitude. The farmers had dined, or I should have found out the most numerous assemblage, and have dined with them. The next best thing was, to go and sit down in the room where they usually dropped in to drink after dinner; and, as they nearly all smoke, to take a pipe with them. This, therefore, I did; and, after a time, we began to talk.

The room was too small, to contain a twentieth part of the people, that would have come in if they could. It was hot to suffocation; but, nevertheless, I related to them the account of the flogging, and of my persecution on that account; and I related to them the account above stated with regard to the English money now sent to the Germans, at which they appeared to be utterly astonished. I had not time sufficient for a lecture, but I explained to them briefly the real cause of the distress which prevailed; I warned the farmers particularly against the consequences of hoping that this distress would remove itself. I portrayed to them the effects of the taxes; and showed them that we owe this enormous burden, to the want of being fairly represented in the Parliament. Above all things, I did that which I never fail to do, showed them the absurdity of grumbling at the six millions a year given in relief to the poor, while they were silent, and seemed to think nothing of the sixty millions of taxes collected by the Government at London, and I asked them how any man of property could have the impudence to call upon the labouring man to serve in the militia, and to deny that that labouring man had, in case of need, a clear right to a share of the produce of the land. I explained to them, how the poor were originally relieved; I told them that the revenues of the livings, which had their foundation in *charity*, were divided for the benefit of the poor, for the repair of the churches, and for the benefit of the clergy themselves; I explained to them how church-rates and poor-rates came to be introduced; how the burden of maintaining the poor came to be thrown upon the people at large; how the nation had sunk by degrees ever since the event, called the Reformation; and, pointing towards the cathedral, I said, "Can you believe, gentlemen, that when that magnificent pile was reared, and when all the fine monasteries, hospitals, schools, and other resorts of piety and charity, existed in this town and neighbourhood; can you believe, that Ely was the miserable little place that it now is; and that England which had never heard of the name of *pauper*, contained the crowds of miserable creatures that it now contains, some starving at stone-cracking by the wayside, and others drawing loaded waggons on that way?"

A young man in the room (I having come to a pause) said; "But, Sir, were there no poor in Catholic times?" "Yes," said I, "to be sure there were. The Scripture says, that the poor shall never cease out of the land; and there are five hundred texts of Scripture, enjoining on all men, to be good and kind to the poor. It is necessary to the existence of civil society, that there should be poor. Men have two motives to industry and care in all the walks of life: one, to acquire wealth; but the other and stronger, to avoid poverty. If there were no poverty, there would be no industry, no enterprise. But this poverty is not to be made a punishment unjustly severe. Idleness, extravagance, are offences against morality; but they are not offences of that heinous nature to justify the infliction of starvation by way of punishment. It is, therefore, the duty of every man that is able; it is particularly the duty of every government, and it was a duty faithfully executed by the Catholic church, to take care that no human being should perish for want in a land of plenty; and to take care, too, that no one should be deficient of a sufficiency of food and raiment, not only to sustain life, but also to sustain health." The young man said: "I thank you, Sir; I am answered."

I strongly advised the farmers to be well with their work-people; for that, unless their flocks were as safe in their fields, as their bodies were in their beds, their lives must be lives of misery; that if their stacks and barns were not places of as safe deposit for their corn, as their drawers were for their money, the life of the farmer was the most wretched upon earth, in place of being the most pleasant, as it ought to be.

Boston, Friday, 9th April, 1830.

Quitting Cambridge and Dr. Chafy and Serjeant Frere,[1]

---

[1] Dr. Chafy was Vice-Chancellor of Cambridge, and Serjeant Frere was Master of Downing. The former had refused the Author permission to hold any meeting in Cambridge of a political character.

on Monday, the 29th of March, I arrived at St. Ives, in Huntingdonshire, about one o'clock in the day. In the evening I harangued about 200 persons, principally farmers, in a wheelwright's shop, that being the only *safe* place in the town, of sufficient dimensions and sufficiently strong. It was market-day; and this is a great cattle-market. As I was not to be at Stamford in Lincolnshire till the 31st, I went from St. Ives to my friend Mr. Wells's, near Huntingdon, and remained there till the 31st in the morning, employing the evening of the 30th in going to Chatteris, in the Isle of Ely, and there addressing a good large company of farmers.

On the 31st, I went to Stamford, and, in the evening, spoke to about 200 farmers and others, in a large room in a very fine and excellent inn, called Standwell's Hotel, which is, with few exceptions, the nicest inn that I have ever been in. On the 1st of April, I harangued here again, and had amongst my auditors some most agreeable, intelligent, and public-spirited yeomen, from the little county of Rutland, who made, respecting the *seat in Parliament*, the proposition, the details of the purport of which, I communicated to my readers in the last Register.

On the 2d of April, I met my audience in the play-house at Peterborough; and though it had snowed all day, and was very wet and sloppy, I had a good large audience; and I did not let this opportunity pass without telling my hearers of the part that their *good* neighbour, Lord Fitzwilliam, had acted with regard to the *French war*, with regard to *Burke and his pension;* with regard to the *dungeoning law*, which drove me across the Atlantic in 1817, and with regard to the putting into the present Parliament, aye, and for that very town, that very Lawyer Scarlett, whose state prosecutions are now become so famous. "Never," said I, "did I say that, behind a man's "back, that I would not say to his face. I wish I had his "face before me: but I am here as near to it, as I can get: "I am before the face of his friends: here, therefore, I will "say what I think of him." When I had described his conduct, and given my opinion on it, many applauded, and not one expressed disapprobation.

On the 3d, I speechified at Wisbeach, in the play-house, to about 220 people, I think it was; and that same night, went to sleep at a friend's (a total stranger to me, however) at St. Edmund's, in the heart of the Fens. I stayed there on the 4th (Sunday), the morning of which brought a hard frost: ice an inch thick, and the total destruction of the apricot blossoms.

After passing Sunday and the greater part of Monday (the 5th) at St. Edmunds, where my daughters and myself received the greatest kindness and attention, we went on Monday afternoon to Crowland, where we were most kindly lodged and entertained at the houses of two gentlemen, to whom also we were personally perfect strangers; and in the evening I addressed a very large assemblage of most respectable farmers and others, in this once famous town. There was another hard frost on the Monday morning; just, as it were, to *finish* the apricot bloom.

On the 6th I went to Lynn, and on that evening and on the evening of the 7th, I spoke to about 300 people in the playhouse. And here there was more *interruption*, than I have ever met with, at any other place. This town, though containing as good and kind friends as I have met with in any other; and though the people are generally as good, contains also, apparently, a large proportion of *dead weight*, the offspring, most likely, of the *rottenness of the borough*. Two or three, or even *one* man, may, if not tossed out at once, disturb and interrupt every thing in a case, where constant attention to *fact* and *argument* is requisite, to insure utility to the meeting. There were but *three* here; and though they were finally silenced, it was not without great loss of time, great noise and hubbub. Two, I was told, were *dead-weight* men, and one a sort of *higgling merchant*.

On the 8th, I went to Holbeach, in this noble county of Lincoln; and good gracious! what a *contrast* with the scene at Lynn? I knew not a soul in the place. Mr. Fields, a bookseller and printer, had invited me by letter, and had, in the nicest and most unostentatious manner, made all the preparations. Holbeach lies in the midst of some of the richest land in the world; a small market-town, but a parish more than twenty miles across, larger, I believe, than the county of Rutland, produced an audience (in a very nice room, with seats prepared) of 178, apparently all wealthy farmers, and men in that rank of life; and an audience so *deeply* attentive to the dry matters on which I had to address it, I have very seldom met with. I was delighted with Holbeach; a neat little town; a most beautiful church with a spire, like that of "the "man of Ross, pointing to the skies;" gardens very pretty; fruit-trees in abundance, with blossom-buds ready to burst; and land, dark in colour, and as fine in substance as flour, as fine as if sifted through one of the sieves, with which we get the dust out of the clover seed; and when cut deep down into with a spade, precisely, as to substance, like a piece of hard butter; yet no where is the *distress* greater than here. I walked on from Holbeach, six miles, towards Boston; and seeing the fatness of the land, and the fine grass and the never-ending sheep lying about like *fat hogs*, stretched in the sun, and seeing the abject state of the labouring people, I could not help exclaiming, "God has given us the best country in the world; our brave and wise and virtuous fathers, who built all these magnificent churches, gave us the best government in the world, and we, their cowardly and foolish and profligate sons have made this once-paradise what we now behold!"

I arrived at Boston (where I am now writing) to-day, (Friday, 9th April) about ten o'clock. I must arrive at Louth before I can say *precisely* what my future route will be. There is an immense fair at Lincoln next week; and a friend has been *here* to point out the proper days to be there; as, however, this Register will not come from the press until after I shall have had an opportunity of writing something at Louth, time enough to be inserted in it, I will here go back, and speak of the country that I have travelled over, since I left Cambridge on the 29th of March.

From Cambridge to St. Ives, the land is generally in open, unfenced fields, and some common fields; generally stiff land, and some of it not very good, and wheat, in many places, looking rather thin. From St. Ives to Chatteris (which last is in the Isle of Ely), the land is better, particularly as you approach the latter place. From Chatteris I came back to Huntingdon, and once more saw its beautiful meadows, of which I spoke when I went thither in 1823. From Huntingdon, through Stilton, to Stamford (the two last in Lincolnshire), is a country of rich arable land and grass fields, and of beautiful meadows. The enclosures are very large, the soil red, with whitish stone below; very much like the soil at, or near, Ross in Herefordshire, and like that near Coventry and Warwick. Here, as all over this country, everlasting fine sheep. The houses all along here are built of the stone of the country; you seldom see brick. The churches are large, lofty, and fine, and give proof that the country was formerly much more populous than it is now, and that the people had a vast deal more of wealth in their hands and at their own disposal. There are three beautiful churches at Stamford, not less, I dare say, than three hundred years old; but two of them (I did not go to the other) are as perfect as when just finished, except as to the *images*, most of which have been destroyed by the ungrateful Protestant barbarians, of different sorts, but some of which (*out of the reach* of their ruthless hands) are still in the niches.

From Stamford to Peterborough is a country of the same description, with the additional beauty of *woods* here and there, and with meadows just like those at Huntingdon, and not surpassed by those on the Severn near Worcester, nor by those on the Avon at Tewkesbury. The cathedral at Peterborough is exquisitely beautiful, and I have great pleasure in saying, that, contrary to the *more magnificent* pile at Ely, it is kept in good order; the Bishop (Herbert Marsh) residing a good deal on the spot; and though he *did* write a pamphlet to justify and urge on the war, the ruinous war, and though he *did* get a *pension* for it, he is, they told me, very good to the poor people. My daughters had a great desire to see, and I had a great desire they should see, the burial-place of that ill-used, that savagely-treated, woman, and that honour to woman-kind, Catherine, queen of the ferocious tyrant, Henry the Eighth. To the infamy of that ruffian, and the shame of after ages, there is no *monument* to record her virtues and her sufferings; and the remains of this daughter of the wise Ferdinand and of the generous Isabella, who sold her jewels to enable Columbus to discover the new world, lie under the floor of the cathedral, commemorated by a short inscription on a plate of brass. All men, Protestants or not Protestants, feel as I feel upon this subject; search the *hearts* of the bishop and of his dean and chapter, and these feelings are there; but to do *justice* to the memory of this illustrious victim of tyranny, would be to cast a reflection on that event to which they owe their rich possessions, and, at the same time, to suggest ideas, not very favourable to the descendants of those, who divided amongst them the plunder of the people arising out of that event, and which descendants are their patrons, and give them what they possess. From this cause, and no other, it is, that the memory of the virtuous Catherine is unblazoned, while that of the tyrannical, the cruel, and the immoral Elizabeth, is recorded with all possible veneration, and all possible varnishing-over of her disgusting amours and endless crimes.

They relate at Peterborough, that the same Sexton who buried Queen Catherine, also buried here Mary Queen of Scots. The remains of the latter, of very questionable virtue, or, rather, of unquestionable vice, were removed to Westminster Abbey by her son, James the First; but those of the virtuous Queen were suffered to remain unhonoured! Good God! what injustice, what a want of principle, what hostility to all virtuous feeling, has not been the fruit of this Protestant Reformation; what plunder, what disgrace to England, what shame, what misery, has that event not produced! There is nothing that I address to my hearers with more visible effect than a statement of *the manner in which the poor-rates and the church-rates came.* This, of course, includes an account of *how the poor were relieved in Catholic times.* To the far greater part of people this is information, *wholly new;* they are *deeply interested* in it; and the impression is very great. Always before we part, Tom Cranmer's church received a considerable blow.

There is in the cathedral a very ancient monument, made to commemorate, they say, the murder of the abbot and his monks by the Danes. Its date is the year 870. Almost all the cathedrals, were, it appears, originally churches of monasteries. That of Winchester and several others, certainly were. There has lately died, in the garden of the bishop's palace, a tortoise that had been *there* more, they say, than two hundred years; a fact very likely to be known; because, at the end of thirty or forty, people would begin to talk about it as something remarkable; and thus the record would be handed down from father to son.

From Peterborough to Wisbeach, the road, for the most part, lies through the *Fens*, and here we passed through the village of Thorney, where there was a famous abbey, which, together with its valuable domain, was given by the savage tyrant, Henry VIII., to John Lord Russell (made a lord by that tyrant), the founder of the family of that name. This man got also the abbey and estate at Woburn; the priory and its estate at Tavistock; and in the next reign, he got Covent Garden and other parts adjoining; together with other things, all then *public property.* A history, a *true history* of this family (which I hope I shall find time to write) would be a most valuable thing. It would be a nice little specimen of the way in which these families became possessed of a great part of their estates. It would show how the poor-rates and the church-rates came. It would set the whole nation *right* at once. Some years ago I had a set of the *Encyclopædia Britannica* (Scotch), which contained an account of every other *great family* in the kingdom; but I could find in it no account of *this* family, either under the word Russell or the word Bedford. I got into a passion with the book, because it contained no account of the mode of raising the birch tree; and it was sold to *a son* (as I was told) of Mr. Alderman Heygate; and if that gentleman look into the book, he will find what I say to be true; but if I should be in error about this, perhaps he will have the goodness to let me know it. I shall be obliged to any one to point me out any printed account of this family; and particularly to tell me where I can get an old folio, containing (amongst other things) Bulstrode's argument and narrative in justification of the sentence and execution of Lord William Russell, in the reign of Charles the Second. It is impossible to look at the now-miserable village of Thorney, and to think of its once-splendid abbey; it is impossible to look at the *twenty thousand acres* of land around, covered with fat sheep, or bearing six quarters of wheat or ten of oats to the acre, without any manure; it is impossible to think of these without feeling a desire that the whole nation should know all about the *surprising merits* of the possessors.

Wisbeach, lying further up the arm of the sea than Lynn, is, like the latter, a little town of commerce, chiefly engaged in exporting to the south, *the corn* that grows in this productive country. It is a good solid town, though not handsome, and has a large market, particularly for corn.

To Crowland, I went, as before stated, from Wisbeach, staying two nights at St. Edmund's. Here I was in the heart of the Fens. The whole country as *level* as the table on which I am now writing. The horizon like the sea in a dead calm: you see the morning sun come up, just as at sea; and see it go down over the rim, in just the same way as at sea in a calm. The land covered with beautiful grass, with sheep lying about upon it, as fat as hogs stretched out sleeping in a stye. The kind and polite friends, with whom we were lodged, had a very neat garden, and fine young orchard. Every thing grows well here: earth without a stone so big as a pin's head; grass as thick as it can grow on the ground; immense bowling-greens separated by ditches; and not the sign of dock or thistle or other weed to be seen. What a contrast between these and the heath-covered sand-hills of Surrey, amongst which I was born! Yet the labourers, who spuddle about the ground in the little *dips* between those sand-hills, are better off than those that exist in this fat of the land. *Here* the grasping system takes *all* away, because it has the means of coming at the value of all: *there*, the poor man enjoys *something*, because he is thought too poor to have any thing: he is there allowed to have what is deemed *worth nothing;* but here, where every inch is valuable, not one inch is he permitted to enjoy.

At Crowland also (still in the Fens) was a great and rich *abbey*, a good part of the magnificent ruins of the church of which are still standing, one corner or part of it being used as the *parish church*, by the worms, which have crept out of the dead bodies of those who lived in the days of the founders;

"And wond'ring man could want the larger pile,
"Exult, and claim the corner with a smile."

They tell you, that all the country at and near Crowland was a mere swamp, a mere bog, *bearing nothing*, bearing nothing worth naming, until the *modern drainings* took place! The thing called the "Reformation," has lied common sense out of men's minds. So *likely* a thing to choose a barren swamp whereon, or wherein, to make the site of an abbey, and of a benedictine abbey too! It has been always observed, that the monks took care to choose for their places of abode, pleasant spots, surrounded by productive land. The likeliest thing in the world for these monks, to choose a swamp for their dwelling-place, surrounded by land that produced nothing good! The thing gives the lie to itself: and it is impossible to reject the belief, that these Fens were as productive of corn and meat a thousand years ago, and more so, than they are at this hour. There is a curious triangular bridge here, on one part of which, stands the statue of one of the ancient kings. It is all of great age; and every thing shows that Crowland was a place of importance in the earliest times.

From Crowland to Lynn, through Thorney and Wisbeach,

is all Fens, well besprinkled, formerly, with monasteries of various descriptions, and still well set with magnificent churches. From Lynn to Holbeach you get out of the real Fens, and into the land that I attempted to describe, when, a few pages back, I was speaking of Holbeach. I say attempted; for I defy tongue or pen to make the description adequate to the matter: to know what the thing is, you must *see* it. The same land continues all the way on to Boston: endless grass and endless fat sheep: not a stone, not a weed.

Boston, Sunday, 11th April, 1830.

Last night, I made a speech at the playhouse to an audience, whose appearance was sufficient to fill me with pride. I had given notice that I should perform *on Friday*, overlooking the circumstance that it was Good Friday. In apologising for this inadvertence, I took occasion to observe, that even if I had persevered, the clergy of the church could have nothing to object, seeing that they were now silent, while a bill was passing in Parliament to put *Jews* on a level with *Christians;* to enable Jews, the blasphemers of the Redeemer, to sit on the bench, to sit in both Houses of Parliament, to sit in council with the King, and to be kings of England, if entitled to the Crown, which, by possibility, they might become, if this bill were to pass; that to this bill, *the clergy had offered no opposition;* and that, therefore, how could they hold sacred, the anniversary appointed, to commemorate the crucifixion of Christ, by the hands of the blaspheming and bloody Jews? That, at any rate, if this bill passed; if those who called Jesus Christ an *impostor* were thus declared to be *as good* as those who adored him, there was not, I hoped, a man in the kingdom who would pretend, that it would be just to compel the people to pay tithes, and fees, and offerings, to men for *teaching Christianity*. This was a *clincher;* and as such it was received.

This morning I went out at six, looked at the town, walked three miles on the road to Spilsby, and back to breakfast at nine. Boston (*bos* is Latin for *ox*) though not above a fourth or fifth part of the size of its *daughter* in New England, which got its name, I dare say, from some persecuted native of this place, who had quitted England and all her wealth and all her glories, to preserve that *freedom*, which was still more dear to him; though not a town like New Boston, and though little, to what it formerly was, when agricultural produce was the great staple of the kingdom, and the great subject of foreign exchange, is, nevertheless, a very fine town; good houses, good shops, pretty gardens about it, a fine open place, nearly equal to that of Nottingham, in the middle of it a river and a canal passing through it, each crossed by a handsome and substantial bridge, a fine market for sheep, cattle, and pigs, and another for meat, butter, and fish; and being, like Lynn, a great place for the export of corn and flour, and having many fine mills, it is altogether a town of very considerable importance; and, which is not to be overlooked, inhabited by people, none of whom appear to be in misery.

The great pride and glory of the Bostonians is *their church*, which is, I think, 400 feet long, 90 feet wide, and has a tower (or steeple, as they call it) 300 feet high, which is both a landmark and a sea-mark. To describe the richness, the magnificence, the symmetry, the exquisite beauty of this pile, is wholly out of my power. It is impossible to look at it without feeling, first, admiration and reverence and gratitude to the memory of our fathers who reared it; and next, indignation at those who affect to believe, and contempt for those who do believe, that, when this pile was reared, the age was *dark*, the people rude and ignorant, and the country *destitute of wealth and thinly peopled.* Look at this church, then; look at the heaps of white rubbish that the parsons have lately stuck up under the "*New-church Act*," and which, after having been built with money forced from the nation by odious taxes, they have stuffed full of *locked-up pens*, called *pews*, which they let for money, as cattle and sheep and pig-pens are let at fairs and markets; nay, after having looked at this work of the "*dark ages*," look at that great, heavy, ugly, unmeaning mass of stone called St. PAUL's, which an American friend of mine, who came to London from Falmouth and had seen the cathedrals at Exeter and Salisbury, swore to me, that when he first saw it, he was at a loss to guess whether it were a *court-house* or a *jail:* after looking at Boston church, go and look at that great, gloomy lump, created by a Protestant Parliament, and by taxes wrung by force from the whole nation; and then say which is the age really meriting the epithet *dark*.

St. Botolph, to whom this church is dedicated, while he (if saints see and hear what is passing on earth) must lament that the piety-inspiring mass has been, in this noble edifice, supplanted by the monotonous hummings of an oaken hutch, has not the mortification to see his church treated in a manner as if the new possessors sighed for the hour of its destruction. It is taken great care of; and though it has cruelly suffered from *Protestant repairs;* though the images are gone and the stained glass; and though the glazing is now in squares, instead of lozenges; though the nave is stuffed with *pens* called pews; and though other changes have taken place, detracting from the beauty of the edifice, great care is taken of it as it now is, and the inside is not disfigured and disgraced by a *gallery*, that great and characteristic mark of Protestant taste, which, as nearly as may be, makes a church like a playhouse. Saint Botolph (on the supposition before mentioned) has the satisfaction to see, that the base of his celebrated church is surrounded by an iron fence, to keep from it all offensive and corroding matter, which is so disgusting to the sight, round the magnificent piles at Norwick, Ely and other places; that the churchyard, and all appertaining to it, are kept in the neatest and most respectable state; that no money has been spared for these purposes; that here the eye tells the heart, that gratitude towards the fathers of the Bostonians is not extinguished in the breasts of their sons; and this the Saint will know that he owes to the circumstances, that the parish is a poor vicarage, and that the care of his church is in the hands of *the industrious people*, and not in those of a fat and luxurious dean and chapter, wallowing in wealth derived from the people's labour.

Horncastle, 12*th April.*

A fine, soft, showery morning saw us out of Boston, carrying with us the most pleasing reflections as to our reception and treatment there by numerous persons, none of whom we had ever seen before. The face of the country, for about half the way, the soil, the grass, the endless sheep, the thickly-scattered and magnificent churches, continue as on the other side of Boston; but, after that, we got out of the low and level land. At Sibsey, a pretty village five miles from Boston, we saw, for the first time since we left Peterborough, land rising above the level of the horizon; and, not having seen such a thing for so long, it had struck my daughters, who overtook me on the road (I having walked on from Boston), that the sight had an effect like that produced by the first *sight of land,* after a voyage across the Atlantic.

We now soon got into a country of hedges and dry land and gravel and clay and stones; the land not bad, however; pretty much like that of Sussex, lying between the forest part and the South Downs. A good proportion of woodland also; and just before we got to Horncastle, we passed the park of that Mr. Dymock who is called "the Champion of England," and to whom, it is said hereabouts, that we pay out of the taxes, eight thousand pounds a year! This never can be, to be sure; but if we pay him only a hundred a year, I will lay down my *glove* against that of the "Champion," that we do not pay him even *that,* for five years longer.

It is curious, that the moment you get out of the *rich land,* the churches become *smaller, mean,* and with scarcely any thing in the way of *tower* or *steeple.* This town is seated in the middle of a large valley, not, however, remarkable for any thing of peculiar value or beauty; a purely agricultural town; well built, and not mean in any part of it. It is a great rendezvous for horses and cattle, and sheep-dealers, and for those who sell these; and accordingly, it suffers severely from the loss of the small paper-money.

Horncastle, 13th April, morning.

I made a speech last evening to from 130 to 150, almost all farmers, and most men of apparent wealth, to a certain extent. I have seldom been better pleased with my audience. It is not the clapping and huzzaing that I value so much as the *silent attention*, the *earnest look* at me from *all eyes* at once, and then when the point is concluded, the *look and nod at each other*, as if the parties were saying, " *Think of that*" *!* And of these, I had a great deal at Horncastle. They say that there are *a hundred parish churches within six miles of this town.* I dare say that there was one farmer, from almost every one of these parishes. This is sowing the seeds of truth, in a very sure manner: it is not scattering broad-cast; it is really *drilling the country.*

There is one deficiency, and that, with me, a great one, throughout this country of corn and grass and oxen and sheep, that I have come over, during the last three weeks; namely, the want of *singing birds.* We are now just in that season when they sing most. Here, in all this country, I have seen and heard only about four sky-larks, and not one other singing bird of any description, and, of the small birds that do not sing, I have seen only one *yellow-hammer*, and it was perched on the rail of a pound between Boston and Sibsey. Oh! the thousands of linnets all singing together on one tree, in the sand-hills of Surrey! Oh! the carolling in the coppices and the dingles of Hampshire and Sussex and Kent! At this moment (5 o'clock in the morning) the groves at Barn-Elm are echoing with the warblings of thousands upon thousands of birds. The *thrush* begins a little before it is light; next the *black bird;* next the *larks* begin to rise; all the rest begin the moment the sun gives the signal; and, from the hedges, the bushes, from the middle and the topmost twigs of the trees, comes the singing of endless variety; from the long dead grass comes the sound of the sweet and soft voice of the *white-throat* or *nettle-tom*, while the loud and merry song of the *lark* (the songster himself out of sight) seems to descend from the skies. MILTON, in his description of paradise, has not omitted the "song of earliest birds." However, every thing taken together, here, in Lincolnshire, are more good things than man could have had the conscience to *ask* of God.

And now, if I had time and room to describe the state of *men's affairs*, in the country through which I have passed, I should show, that the people at Westminster would have known how to turn paradise itself into h—. I must, however, defer this until my next, when I shall have been at Hull and Lincoln, and have had a view of the whole of this rich and fine country. In the mean while, however, I cannot help congratulating that *sensible* fellow, Wilmot Horton, and his co-operator, Burdett, that Emigration is going on at a swimming rate. Thousands are going, and that, too, *without mortgaging the poor rates*. But, *sensible* fellows! it is not the *aged*, the *halt*, the *ailing* ; it is not the *paupers* that are going; but men with from 200*l.* to 2,000*l.* in their pocket! This very year, from two to five millions of pounds sterling will actually be carried *from England* to the United States. The Scotch, who have money to pay their passages, go to New York; those who have none get carried to Canada, that they may thence, get into the United States. I will inquire, one of these days, what *right* Burdett has to live in England, more than those whom he proposes to send away.

Spittal, near Lincoln, 19*th April,* 1830.

Here we are, at the end of a pretty decent trip, since we left Boston. The next place, on our way to Hull, was Horncastle, where I preached politics, in the playhouse, to a most respectable body of farmers, who had come in the wet to meet me. Mr. John Peniston, who had invited me to stop there, behaved in a very obliging manner, and made all things very pleasant.

The country *from* Boston continued, as I said before, flat for about half the way to Horncastle, and we then began to see the high land. From Horncastle I set off two hours before the carriage, and going through a very pretty village called Ashby, got to another at the foot of a hill, which, they say, forms part of the *Wolds;* that is, a ridge of hills. This second village is called Scamblesby. The vale in which it lies is very fine land. A hazel mould, rich and light too. I saw a man here ploughing for barley, after turnips, with *one horse:* the horse did not seem to work hard, and the man was *singing:* I need not say that he was young; and I dare say he had the good sense to keep his legs under another man's table, and to stretch his body on another man's bed.

This is a very fine *corn country:* chalk at bottom : stony near the surface, in some places : here and there a chalk pit in the hills : the shape of the ground somewhat like that of the broadest valleys in Wiltshire; but the fields not without fences as they are there : fields from fifteen to forty acres : the hills not downs, as in Wiltshire; but cultivated all over. The houses white and thatched, as they are in all chalk-countries. The valley at Scamblesby has a little rivulet running down it, just as in all the chalk countries. The land continues nearly the same to Louth, which lies in a deep dell, with beautiful pastures on the surrounding hills, like those that I once admired at Shaftesbury, in Dorsetshire, and like that near St. Austle, in Cornwall, which I described in 1808.

At Louth the wise corporation had *refused* to let us have the playhouse; but my friends had prepared a very good place; and I had an opportunity of addressing crowded audiences, two nights running. At no place have I been better pleased, than at Louth. Mr. Paddison, solicitor, a young gentleman whom I had the honour to know slightly before, and to know whom, whether I estimate by character or by talent, would be an honour to any man, was particularly attentive to us. Mr. Naull, ironmonger, who had had the battle to fight for me, for twenty years, expressed his exultation at my triumph, in a manner that showed that he justly participated it with me. I breakfasted, at Mr. Naull's with a gentleman 88 or 89 years of age, whose joy, at shaking me by the hand, was excessive. "Ah!" said he, "where are *now* "those savages who, at Hull, threatened to kill me for raising "my voice against this system?" This is a very fine town, and has a beautiful church, nearly equal to that at Boston.

We left Louth on the morning of Thursday the 15th, and got to Barton on the Humber by about noon, over a very fine country, large fields, fine pastures, flocks of those great sheep, of from 200 to 1000 in a flock; and here at Barton, we arrived at the northern point of this noble county, having never seen one single acre of waste land, and not one acre that would be called bad land, in the south of England. The *Wolds*, or highlands, lie away to our right, from Horncastle to near Barton; and, on the other side of the Wolds, lie the *Marshes of Lincolnshire*, which extend along the coast, from Boston to the mouth of the Humber, on the bank of which we were at Barton, Hull being on the opposite side of the river, which is here about five miles wide, and which we had to cross in a steam-boat.

But let me not forget Great Grimsby, at which we changed horses, and breakfasted, on our way from Louth to Barton. "What the d———!" the reader will say, "should you want to "recollect *that* place for? Why do you want not to forget "that sink of corruption? What could you find there to be "snatched from everlasting oblivion, except for the purpose "of being execrated?" I did, however, find something there worthy of being made known, not only to every man in England but to every man in the world; and not to mention it here, would be to be guilty of the greatest injustice.

To my surprise, I found a good many people assembled at the inn-door, evidently expecting my arrival. While breakfast was preparing, I wished to speak to the bookseller of the place, if there were one, and to give him a list of my books and writings, that he might place it in his shop. When he came, I was surprised to find that he had it already, and that he, occasionally, sold my books. Upon my asking him how he got it, he said that it was brought down from London and given to him by a Mr. Plaskitt, who, he said, had all my writings, and who, he said, he was sure, would be very glad to see me; but that he lived above a mile from the town. A messenger, however, had gone off to carry the news, and Mr. Plaskitt arrived, before we had done breakfast, bringing with him a son, and a daughter. And from the lips of this gentleman, a man of as kind and benevolent appearance and manners as I ever beheld in my life, I had the following facts; namely, "that one of his sons sailed for New York some years ago; that the ship was cast away on the shores of Long Island; that the captain, crew, and passengers, all perished; that the wrecked vessel was taken possession of by people on the coast; that his son had a watch in his trunk, or chest, a purse with fourteen shillings in it, and divers articles of wearing apparel; that the Americans, who searched the wreck, "*sent all these articles safely to England to him;* and," said he, "I keep the purse and the money at home, and *here is the watch in my pocket!*"

It would have been worth the expense of coming from London to Grimsby, if for nothing but to learn this fact, which I record, not only in justice to the free people of America, and particularly in justice to my late neighbours in Long Island, but in justice to the character of mankind. I publish it as something to counterbalance the conduct of the atrocious monsters, who plunder the wrecks on the coast of Cornwall, and, as I am told, on the coasts here in the east of the island.

Away go, then, all the accusations upon the character of the Yankees. People may call them *sharp, cunning, over-reaching;* and when they have exhausted the vocabulary of their abuse, the answer is found in this one fact, stated by Mr. Joshua Plaskitt, of Great Grimsby, in Lincolnshire, Old England. The person who sent the things to Mr. Plaskitt, was named Jones. It did not occur to me to ask his christian name, nor to inquire what was the particular place where he lived in Long Island. I request Mr. Plaskitt to contrive to let me know these particulars; as I should like to communicate them to friends that I have on the north side of that island.

However, it would excite no surprise there, that one of their countrymen had acted this part; for every man of them, having the same opportunity, would do the same. Their forefathers carried to New England the nature and character of the people of Old England, before national debts, paper-money, septennial bills, standing armies, dead-weights, and jubilees, had beggared and corrupted the people.

At Hull I *lectured* (I laugh at the word) to about seven hundred persons, on the same evening that I arrived from Louth, which was on Thursday the 15th. We had what they call the summer theatre, which was crowded in every part except on the stage; and the next evening, the stage was crowded too. The third evening was merely accidental, no previous notice having been given of it. On the Saturday, I went in the middle of the day to Beverley; saw there the beautiful minster, and some of the fine horses which they show there at this season of the year; dined with about fifty farmers; made a speech to them and about a hundred more, perhaps; and got back to Hull time enough to go to the theatre there.

The country round Hull appears to exceed even that of Lincolnshire. The three mornings that I was at Hull, I walked out in three different directions, and found the country everywhere fine. To the east lies the Holderness country. I used to wonder that Yorkshire, to which I, from some false impression in my youth, had always attached the idea of *sterility*, should send us of the south those beautiful cattle with short horns and straight and deep bodies. You have only to see the country, to cease to wonder at this. It lies on the north side of the mouth of the Humber; is as flat and fat as the land between Holbeach and Boston, without, as they tell me, the necessity of such numerous ditches. The appellation "Yorkshire *bite;*" the acute sayings ascribed to Yorkshiremen; and their quick manner, I remember, in the army. When speaking of what country a man was, one used to say, in defence of the party, "York, but honest." Another saying was, that it was a bare common that a Yorkshireman would go over without taking a bite. Every one knows the story of the gentleman, who, upon finding that a boot-cleaner, in the south, was a Yorkshireman, and expressing his surprise that he was not become master of the inn, received for answer, "Ah, sir, but master is York too!" And that of the Yorkshire boy, who, seeing a gentleman eating some eggs, asked the cook to give him a little *salt;* and upon being asked what he could want with salt, he said, "perhaps that gentleman may give me an egg presently."

It is surprising what effect sayings like these produce upon the mind. From one end to the other of the kingdom, Yorkshiremen are looked upon as being keener than other people; more eager in pursuit of their own interests; more sharp and more selfish. For my part, I was cured with regard to the *people* long before I saw Yorkshire. In the army, where we see men of all counties, I always found Yorkshiremen, distinguished for their frank manners, and generous disposition. In the United States, my kind and generous friends of Pennsylvania were the children and descendants of Yorkshire parents[1] and, in truth, I long ago made up my mind, that this hardness and sharpness ascribed to Yorkshiremen, arose from the sort of envy excited by that quickness, that activity, that buoyancy of spirits, which bears them up through adverse circumstances, and their consequent success in all the situations of life. They, like the people of Lancashire, are just the very reverse of being *cunning* and *selfish;* be they farmers, or be they what they may, you get at the bottom of their hearts in a minute. Every thing they think soon gets to the tongue, and out it comes, heads and tails, as fast as they can pour it. Fine materials for Oliver to work on! If he had been sent to the *west*, instead of the north, he would have found people there, on whom he would have exercised his

---

[1] These friends were two brothers, James and Thomas Paull, Quaker farmers, with whom the Author stayed, at their residence at Bustleton, near Philadelphia, in 1798, and with whom he was on intimate terms. He makes these gentlemen an exception, to the sweeping charges which he pronounces generally against the Society of Friends.

powers in vain. You are not to have every valuable quality in the same man and the same people: you are not to have prudent caution, united with quickness, and volubility.

But though, as to the character of the *people*, I, having known so many hundreds of Yorkshiremen, was perfectly enlightened, and had quite got the better of all prejudices many years ago, I still, in spite of the matchless horses and matchless cattle, had a general impression that Yorkshire was a *sterile* county, compared with the counties in the south and the west; and this notion was confirmed in some measure, by my seeing the moory and rocky parts in the West Riding, last winter. It was necessary for me to come and see the country on the banks of the Humber. I have seen the vale of Honiton, in Devonshire, that of Taunton and of Glastonbury, in Somersetshire: I have seen the vales of Gloucester and Worcester, and the banks of the Severn and the Avon; I have seen the vale of Berkshire, that of Aylesbury, in Buckinghamshire: I have seen the beautiful vales of Wiltshire; and the banks of the Medway, from Tunbridge to Maidstone, called the Garden of Eden; I was born at one end of Arthur Young's "finest ten miles in England:" I have ridden my horse across the Thames at its two sources; and I have been along every inch of its banks, from its sources, to Gravesend, whence I have sailed out of it into the channel; and, having seen and had ability to judge of the goodness of the land in all these places, I declare that I have never seen any to be compared with the land on the banks of the Humber, from the Holderness country included, and with the exception of the land from Wisbeach to Holbeach, and Holbeach to Boston. Really, the single parish of Holbeach, or a patch of the same size in the Holderness country, seems to be equal in value to the whole of the county of Surrey, if we leave out the little plot of hop-garden, at Farnham.

Nor is the town of Hull itself to be overlooked. It is a little city of London: streets, shops, everything like it; clean as the best parts of London, and the people as bustling and attentive. The town of Hull is *surrounded* with commodious docks for shipping. These docks are separated, in three or four places, by draw-bridges; so that, as you walk round the town, you walk by the side of the docks and the ships. The town on the outside of the docks is pretty considerable, and the walks from it into the country beautiful. I went about a good deal, and I nowhere saw marks of beggary or filth, even in the outskirts; none of those nasty, shabby, thief-looking sheds that you see in the approaches to London: none of those off-scourings of pernicious and insolent luxury. I hate commercial towns in general: there is generally something so loathsome in the look, and so stern and unfeeling in the manners of sea-faring people, that I have always, from my very youth, disliked sea-ports; but really, the sight of this nice town, the manners of its people, the civil, and kind and cordial reception that I met with, and the clean streets, and especially the pretty gardens in every direction, as you walk into the country, has made Hull, though a sea-port, a place that I shall always look back to with delight.

Beverley, which was formerly a very considerable city, with three or four gates, one of which is yet standing, had a great college, built in the year 700, by the Archbishop of York. It had three famous hospitals and two friaries. There is one church, a very fine one, and the minster still left; of which a bookseller in the town, was so good as to give me copper-plate representations. It is still a very pretty town; the market large; the land all round the country, good; and it is particularly famous for horses; those for speed being shown off here, on the market-days at this time of the year. The farmers and gentlemen assemble in a very wide street, on the outside of the western gate of the town; and at a certain time of the day, the grooms come from their different stables to show off their beautiful horses; blood horses, coach horses, hunters, and cart horses; sometimes, they tell me, forty or fifty in number. The day that I was there (being late in the season), there were only seven or eight, or ten, at the most. When I was asked at the inn to go and see "*the horses,*" I had no curiosity, thinking it was such a parcel of horses as we see at a market in the south; but I found it a sight worth going to see; for, besides the beauty of the horses, there were the adroitness, the agility, and the boldness of the grooms, each running alongside of his horse, with the latter trotting at the rate of ten or twelve miles an hour, and then swinging him round, and showing him off to the best advantage. In short, I was exceedingly gratified by the trip to Beverley: the day was fair and mild; we went by one road and came back by another, and I have very seldom passed a pleasanter day in my life.

I found, very much to my surprise, that at Hull, I was very nearly as far north as at Leeds, and, at Beverley, a little farther north. Of all things in the world, I wanted to speak to Mr. Foster, of the *Leeds Patriot;* but was not aware of the relative situation, till it was too late to write to him. Boats go up the Humber, and the Ouse, to within a few miles of Leeds. The Holderness country is that piece of land, which lies between Hull and the sea: it appears to be a perfect flat; and is said to be, and I dare say is, one of the very finest spots in the whole kingdom. I had a very kind invitation to go into it; but I could not stay longer on that side of the Humber, without neglecting some duty or other. In quitting Hull, I left behind me but one thing, the sight of which had not pleased me; namely, a fine gilded equestrian statue of the Dutch "*Deliverer,*" who gave to England the national debt, that fruitful mother of mischief and misery. Until this statue, be replaced by that of Andrew Marvell, that real honour of this town, England will never be what it ought to be.

We came back to Barton, by the steam boat, on Sunday, in the afternoon of the 18th, and in the evening reached this place, which is an inn, with three or four houses near it, at the distance of ten miles from Lincoln, to which we are going on Wednesday, the 21st. Between this place and Barton, we passed through a delightfully pretty town, called Brigg. The land in this, which is called the high part of Lincolnshire, has generally stone, a solid bed of stone of great depth, at different distances from the surface. In some parts, this stone is of a yellowish colour, and in the form of very thick slate; and in these parts the soil is not so good; but, generally speaking, the land is excellent; easily tilled; no surface water; the fields very large; not many trees; but what there are, particularly the ash, very fine, and of free growth; and innumerable flocks of those big, long-woolled sheep, from one hundred to a thousand in a flock, each having from eight to ten pounds of wool upon his body. One of the finest sights in the world is one of these thirty or forty-acre fields, with four or five or six hundred ewes, each with her one or two lambs skipping about upon grass, the most beautiful that can be conceived, and on lands as level as a bowling-green. I do not recollect having seen a mole-hill or an ant-hill since I came into the country; and not one acre of waste land, though I have gone the whole length of the country one way, and am now got nearly half way back another way.

Having seen this country, and having had a glimpse at the Holderness country, which lies on the banks of the sea, and to the east and north-east of Hull, can I cease to wonder that those devils, the Danes, found their way hither so often. There were the fat sheep then, just as there are now, depend upon it; and these numbers of noble churches, and these magnificent minsters, were reared, because the wealth of the country remained *in the country*, and was not carried away to the south, to keep swarms of devouring tax-eaters, to cram the maws of wasteful idlers, and to be transferred to the grasp of luxurious and blaspheming Jews.

You always perceive that the churches are large and fine and lofty, in proportion to the richness of the soil and the extent of the parish. In many places, where there are *now* but a very few houses, and those comparatively miserable, there are churches that look like cathedrals. It is quite curious to observe the difference in the style of the churches of Suffolk, and Norfolk, and those of Lincolnshire, and of the other bank of the Humber. In the former two counties the churches are good, large, and with a good, plain, and pretty lofty tower. And, in a few instances, particularly at Ipswich and Long Melford, you find magnificence in these buildings; but in Lincolnshire the magnificence of the churches is surprising. These churches are the indubitable proof of great and solid wealth, and formerly of great population. From every thing that I have heard, the *Netherlands* is a country very much resembling Lincolnshire; and they say, that the church at Antwerp is like that at Boston; but my opinion is, that Lincolnshire alone, contains more of these fine buildings than the whole of the continent of Europe.

Still, however, there is the almost total want of the *singing birds*. There had been a shower a little while before we arrived at this place; it was about six o'clock in the evening; and there is a thick wood, together with the orchards and gardens, very near to the inn. We heard a little twittering from one thrush; but, at that very moment, if we had been as near to just such a wood in Surrey, or Hampshire, or Sussex, or Kent, we should have heard ten thousand birds singing altogether; and the thrushes continuing their song till twenty minutes after sunset. When I was at Ipswich, the gardens and plantations round that beautiful town began in the morning to ring with the voices of the different birds. The nightingale is, I believe, *never heard* any where on the eastern side of Lincolnshire; though it is sometimes heard in the same latitude in the dells of Yorkshire.[1] How ridiculous it is to suppose, that these frail birds, with their slender wings and proportionately heavy bodies, *cross the sea*, and come back again! I have not yet heard, more than half a dozen skylarks; and I have, only last year, heard ten at a time make the air ring, over one of my fields at Barn-Elm. This is a great drawback from the pleasure of viewing this fine country.

It is time for me now, withdrawing myself from these objects visible to the eye, to speak of the state of *the people*, and of the manner in which their affairs are affected by the workings of

---

[1] Some birds known as "night warblers" are sometimes mistaken for the nightingale. In Lancashire and Cheshire a bird commonly called the "pitsparrow" is heard warbling at night, but its note is very inferior to that of the nightingale.

the system. With regard to the labourers, they are, every where, miserable. The wages for those who are employed on the land are, through all the counties that I have come, twelve shillings a week for married men, and less for single ones; but a large part of them are not even at this season employed on the land. The farmers, for want of means of profitable employment, suffer the men to fall upon the parish; and they are employed in digging and breaking stone for the roads; so that the roads are nice, and smooth, for the sheep and cattle to walk on, in their way to the all-devouring jaws of the Jews and other tax-eaters in London and its vicinity. None of the best meat, except by mere accident, is consumed here. To-day (the 20th of April), we have seen hundreds upon hundreds of sheep, as fat as hogs, go by this inn door, their toes, like those of the foot-marks at the entrance of the lion's den, all pointing towards the Wen; and the landlord gave us for dinner a little skinny, hard leg of old ewe mutton! Where the man got it, I cannot imagine. Thus it is: every good thing is literally driven or carried away out of the country. In walking out yesterday, I saw three poor fellows digging stone for the roads, who told me that they never had anything, but bread to eat, and water to wash it down. One of them was a widower, with three children; and his pay was eighteen-pence a-day; that is to say, about three pounds of bread a day each, for six days in the week; nothing for Sunday, and nothing for lodging, washing, clothing, candle-light, or fuel! Just such was the state of things in France, at the eve of the revolution! Precisely such; and precisely the same were the *causes*. Whether the effect will be the same, I do not take upon myself positively to determine. Just on the other side of the hedge, while I was talking to these men, I saw about two hundred fat sheep in a rich pasture. I did not tell them what I might have told them; but I explained to them why the farmers were unable to give them a sufficiency of wages. They listened with great attention; and said that they did believe, that the farmers were in great distress themselves.

With regard to the farmers, it is said here, that the far

greater part, if sold up, would be found to be insolvent. The tradesmen in country towns are, and must be, in but little better state. They all tell you, they do not sell half so many goods as they used to sell; and, of course, the manufacturers must suffer in the like degree. There is a diminution and deterioration, every one says, in the stocks upon the farms. *Sheep-washing* is a sort of business in this country; and I heard at Boston, that the sheep-washers say, that there is a gradual falling off, in point of the numbers, of sheep washed.

The farmers are all gradually sinking in point of property. The very rich ones, do not feel that ruin is absolutely approaching; but they are all alarmed; and, as to the poorer ones, they are fast falling into the rank of paupers. When I was at Ely, a gentleman who appeared to be a great farmer, told me in presence of fifty farmers, at the White Hart inn, that he had seen that morning, *three men* cracking stones on the road, as paupers of the parish of Wilbarton; and that all these men had been *overseers of the poor of that same parish within the last seven years.* Wheat keeps up in price to about an average of seven shillings a bushel; which is owing to our two successive bad harvests; but fat beef, and pork are at a very low price, and mutton not much better. The beef was selling at Lynn, for five shillings the stone of fourteen pounds, and the pork at four and sixpence. The wool (one of the great articles of produce in these countries) selling for less than half of its former price.

And here let me stop to observe, that I was well informed before I left London, that merchants were exporting our long wool to France, where it paid *thirty per cent. duty.* Well, say the landowners, but we have to thank Huskisson for this, at any rate; and that is true enough; for the law was most rigid against the export of wool; but what will the *manufacturers* say? Thus the collective goes on, smashing one class and then another; and, resolved to adhere to the taxes, it knocks away, one after another, the props of the system itself. By every measure that it adopts for the sake of obtaining security, or of affording relief to the people, it does some act of crying injustice. To save itself from the natural effects of its own measures, it knocked down the country bankers, in direct violation of the law in 1822. It is now about to lay its heavy hand on the big brewers and the publicans, in order to pacify the call for a reduction of taxes, and with the hope of preventing such reduction in reality. It is making a trifling attempt to save the West Indians from total ruin, and the West India colonies from revolt; but by that same attempt, it reflects injury on the British distillers, and on the growers of barley. Thus it cannot do justice without doing injustice; it cannot do good without doing evil; and thus it must continue to do, until it take off, in reality, more than one half of the taxes.

One of the great signs of the poverty of people in the middle rank of life, is the falling off of the audiences at the playhouses. There is a playhouse in almost every country town, where the players used to act occasionally; and in large towns almost always. In some places they have of late abandoned acting altogether. In others they have acted, very frequently, to not more than *ten or twelve persons*. At Norwich, the playhouse had been shut up for a long time. I heard of one manager who has become a porter to a warehouse, and his company dispersed. In most places, the insides of the buildings seem to be tumbling to pieces; and the curtains and scenes that they let down, seem to be abandoned to the damp and the cobwebs. *My* appearance on the boards seemed to give new life to the drama. I was, until the birth of my third son, a constant haunter of the playhouse, in which I took great delight; but when *he* came into the world, I said, "Now, Nancy, it is time for us to leave off going to the play." It is really melancholy to look at things now, and to think of things then. I feel great sorrow on account of these poor players; for, though they are made the tools of the Government and the corporations and the parsons, it is not their fault, and they have uniformly, whenever I have come in contact with them, been very civil to me. I am not sorry that they are left out of the list of vagrants in the new act; but, in this case, as in so many others, the men have to be grateful to the *women;* for who believes that this merciful omission would have taken place, if so many of the peers had not contracted matrimonial alliances with players; if so many playeresses had not become peeresses. We may thank God for disposing the hearts of our law-makers, to be guilty of the same sins, and foibles as ourselves; for when a lord had been sentenced to the pillory, the use of that ancient mode of punishing offences was abolished; when a lord (CASTLEREAGH), who was also a minister of state, had cut his own throat, the degrading punishment of burial in cross-roads was abolished; and now, when so many peers, and great men have taken to wife playactresses, which the law termed *vagrants*, that term, as applied to the children of Melpomene and Thalia, is abolished! Laud we the Gods, that our rulers cannot, after all, divest themselves of flesh and blood! For the Lord have mercy upon us, if their great souls were once to soar above that tenement!

Lord Stanhope cautioned his brother peers, a little while ago, against the angry feeling which was *rising up in the poor against the rich.* His Lordship is a wise and humane man, and this is evident from all his conduct. Nor is this angry feeling confined to the counties in the south, where the rage of the people, from the very nature of the local circumstances, is more formidable; woods and coppices and dingles and byelanes and sticks and stones ever at hand, being resources unknown in counties like this. When I was at St. Ives, in Huntingdonshire, an open country, I sat with the farmers, and smoked a pipe by way of preparation for evening service, which I performed on a carpenter's bench in a wheelwright's shop; my friends, the players, never having gained any regular settlement in that grand mart for four-legged fat meat, coming from the Fens, and bound to the Wen. While we were sitting, a hand-bill was handed round the table, advertising *farming stock* for sale; and amongst the implements of husbandry, "an *excellent fire-engine, several steel traps, and spring guns*"! And that is the life, is it, of an *English farmer?* I walked on about six miles of the road from Holbeach to Boston. I have before observed upon the inexhaustible riches of this land. At the end of about five miles and three quarters, I came to a public-house, and thought I would get some breakfast; but the poor woman, with a tribe of children about her, had not a morsel of either meat or bread! At a house called an inn, a little further on, the landlord had no meat except a little bit of chine of bacon; and though there were a good many houses near the spot, the landlord told me that the people were become so poor, that the butchers had left off killing meat in the neighbourhood. Just the state of things that existed in France on the eve of the Revolution. On that very spot I looked round me, and counted more than two thousand fat sheep in the pastures! How long; how long, good God! is this state of things to last? How long will these people starve in the midst of plenty? How long will fire-engines, steel traps, and spring guns be, in such a state of things, a protection to property? When I was at Beverley, a gentleman told me (it was Mr. Dawson of that place) that some time before a farmer had been sold up by his landlord; and that, in a few weeks afterwards, the farm-house was on fire, and that when the servants of the landlord arrived to put it out, they found the handle of the pump taken away, and that the homestead was totally destroyed. This was told me in the presence of several gentlemen, who all spoke of it as a fact of perfect notoriety.

Another respect in which our situation so exactly resembles that of France on the eve of the Revolution, is, the *fleeing from the country* in every direction. When I was in Norfolk, there were four hundred persons, generally young men, labourers, carpenters, wheelwrights, millwrights, smiths, and bricklayers; most of them with some money, and some farmers and others with good round sums. These people were going to Quebec, in timber-ships, and from Quebec, by land, into the United States. They had been told that they would not be suffered to land in the United States from board ship. The roguish villains had deceived them: but no matter; they will get into the United States; and going through Canada will do them good, for it will teach them to detest every thing belonging to it. From Boston, two great barge loads had just gone off by canal, to Liverpool, most of them farmers; all carrying some money, and some as much as two thousand pounds each. From the North and West Riding of Yorkshire, numerous waggons have gone carrying people to the canals, leading to Liverpool; and a gentleman, whom I saw at Peterboro', told me that he saw some of them; and that the men all appeared to be respectable farmers. At Hull, the scene would delight the eyes of the wise Burdett; for here the emigration is going on in the "Old Roman Plan." Ten large ships have gone this spring, laden with these fugitives, from the fangs of taxation; some bound direct to the ports of the United States; others, like those at Yarmouth, for Quebec. Those that have most money, go direct to the United States. The single men, who are taken for a mere trifle in the Canada ships, go that way, have nothing but their carcasses to carry over the rocks and swamps, and through the myriads of place-men and pensioners in that miserable region; there are about fifteen more ships going from this one port this spring. The ships are fitted up with berths as transports for the carrying of troops. I went on board one morning, and saw the people putting their things on board and stowing them away. Seeing a nice young woman, with a little baby in her arms, I told her that she was going to a country where she would be sure that her children would never want victuals; where she might make her own malt, soap, and candles, without being half put to death for it, and where the blaspheming Jews, would not have a mortgage on the life's labour of her children.

There is at Hull one farmer going who is seventy years of age; but who takes out five sons and fifteen hundred pounds! Brave and sensible old man! and good and affectionate father! He is performing a truly parental and sacred duty; and he will die with the blessing of his sons on his head, for having rescued them from this scene of slavery, misery, cruelty, and crime. Come, then, Wilmot Horton, with your sensible associates, Burdett and Poulett Thomson; come into Lincolnshire, Norfolk, and Yorkshire; come and bring Parson Malthus along with you; regale your sight with this delightful "stream of emigration"; congratulate the "greatest captain of the age," and your brethren of the Collective: congratulate the "noblest assembly of free men," on these the happy effects of their measures. Oh! no, Wilmot! Oh! no, generous and sensible Burdett, it is not the aged, the infirm, the halt, the blind, and the idiots, that go: it is the youth, the strength, the wealth, and the spirit, that will no longer brook hunger and thirst, in order that the maws of tax-eaters and Jews may be crammed. You want the Irish to go, and so they will *at our expense*, and all the best of them, to be kept at our expense on the rocks and swamps of Nova Scotia and Canada. You have no money to send them away with: the tax-eaters want it all; and, thanks to the "improvements of the age," the steam-boats will continue to bring them in shoals in pursuit of the orts of the food, that their task-masters have taken away from them.

After evening lecture, at Horncastle, a very decent farmer came to me, and asked me about America, telling me that he was resolved to go, for that, if he staid much longer, he should not have a shilling to go with. I promised to send him a letter from Louth, to a friend at New York, who might be useful to him there, and give him good advice. I forgot it at Louth; but I will do it before I go to bed. From the Thames, and from the several ports down the Channel, about two thousand have gone this spring. All the flower of the labourers of the east of Sussex, and west of Kent, will be culled out and sent off in a short time. From Glasgow, the sensible Scotch are pouring out amain. Those that are poor and cannot pay their passages, or can rake together only a trifle, are going to a rascally heap of sand and rock and swamp, called Prince Edward's Island, in the horrible Gulf of St. Lawrence; but when the American vessels come over with Indian corn, and flour, and pork, and beef, and poultry, and eggs, and butter, and cabbages, and green peas, and asparagus, for the soldier-officers, and other tax-eaters, that we support upon that lump of worthlessness; for the lump itself bears nothing but potatoes; when these vessels come, which they are continually doing, winter and summer; towards the fall, with apples and pears and melons and cucumbers; and, in short, everlastingly coming and taking away the amount of taxes raised in England; when these vessels return, the sensible Scotch will go back in them for a dollar a head, till at last, not a man of them will be left, but the bed-ridden. Those villanous colonies are held for no earthly purpose but that of furnishing a pretence of giving money to the relations and dependents of the aristocracy; and they are the nicest channels in the world through which to send English taxes, to enrich, and strengthen, the United States. Withdraw the English taxes, and, except in a small part in Canada, the whole of those horrible regions would be left to the bears and the savages in the course of a year.

This emigration is a famous blow given to the borough-mongers. The way to New York is now as well known and as easy, and as little expensive as from old York to London. First, the Sussex parishes sent their paupers: they invited over others that were not paupers: they invited over people of some property; then persons of greater property; now substantial farmers are going; men of considerable fortune will follow. It is the letters written across the Atlantic that do the business. Men of fortune will soon discover, that to secure to their families their fortunes, and to take these out of the grasp of the inexorable tax-gatherer, they must get away. Every one that goes will take twenty after him; and thus it will go on. There can be no interruption but *war;* and war, the Thing dare not have. As to France or the Netherlands, or any part of that h— called Germany, Englishmen can never settle there. The United States form another England without its unbearable taxes, its insolent game-laws, its intolerable dead-weight, and its tread-mills.[1]

---

[1] The number of Immigrants into the United States, from 1820 to 1880, with their nationality, has been computed as follows:—

EASTERN TOUR ENDED; MIDLAND TOUR BEGUN.

Lincoln, 23rd *April*, 1830.

From the inn at Spittal, we came to this famous ancient Roman station, and afterwards, grand scene of Saxon and Gothic splendour, on the 21st. It was the third or fourth day of the *Spring fair*, which is one of the greatest in the kingdom, and which lasts for a whole week. Horses begin the fair; then come sheep; and to-day, the horned-cattle. It is supposed that there were about 50,000 sheep, and I think the whole of the space in the various roads and streets, covered by the cattle, must have amounted to ten acres of ground, or more. Some say that they were as numerous as the sheep. The number of horses I did not hear; but they say that there were 1,500 fewer in number than last year. The sheep sold 5s. a head, on an average, lower than last year; and the cattle in the same proportion. High-priced horses sold well; but the horses, which are called tradesmen's horses, were very low. This is the natural march of the Thing: those who live on the taxes have money to throw away, but those who *pay* them are ruined, and have, of course, no money to lay out on horses.

The country from Spittal to Lincoln continued to be much about the same as from Barton to Spittal. Large fields, rather light loam at top, stone under, about half corn-land and the rest grass. Not so many sheep as in the richer lands,

From	Ireland	3,538,000
,,	England	1,105,000
,,	Scotland	195,000
,,	Germany	3,212,000
,,	Canada	826,000
,,	Scandinavia	427,000
,,	France	345,000
,,	China	231,000
,,	Various Countries	402,000
	Total	10,281,000

but a great many still. As you get on towards Lincoln, the ground gradually rises, and you go on the road made by the Romans. When you come to the city, you find the ancient castle, and the magnificent cathedral, on the *brow* of a sort of ridge which ends here; for you look all of a sudden down into a deep valley, where the greater part of the remaining city lies. It once had *fifty-two churches;* it has now only eight, and only about 9,000 inhabitants! The cathedral is, I believe, the *finest building in the whole world.* All the others that I have seen (and I have seen all in England except Chester, York, Carlisle, and Durham), are little things compared with this. To the task of describing a thousandth-part of its striking beauties I am inadequate; it surpasses greatly all that I had anticipated; and oh! how loudly it gives the lie to those brazen Scotch historians who would have us believe that England was formerly *a poor* country! The whole revenue raised from Lincolnshire, even by this present system of taxation, would not rear such another pile in two hundred years. Some of the city gates are down; but there is one standing, the arch of which is said to be two thousand years old; and a most curious thing it is. The sight of the cathedral fills the mind alternately with wonder, admiration, melancholy, and rage: wonder at its grandeur and magnificence; admiration of the zeal and disinterestedness of those who here devoted to the honour of God, those immense means which they might have applied to their own enjoyments; melancholy at its present neglected state; and indignation against those who now enjoy the revenues belonging to it, and who creep about it, merely as a pretext, for devouring a part of the fruit of the people's labour. There are no men in England who ought to wish for *reform* so anxiously as the working clergy of the church of England; we are all oppressed; but they are oppressed and insulted, more than any men that ever lived in the world. The clergy in America; I mean in free America, not in our beggarly colonies, where clerical insolence and partiality prevail still more than here; I mean in the United States, where every man gives what he pleases, and no more : the clergy of the episcopal church, are a hundred times better off than the working clergy are here. They are, also, much more respected, because their *order* has not to bear the blame of enormous exactions ; which exactions here are swallowed up by the aristocracy and their dependents ; but which swallowings, are imputed to every one bearing the name of parson. Throughout the whole country, I have maintained the necessity and the justice of resuming the church property ; but I have never failed to say, that I know of no more meritorious, and ill-used men, than the working clergy of the established church.[1]

Leicester, 26*th April*, 1830.

At the famous ancient city of Lincoln I had crowded

---

[1] No greater scandal exists in the Church of England (except the sale of livings, and the frequently erratic manner in which patronage is exercised) than the frightful disparity in Church incomes. The prizes of the Church have hitherto unfortunately but rarely fallen to the lot of the working clergy, who, however, in the present day are rapidly increasing in number and influence. Mr. Mulhall, in his statistics, furnishes the following statement of the incomes of the clergy :—

Clergy.	No.	Income.	Per Head.
Bishops	33	£168,000	£5,100
Canons	166	240,000	1,440
Rectors and Vicars	11,780	4,830,000	408
Curates	5,050	565,000	112
Total	17,029	5,803,000	

The average income of a bishop of the Roman Church (in the United Kingdom) is £400 per annum, and £80 for a priest.

Patrons.	Number of Livings.
Crown	967
Noblemen	5,357
Bishops	2,088
Various	4,476
Total	12,888

audiences, principally consisting of farmers, on the 21st and 22nd; exceedingly well-behaved audiences; and great impression produced. One of the evenings, in pointing out to them the wisdom of explaining to their labourers the cause of their distress, in order to ward off the effects of the resentment, which the labourers now feel every where against the farmers, I related to them, what my labourers at Barn-Elm, had been doing since I left home : and I repeated to them the complaints that my labourers made, stating to them, from memory, the following parts of that spirited petition :

"That your petitioners have recently observed, that many great sums of the money, part of which we pay, have been voted to be given to persons who render no services to the country; some of which sums we will mention here; that the sum of 94,900*l.* has been voted for disbanded *foreign* officers, their *widows* and *children ;* that your petitioners know that ever since the peace, this charge has been annually made ; that it has been on an average, 110,000*l.* a-year, and that, of course, this band of foreigners have actually taken away out of England, since the peace, one million and seven hundred thousand pounds; partly taken from the fruit of our labour; and if our dinners were actually taken from our table, and carried over to Hanover, the process could not be, to our eyes, more visible than it is now; and we are astonished, that those who fear that we, who make the land bring forth crops, and who make the clothing and the houses, shall swallow up the rental, appear to think nothing at all, of the swallowings of these Hanoverian men, women, and children, who may continue thus to swallow, for half a century to come.

"That the advocates of the project for sending us out of our country to the rocks and snows of Nova Scotia, and the swamps and wilds of Canada, have insisted on the necessity of *checking marriages* amongst us, in order to cause a decrease in our numbers; that, however, while this is insisted on in your honourable House, we perceive a part of our own earnings voted away to encourage marriage amongst those who do no work, and who live at our expense; and that to your petitioners it does seem most wonderful, that there should be persons to fear that we, the labourers, shall, on account of our numbers, swallow up the rental, while they actually vote away our food and raiment to increase the numbers of those, who never have produced, and who never will produce, any thing useful to man.

"That your petitioners know that more than one-half of the whole of their wages is taken from them by the taxes; that these taxes go chiefly into the hands of idlers; that your petitioners are the bees, and that the tax-receivers are the drones; and they know, further, that while there is a project for sending the bees out of the country, no one proposes to send away the drones; but that your petitioners hope to see the day when the checking of the increase of the drones, and and not of the bees, will be the object of an English Parliament.

"That, in consequence of taxes, your petitioners pay sixpence for a pot of worse beer than they could make for one penny;[1] that they pay ten shillings for a pair of shoes that

---

[1] The last Editor remarks on this subject, that "the importance to farm labourers, of having beer to drink, can be fully known, to those only who are aware of the amount of work done by these men, which is perhaps greater than is performed by any other class in the world." This remark naturally touches upon one of the burning questions of the day. On the one hand there are many of the most courageous and self-denying leaders of society, who press total abstinence upon the labouring classes, as the panacea for all evils (moral and social), but this is done by some of them so intemperately and unwisely, that it may be feared that a terrible reaction will one day take place. On the other hand, it is not denied that drinking is closely connected with (or that it greatly exasperates) the misery undergone by the labouring classes, but it is denied that it is "the cause" of the misery. It is maintained that drinking must be regarded as an effect of the bad conditions inherited by the labouring classes and under which they live. It is affirmed that the fluctuations of crime (properly so called) do not depend upon the amount of drinking, but that it is destitution, not drunkenness, that contributes most largely to the increase of crime. In short, that the drunkenness, the crime, and the pauperism cannot be permanently reduced, except through a material and moral improvement of the labouring classes. May not the summing up of these conflicting opinions, lead us to regard total abstinence as of little value, except it become a sign of moral improvement, and that by far the safest plan is to help the labouring classes to face the temptations of their several callings,

they could have for five shillings; that they pay seven-pence for a pound of soap or candles that they could have for three-pence ; that they pay seven-pence for a pound of sugar that they could have for three-pence; that they pay six shillings for a pound of tea that they could have for two shillings ; that they pay double for their bread and meat, of what they would have to pay, if there were no idlers to be kept out of the taxes; that, therefore, it is the taxes that make their wages insufficient for their support, and that compel them to apply for aid to the poor-rates; that, knowing these things, they feel indignant at hearing themselves described as *paupers*, while so many thousands of idlers, for whose support they pay taxes, are called *noble Lords* and *Ladies, honourable Gentlemen, Masters,* and *Misses;* that they feel indignant at hearing themselves described as a nuisance

---

trying to fortify them against those temptations, by education and by moral and religious teaching, at the same time holding up to them, the happiness and freedom of being "temperate in all things," and the debasing effects of intemperance, in morals, as well as in beer.

With regard to the beer consumed by the farm labourer, it is to be feared that he suffers more frequently from the infamous "quality" of the beer than from the "quantity." In poor agricultural districts, the beer is "doctored," if not "drugged," by many beer-house sellers. The attention of the excisemen ought to be most keenly directed to this matter. Much of the beer which finds its way into the hay and harvest field is rather "poison" than pure malt and hops, and produces disease and engenders drunkenness. It were much to be wished that employers of labour would encourage their men to substitute some other wholesome beverage for beer, in hay and harvest time. The following comparative statement shows that a great reduction might be made throughout the United Kingdom in the consumption of beer:—

	Number of Breweries.	Millions of Gallons.	Gallons per Inhabitant.
United Kingdom	16,114	1,025	29.0
France	3,100	190	5.2
Germany	23,940	880	19.4
Austria	2,297	245	6.4
Italy	200	20	0.7
Belgium	2,500	170	31.5
United States	3,293	340	6.6

to be got rid of, while the idlers who live upon their earnings are upheld, caressed and cherished, as if they were the sole support of the country."

Having repeated to them these passages, I proceeded: " My workmen were induced thus to petition, in consequence of the information which I, their master, had communicated to them; and, Gentlemen, why should not your labourers petition in the same strain? Why should you suffer them to remain in a state of ignorance, relative to the cause of their misery? The eye sweeps over in this county more riches, in one moment, than are contained in the whole county in which I was born, and in which the petitioners live. Between Holbeach and Boston, even at a public-house, neither bread nor meat was to be found; and while the landlord was telling me that the people were become so poor, that the butchers killed no meat in the neighbourhood, I counted more than two thousand fat sheep lying about in the pastures of that richest spot in the whole world. Starvation in the midst of plenty; the land covered with food, and the working people without victuals: every thing taken away by the tax-eaters of various descriptions: and yet you take no measures for redress; and your miserable labourers seem to be doomed to expire with hunger, without an effort to obtain relief. What! cannot you point out to them the real cause of their sufferings? cannot you take a piece of paper and write out a petition for them? cannot your labourers petition as well as mine? are God's blessings bestowed on you without any spirit to preserve them? is the fatness of the land, is the earth teeming with food for the body, and raiment for the back, to be an apology for the want of that courage, for which your fathers were so famous? is the abundance which God has put into your hands, to be the excuse for your resigning yourselves to starvation? My God! is there no spirit left in England except in the miserable sand-hills of Surrey?" These words were not uttered without effect, I can assure the reader. The assemblage was of that stamp, in which thought goes before expression; but the effect of this example of my men in Surrey, will

I am sure, be greater than anything that has been done in the petitioning way for a long time past.

We left Lincoln on the 23rd, about noon, and got to Newark, in Nottinghamshire, in the evening, where I gave a lecture at the theatre, to about three hundred persons. Newark is a very fine town, and the Castle Inn, where we stopped, extraordinarily good and pleasantly situated. Here I was met by a parcel of the printed petitions of the labourers at Barn-Elm.

I shall continue to *sow these*, as I proceed on my way. It should have been stated at the head of the printed petition, that it was presented to the House of Lords, by his Grace the Duke of Richmond, and by Mr. Pallmer to the House of Commons.

The country from Lincoln to Newark (sixteen miles), is by no means so fine as that which we have been in for so many weeks. The land is clayey in many parts. A pleasant country; a variety of hill and valley; but not that richness which we had so long had, under our eye: fields smaller; fewer sheep, and those not so large, and so manifestly loaded with flesh. The roads always good. Newark is a town very much like Nottingham, having a very fine and spacious market-place; the buildings every where good; but it is in the villages that you find the depth of misery.

Having appointed positively to be at Leicester in the evening of Saturday, the 24th, we could not stop either at Grantham or at Melton Mowbray, not even long enough to view their fine old magnificent churches. In going from Newark to Grantham, we got again into Lincolnshire, in which last county Grantham is. From Newark nearly to Melton Mowbray, the country is about the same as between Lincoln and Newark; by no means bad land, but not so rich as that of Lincolnshire, in the middle and eastern parts; not approaching to the Holderness country, in point of riches; a large part arable land, well tilled; but not such large homesteads, such numerous great stacks of wheat, and such endless flocks of lazy sheep.

Before we got to Melton Mowbray, the beautiful pastures of this little verdant county of Leicester began to appear. Meadows and green fields, with here and there a corn field, all of smaller dimensions than those of Lincolnshire, but all very beautiful; with gentle hills and woods too; not beautiful woods, like those of Hampshire and of the wilds of Surrey, Sussex and Kent; but very pretty, all the country around being so rich. At Mowbray we began to get amongst the Leicestershire sheep, those fat creatures which we see the butchers' boys battering about so unmercifully, in the streets and the outskirts of the Wen. The land is warmer here than in Lincolnshire; the grass more forward, and the wheat between Mowbray and Leicester, six inches high, and generally looking exceedingly well. In Lincolnshire and Nottinghamshire, I found the wheat in general rather thin, and frequently sickly; nothing like so promising as in Suffolk and Norfolk.

We got to Leicester on the 24th, at about half-past five o'clock; and the time appointed for the lecture was six. Leicester is a very fine town; spacious streets, fine inns, fine shops, and containing, they say, thirty or forty thousand people. It is well stocked with jails, of which a new one, in addition to the rest, has just been built, covering three acres of ground! And, as if *proud* of it, the grand portal has little turrets, in the castle style, with *embrasures* in miniature on the caps of the turrets. Nothing speaks the want of reflection in the people so much, as the self-gratulation which they appear to feel in these edifices in their several towns. Instead of expressing shame at these indubitable proofs of the horrible increase of misery and of crime, they really boast of these " improvements," as they call them. Our forefathers built abbeys and priories and churches, and they made such use of them that jails were nearly unnecessary. We, their sons, have knocked down the abbeys and priories; suffered half the parsonage-houses and churches to pretty nearly tumble down, and make such uses of the remainder, that jails and tread-mills and dungeons, have now become the most striking edifices in every county in the kingdom.

Yesterday morning (Sunday the 25th), I walked out to the village of Knighton, two miles on the Bosworth road, where I breakfasted, and then walked back. This morning I walked out to Hailstone, nearly three miles on the Lutterworth road, and got my breakfast there. You have nothing to do but to walk through these villages, to see the cause of the increase of the jails. Standing on the hill at Knighton, you see the three ancient and lofty and beautiful spires rising up at Leicester: you see the river winding down through a broad bed of the most beautiful meadows that man ever set his eyes on; you see the bright verdure covering all the land, even to the tops of the hills, with here and there a little wood, as if made by God to give variety to the beauty of the scene, for the river brings the coal in abundance, for fuel, and the earth gives the brick and the tile in abundance. But go down into the villages; invited by the spires, rising up amongst the trees in the dells, at scarcely ever more than a mile or two apart; invited by these spires, go down into these villages, view the large, and once the most beautiful, churches; see the parson's house, large, and in the midst of pleasure-gardens; and then look at the miserable sheds in which the labourers reside! Look at these hovels, made of mud and of straw; bits of glass, or of old off-cast windows, without frames or hinges, frequently, but merely stuck in the mud wall. Enter them, and look at the bits of chairs or stools; the wretched boards tacked together, to serve for a table; the floor of pebble, broken brick, or of the bare ground; look at the thing called a bed; and survey the rags on the backs of the wretched inhabitants; and then wonder if you can, that the jails and dungeons and tread-mills increase, and that a standing army and barracks are become the favourite establishments of England!

At the village of Hailstone, I got into the purlieu, as they call it in Hampshire, of a person well known in the Wen; namely, the Reverend Beresford, rector of that fat affair, St. Andrew's, Holborn! In walking through the village, and surveying its deplorable dwellings, so much worse than the cow-sheds of the cottagers on the skirts of the forests in Hampshire, my attention was attracted by the surprising contrast between them and the house of their religious teacher. I met a labouring man. Country people *know everything.* If you have ever made a *faux-pas,* of any sort of description; if you have anything about you, of which you do not want all the world to know, never retire to a village, keep in some great town; but the Wen, for your life, for there the next-door neighbour will not know even your name; and the vicinage, will judge of you solely by the quantity of money, that you have to spend. This labourer seemed not to be in a very great hurry. He was digging in his garden; and I, looking over a low hedge, *pitched him up* for a gossip, commencing by asking whether that was the parson's house. Having answered in the affirmative, and I, having asked the parson's name, he proceeded thus : "His name is Beresford; but though he lives there, he has not this living now, he has got the living of St. Andrew's, Holborn; and they say it is worth a great many thousands a year. He could not, they say, keep this living and have that too, because they were so far apart. And so this living was given to Mr. Brown, who is the rector of Hobey, about seven miles off." "Well," said I, "but *how comes Beresford to live here now,* if the living be given to another man?" "Why, Sir," said he, "this Beresford married a daughter of Brown; and so, you know (smiling and looking very archly), Brown comes, and takes the payment for the tithes, and pays a curate that lives in that house there in the field; and Beresford lives at that fine house still, just as he used to do." I asked him what the living was worth, and he answered twelve hundred pounds a year. It is a rectory, I find, and of course the parson has great tithes, as well as small.

The people of this village know a great deal more about Beresford, than the people of St. Andrew's, Holborn, know about him. In short, the country people know all about the whole thing. They will be long before they act; but they will make no noise as a signal for action. They will be moved by nothing but actual want of food. This the Thing seems to be aware of; and hence, all the innumerable schemes for keeping them quiet: hence, the endless jails and all the terrors of hardened law: hence, the schemes for coaxing them, by letting them have bits of land: hence the everlasting bills and discussions of committees about the state of the poor, and the state of the poor-laws: all of which will fail: and at last, unless reduction of taxation speedily take place, the schemers will find what the consequences are of reducing millions to the verge of starvation.

The labourers here, who are in need of parochial relief, are formed into what are called *roundsmen;* that is to say, they are sent round from one farmer to another, each maintaining a certain number for a certain length of time; and thus they go round from one to the other. If the farmers did not pay three shillings in taxes out of every six shillings that they give in the shape of wages, they could afford to give the men four and sixpence in wages, which would be better to the men than the six. But as long as this burden of taxes shall continue, so long the misery will last, and it will go on increasing with accelerated pace. The march of circumstances is precisely what it was in France, just previous to the French revolution. If the aristocracy were wise, they would put a stop to that march. The middle class are fast sinking down to the state of the lower class. *A community of feeling* between these classes; and that feeling an angry one, is what the aristocracy has to dread. As far as the higher clergy are concerned, this community of feeling is already complete. A short time will extend the feeling to every other branch; and then, the hideous consequences make their appearance. Reform; a radical reform of the Parliament; this reform *in time;* this reform, which would reconcile the middle class to the aristocracy, and give renovation to that which has now become a mass of decay and disgust; this reform, given with a good grace, and not taken by force, is the only refuge for the aristocracy of this kingdom. Just as it was in France. All the tricks of financiers have been tried in vain; and by-and-by some trick more pompous and foolish than the rest; Sir Henry Parnell's trick, perhaps, or something equally foolish, would blow the whole concern into the air.[1]

Worcester, 18th May, 1830.

In tracing myself from Leicester to this place, I begin at Lutterworth, in Leicestershire, one of the prettiest country towns that I ever saw; that is to say, prettiest *situated*. At this place they have, in the church (they say), the identical *pulpit* from which Wickliffe preached! This was not his birthplace; but he was, it seems, priest of this parish.

I set off from Lutterworth early on the 29th of April, stopped to breakfast at Birmingham, got to Wolverhampton by two o'clock (a distance altogether of about 50 miles), and lectured at six in the evening. I repeated, or rather continued, the lecturing, on the 30th, and on the 3rd of May. On the 6th of May went to Dudley, and lectured there: on the 10th of May, at Birmingham; on the 12th and 13th, at Shrewsbury; and on the 14th, came here.

Thus have I come through countries of corn, and meat, and iron, and coal; and from the banks of the Humber to those of the Severn, I find all the people, who do not share in the taxes, in a state of distress, greater or less, *Mortgagers* all frightened out of their wits; *fathers* trembling for the fate of their children; and *working people* in the most miserable state, and, as they ought to be, in the *worst of temper*. These will, I am afraid, be the *state-doctors* at last! The farmers are cowed down: the poorer they get, the more cowardly they are. Every one of them, sees the cause of his suffering,

---

[1] The "trick" referred to was the scheme for "Joint-Stock Banks." Since the Act of 1826, a number of joint-stock banks have been established. Sir Henry Parnell (afterwards Lord Congleton) was a promoter of them. At the present time, there are about 120 of these banks in England and Wales, but the number is increasing. A large proportion of these joint-stock banks (in the provinces) are entitled to issue notes to the extent of nearly £3,000,000 "without its being compulsory to hold any gold in reserve against them." Several severe failures however have occurred even among joint-stock banks.

and sees general ruin at hand; but every one hopes, that by some trick, some act of meanness, some contrivance, *he shall escape*. So that there is no hope of any change for the better, but from the *working people*. The farmers will sink to a very low state; and thus the Thing (barring *accidents*) may go on, until neither farmer nor tradesman will see a joint of meat on his table once in a quarter of a year. It appears likely to be precisely, as it was in France: it is now just what France was at the close of the reign of Louis XV. It has been the fashion to ascribe the *French Revolution* to the writings of Voltaire, Rousseau, Diderot, and others. These writings had *nothing at all* to do with the matter: no, *nothing at all*. The *Revolution* was produced by *taxes*, which at last became unbearable; by debts of the State; but, in fact, by the despair of the people, produced by the weight of the taxes.

It is curious to observe how ready the supporters of tyranny and taxation are to ascribe rebellions and revolutions to disaffected leaders; and particularly to writers; and, as these supporters of tyranny and taxation have had the press at their command; have had generally the absolute command of it, they have caused this belief to go down from generation to generation. It will not do for them to ascribe revolutions, and rebellions, to the true cause; because then the rebellions, and revolutions, would be justified; and it is their object to cause them to be condemned. Infinite delusion has prevailed in this country, in consequence of the efforts of which I am now speaking. Voltaire was just as much a cause of the French Revolution, as I have been the cause of imposing these sixty millions of taxes. The French Revolution was produced by the grindings of taxation; and this I will take an opportunity very soon of proving, to the conviction of every man in the kingdom who chooses to read.

In the iron country, of which Wolverhampton seems to be a sort of central point, and where thousands, and perhaps two or three hundred thousand people, are assembled together, the *truck* or *tommy* system generally prevails; and this is a very remarkable feature in the state of this country. I have made inquiries with regard to the origin, or etymology, of this word *tommy*, and could find no one to furnish me with the information. It is certainly, like so many other good things, to be ascribed to *the army;* for, when I was a recruit at Chatham barracks, in the year 1783, we had brown bread served out to us twice in the week. And, for what reason God knows, we used to call it *tommy*. And the sergeants, when they called us out to get our bread, used to tell us to come and get our *tommy*. Even the officers used to call it tommy. Any one that could get white bread, called it bread; but the brown stuff that we got in lieu of part of our pay, was called *tommy;* and so we used to call it when we got abroad. When the soldiers came to have bread served out to them in the several towns in England, the name of "tommy" went down by tradition; and, doubtless, it was taken up and adapted to the truck system in Staffordshire and elsewhere.

Now, there is nothing wrong, nothing *essentially* wrong, in this system of barter. Barter is in practice in some of the happiest communities in the world. In the new settled parts of the United States of America, to which money has scarcely found its way, to which articles of wearing apparel are brought from a great distance, where the great and almost sole occupations are, the rearing of food, the building of houses, and the making of clothes, barter is the rule and money payment the exception. And this is attended with no injury and with very little inconvenience. The bargains are made, and the accounts kept *in money;* but the payments are made in produce or in goods, the price of these being previously settled on. The store-keeper (which we call shop-keeper) receives the produce in exchange for his goods, and exchanges that produce for more goods; and thus the concerns of the community go on, every one living in abundance, and the sound of misery never heard.

But when this tommy system; this system of barter; when this makes its appearance where money has for ages been the medium of exchange, and of payments for labour; when this system makes its appearance in such a state of society, there is something wrong; things are out of joint; and it becomes us to inquire into the real cause of its being resorted to; and it does not become us to join in an outcry against the employers who resort to it, until we are perfectly satisfied that those employers are guilty of oppression.

The manner of carrying on the tommy system is this: suppose there to be a master who employs a hundred men. That hundred men, let us suppose, to earn a pound a week each. This is not the case in the iron-works; but no matter, we can illustrate our meaning by one sum as well as by another. These men lay out weekly the whole of the hundred pounds in victuals, drink, clothing, bedding, fuel, and house-rent. Now, the master finding the profits of his trade fall off very much, and being at the same time in want of money to pay the hundred pounds weekly, and perceiving that these hundred pounds are carried away at once, and given to shopkeepers of various descriptions; to butchers, bakers, drapers, hatters, shoemakers, and the rest; and knowing that, on an average, these shopkeepers must all have a profit of thirty *per cent.*, or more, he determines to *keep this thirty per cent. to himself;* and this is thirty pounds a week gained as a shop-keeper, which amounts to 1,560*l.* a year. He, therefore, sets up a tommy shop: a long place containing every commodity that the workman can want, liquor and house-room excepted. Here the workman takes out his pound's worth; and his house-rent he pays in truck, if he does not rent of his master; and if he will have liquor, beer, or gin, or any thing else, he must get it by trucking with the goods that he has got at the tommy shop.[1]

---

[1] The Truck system, "of paying workmen's wages in goods (sold at tommy shops) instead of in money," was prohibited by the Truck Act of 1831 (1 and 2 William. IV. c. 37). By a more recent Act, not only must wages *not be paid in kind*, but it is prohibited to pay wages "in a public-house." *Moreover*, the workman who is now paid upon the Truck system, has still an action for wages, and all wages paid him by *Truck* are regarded as *nil*. Notwithstanding, however, the stringency of the law, the Truck system still prevails greatly in the iron and mining districts, under different forms. For instance, a very simple form is this:—Wages are paid monthly in cash. The men are always requiring advances, which are also paid in cash. There is a large neighbouring store indirectly connected with the

Now, there is nothing essentially unjust in this. There is a little inconvenience as far as the house-rent goes; but not much. The tommy is easily turned into money; and if the single saving man does experience some trouble in the sale of his goods, that is compensated for in the more important case of the married man, whose wife and children generally experience the benefit of this payment in kind. It is, to be sure, a sorrowful reflection, that such a check upon the drinking propensities of the fathers should be necessary; but *the necessity exists;* and, however sorrowful the fact, the fact, I am assured, is, that thousands upon thousands of mothers have to bless this system, though it arises from a loss of trade and the poverty of the masters.

I have often had to observe on the cruel effects of the suppression of markets and fairs, and on the consequent power of extortion possessed by the country shop-keepers. And what a thing it is to reflect on, that these shop-keepers have the whole of the labouring men of England constantly in their debt; have, on an average, a mortgage on their wages to the amount of five or six weeks, and make them pay any price that they choose to extort. So that, in fact, there is a tommy system, in every village, the difference being, that the shop-keeper, is the tommy man, instead of the farmer.

The only question is in this case of the manufacturing tommy work, whether the master charges a higher price than the shop-keepers would charge; and, while I have not heard that the masters do this, I think it improbable that they should. They must desire to avoid the charge of such extortion; and they have little temptation to it; because they buy at best hand and in large quantities; because they are sure of their customers, and know to a certainty the quantity that they want;

---

iron works, or mine; all purchases are made here in cash. The books of this store, however, show how much each man spends there, and if that amount does not reach a certain proportion of his wages, his next application for an advance is refused, for reasons known to both parties but not explained: indeed, the rate of wages is adjusted on the profits of purchases at the store.

and because the distribution of the goods is a matter of such perfect regularity, and attended with so little expense, compared with the expenses of the shop-keeper. Any farmer who has a parcel of married men working for him, might supply them with meat for four-pence the pound, when the butcher must charge them seven-pence, or lose by his trade : and to me, it has always appeared astonishing, that farmers (where they happen to have the power completely in their hands) do not compel their married labourers, to have a sufficiency of bread and meat, for their wives and children. What would be more easy than to reckon what would be necessary for house-rent, fuel, and clothing; to pay that in money once a month, or something of that sort, and to pay the rest in meat, flour, and malt? I may never occupy a farm again; but if I were to do it, to any extent, the East and West Indies, nor big brewer, nor distiller, should ever have one farthing out of the produce of my farm, except he got it through the throats of those who made the wearing apparel. If I had a village at my command, not a tea-kettle should sing in that village : there should be no extortioner under the name of country shop-keeper, and no straight-backed, bloated fellow, with red eyes, unshaven face, and slip-shod till noon, called a publican, and generally worthy of the name of *sinner*. Well-covered backs and well-lined bellies would be my delight; and as to talking about controlling, and compelling, what a controlling, and compelling are there now! It is everlasting control and compulsion. My bargain should be so much in money, and so much in bread, meat, and malt.

And what is the bargain, I want to know, *with yearly servants?* Why, so much in money and the rest in bread, meat, beer, lodging and fuel. And does any one affect to say that this is wrong? Does any one say, that it is wrong to exercise control, and compulsion, over these servants; such control, and compulsion, is not only the master's right, but they are included in his bounden *duties*. It is his duty to make them rise early, keep good hours, be industrious and careful, be cleanly in their persons and habits, be civil in their language.

These are amongst the uses of the means which God has put into his hands; and are these means to be neglected towards married servants, any more than towards single ones?

Even in the well-cultivated and thickly-settled parts of the United States of America, it is the general custom, and a very good custom it is, to pay the wages of labour *partly in money and partly in kind;* and this practice is extended to carpenters, bricklayers, and other workmen about buildings, and even to tailors, shoemakers, and weavers, who go (a most excellent custom) to farm-houses to work. The bargain is, so much money *and found;* that is to say, found in food, and drink, and sometimes in lodging. The money then used to be, for a common labourer, in Long Island, at common work (not haying or harvesting), three York shillings a day, and found; that is to say, three times seven-pence halfpenny of our money; and three times seven-pence halfpenny a day, which is eleven shillings, and three-pence a week, and found. This was the wages of the commonest labourer at the commonest work. And the wages of a good labourer now, in Worcestershire, *is eight shillings a week, and not found.* Accordingly they are miserably poor and degraded.

Therefore, there is in this mode of payment, nothing *essentially* degrading; but the tommy system of Staffordshire, and elsewhere, though not unjust in itself, indirectly inflicts great injustice on the whole race of shop-keepers, who are necessary for the distribution of commodities in great towns, and whose property is taken away from them by this species of monopoly, which the employers, of great numbers of men, have been compelled to adopt for their own safety. It is not the fault of the masters, who can have no pleasure in making profit in this way: it is the fault of the taxes, which, by lowering the price of their goods, have compelled them to resort to this means of diminishing their expenses, or to quit their business altogether, which a great part of them cannot do, without being left without a penny; and if a law could be passed and enforced (which it cannot), to put an end to the tommy system, the consequence would be, that instead of a fourth part of the furnaces being let out of blast in this neighbourhood, one-half would be let out of blast, and additional thousands of poor creatures would be left solely dependent on parochial relief.

A view of the situation of things at Shrewsbury, will lead us in a minute to the real cause of the tommy system. Shrewsbury is one of the most interesting spots that man ever beheld. It is the capital of the county of Salop, and Salop appears to have been the original name of the town itself. It is curiously enclosed by the river Severn, which is here large and fine, and which, in the form of a *horse-shoe*, completely surrounds it, leaving, of the whole of the two miles round, only one little place whereon to pass in and out on land. There are two bridges, one on the east, and the other on the west; the former called the English, and the other, the Welsh bridge. The environs of this town, especially on the Welsh side, are the most beautiful that can be conceived. The town lies in the midst of a fine agricultural country, of which it is the great and almost only mart. Hither come the farmers to sell their produce, and hence they take, in exchange, their groceries, their clothing, and all the materials for their implements and the domestic conveniences. It was fair-day when I arrived at Shrewsbury. Every thing was on the decline. Cheese, which four years ago sold at sixty shillings the six-score pounds, would not bring forty. I took particular pains to ascertain the fact with regard to the cheese, which is a great article here. I was assured that shop-keepers in general did not now sell half the quantity of goods in a month, that they did in that space of time, four or five years ago. The *ironmongers* were not selling a fourth-part of what they used to sell five years ago.

Now, it is impossible to believe that a somewhat similar falling off in the sale of iron, must not have taken place all over the kingdom; and need we then wonder that the iron in Staffordshire has fallen, within these five years, from thirteen pounds to five pounds a ton, or perhaps a great deal more; and need we wonder that the *iron-masters*, who have the same rent and taxes to pay that they had to pay before, have resorted to the tommy system; in order to assist in saving themselves from ruin! Here is the real cause of the tommy system; and if Mr. Littleton really wishes to put an end to it, let him prevail upon the Parliament to take off taxes to the amount of forty millions a year.

Another article had experienced a still greater falling off at Shrewsbury; I mean the article of corn-sacks, of which there has been a falling off of *five-sixths*. The sacks are made by weavers in the North; and need we wonder, then, at the low wages of those industrious people, whom I used to see weaving sacks in the miserable cellars at Preston!

Here is the true cause of the tommy system, and of all the other evils which disturb and afflict the country. It is a great country; an immense mass of industry and resources of all sorts, *breaking up ;* a prodigious mass of enterprise and capital diminishing and dispersing. The enormous taxes co-operating with the Corn-bill, which those taxes have engendered, are driving skill and wealth out of the country in all directions; are causing iron-masters, to make France, and particularly Belgium, blaze with furnaces, in the lieu of those which have been extinguished here; and that have established furnaces and cotton mills in abundance. These same taxes and this same Corn-bill are sending the long wool from Lincolnshire to France, there to be made into those blankets, which for ages, were to be obtained nowhere but in England.

This is the true state of the country, and here are the true causes of that state; and all that the corrupt writers and speakers say about over-population and poor-laws, and about all the rest of their shuffling excuses, is a heap of nonsense and of lies.

I cannot quit Shrewsbury without expressing the great satisfaction that I derived from my visit to that place. It is the only town into which I have gone in all England, without knowing, beforehand, something of some person in it. I could find out no person, that took the Register; and could discover but one person who took the *Advice to young Men.*

The number of my auditors was expected to be so small, that I doubled the price of admission, in order to pay the expense of the room. To my great surprise, I had a room full of gentlemen, at the request of some of whom, I repeated the dose, the next night; and if my audience were as well pleased with me as I was with them, their pleasure must have been great indeed. I saw not one single person in the place that I had ever seen before; yet I never had more cordial shakes by the hand; in proportion to their numbers not more at Manchester, Oldham, Rochdale, Halifax, Leeds, or Nottingham or even Hull. I was particularly pleased with the conduct of the *young* gentlemen at Shrewsbury, and especially when I asked them, whether they were prepared to act upon the insolent doctrine of Huskisson, and quietly submit to this state of things "*during the present generation*"?

TOUR IN THE WEST.

3rd July, 1830.

Just as I was closing my third Lecture (on Saturday night), at Bristol, to a numerous and most respectable audience, the news of the death of George IV. arrived. I had advertised and made all the preparations for lecturing at Bath on Monday, Tuesday, and Wednesday; but, under the circumstances, I thought it would not be proper to proceed thither, for that purpose, until after the burial of the King. When that has taken place, I shall, as soon as may be, return to Bath, taking Hertfordshire and Buckinghamshire in my way; from Bath, through Somerset, Devon, and into Cornwall; and back through Dorset, South Wilts, Hants, Sussex, Kent, and then go into Essex, and, last of all, into my native county of Surrey. I shall then have seen all England with my own eyes, except Rutland, Westmoreland, Durham, Cumberland, and Northumberland; and these, if I have life and health till next spring, I shall see, in my way to Scotland. But never shall I see another place to interest me, and so pleasing to me, as Bristol and its environs, taking the whole together. A good and solid and wealthy city: a people of plain and good manners; private virtue and public spirit united; no empty noise, no insolence, no flattery; men very much like the Yorkers and Lancastrians. And, as to the seat of the city and its environs, it surpasses all that I ever saw. A great commercial city in the midst of corn-fields, meadows and woods, and the ships coming into the centre of it, miles from any thing like sea, up a narrow river, and passing between two clefts of a rock probably a hundred feet high; so that from the top of these clefts you *look down* upon the main-top gallant masts of lofty ships, that are gliding along!

PROGRESS IN THE NORTH.

Newcastle-upon-Tyne, 23 *September,* 1832.

From Bolton, in Lancashire, I came, through Bury and Rochdale, to Todmorden, on the evening of Tuesday, the 18th September. I have formerly described the valley of Todmorden as the most curious and romantic that was ever seen, and where the water and the coal seemed to be engaged in a struggle for getting foremost in point of utility to man. On the 19th I staid all day at Todmorden to write and to sleep. On the 20th I set off for Leeds by the stage coach, through Halifax and Bradford; and as to *agriculture,* certainly the poorest country that I have ever set my eyes on, except that miserable *Nova Scotia,* where there are the townships of Horton and of Wilmot, and whither the sensible suckling statesman, Lord Howick, is wanting to send English country girls, lest they should breed if they stay in England! This country, from Todmorden to Leeds, is, however, covered over with population, and the two towns of Halifax and Bradford are exceedingly populous. There appears to be nothing produced by the earth but the natural grass of the country, which, however, is not bad. The soil is a sort of yellow-looking, stiffish stuff, lying about a foot thick, upon a bed of rocky stone, lying upon solid rock beneath. The grass does not seem to burn here; nor is it bad in quality; and all the grass appears to be wanted to rear milk for this immense population, that absolutely covers the whole face of the country. The only grain crops that I saw were those of very miserable oats; some of which were cut and carried; some standing in *shock*, the sheaves not being more than about a foot and a half long; some still standing, and some yet *nearly green*. The land is very high from Halifax to Bradford, and proportionably cold. Here are some of those "Yorkshire Hills" that they see from Lancashire and Cheshire.

I got to Leeds about four o'clock, and went to bed at eight precisely. At five in the morning of the 21st, I came off by the coach to Newcastle, through Harrowgate, Ripon, Darlington, and Durham. As I never was in this part of the country before, and can, therefore, never have described it upon any former occasion, I shall say rather more about it now than I otherwise should do. Having heard and read so much about the "Northern Harvest," about the "Durham ploughs," and the "Northumberland system of husbandry," what was my surprise at finding, which I verily believe to be the fact, that there is not as much corn grown in the North-Riding of Yorkshire, which begins at Ripon, and in the whole county of Durham, as is grown in the Isle of Wight alone. A very small part, comparatively speaking, is *arable* land; and all the outward appearances show, that that which is arable was formerly pasture. Between Durham and Newcastle there is a pretty general division of the land into grass fields and corn fields; but, even here, the absence of *homesteads*, the absence of barns, and of labourers' cottages, clearly show, that agriculture is a sort of novelty; and that nearly all was pasturage not many years ago, or at any rate, only so much of the land was cultivated as was necessary to furnish straw for the horses kept for other purposes than those of agriculture, and oats for those horses, and bread corn sufficient for the graziers and their people. All along the road from Leeds to

Durham I saw hardly any wheat at all, or any wheat stubble, no barley, the chief crops being oats and beans mixed with peas. These everywhere appeared to be what we should deem most miserable crops. The oats, tied up in sheaves, or yet uncut, were scarcely ever more than two feet and a half long, the beans were about the same height, and in both cases the land so full of grass, as to appear to be *a pasture*, after the oats and the beans were cut.

The land appears to be divided into very extensive farms. The corn, when cut, you see put up into little stacks of a circular form, each containing about *three* of our southern waggon-loads of sheaves, which stacks are put up round about the stone house and the buildings of the farmer. How they thrash them out I do not know, for I could see nothing resembling a barn, or a barn's door. By the corn being put into such small stacks, I should suppose the thrashing places to be very small, and capable of holding only one stack at a time. I have many times seen one single rick containing a greater quantity of sheaves than fifteen or twenty of these stacks; and I have seen more than twenty stacks, each containing a number of sheaves equal to, at least, fifteen of these stacks; I have seen more than twenty of these large stacks, standing at one and the same time, in one single homestead in Wiltshire. I should not at all wonder if Tom Baring's farmers at Micheldever had a greater bulk of wheat-stacks standing now than any one would be able to find of that grain, especially, in the whole of the North Riding of Yorkshire, and in one half of Durham.

But this by no means implies that these are beggarly counties, even exclusive of their waters, coals, and mines. They are not *agricultural* counties; they are not counties for the producing of bread, but they are counties made for the express purpose of producing meat; in which respect they excel the southern counties, in a degree beyond all comparison. I have just spoken of the *beds of grass* that are everywhere seen after the oats and the beans have been cut. Grass is the natural produce of this land, which seems to have been made on purpose to produce it; and we are not to call land *poor* because it will produce nothing but meat. The size and shape of the fields, the sort of fences, the absence of all homesteads and labourers' cottages, the thinness of the country churches, every thing shows that this was always a country purely of pasturage. It is curious, that, belonging to every farm, there appears to be a large quantity of turnips. They are sowed in drills, cultivated between, beautifully clean, very large in the bulb, even now, and apparently having been sowed early in June, if not in May. They are generally the white globe turnip, here and there a field of the Swedish kind. These turnips are not fed off by sheep and followed by crops of barley and clover, as in the South, but are raised, I suppose, for the purpose of being carried in and used in the feeding of oxen, which have come off the grass lands in October and November. These turnip lands seem to take all the manure of the farm; and, as the reader will perceive, they are merely an adjunct to the pasturage, serving, during the winter, instead of hay, wherewith to feed the cattle of various descriptions.

This, then, is not a country of farmers, but a country of graziers; a country of pasture, and not a country of the plough; and those who formerly managed the land here were not husbandmen, but herdsmen. Fortescue was, I dare say, a native of this country; for he describes England as a country of shepherds and of herdsmen, not working so very hard as the people of France did, having more leisure for contemplation, and, therefore, more likely to form a just estimate of their rights and duties: and he describes them as having, at all times, in their houses, plenty of flesh to eat and plenty of woollen to wear. St. Augustine, in writing to the Pope an account of the character and conduct of his converts in England, told him that he found the English an exceedingly good and generous people; but they had one fault, their fondness for flesh-meat was so great, and their resolution to have it so determined, that he could not get them to abstain from it, even on the fast-days; and that he was greatly afraid that they would return to their state of horrible heathenism, rather than submit to the discipline of the church in this respect. The Pope, who had more sense than the greater part of bishops have ever had, wrote for answer: " Keep them within the pale of the church at any ' rate, even if they slaughter their oxen in the churchyards : "let them make shambles of the churches, rather than suffer "the devil to carry away their souls." The taste of our fathers was by no means for the potato ; for the " nice *mealy* "potato." The Pope himself would not have been able to induce them to carry " cold potatoes in their bags " to the ploughfield, as was, in evidence before the special commissions, proved to have been the common practice in Hampshire and Wiltshire, and which had been before proved by evidence taken by unfeeling committees of the boroughmonger House of Commons. Faith! these old papas of ours would have burnt up, not only the stacks, but the ground itself, rather than have lived upon miserable roots, while those who raised none of the food were eating up all the bread and the meat.

Brougham and Birkbeck, and the rest of the Malthusian crew, are constantly at work preaching *content to the hungry and naked*. To be sure, they themselves, however, are not content to be hungry and naked. Amongst other things, they tell the working-people that the working-folks, especially in the North, used to have no bread, except such as was made of oats and of barley. That was better than potatoes, even the "nice mealy ones ; " especially when carried cold to the field in a bag. But these literary impostors, these deluders, as far as they are able to delude; these vagabond authors, who thus write and publish for the purpose of persuading the working-people to be quiet, while they suck luxuries and riches out of the fruit of their toil ; these literary impostors take care not to tell the people, that these oat-cakes and this barley-bread were always associated with great lumps of flesh-meat ; they forget to tell them this, or rather these half-mad, perverse, and perverting literary impostors suppress the facts, for reasons far too manifest to need stating.[1]

The cattle here are the most beautiful by far that I ever saw. The sheep are very handsome; but the horned cattle are the prettiest creatures that my eyes ever beheld. My sons will recollect that when they were little boys I took them to see the "Durham Ox," of which they drew the picture, I dare say, a hundred times. That was upon a large scale, to be sure, the model of all these beautiful cattle: short horns, straight back, a taper neck, very small in proportion where it joints on the small and handsome head, deep dewlap, small-boned in the legs, hoop-ribbed, square hipped, tail slender. A great part of them are white, or approaching very nearly to white: they all appear to be half fat, cows and oxen and all; and the meat from them is said to be, and I believe it is, as fine as that from Lincolnshire, Herefordshire, Romney Marsh, or Pevensey Level; and I am ready, at any time, to swear, if need be, that one pound of it fed upon this grass is worth more, to me at least, than any ten pounds or twenty pounds fed upon oil-cake, or the stinking stuff of distilleries; aye, or even upon turnips. This is all *grass-land*, even from Stafford-shire to this point. In its very nature it produces grass that fattens. The little producing-land that there is even in Lancashire and the West-Riding of Yorkshire, produces grass that would fatten an ox, though the land be upon the tops of hills. Everywhere, where there is a sufficiency of grass, it will fatten an ox; and well do we Southern people know,

---

[1] Lord Brougham was frequently the object of the Author's keenest satire, being styled "the shallow and noisy man," "bawler," "barker," "ramper," and "swamper," the two latter sobriquets applying to the circumstance of Brougham, after thrusting himself into office, shortly afterwards (by his fierce crusade against the pauper) bringing his party into a great dilemma. The strong dislike which Cobbett entertained for Brougham, arose from reasons of a personal nature. Brougham charged Cobbett "with direct incitements to the invasion of private property," to plunder, and to incendiarism, and indeed he appeared to take every opportunity for speaking vindictively of him. At the same time, no one had a greater dread of the Author's lash in the *Register* than Brougham.

that, except in mere vales and meadows, we have no land that will do this; we know that we might put an ox up to his eyes in our grass, and that it would only just keep him from growing worse: we know that we are obliged to have turnips, and meal, and cabbages, and parsnips, and potatoes, and then, with some of our hungry hay for them to *pick their teeth with*, we make shift to put fat upon an ox.

Yet, so much are we like the beasts which, in the fable, came before Jupiter to ask him to endow them with faculties incompatible with their divers frames, and divers degrees of strength, that we, in this age of "*waust improvements, Ma'am*," are always hankering after laying fields down in pasture, in the South, while these fellows in the North, as if resolved to rival us in "improvement" and perverseness, must needs break up their pasture-lands, and proclaim defiance to the will of Providence, and, instead of rich pasture, present to the eye of the traveller half green starveling oats and peas, some of them in blossom in the last week of September. The land, itself, the earth, of its own accord, as if resolved to vindicate the decrees of its Maker, sends up grass under these miserable crops, as if to punish them for their intrusion; and, when the crops are off, there comes a pasture, at any rate, in which the grass, like that of Herefordshire and Lincolnshire, is not (as it is in our Southern countries), mixed with weeds; but, standing upon the ground as thick as the earth can bear it, and fattening everything that eats of it, it forbids the perverse occupier to tear it to pieces. Such is the land of this country; all to the North of Cheshire, at any rate, leaving out the East-Riding of Yorkshire and Lincolnshire, which are adapted for corn in some spots and for cattle in others.

These Yorkshire and Durham cows are to be seen in great numbers in and about London, where they are used for the purpose of giving milk, of which I suppose they give great quantities; but it is always an observation that, if you have these cows, you must *keep them exceedingly well:* and this is very true; for, upon the food which does very well for the common cows of Hampshire and Surrey, they would dwindle away directly and be good for nothing at all; and these sheep, which are as beautiful as even imagination could make them, so round and so loaded with flesh, would actually perish upon those downs and in those folds where our innumerable flocks not only live but fatten so well, and with such facility are made to produce us such quantities of fine mutton and such bales of fine wool. There seems to be something in the soil and climate, and particularly in the soil, to create everywhere a sort of cattle and of sheep fitted to it; Dorsetshire, and Somersetshire, have sheep different from all others, and the nature of which, it is to have their lambs in the fall, instead of having them in the spring. I remember when I was amongst the villages on the Cotswold-hills, in Gloucestershire, they showed me their sheep in several places, which are a stout big-boned sheep. They told me that many attempts had been made to cross them, with the small-boned Leicester breed, but that it had never succeeded, and that the race always got back to the Cotswold breed immediately.

Before closing these rural remarks, I cannot help calling to the mind of the reader an observation of LORD JOHN SCOTT ELDON, who, at a time when there was a great complaint about "agricultural distress" and about the fearful increase of the poor-rates, said, "that there was no such distress *in* "*Northumberland*, and no such increase of the poor-rates:" and so said my dignitary, Dr. Black, at the same time: and this, this wise lord, and this not less wise dignitary of mine, ascribed to "the bad practice of the farmers o' the Sooth "paying the labourers their wages out of the poor-rates, which "was not the practice in the North." I thought that they were telling what the children call *stories;* but I now find that these observations of theirs arose purely from that want of knowledge of the country, which was, and is, common to them both. Why, Lord John, there are no such persons here as we call farmers, and no such persons as we call farm-labourers. From Cheshire to Newcastle, I have never seen *one single labourer's cottage by the side of the road!* Oh, Lord! if the good people of this country could but see the endless strings of vine-covered cottages and flower-gardens of the labourers of Kent, Sussex, Surrey, and Hampshire; if they could go down the vale of the Avon in Wiltshire, from Marlborough Forest to the city of Salisbury, and there see *thirty* parish churches in a distance of thirty miles; if they could go up from that city of Salisbury up the valley of Wylly to Warminster, and there see one-and-thirty churches in the space of twenty-seven miles; if they could go upon the top of the down, as I did, not far (I think it was) from St. Mary Cotford, and there have under the eye, in the valley below, *ten parish churches within the distance of eight miles*, see the downs covered with innumerable flocks of sheep, water meadows running down the middle of the valley, while the sides rising from it were covered with corn, sometimes a hundred acres of wheat in one single piece, while the stack-yards were still well stored from the previous harvest; if John Scott Eldon's countrymen could behold these things, their quick-sightedness would soon discover why poor-rates should have increased in the South and not in the North; and, though their liberality would suggest an apology for my dignitary, Dr. Black, who was freighted to London in a smack; and has ever since been impounded in the Strand, relieved now and then by an excursion to Blackheath or Clapham Common; to find an apology, for their countryman, Lord John, would be putting their liberality to an uncommonly severe test; for he, be it known to them, has chosen his country abode, not in the Strand, like my less-informed dignitary, Dr. Black, nor in his native regions in the North; but has, in the beautiful county of Dorset, amidst valleys and downs precisely like those of Wiltshire, got as near to the sun as he could possibly get, and there, from the top of his mansion, he can see a score of churches, and from his lofty and ever-green downs, and from his fat valleys beneath, he annually sends his flocks of long-tailed ewes to Appleshaw fair, thence to be sold to all the southern parts of the kingdom, having L. E. marked upon their beautiful wool; and, like the two factions at Maidstone, all tarred with the same brush. It is curious, too, notwithstanding the old maxim, that we all try to get as nearly as possible in our old age, to the spot whence we first sprang. Lord John's brother William (who has some title that I have forgotten) has taken up his quarters on the healthy and I say beautiful Cotswold of Gloucestershire, where, in going in a postchaise from Stowe-in-the-Wold to Cirencester, I thought I should never get by the wall of his park; and I exclaimed to Mr. Dean, who was along with me, "Curse this Northumbrian ship-broker's son, he has got one half of the county;" and then all the way to Cirencester I was explaining to Mr. Dean *how the man had got his money*, at which Dean, who is a Roman Catholic, seemed to me to be ready to cross himself several times.

No, there is no apology for Lord John's observations on the difference between the poor-rates of the South and the North. To go from London to his country-houses he must go across Surrey and Hampshire, along one of the vales of Wiltshire, and one of the vales of Dorsetshire, in which latter county he has many a time seen in one single large field *a hundred wind-rows* (stacks made in the field in order that the corn may get quite dry before it be put into great stacks); he has many a time seen, on one farm, two or three hundred of these, each of which was very nearly as big as the stacks which you see in the stack-yards of the North Riding of Yorkshire and of Durham, where a large farm seldom produces more than ten or a dozen of these stacks, and where the farmer's property consists of his cattle and sheep, and where little, very little, agricultural labour is wanted. Lord John ought to have known the cause of the great difference, and not to have suffered such nonsense to come out of a head covered with so very large a wig.

I looked with particular care on the sides of the road all the way through Yorkshire and Durham. The distance, altogether, from Oldham in Lancashire, to Newcastle-upon-Tyne, is about a hundred and fifty miles; and, leaving out the *great* towns, I did not see so many churches, as are to be seen in any twenty miles, of any of the valleys of Wiltshire.

All these things prove that these are by nature counties of pasturage, and that they were formerly used solely for that purpose. It is curious that there are none of those lands here which we call "meadows." The rivers run in *deep beds*, and have generally very steep sides; no little rivulets and occasional overflowings that make the meadows in the South, which are so very beautiful, but the grass in which is not of the rich nature that the grass is in these counties in the North: it will produce milk enough, but it will not produce beef. It is hard to say which part of the country is the most valuable gift of God; but every one must see how perverse and injurious it is, to endeavour to produce in the one, that which nature has intended to confine to the other. After all the unnatural efforts that have been made here to ape the farming of Norfolk and Suffolk, it is only *playing at farming*, as stupid and "loyal" parents used to set their children *to play at soldiers during the last war.*

If any of these sensible men of Newcastle were to see the farming in the South Downs, and to see, as I saw in the month of July last, four teams of large oxen, six in a team, all ploughing in one field in preparation for wheat, and several pairs of horses, in the same field, dragging, harrowing, and rolling, and had seen on the other side of the road from five to six quarters of wheat, standing upon the acre, and from nine to ten quarters of oats, standing along side of it, each of the two fields from fifty to a hundred statute acres; if any of these sensible men of Newcastle could see these things, they would laugh at the childish work that they see going on here under the name of farming; the very sight would make them feel how imperious is the duty on the lawgiver to prevent distress from visiting the fields, and to take care that those whose labour produced all the food and all the raiment, shall not be fed upon potatoes and covered with rags; contemplating the important effects of their labour, each man of them could say, as I said when this mean and savage faction had me at my trial, " I would see all these labourers hanged, "and be hanged along with them, rather than see them live "upon potatoes." [1]

Newcastle-upon-Tyne, 24 September, 1832.

Since writing the above I have had an opportunity of receiving information from a very intelligent gentleman of this county, who tells me, that in Northumberland there are some lands which bear very heavy crops of wheat; that the agriculture in this county is a great deal better than it is farther south; that, however, it was a most lamentable thing, that the paper-money price of corn tempted so many men to break up these fine pastures; that the turf thus destroyed, cannot be restored probably in a whole century; that the land does not now, with present prices, yield a clear profit, anything like what it would have yielded in the pasture; and that thus was destroyed the *goose with the golden eggs.* Just so was it with regard to the *downs* in the south and the west of England, where there are hundreds of thousands of acres, where the turf was the finest in the world, broken up for the sake of the paper-money prices, but now left to be *downs again;* and which will not be *downs* for more than a century to come. Thus did this accursed paper-money cause even the fruitful qualities of the earth to be anticipated, and thus was the soil made *worth less* than it was before the accursed

---

[1] The Author refers here to his last prosecution, by the Whig Government in 1831, for libel. Although in his seventieth year, he defended himself with marvellous ability. His speech occupied several hours. No one was spared. Even the Cabinet Ministers (who were seated before him) were severely taken to task for their perfidy towards the people; and he wound up his address in these words:—"The Whigs know that my intention is not bad. This is a mere pretence to inflict pecuniary ruin on me, or to cause me to die in jail, so that they may get rid of me, for they can neither buy, nor silence me. In that object they will be defeated; for (thank Heaven) you stand between me and destruction. If, however, your verdict should be (which I do not anticipate) one that will consign me to death by consigning me to a loathsome dungeon, I will, with my last breath, pray to God, to bless my country and to curse the Whigs, and I bequeath my revenge to my children and the labourers of England." The result of the trial was that he was acquitted; and from that day (31 July 1831) the press of England has been free from political persecution.

invention appeared: This gentleman told me, that this breaking up of the pasture-land in this country had made the land, though covered again with artificial grasses, unhealthy for sheep; and he gave as an instance the facts, that three farmers purchased a hundred and fifty sheep each, out of the same flock; that two of them, who put their sheep upon these recently broken-up lands, lost their whole flocks by the rot, with the exception of four, in the one case, and four, in the other, out of the three hundred: and that the third farmer, who put his sheep upon the old pastures, and kept them there, lost not a single sheep out of the hundred and fifty! These, ever accursed paper-money, are amongst thy destructive effects!

I shall now, laying aside for the present these rural affairs, turn to the politics of this fine, opulent, solid, beautiful, and important town; but as this would compel me to speak of particular transactions and particular persons, and as this *Register* will come back to Newcastle before I am likely to quit it, the reader will see reasons quite sufficient for my refraining to go into matters of this sort, until the next *Register*, which will in all probability be dated from Edinburgh.

While at Manchester, I received an invitation to lodge while here, at the house of a friend, of whom I shall have to speak more fully hereafter; but every demonstration of respect and kindness met me at the door of the coach in which I came from Leeds, on Friday, the 21st September. In the early part of Saturday, the 22d, a deputation waited upon me with *an address*. Let the readers, in my native county and parish, remember, that I am now at the end of thirty years of calumnies, poured out incessantly upon me from the poisonous mouths and pens, of three hundred mercenary villains, called newspaper editors and reporters; that I have written and published more than three hundred volumes in those thirty years; and that more than a thousand volumes (chiefly paid for out of the taxes) have been written and published for the sole purpose of impeding the progress of these truths that dropped from my pen; that my whole life has been a life of sobriety and labour; that I have invariably shown that I loved and honoured my country, and that I preferred its greatness and happiness far beyond my own; that, at four distinct periods, I might have rolled in wealth derived from the public money, which I always refused in any way to touch; that, for having thwarted this Government in its wastefulness of the public resources, and particularly for my endeavours to produce that Reform of the Parliament which the Government itself has at last been compelled to resort to; that, for having acted this zealous and virtuous part, I have been twice stripped of all my earnings by the acts of this Government; once lodged in a felon's jail for two years, and once driven into exile for two years and a half; and that, after all, here I am on a spot within a hundred miles of which I never was before in my life; and here I am receiving the unsolicited applause of men amongst the most intelligent in the whole kingdom, and the names of some of whom have been pronounced accompanied with admiration, even to the southernmost edge of the kingdom.

Hexham, 1 *Oct.*, 1832.

I left Morpeth this morning pretty early, to come to this town, which lies on the banks of the Tyne, at thirty-four miles distant from Morpeth, and at twenty distant from Newcastle. Morpeth is a great market-town, for cattle especially. It is a solid old town; but it has the disgrace of seeing an enormous new jail rising up in it. From cathedrals and monasteries we are come to be proud of our jails, which are built in the grandest style, and seemingly as if to imitate the Gothic architecture.

From Morpeth to within about four miles of Hexham, the land is but very indifferent; the farms of an enormous extent. I saw in one place more than a hundred corn-stacks in one yard, each having from six to seven Surrey waggon-loads of sheaves in a stack; and not another house to be seen within a mile or two of the farm-house. There appears to be no such thing as barns, but merely a place to take in a stack at a time, and thrash it out by a machine. The country seems to be almost wholly destitute of people. Immense tracks of corn-land, but neither cottages nor churches. There is here and there a spot of good land, just as in the deep valleys that I crossed; but, generally speaking, the country is poor; and its bleakness is proved by the almost total absence of the oak tree, of which we see scarcely one, all the way from Morpeth to Hexham. Very few trees of any sort, except in the bottom of the warm valleys; what there are, are chiefly the *ash*, which is a very hardy tree, and will live and thrive where the *oak* will not grow at all, which is very curious, seeing that it comes out into leaf so late in the spring, and sheds its foliage so early in the fall. The trees, which stand next in point of hardiness, are the *sycamore*, the *beech*, and the *birch*, which are all seen here; but none of them fine. The *ash* is the most common tree, and even it flinches upon the hills, which it never does in the South. It has generally become yellow in the leaf already; and many of the trees are now bare of leaf before any frost has made its appearance.

The cattle all along here are of a coarse kind; the cows swag-backed and badly shaped; Kiloe oxen, except in the dips of good land by the sides of the bourns which I crossed. Nevertheless, even here, the fields of turnips, of both sorts, are very fine. Great pains seem to be taken in raising the crops of these turnips: they are all cultivated in rows, are kept exceedingly clean, and they are carried in, as winter food, for all the animals of a farm, the horses excepted.

As I approached Hexham, which, as the reader knows, was formerly the seat of a famous abbey, and the scene of a not less famous battle, and was, indeed, at one time, the *see* of a bishop, and which has now churches of great antiquity and cathedral-like architecture [1] as I approached this town,

---

[1] At the time the See of Newcastle was erected (1882) the question was raised whether the seat of the new Bishopric, should be Hexham, or Newcastle. The claim of the former town, rested upon the fact, that it had already been the seat of an ancient see, which was founded A.D. 678, and that ten bishops successively had occupied it (the last prelate having

along a valley down which runs a small river that soon after empties itself into the Tyne, the land became good, the ash trees more lofty, and green as in June; the other trees proportionably large and fine; and when I got down into the vale of Hexham itself, there I found the *oak tree*, certain proof of a milder atmosphere; for the *oak*, though amongst the hardest *woods*, is amongst the tenderest of plants known as natives of our country. Here everything assumes a different appearance. The Tyne, the southern and northern branches of which, meet a few miles above Hexham, runs close by this ancient and celebrated town, all round which, the ground rises gradually away towards the hills, crowned here and there, with the remains of those castles, which were formerly found necessary for the defence of this rich and valuable valley, which, from tip of hill to tip of hill, varies, perhaps, from four to seven miles wide, and which contains as fine corn-fields as those of Wiltshire, and fields of turnips, of both kinds, the largest, finest, and best cultivated, that my eyes ever beheld. As a proof of the goodness of the land and the mildness of the climate here, there is, in the grounds of the gentleman who had the kindness to receive and to entertain me (and that in a manner which will prevent me from ever forgetting either him or his most amiable wife); there is, standing in his ground, *about an acre of my corn*, which will ripen perfectly well; and, in the same grounds, which, together with the kitchen-garden, and all the appurtenances belonging to a house, and the house itself, are laid out, arranged, and contrived, in a manner so judicious, and to me so original, as to render them objects of great interest, though, in general, I set very little value on the things which appertain merely to the enjoyments of the rich. In these same grounds (to come back again to the climate),

---

been consecrated to it A.D. 810). The western end of its old Priory Church, still exhibits the remains of the magnificent monastery erected in the seventh century by S. Wilfred. The population of the town, however, is small. Notwithstanding these circumstances, the claims of Newcastle predominated, with its population of 200,000, and its world-renowned trade in coal, iron, steel, and lead. A worthy son of the great Bishop Wilberforce, has been consecrated the first Bishop of Newcastle.

I perceived that the rather tender evergreens not only lived, but throve perfectly well, and (a criterion infallible), the *biennial stocks* stand the winter without any covering, or any pains taken to shelter them; which, as every one knows, is by no means always the case, even at Kensington and Fulham.

At night I gave a lecture at an inn, at Hexham, in the midst of the domains of that impudent and stupid man, Mr. Beaumont, who, not many days before, in what he called a speech, I suppose, made at Newcastle, thought proper, as was reported in the newspapers, to utter the following words with regard to me, never having, in his life, received the slightest provocation for so doing. "The liberty of the "press had nothing to fear from the Government. It was "the duty of the administration to be upon their guard to "prevent extremes. There was a crouching servility on the "one hand, and an excitement to disorganization and to "licentiousness on the other, which ought to be discounten- "anced. The company, he believed, as much disapproved "of that political traveller, who was now going through the "country—he meant Cobbett—as they detested the servile "effusions of the Tories." Beaumont, in addition to his native stupidity and imbecility, might have been drunk when he said this, but the servile wretch who published it, was not drunk; and, at any rate, Beaumont was my mark, it not being my custom to snap at the stick, but at the cowardly hand that wields it.

Such a fellow cannot be an object of what is properly called *vengeance* with any man who is worth a straw; but, I say, with SWIFT, "If a *flea* or a *bug* bite me, I will kill it if I can;" and, acting upon that principle, I, being at Hexham, put my foot, upon this contemptible creeping thing, who is offering himself as a canditate for the southern division of the county, being so eminently fitted to be a maker of the laws!

The newspapers have told the whole country that Mr. John Ridley, who is a tradesman at Hexham, and occupies some land close by, has made a stand against the demand for tithes;

and that the tithe-owner recently broke open, in the night, the gate of his field, and carried away what he deemed to be the tithe; that Mr. Ridley applied to the magistrates, who could only refer him to a court of law to recover damages for the trespass. When I arrived at Hexham, I found this to be the case. I further found that Beaumont, that impudent, silly and slanderous Beaumont, is the *lay-owner* of the tithes in, and round about, Hexham; he being, in a right line, doubtless, the heir or successor of the abbot and monks of the Abbey of Hexham; or, the heir of the donor, Egfrid, *king of Northumberland.* I found that Beaumont had leased out his tithes to *middle men*, as is the laudable custom with the pious bishops and clergy of the law-church in Ireland.

North Shields, 2d Oct., 1832.

These sides of the Tyne are very fine: corn-fields, woods, pastures, villages; a church every four miles, or thereabouts; cows and sheep beautiful; oak trees, though none very large; and, in short, a fertile and beautiful country, wanting only the gardens and the vine-covered cottages, that so beautify the counties in the South and the West. All the buildings are of stone. Here are coal-works and railways every now and then. The working people seem to be very well off; their dwellings solid and clean, and their furniture good; but the little gardens and orchards are wanting. The farms are all large; and the people who work on them, either live in the farm-house, or in buildings appertaining to the farm-house; and they are all well fed, and have no temptation to acts like those which sprang up out of the ill-treatment of the labourers in the South. Besides, the mere country people are so few in number, the state of society is altogether so different, that a man who has lived here, all his life-time, can form no judgment at all, with regard to the situation, the wants, and the treatment of the working people in the counties of the South.

They have begun to make a rail-way from Carlisle to Newcastle; and I saw them at work at it as I came along. There are great *lead mines* not far from Hexham; and I saw a great number of little one-horse carts, bringing down the *pigs of lead* to the point where the Tyne becomes navigable to Newcastle; and sometimes I saw loads of these *pigs* lying by the roadside, as you see parcels of timber lying in Kent and Sussex, and other timber counties. No fear of their being stolen: their weight is their security, together with their value, compared with that of the labour of carrying. Hearing that Beaumont was, somehow or other, connected with this leadwork, I had got it into my head that he was a pig of lead himself, and half expected to meet with him, amongst these groups of his fellow-creatures; but, upon inquiry, I found that some of the lead-mines belonged to him; descending, probably, in that same right line in *which the tithes descended to him;* and, as the Bishop of Durham is said to be the owner of great lead-mines, Beaumont, and the bishop, may possibly be in the *same boat* with regard to the subterranean estate as well as that upon the surface; and, if this should be the case, it will, I verily believe, require all the piety of the bishop, and all the wisdom of Beaumont, to keep the boat above water, for another five years.

North Shields, 3d *Oct.,* 1832.

I lectured at South Shields last evening, and here this evening. I came over the river from South Shields about eleven o'clock last night, and made a very firm bargain with myself, never to do the like again. This evening, after my lecture was over, some gentlemen presented an address to me upon the stage, before the audience, accompanied with the valuable and honourable present, of the late Mr. Eneas Mackenzie's *History of the County of Northumberland;* a very interesting work, worthy of every library in the kingdom.

From Newcastle to Morpeth; from Morpeth to Hexham; and then all the way down the Tyne; though, everywhere such abundance of fine turnips, and, in some cases of mangelwurzel, you see scarcely any *potatoes;* a certain sign that the working people, do not live like hogs. This root is raised in

Northumberland and Durham, to be used merely as garden stuff; and, used in that way, it is very good; the contrary of which, I never thought, much less did I ever say it. It is the using of it, as a *substitute* for bread and for meat, that I have deprecated it; and when the Irish poet, Dr. Drennen, called it "the lazy root, and the root of misery," he gave it its true character. Sir Charles Wolseley, who has travelled a great deal in France, Germany, and Italy, and who, though Scott Eldon scratched him out of the commission of the peace, and though the sincere patriot Brougham, will not put him in again, is a very great and accurate observer as to these interesting matters, has assured me, that, in whatever proportion the cultivation of potatoes prevails in those countries, in that same proportion the working-people are wretched.[1]

From this degrading curse; from sitting round a dirty board, with potatoes trundled out upon it, as the Irish do; from going

---

[1] Notice has already been taken respecting "potatoes (as a staple of food) affecting the population." It may, however, be well to supply here a short statement (from Mulhall's statistics) showing the quantity of potatoes grown in different countries. :—

	Thousands Omitted.		lbs. per Inhabitant.
	Acres.	Tons.	
England	400	1,400	120
Scotland	189	665	390
Ireland	854	2,970	1,320
France	3,200	9,500	550
Germany	6,800	21,300	-1,060
Austria	3,500	8,100	510
Russia	3,100	9,200	250
Italy and Spain . . .	450	1,120	55
Holland and Belgium .	750	2,800	580
Scandinavia	560	1,750	460
United States	1,900	3,500	150

The potato was brought to Ireland from Virginia by Sir John Hawkins A.D. 1565; to England by Sir Francis Drake A.D. 1585, but without attracting much notice. It was for the third time imported from America by Sir Walter Raleigh about 1610.

to the field with cold potatoes in their bags, as the working-people of Hampshire and Wiltshire *did*, but which they have not done since the appearance of certain *coruscations*, which, to spare the feelings of the "Lambs, the Broughams, the Greys, and the Russells," and their dirty bill-of-indictment-drawer Denman, I will not describe, much less will I eulogise; from this degrading curse, the county of Northumberland is yet happily free!

Sunderland, 4*th Oct.* 1832.

This morning I left North Shields in a post-chaise, in order to come hither through Newcastle and Gateshead, this affording me the only opportunity that I was likely to have of seeing a plantation of Mr. Annorer Donkin, close in the neighbourhood of Newcastle; which plantation had been made according to the method prescribed in my book, called the "Woodlands;" and to see which plantation I previously communicated a request to Mr. Donkin. That gentleman received me in a manner which will want no describing to those who have had the good luck to visit Newcastle. The plantation is most advantageously circumstanced to furnish proof of the excellence of my instructions as to planting. The predecessor of Mr. Donkin also made plantations upon the same spot, and consisting precisely of the same sort of trees. The two plantations are separated from each other merely by a road going through them. Those of the predecessor have been made *six-and-twenty years;* those of Mr. Donkin *six years;* and, incredible as it may appear, the trees in the latter are full as lofty as those in the former; and besides the equal loftiness, are vastly superior in point of shape, and, which is very curious, retain all their freshness at this season of the year, while the old plantations are brownish, and many of the leaves falling off the trees, though the sort of trees is precisely the same. As a sort of reward for having thus contributed to this very rational source of his pleasure, Mr. Donkin was good enough to give me an elegant copy of the Fables of the celebrated Bewick, who was once a native of Newcastle and an honour to the town, and whose books I had had, from the time that my children began to look at books, until taken from me by that sort of rapine, which I had to experience, at the time of my memorable flight across the Atlantic, in order to secure the use of that long arm which I caused to reach them from Long Island, to London.

In Mr. Donkin's kitchen-garden (my eyes being never closed in such a scene), I saw what I had never seen before in any kitchen-garden, and which it may be very useful to some of my readers to have described to them. *Wall-fruit* is, when destroyed in the spring, never destroyed by *dry-cold;* but ninety-nine times out of a hundred, by wet-frosts, which descend always perpendicularly, and which are generally fatal if they come between the expansion of the blossom and the setting of the fruit; that is to say, if they come after the bloom is quite open, and before it has disentangled itself from the fruit. The great thing, therefore, in getting *wall-fruit*, is to keep off these frosts. The French make use of boards, in the neighbourhood of Paris, projecting from the tops of the walls and supported by poles; and some persons contrive to have curtains to come over the whole tree at night and to be drawn up in the morning. Mr. Donkin's walls have a top of stone; and this top, or cap, projects about eight inches beyond the face of the wall, which is quite sufficient to guard against the wet-frosts which always fall perpendicularly. This is a country of stone to be sure; but those who can afford to build walls for the purpose of having wall-fruit, can afford to cap them in this manner: to rear the wall, plant the trees, and then to save the expense of the cap, is really like the old proverbial absurdity, "of losing the ship for the sake of saving a pennyworth of tar."

At Mr. Donkin's I saw a portrait of Bewick, which is said to be a great likeness, and which, though imagination goes a great way in such a case, really bespeaks that simplicity, accompanied with that genius, which distinguished the man. Mr. Wm. Armstrong was kind enough to make me a present of a copy of the last performance of this so justly celebrated man. It is entitled "*Waits for Death,*" exhibiting a poor old horse just about to die, and preceded by an explanatory writing, which does as much honour to the heart of Bewick as the whole of his designs put together do to his genius. The sight of the picture, the reading of the preface to it, and the fact that it was the last effort of the man; altogether make it difficult to prevent tears from starting from the eyes of any one not uncommonly steeled with insensibility.[1]

You see nothing here that is pretty; but everything seems to be abundant in value; and one great thing is, the working people live well. Theirs is not a life of ease to be sure, but it is not a life of hunger. The pitmen have twenty-four shillings a week; they live rent-free, their fuel costs them nothing, and their doctor costs them nothing. Their work is terrible, to be sure; and, perhaps, they do not have what they ought to have; but, at any rate, they live well, their houses are good and their furniture good; and though they live not in a beautiful scene, they are in the scene where they were born, and their lives seem to be as good as that of the working part of mankind can reasonably expect. Almost the whole of the country hereabouts is owned by that curious thing, called the *Dean and Chapter* of Durham. Almost the whole of South Shields is theirs, granted upon leases with fines at stated periods. This Dean and Chapter are the *lords of the Lords.* Londonderry, with all his huffing and strutting, is but a tenant of the Dean and Chapter of Durham, who souse him so often with their *fines* that it is said that he has had to pay them, more than a hundred thousand pounds, within the last ten or twelve years. What will Londonderry bet that he is not the *tenant of the public* before this day five years? There would be no difficulty in these cases, but on the contrary a very great

---

[1] Thomas Bewick, a native of Cherryburn, near Newcastle, was an engraver of great art. He illustrated Gay's Fables (probably the work to which reference is here made), and obtained for one of the cuts—"The Old Hound"—the prize of the Society of Arts (A.D. 1775). Subsequently he published "A History of British Birds." His last work (as an engraver) was called "Waiting for Death," and represents an old worn-out horse, which is an universal favourite. He died in 1828.

convenience; because all these tenants of the Dean and Chapter might then purchase out-and-out, and make that property freehold, which they now hold by a tenure so uncertain and so capricious.

Alnwick, 7th Oct., 1832.

From Sunderland I came, early in the morning of the 5th of October, once more (and I hope not for the last time) to Newcastle, there to lecture on the paper-money, which I did, in the evening. But before I proceed further, I must record something that I heard at Sunderland respecting that babbling fellow Trevor! My readers will recollect the part which this fellow acted with regard to the "liberal Whig prosecution;" they will recollect that it was he who first mentioned the thing in the House of Commons, and suggested to the wise Ministers the propriety of prosecuting me; that Lord Althorp and Denham *hummed* and *ha'd* about it; that the latter had *not read it*, and that the former would offer no opinion upon it; that Trevor came on again, encouraged by the works of the curate of Crowhurst,[1] and by the old *Times*, whose former editor and now printer, is actually a candidate for Berkshire[2]

---

[1] The last prosecution of Mr. Cobbett by the Whig Government, for political libel, was brought about by Mr. Trevor, M.P. for New Romney, Kent. He drew the attention of the House to the *Register* of 11th December 1830, which, he said, "contained a malicious libel on the authorities of the State, and a gross and unwarrantable attack on the members of the Church by law established." Mr. Trevor moved a motion on the subject, and a discussion ensued, but it was ultimately agreed to leave the matter to the discretion of the Ministers. The curate of Crowhurst, to whom reference is here made, was reported, by the *Times* newspaper, to have received the confession of Thomas Goodman, a Sussex labourer, who was sentenced to death for arson, but was afterwards respited. The confession (which was a clumsy forgery) attributed the commission of his crime to Cobbett's teaching.

[2] Mr. John Walter, the original founder of *The Times* newspaper, was a London printer, and the publisher, in 1785, of the *Daily Universal Register*, which he continued to publish until 1788. Then he changed the name of his paper to *The Times*. His son, Mr. John Walter, junior, became sole manager in 1803. It is this latter gentleman, to whom the Author is here referring. The representation of Berks, still remains in the same family. In 1814, steam was first used for working the printing press in the

supported by that unprincipled political prattler, Jepthah Marsh, whom I will call to an account as soon as I get back to the South. My readers will further recollect that the old *Times* then put forth another document as a confession of Goodman, made to Burrell, Tredcroft, and Scawen Blunt, while the culprit was in Horsham jail with a halter actually about his neck. My readers know the *result* of this affair; but they have yet to learn some circumstances belonging to its progress, which circumstances are not to be stated here. They recollect, however, that from the very first I treated this TREVOR with the utmost disdain; and that at the head of the articles which I wrote about him, I put these words, "TREVOR AND POTATOES;" meaning that he hated me because I was resolved, fire or not fire, that working men should not live upon potatoes in my country. Now, mark; now, chopsticks of the South, mark the sagacity, the justice, the promptitude, and the excellent taste of these lads of the North! At the last general election, which took place after the "liberal Whig prosecution" had been begun, Trevor was a candidate for the city of Durham, which is about fourteen miles from this busy town of Sunderland. The freemen of Durham are the voters in that city, and some of these freemen reside at Sunderland. Therefore, this fellow (I wish to G—— you could *see* him!) went to Sunderland to canvass these freemen residing there; and they pelted him out of the town; and (oh appropriate missiles!) pelted him out with the "accursed root," hallooing and shouting after him—"*Trevor and potatoes!*" Ah! stupid coxcomb! little did he imagine, when he was playing his game with Althorp and Denman, what would be the ultimate effect of that game!

From Newcastle to Morpeth (the country is what I before

---

publication of *The Times*. *The Times* has always boasted of its being able, by means of its wonderful organisation, to give to the public the earliest "foreign" news. On two occasions recently, however, it has been the victim of a cruel hoax. Perhaps in the matter referred to—viz., the publication of the dying confession of Thomas Goodman—*The Times* was equally "unfortunate" in its "home news."

described it to be). From Morpeth to this place (Alnwick) the country, generally speaking, is very poor as to land, scarcely any trees at all; the farms enormously extensive; only two churches, I think, in the whole of the twenty miles; scarcely anything worthy the name of a tree, and not one single dwelling having the appearance of a labourer's house. Here appears neither hedging nor ditching; no such thing as a sheep-fold or a hurdle to be seen; the cattle and sheep very few in number; the farm servants living in the farm-houses, and very few of them; the thrashing done by machinery and horses; a country without people. This is a pretty country to take a minister from, to govern the South of England! A pretty country to take a Lord Chancellor from, to prattle about *Poor Laws* and about *surplus population!* My Lord Grey has, in fact, spent his life here, and Brougham has spent his life in the Inns of Court, or in the botheration of speculative books. How should either of them know anything about the eastern, southern, or western counties? I wish I had my dignitary Dr. Black here; I would soon make him see that he has all these number of years been talking about the bull's horns, instead of his tail and his buttocks. Besides the indescrible pleasure of having seen Newcastle, the Shields, Sunderland, Durham, and Hexham, I have now discovered the true ground of all the errors of the Scotch *feelosofers* with regard to population, and with regard to poor-laws. The two countries are as different as any two things of the same nature can possibly be; that which applies to the one, does not at all apply to the other. The agricultural counties are covered all over with parish churches, and with people thinly distributed here and there.

Only look at the two counties of Dorset and Durham. Dorset contains 1,005 square miles; Durham contains 1,061 square miles. Dorset has 271 *parishes;* Durham has 75 parishes. The population of Dorset is scattered over the whole of the county, there being no town of any magnitude in it. The population of Durham, though larger than that of Dorset, is almost all gathered together, at the mouths of the Tyne, the

Wear, and the Tees. Northumberland has 1,871 square miles; and Suffolk has 1,512 square miles. Northumberland has *eighty-eight parishes;* and Suffolk has *five hundred and ten parishes.* So that here is a county one third part smaller than that of Northumberland, with six times as many villages in it! What comparison is there to be made between states of society so essentially different? What rule is there, with regard to population and poor-laws, which can apply to both cases? And how is my Lord Howick, born and bred up in Northumberland, to know how to judge of a population suitable to Suffolk? Suffolk is a county teeming with production, as well as with people; and, how brutal must that man be, who would attempt to reduce the agricultural population of Suffolk to that of the number of Northumberland! The population of Northumberland, larger than Suffolk as it is, does not equal it in total population by nearly one-third, notwithstanding that one half of its whole population have got together on the banks of the Tyne. And are we to get rid of our people in the South, and supply the places of them by horses and machines? Why not have the people in the fertile counties of the South, where their very existence causes their food and their raiment to come? Blind and thoughtless must that man be, who imagines that all, but *farms* in the South, are unproductive. I much question whether, taking a strip three miles each way from the road, coming from Newcastle to Alnwick, an equal quantity of what is called *waste ground*, together with the cottages that skirt it, do not exceed such strip of ground in point of produce. Yes, the cows, pigs, geese, poultry, gardens, bees and fuel that arise from those *wastes*, far exceed, even in the capacity of sustaining people, similar breadths of ground, distributed into these large farms in the poorer parts of Northumberland. I have seen not less than ten thousand geese in one tract of common, in about six miles, going from Chobham towards Farnham in Surrey. I believe these geese alone, raised entirely by care and by the common, to be worth more than the clear profit that can be drawn from any similar breadth of land between Morpeth and Alnwick. What folly is it to talk, then, of applying to the counties of the South, principles and rules applicable to a country like this!

To-morrow morning I start for "Modern Athens"! My readers will, I dare say, perceive how much my "*antalluct*" has been improved since I crossed the Tyne. What it will get to when I shall have crossed the Tweed, God only knows. I wish very much that I could stop a day at Berwick, in order to find some *feelosofer* to ascertain, by some chemical process, the exact degree of the improvement of the "*antalluct*." I am afraid, however, that I shall not be able to manage this; for I must get along; beginning to feel devilishly home-sick since I have left Newcastle.

They tell me that Lord Howick, who is just married by-the-by, made a speech here the other day, during which he said, "that the Reform was only the means to an end; and "that the end was cheap government." Good! stand to that, my Lord, and, as you are now married, pray let the country fellows and girls marry too: let us have *cheap government*, and I warrant you, that there will be room for us all, and plenty for us to eat and drink. It is the drones, and not the bees, that are too numerous; it is the vermin who live upon the taxes, and not those who work to raise them, that we want to get rid of. We are keeping fifty thousand tax-eaters to breed gentlemen and ladies for the industrious and laborious to keep. These are the opinions which I promulgate; and whatever your flatterers may say to the contrary, and whatever *feelosofical* stuff Brougham and his rabble of writers may put forth, these opinions of mine will finally prevail. I repeat my anxious wish (I would call it a *hope* if I could), that your father's resolution may be equal to his sense, and that he will do that, which is demanded by the right which the people have, to insist upon measures necessary, to restore the greatness and happiness of the country; and, if he show a disposition to do this, I should deem myself the most criminal of all mankind, if I were to make use of any influence that I possess, to render his undertaking more difficult than it naturally must be; but, if he show not that disposition, it will be my bounden duty to endeavour to drive him from the possession of power; for, be the consequences to individuals what they may, the greatness, the freedom, and the happiness of England must be restored.

INDEX.

Abrotson, i. 169, 396
Abergavenny, Lord, i. 285, 286
Abingdon, i. 24, 41, 42
Acacia (or Locust tree), ii. 121
Acres, Mr., ii. 184
Addington, Dr. A., i. 186
Addington, Mr. H., i. 182, 222
Address to journeymen and labourers, ii. 199
Address to Prince Regent, i. 372
Admiralty, i. 361
Agricultural distress, i. 9 ; ii. 6, 199
Agricultural interests, i. 148
Agricultural, report of committee, i. 264 ; ii. 202
Albans, S., i. 103, 105, 108, 328
Albourne, ii. 183, 184
Albury, i. 193, 194, 198, 309, 359, 395 ; ii. 268
Alderbridge, i. 157
Alderminster, i. 164
Alfred, King, i. 212, 375, 377 ; ii. 10, 110, 111
Aldhelm, S., ii. 135, 136
Allies, Holy, i. 4 ; ii. 220
Allington, ii. 223, 256
Alnwick, ii. 384, 386, 387
Althæa frutex, i. 329
Althorp, Lord, ii. 384, 385
Alresford, i. 83, 128, 166, 169, 170, 171, 173, 244, 246, 252, 253, 254, 331, 372, 396
Alton, i. 124, 128, 236, 253, 255, 257, 259, 330, 331, 372, 378
America, arbitrations with, i. 398
American stoves, i. 360 ; ii. 32
Amesbury, i. 153 ; ii. 60

Andover, i. 15, 132, 148, 150, 152, 331, 377 ; ii. 4, 49, 50, 201, 214, 216, 221, 223
Anne de Boleyne, i. 59
Annes Hill, i. 114
Antwerp, ii. 330
Appledore, i. 302, 303, 306
Apples, i. 56
Appleshaw, i. 14, 15, 16 ; ii. 193, 194, 195, 369
Arbuthnot, ii. 227
Arkall, Mr., ii. 179
Armstong, Wm., ii. 382.
Arundel, ii. 261
Arun River, i. 219, 224, 225, 257 ; ii. 18
Ashburton, Lord, i. 33, 74, 96
Ashby, ii. 321
Ashdown Forest, i. 303
Ashdown, Lord, ii. 246
Ashe, i. 361
Ashendon, i. 246
Ashmansworth, i. 180, 255, 310, 326, 327, 331
Ash trees, ii. 272
Ashurst Forest, i. 83, 281, 283
Assignats, French, i. 141, 143, 166
Astley, Sir John, ii. 55
Atheism, ii. 132
Atlantic, the, i. 225
Attleborough, ii. 53, 294
Atwood, Mr. W., ii. 75, 158, 159
Augustine, priories, ii. 295
Augustine, S., ii. 364
Aumil, ii. 129
Austin, S., ii. 299
Austle, S., ii. 321

Australia, ii. 43
Avening, ii. 140, 141
Avington, i. 244, 245, 246, 247 ; ii. 6, 8
Avon, river, ii. 54, 87, 134, 135, 153, 171, 175, 241, 243, 310, 326
Avon, valley of, ii. 54, 55, 56, 57, 62, 64, 69, 71, 73, 75, 76, 79, 85, 96
Aylesbury, ii. 280, 283, 326
Aylesbury, Lord, i. 20
Aylsham, i. 59

BAGSHOT, i. 23, 176, 207 ; ii. 174, 237, 244
Bagshot Heath, i. 304
Bailey, Judge, i. 3, 241, 242
Bailey, Mr. Hinton, i. 380, 381, 391, 392
Baines, Parson, i. 172
Baker, Rev. R., i. 65 ; ii. 200
Baltimore, ii. 59
Bank bill, Peel's, i. 142, 143
Bankhead, Dr., i. 166
Bank holidays, ii. 77
Bank notes, i. 9, 18, 194, 394
Bank restriction, ii. 282
Banks, i. 189
Banstead Downs, i. 274
Baring, Mr., ii. 140, 151, 152, 155, 194, 215, 363
Baring, Sir T., i. 33, 64, 111, 129, 130, 131, 167, 168, 169, 249, 251, 397
Barn Elm, ii. 272, 319, 330, 342, 346
Barnes, i. 113
Barn orator, ii. 12
Barnsley, ii. 286
Barracks, the, ii. 296
Barretto, Mr., i. 328
Barrie, Capt., ii. 53
Barton, ii. 322, 328, 339
Basham, Lord, i. 328
Basingstoke, ii. 4
Bath, i. 40 ; ii. 97, 112, 134, 173, 360
Bathurst, Lord, ii. 92
Battle, i. 68, 71, 72, 74, 78, 86, 87, 94, 95, 96, 331
Baughton Hill, i. 325

Baxter, Mr., i. 91
Bayside, i. 25
Beach, Mr., i. 153, 154 ; ii. 83
Beacon Hill, i. 172, 379, 392 ; ii. 1
Beaconsfield, i. 111
Beaulieu, ii. 223, 230, 231, 232, 233, 234, 235, 236, 237
Beaumont, Mr., ii. 377, 378, 379
Beauworth, i. 170, 171
Beccles, i. 66
Beckenham, i. 332
Becket, Sir John, ii. 286
Beckford, Mr., ii. 118
Bedford, Duke of, i. 129, 168 ; ii. 313
Bedwin, Great, i. 19, 35, 229
Bedhampton, i. 233, 234
Beer-drinking, statistics of, ii. 343, 344
Beevor, Sir Thomas, ii. 53, 271, 294
Beggars, ii. 106
Belgium, ii. 288
Bell's Weekly Messenger, i. 276, 278
Benedictine Order, ii. 234, 252, 295
Benendin, i. 285, 293, 294, 296, 297 ; ii. 274
Bennet, Justice, ii. 260
Bennet, Mr. John, i. 21 ; ii. 55, 74, 98, 300
Bentham, i. 44, 53
Bere, i. 72
Beresford, Rev., ii. 348, 349
Bergh Apton, i. 23, 57, 64, 68
Berghclere, i. 1, 6, 23, 24, 41, 43, 45, 46, 60, 152, 156, 164, 377, 379, 380, 382 ; ii. 1, 10, 47, 57, 163, 180, 183, 187, 191, 193, 210
Berkshire, Vale of, i. 42
Berwick, ii. 88, 388
Betchworth, i. 199, 273, 359, 395
Beverley, ii. 324, 327, 328, 335
Bewick, Mr., ii. 382, 383
Bey of Tunis, ii. 202
Biel, Mr., ii. 232, 233, 234, 236, 237
Big upon little, i. 282
Billinghurst, i. 216, 219, 273
Binfield, i. 162, 164
Binley, ii. 1
Binstead, i. 179
Bird, Mr., i. 247

Index.

Bird singing, ii. 319
Birkbeck, Mr., i. 53, 119, 304, 368; ii. 59, 60, 365
Birket, Mr., i. 353
Birnie, Sir R., ii. 123
Birmingham, ii. 351
Bishops Sutton, i. 253; ii. 9
Bishopstrow, ii. 98, 99, 183
Bishops Waltham, i. 243; ii. 10
Black, Dr., i. 368, 375, 376, 390, 399; ii. 108, 125, 146, 147, 175, 368, 369
Blackburn, ii. 271
Blackman, i. 86
Blackdown, i. 215, 218, 221, 225, 243, 257, 271, 272, 378
Blackheath, ii. 369
Black Sea, ii. 281
Blackstone, ii. 205, 207, 296
Blackwater, i. 157; ii. 244
Blandy, Mr., i. 45; ii. 184, 188
Blanketteers, i. 222
Blechingley, i. 83, 191
Blenheim, i. 7
Blount, Mr., i. 22, 47; ii. 195
Blucher, ii. 125
Blunsdon, ii. 119
Blunt Scawen, ii. 385
Boar, wild, ii. 239
Bobadil, i. 11
Bognor, i. 40
Bolder, ii. 241
Bolingbroke, Lord, ii. 118
Bollitree, i. 24, 31, 34, 37, 39; ii. 136, 142, 143, 144, 264
Bolton, Duke of, ii. 253
Bolton, ii. 271, 361
Boniface, Mr., i. 234
Bootle, i. 316
Bordeaux, ii. 184, 185
Boston, ii. 59, 306, 309, 315, 316, 317, 319, 320, 324, 326, 330, 334, 336, 345
Boston, New, ii. 316
Botley, i. 14, 23, 65, 136, 204, 237, 238, 239, 240, 273, 374; ii. 3, 121, 209, 223, 237, 247, 254, 260, 262, 263
Bough Beach, i. 329, 330
Boulogne, i. 307, 317
Bourbons, i. 192, 315, 400

Bourne, ii. 4, 56, 87
Bourne, Mr. Sturges, ii. 147, 199, 256
Bourn, the, i. 124, 125, 126, 165
Bovant, north, ii. 183
Bower, i. 177, 178
Bradford, ii. 79, 95, 105, 116, 361 362
Bralton Castle, ii. 110, 111
Brazier, Mr., i. 23, 84
Bredon Hill, ii. 153, 154
Brenzett, i. 303
Brewing, ii. 250
Bric, Counsellor, ii. 187
Brigg, ii. 328
Brighton, i. 40, 81, 91, 92, 206, 215 282; ii. 244, 261, 274
Brighton Chronicle, i. 95
Brimton, i. 157
Bristol, ii. 41, 112, 360, 361
Bristol riots, i. 201
Broadlands, ii. 203, 222
Brodie and Dowding, ii. 93, 94
Brodie, Anna, ii. 266
Brook, ii. 13
Brooke, Mr., ii. 157
Broomsborough, ii. 156
Bromley, i. 71, 72, 82
Brougham, Lord, i. 8. 49, 107, 236, 387; ii. 11, 47, 78, 80, 92, 124
Brown, i. 367
Brown-Candover, i. 128
Brown, Miss, ii. 17
Brown, Sir A., ii. 17
Buccleugh, Duchess of, ii. 233, 236, 237
Buckingham, Duke of, ii. 8
Buckland, i. 199, 359
Buckle, History of Civilization, i. 108, 131
Bucks Gazette, ii. 276
Budd, Mr., ii. 34, 191
Buenos Ayres, i. 213
Bullington, ii. 4
Bulstrode, ii. 313
Bumpers, ii. 22
Bungay, ii. 290, 294
Buonaparte, Joseph, i. 338
Burdett, Sir F., i. 158, 163, 189, 190, 294
Burford, i. 39

Burke, i. 168, 313; ii. 307
Burlip Hill, i. 23, 41
Burnet, Bishop, i. 260
Burrough, Judge, i. 279; ii. 84, 203
Bury, i. 241; ii. 361
Bury S. Edmunds, i. 58; ii. 290, 293, 297, 299, 308, 313
Bushey Park, ii. 229
Bustleton, ii. 325
Butler, Dr. S., i. 44, 45; ii. 243
Butser Hill, ii. 262, 264, 265, 272
Butterworth, Mr., i. 316, 392
Buxton, Mr., i. 383, 385; ii. 14
Byron, Lord, ii. 163, 223

CABBAGE, ii. 139, 169, 269
Cadiz, i. 176; ii. 126, 289
Calais, i. 307, 315
Calshot Castle, ii. 232, 237, 243
Cambridge, ii. 300, 301, 306, 309, 310
Camden, Marquis, i. 286, 287, 288
Camelford, Lord, i. 328
Canada, ii. 288
Canadian corn, i. 333
Candovers, i. 165
Canning, Mr., i. 63, 67, 126, 161, 176, 183, 186, 193, 199, 200, 204, 205, 222, 317, 339, 340, 400
Canterbury, i. 56, 72, 102, 308, 311, 317, 319, 323, 325
Canute, i. 378
Captain of the age, greatest, i. 158
Carlisle, Mr., i. 280
Carmelite Friary, ii. 295
Carnarvon, Lord, i. 6, 8, 47, 60, 398
Caroline, Queen, i. 8, 56, 60, 65, 342, 357; ii. 150
Cartwright, Major, i. 60; ii. 186
Castlereagh, Lord, i. 49, 59, 63, 66, 69, 120, 121, 163, 183, 199, 307
Catharine, Queen, ii. 311
Catholic Emancipation, i. 12
Cathedrals, i. 5
Cato Street conspiracy, i. 151
Cawston, i. 64, 65
Caxton, i. 101
Chafy, Dr., ii. 306
Chalmers, Mr. ii. 99, 144, 179, 239, 240
Chamberlayne, Mr., ii. 247, 248, 249, 250, 251, 252, 253, 254

Change Alley, ii. 202
Channel, The, i. 225
Chapels, ii. 129
Charles I., ii. 226-239
Charles II., ii. 19, 226, 313
Charrington, i. 344, 345, 346
Chatfield, i. 86
Chatham, i. 49, 50, 51, 53; ii. 353
Chatteris, ii. 310
Chedworth, ii. 173
Cheer, Mr., i. 101
Cheese, ii. 358
Chelsea, ii. 246
Cheltenham, i. 24, 39, 40; ii. 82, 171, 172, 173, 175
Cheriton, i. 171
Chertsey, i. 113, 114, 331; ii. 189
Chesham, i. 103, 105, 107, 108, 109, 111
Cheshire, ii. 362
Chichester, i. 97, 227, 231, 232, 268, 271, 360
Chichester, Bishop of, i. 231
Chichester, Lord, i. 85
Chiddingfold, ii. 13, 22, 23, 24, 25, 33
Chilton-Candover, i. 128
Chilworth, i. 113, 117, 119, 193, 198, 309, 331, 359, 360, 369, 395; ii. 6, 268
Chisenbury Priory, ii. 62
Chittingstone, i. 329
Chorley, ii. 50
Christchurch, ii. 87, 241, 243
Christ's Hospital, i. 343
Christian Knowledge Society, i. 291, 292
Church and Poor, i. 349
Churches, ii. 54, 55, 56, 65, 69, 100, 112; highest use of, i. 299
Church-going and Labouring Class, i. 298
Church Property, i. 133, 388
Church Revival, i. 169
Churchyards, ii. 100
Churt, i. 262, 263
Chute, ii. 50
Cinque Ports, i. 307, 308
Cirencester, ii. 173, 370
Clergy, ii. 102, 129
Clergy, Cobbett's call upon, i. 134

Index. 395

Cobbett, James P., i. 166
Cobbett, Mr., i. 197, 266, 271, 275, 276, 277, 278, 279, 281, 283, 304, 366, 372, 377, 384 ; ii. 41, 53, 113, 121, 148, 155, 186, 187, 367, 368, 370
Cobbett's Indian Corn, ii. 275, 376
Cobbold, Rev., i. 259
Cobden, Mr., i. 64
Cobham, ii. 387
Cochrane, Lord, i. 116, 172 ; ii. 186, 255
Cockbain, John, i. 256
Codford, ii. 97, 100
Coke, ii. 11, 195
Colchicum, ii. 143, 144
Coleshill, ii. 120, 122, 123
Collective Wisdom, i. 69, 111, 185, 199, 204. 235, 236, 284 ; ii. 74, 125, 177, 271, 332
Colley Farm, ii. 268, 269
Collingwood, Admiral, i. 4, 8
Colne, ii. 173, 176
Colossus, i. 4
Commons Acts, i. 35
Commons, House of, i. 9
Commonwealth, ii. 76
Congleton, Lord, ii. 351
Constantinople, ii. 289
Cooke, Mr., ii. 241
Coombe, i. 331
Cooper, Mr. Thomas, i. 16
Corhampton, i. 172
Corn Bill, Mr. Cobbett's speech on, i. 75, 76, 77
Corn Exchange, i. 235
Corn Laws, i. 405, 406 ; repeal of, ii. 6, 12, 91, 145, 185, 359
Corsley, ii. 113
Corunna, i. 213
Cosham, i. 232
Cotford, St. Mary, ii. 369
Cotswold sheep, i. 303
Cotswold Hill, ii. 173, 175, 176, 178, 181, 182, 187, 367, 370
Cottage Economy, i. 363
Courier, The, i. 96, 241, 318, 332, 336
Coursing, ii. 97
Court Martial, i. 241
Court of Pie Powder and Dustyfoot, ii. 209

Covent Garden, ii. 312
Coventry, i. 243
Cowdry House, ii. 3, 17
Cowes, ii, 233–367
Cracow, i. 320
Cranberry, American, i. 198
Cranbrook, ii. 262
Cranmer, Archbishop, i. 59 ; ii. 312
Crawley, i. 207, 215, 216, 272, 273
Cray, North, ii. 88, 147
Crevey, i. 114
Cricklade, i. 20, 22, 35, 229 ; ii. 128, 131
Crimean War, i. 3 ; ii. 281
Criminal Code, i. 154, 391
Cromwell, O., ii. 179, 226, 227
Cromwell, Thomas, ii. 17
Crookham, i. 157, 164
Crooksbury Hill, i. 263
Cropper, Benson & Co., i. 264, 265
Cropper, Mr. J., ii. 107, 108
Crowdy, Mr. J., ii. 179
Crowhurst, Curate of, ii. 384
Crowland, ii. 308, 313, 314
Crown Lands, i. 35, 121
Croydon, i. 81, 82, 93, 209, 211
Crucifixes, i. 5
Crudwell, ii. 133, 159
Crux, Easton, ii. 195
Cuckfield, i. 81, 93
Currency Question, ii. 159
Curties, Mr. J., ii. 81, 82, 124
Curwen, i. 68
Custom House, ii. 229
Customs Returns, ii. 402
Cyprus Island, ii. 281

DAMPIER, Mr., ii. 89, 90
Danube, i. 306, 315
Danes, ii. 10
Darlington, ii. 362
Davidson, Rev., i. 230
Davis, Col., ii. 157
Dawkins, ii. 227
Dawson, Mr., ii. 335
Deadweight, i. 121, 138, 188, 223, 268, 269, 401 ; ii. 102
Deal, i. 318, 319
Deanery, ii. 129
Dean, Forest of, i. 25, 34, 37 ; ii. 30

Deer, ii. 239
Debt, National, ii. 192, 193, 195, 202, 229, 241, 247, 253, 255, 328
Deller, Mr., i. 245, 246, 247, 248, 265
Denison, Mr. Becket, ii. 286
Denman, Lord Chief Justice, i. 1, 8; ii. 385
Deptford, i. 49
Devizes, i. 18, 186; ii. 77, 85, 106, 110, 111, 112, 113, 115, 117, 134, 136, 189
Dewsbury, ii. 289
Dickens, C., i. 376
Dickenson, ii. 55
Dick, Mr., i. 120, 199
Diet, ii. 225
Dimchurch, i. 305
Dippinghall, i. 331
Dipten, ii. 231, 241
Dissenters, i. 350
Doddington, i. 326
Dodeswell, ii. 173
Dog, American, i. 367
Domesday Book, i. 118; ii. 241
Domingo, S., i. 299, 398, 400, 404
Doncaster, ii. 285
Donkin, Mr. A., ii. 381
Donnington Hill, i. 224, 226, 227, 230, 231, 272
Donovan, Mr., i. 86
Donton, i. 225, 226
Dorchester, ii. 183
Dorking, ii. 268
Dorset, Duchess of, i. 72
Dorset, county of, ii. 386
Dover, i. 56, 279, 297, 305, 308, 309, 310, 311, 314, 316, 317, 321, 325, 330
Down Hursthourn, i. 165, 166; ii. 4
Drake, Admiral, i. 176
Draycot Foliot, ii. 166, 194, 210
Drennen, Dr., ii. 380
Droxford, i. 172
Drummond, Mr., i. 194, 195, 196, 197, 198, 395
Dublin, ii. 123
Duchy, Cornwall, i. 262
Duchy, Lancaster, i. 262
Dudley, ii. 351
Dumbleton, ii. 155

Dundas, i. 151, 156, 305, 312, 313, 318, 320, 323; ii. 150
Durham, ii. 362, 363, 385, 386
Durham, Bishop of, ii. 379
Durham, Dean and Chapter of, ii. 383, 384
Durham Ox, ii. 366
Durham Ploughs, ii. 362
Duthy, i. 240, 241
Dutch Deliverer, ii. 328
Dutley, Mr., i. 255
Dymock, Mr., ii. 318

EALING, i. 111
Earls Court, i. 275
Earl's Stoke, ii. 111
Eastbourne, ii. 260
Eastdean, i. 227, 229, 231
Easter lambs, ii. 193
East Grinstead, i. 81, 123, 191, 271, 281, 282, 297
Eastmeon, i. 175, 177
Eastnor Castle, ii. 156
Eastnor, Lord, i. 353; ii. 156
Easton, i. 236, 239, 246, 273, 372, 396; ii. 3, 8, 56, 58
East Woody, i. 44, 45
Economist, ii. 71
Eddington, ii. 111
Eden, Garden of, ii. 183, 326
Edgar, King, ii. 136
Edgeware, i. 103
Edinburgh, ii. 373, 388
Edinburgh Review, i. 36, 270, 300; ii. 128
Education, National, i. 292, 386, 387, 391
Edward I., ii. 150
Edward III., ii. 118, 241
Edward VI., ii. 106, 252
Egham, i. 160, 161, 162
Egremont, Lord, i. 88, 221, 228, 246, 272; ii. 19, 24
Eldon, Lord, ii. 368, 369, 380
Elementary Education Act, i. 130
Eling, ii. 231, 241, 246
Elizabeth, Queen, ii. 157, 178, 239, 252, 311
Ellenborough's Act, ii. 102
Ellenborough, Lord, i. 241, 289; ii. 150, 204

Index. 397

Elliman, Mr., ii. 272, 273, 275, 276
Ellman, Mr., i. 84, 85, 90, 91, 161
Elm Trees, ii. 122
Elverton, i. 49, 324
Ely, i. 241; ii. 301, 302, 303, 304, 305, 332
Ely Cathedral, ii. 302, 317
Ely, Isle of, ii. 302
Emigration, i. 384, 385; ii. 60, 70, 71, 81, 100, 127, 177
Emigration Scheme, ii. 60
Enclosure Acts, i. 35
Endowments, Church, ii. 86, 87
Enford, ii. 60, 74
England, Church of, and elementary education, i. 292
English Leghorn, ii. 274
Envy of surrounding Nations, i. 333
Epping Forest, i. 35
Epsom, i. 82, 120
Equitable Adjustment, ii. 11
Erskine, Lord, i. 215, 278, 288, 303
Esher, i. 116
Established Church, i. 139
Etwall, i. 153
Evelyn, i. 195
Evening Mail, ii. 265, 266, 267
Everley, ii. 51, 58, 89
Eversham, ii. 183
Eversley, i. 157
Ewhurst, i. 272
Ewing, i. 366, 367
Excise, i. 17
Exeter, i. 102
Exton, i. 170, 172
Eye, ii. 291, 294, 297

FAIRFORD, ii. 170, 173, 175, 178
Faithful, ii. 277
Falmouth, ii. 317
Fareham, i. 204, 232, 233, 235, 236, 237; ii. 263
Farmer's Journal, i. 27, 28
Farnham, i. 18, 23, 82, 102, 118, 123, 124, 125, 151, 173, 236, 244, 259, 261, 309, 331, 362; ii. 88, 158, 215, 326, 387
Farquhar, ii. 118
Faversham, i. 49, 54, 55, 98, 308, 325
Fawkes, Guy, ii. 154
Fawley, ii. 241

Featherstone, Sir H., ii. 10
Fellbridge, i. 191
Fellowes, i. 357, 358, 395
Fens, the, ii. 312, 313, 314, 315, 334
Ferdinand, King, ii. 311
Fields, Mr., ii. 308
Fifield, ii. 58, 60, 72
Figheldean, ii. 62
Fire Shovels, i. 406
Firs, Scotch, ii. 230
Fisherton, ii. 69, 98, 99
Fitzwilliam, Lord, ii. 307
Flaying, i. 73
Fleet Street, i. 208, 232, 332; ii. 29
Flemming, i. 250, 372
Flogging of Militia Men, ii. 303
Florida, ii. 289
Flower, Mr., ii. 60
Flukes, i. 356
Foley, Lord, ii. 160
Folkstone, i. 297, 302, 305, 307, 308, 309, 311, 317, 326, 330, 331
Folkstone, Lord, ii. 120, 121, 122, 128
Fonthill, i. 7
Fordingbridge, ii. 241
Fordyce, i. 114
Foreign Loans, ii. 152
Forest Lands, i. 35
Forest Row, i. 83
Fortescue, i. 400
Fortescue, Sir J., ii. 100, 101, 364
Foster, Mr., ii. 328
Fountain Abbey, i. 129
Four Elms, i. 329
Fox, George, ii. 260
Fox, Mr., i. 114, 314
Foxe's Book of Martyrs, i. 59
Fox, Mrs., ii. 124
France, ii. 43, 288
Franco-German War, ii. 281
Frant, i. 285, 286, 288
Fredericton, ii. 7
Free Trade, i. 314, 402
French Farmer, i. 333
French, the, ii. 281
French wine, i. 401
French Revolution, i. 9
Frensham, i. 179
Frere, Sergeant, ii. 306

Index.

Friend, Mr. W., ii. 184
Friends, Society of, ii. 260
Frome, ii. 85, 103, 104, 105
Froyle, i. 259
Fry, Mrs., ii. 14.
Fulham, i. 113, 256; ii. 77, 111, 377
Fuller, Mr., i. 74, 96
Funtington, i. 227, 232, 233

GADBROOK COMMON, 273
Gallon Loaf Man, i. 21
Galloway, Mr., ii. 152, 239
Gamblet, Mr. i. 101
Game, i, 363
Gamekeepers, i. 295
Game laws, i. 154; ii. 204, 206, 207, 209, 210
Gardening, Ornamental, ii. 298
Garden of Eden, i. 327, 379
Gatcomb, ii. 141
Gateshead, ii. 381
Gatton, i. 161, 199, 206, 214
George, Mr., i. 85
George III., ii. 9, 90
George IV., ii. 211; death of, ii. 360
German Legion, i. 241
German Ocean, i. 225
German Troops, ii. 303, 305
Gibbs, ii. 150
Giddy, Mr. D., i. 85, 86, 189
Giles, S., i. 113
Gladstone, Rt. Hon. W. E., i. 388
Glanville, Lord, ii. 220
Glasgow, ii. 163, 337
Glastonbury, ii. 183, 326
Glebe land, ii. 165
Gloucester, i. 22, 24, 39, 40, 101, 102, 118; ii. 89, 136, 142, 143, 153, 173, 182, 183, 326
Glove manufacture, ii. 163, 164
Glover, Mr., ii. 139
Goal, a magnificent, ii. 115
Goddard, i. 44
Godalming, i. 268, 271, 331, 119, 120, 123, 164, 190, 191, 193, 225, 257, 359, 360, 377; ii. 25, 26, 32, 33, 36, 223, 268
Godmanchester, i. 102
Godschall, i. 395
Godstone, i. 81, 82, 83, 93, 191, 271, 272; ii. 262

Golden Farmer Hill, ii. 244
Goldfinches, ii. 133, 137
Goldsmith, Mr., ii. 262
Gooch, Gaffer, i. 66, 335
Goodlad, ii. 260
Goodman, Thos., ii. 384, 385
Goose Green, i. 272
Goulburn, Mr., ii. 279
Gouldhurst, i. 285, 289, 291, 298
Gourlay, ii. 92, 93, 94
Gosport, i. 243, 255, 304; ii. 263
Græme, Squire, ii. 10
Graham, Sir James, ii. 102, 104, 144, 166, 200
Grain, i. 333
Grange Park, i. 167, 169
Grantham, ii. 346
Gravesend, i. 50
Greame, i. 373
Great Britain, ii. 43
Great Council of Nations, i. 42
Greatham, i. 175, 178, 179, 180, 181, 185
Greek Cause, ii. 269
Greek Loan, ii. 151, 239
Greene, Mr., i. 253
Green Street, i. 326
Greenwich, i. 361
Grenvill, Lord, ii. 286
Grey, Lord, i. 314; ii. 386
Gridiron, prophecy of, i. 66; ii. 161
Grimbald, St., i. 375
Grimshaw, ii. 53
Grimsby, Great, ii. 322, 323
Grinstead, i. 83, 93
Grose, Judge, i. 241, 371
Grosvenor, Lord, i. 187
Grove, near Holt, i. 59
Guilford, i. 82, 102, 113, 115, 116, 119, 123, 193, 272, 231, 359, 360, 362
Gunner, ii. 10
Gunpowder, i. 194
Gunter, ii. 27
Gurney, ii. 11
Guthrie, ii. 241
Guy Fawkes, ii. 236

HABEAS Corpus Act, i. 314
Hadlow, i. 329
Halifax, ii. 360, 361, 362

Index.

Hallett, Mr., ii. 255
Hambledon, i. 170, 173, 174, 175, 177, 204, 261, 268, 271, 360; ii. 10, 223, 254, 257, 262
Hamble River, ii. 247
Hamlin, i. 120
Hammersmith, i. 8, 161
Hampshire, ii. 40, 51
Hampshire Down, i. 2
Hampshire Hills, i. 1
Hampshire Journal, i. 16
Hampshire Petition, ii. 255
Hampton, i. 113
Hampton Court, ii. 296
Hampton Court Park. i. 129
Hanford, Mr., ii. 153, 154
Hannington, i. 20
Hanoverians, ii. 102
Hanson, Mr., i. 394
Harbord, Mr., i. 60
Hardwicke, Lord, i. 99, 100, 288
Hardy, Mr., i. 60, 61
Harewood, ii. 287
Hargham, ii. 53, 290, 293, 300
Harlow, ii. 60
Harleston, ii. 291, 294
Harmony Hall, ii. 116
Harold, King, i. 378
Harrowgate, ii. 362
Harrisburgh, i. 217
Hartley Row, i. 48
Hartswood, i. 343
Harwich, ii. 294, 361
Hascombe, i. 271, 272, 360
Haselmere, i. 23, 120; ii. 25
Hastings, i. 74, 306
Havant, i. 215, 227, 232, 275
Hawkers' licenses, ii. 147
Hawkley, i. 175, 178, 179, 180, 185, 193, 256, 257
Hayden, ii. 170
Hay, Rev., ii. 108
Headley, i. 175, 179, 181, 183, 185, 261, 262, 263
Heckfield Heath, i. 157
Hector, i. 145
Hedingham, i. 281
Hempstead, i. 103, 105, 106, 107, 108, 109, 110, 111
Henry II., ii. 295
Henry III., ii. 248, 252

Henry VII., ii. 178
Henry VIII., ii. 17, 87, 106, 234, 235, 248, 252, 253, 311, 312
Herbert, Mr. John, ii. 195
Herbert, Rev. G., ii. 211
Hereford, i. 24, 29, 102
Hertford, i. 69
Hexham ii. 374, 375, 377, 379, 386
Heygate, ii. 313
Heytesbury, ii. 85, 87, 95, 96, 99, 105, 183
Hibiscus, i. 329
Highclere, i. 6, 8, 43, 60, 157, 164, 172, 175, 331, 379
Highworth, i. 22
High Wycombe, i. 105, 109, 110
Hindhead, i. 120, 123, 164, 174, 177, 178, 179, 181, 183, 184, 185, 215, 218, 220, 225, 257, 262, 309, 360, 378; ii. 10, 174, 268
Hoare, Sir Richard, i. 15
Hobart, Mr., i. 59
Hobey, ii. 349
Hobhouse, i. 189, 294; ii. 152
Hodges, Mr., i. 293
Hodgson, i. 265
Hoggart, Mr., i. 324
Hogsback, i. 82, 331, 362
Holbeach, ii. 308, 309, 315, 324, 326, 334, 345
Holderness country, ii. 324, 326, 328, 346
Holland, ii. 155
Hollest, Mr. George, ii. 5
Hollingbourne, i. 326, 327, 331
Hollis, George, i. 249, 250, 251, 252
Holloway, Mr., i. 74
Hollyhock, i. 329
Holmwood, i. 272, 273
Holt, i. 60, 61, 64, 65, 125
Holt Forest, i. 178, 179; ii. 30
Holthigh Common, i. 281
Home Dale, i. 198
Hone, Mr. William, ii. 211
Honeywood, Mr., i. 55
Honiton, i. 297; ii. 183, 326
Hopkins, i. 280
Hops, i. 258, 259, 260, 293, 326, 330; ii. 158

400 Index.

Horley, i. 211, 271
Horncastle, ii. 318, 319, 321, 337
Horsham, i. 215, 216, 217, 257, 272, 273, 360; ii. 13, 23, 385
Horton, Mr. Wilmot, ii. 294, 320, 336, 361
Hoseason, Mr., i. 384
Hounslow, i. 395
Hounslow Heath, i. 157, 161, 162, 176
Howards, i. 195, 395
Howick, Lord, ii. 387, 388
Huddersfield, ii. 285, 289
Huguenots, i. 352
Hulbert, i. 46
Hull, ii. 320, 322, 324, 326, 327, 328, 329, 336, 360
Hume, Mr., i. 55, 228
Hungerford, i. 164; ii. 181, 183
Hunter, Orby, i. 371
Hunting, ii. 97
Huntingdon, i. 97, 98, 101, 102, 103; ii. 13, 310
Huntley, ii. 142
Hurstbourne, i. 1, 6, 149, 165, 398
Hurstbourne Tarrant, ii. 1, 193
Hurst Castle, ii. 232
Huskisson, Mr., i. 144, 182, 203, 261, 339, 340, 400, 401; ii. 126, 278, 332, 360
Hyde, Mr., ii. 157
Hyde Park, ii. 125, 229
Hythe, i. 297, 305, 306, 307

ILES, Mr., ii. 178
Illinois, ii. 60
Ilsley, i. 42
Immigration into United States, ii. 338
Imprisonment in Newgate, i. 241
Incomes of Bishops and Clergy, ii. 341
Ingram, Mr., i. 88
Ipswick, ii. 291, 293, 294, 295, 296, 297, 298, 299, 330
Irish Tithe Bill, i. 224
Iron Masters, ii. 358
Isabella, Queen, ii. 311
Isis, river, ii. 128
Isle of Thanet, i. 309, 319, 320, 321, 323, 324, 325

Isle of Wight, i. 157, 165, 192, 193, 226, 244; ii. 213, 263, 362
Islington, ii. 238
Itchen Abas, i. 252
Itchen, river, i. 247, 252, 253, 454, 262, 275, 372; ii. 4, 6, 8, 9, 10, 56, 247
Itchen Stoke, i. 252
Ives, S., ii. 301, 307, 310, 334

JABET, Mr., ii. 193
Jacob and Johnson, ii. 93, 94
Jacobins, i. 115, 121, 198, 223, 306, 307, 308
James I., ii. 154, 179, 311
Jefferson, i. 10
Jenkinson, i. 318, 322, 339
Jennets, Spanish, ii. 239
Jesse's "Gleanings," i. 129
Jews, the, i. 318, 401; ii. 45, 177, 183, 197, 202, 315, 331, 336
Jews and jobbers, ii. 108, 109, 180, 181, 222
Jobbers, i. 401
John, King, ii. 213, 234, 295
John of Gaunt, ii. 179
Johnson, Mr., i. 48
Johnstone, Mr., i. 87
Joint Stock Banks, ii. 351
Joliff, Mr., ii. 195
Joliffe, Col., i. 210
Jones, Mr., ii. 41, 42, 323
Jubilee reign, ii. 115, 128, 135, 238
Judges' wigs, i. 226, 262
Judson, Mr., i. 360
Justices of the Peace, ii. 113

KEBLE, John, i. 170
Keines, Ashton, ii. 131
Kemp, i. 87, 88
Kempsford, ii. 178, 179
Kendrick, i. 395
Kennet River, ii. 187
Kensington, i. 11, 24, 48, 49, 68, 71, 78, 93, 103, 105, 113, 116, 163, 206, 275, 279, 325; ii. 13, 32, 71, 103, 110, 161, 212, 240
Kent, ii. 51
Kenyon, i. 289
Kew Gardens, ii. 229
Kingsclere, i. 157, 331

Index.

Kildare Farming Society, i. 11
Kilmston, i. 170, 171, 172, 173
Kiloe Oxen, ii. 375
Kingston, i. 52
Kings Worthy, i. 377; ii. 4, 189
Knatchbull, Sir E., i. 55, 57
Knaresborough, i. 280
Knight, ii. 123
Knighton, ii. 348
Knightsbridge, i. 247
Knights Templars, ii. 235, 236, 237
Knowle, i. 72
Knowles, Mr., ii. 28, 32, 216, 217, 218, 268
Kremlin, The Brighton, i. 92, 93

LABOURERS, Agricultural, ii. 103, 342
Labourers, English, ii. 7, 65, 66, 67, 68
Laing, i. 371, 396
Lambe, Mr., i. 74, 189
Lamberhurst, i. 285, 288, 289
Lancashire, ii. 362
Landlords' distress meeting, i. 69
Landlords, ii. 209
Langford, Little, ii. 130
Lansdowne, Lord, i. 111, 120, 280, 340, 342; ii. 117, 226
Larches, ii. 272
Launceston, i. 73
Lavant, i. 224, 232, 253
Laverstoke, i. 48; ii. 3, 61, 83, 84
Law, New Game, i. 256, 280
Law, New Trespass, i. 256, 265
Le Blanc, Judge, i. 241
Lea, i. 119, 120, 123, 266; ii. 27
Leach, Mr., i. 266
Leech, ii. 27, 32, 268
Leeds, ii. 163, 285, 286, 328, 362, 373
Leeds Patriot, ii. 328, 360, 362
Leghorn Plat, i. 220, 296
Leicester, i. 24; ii. 341, 346, 347, 348, 351
Leigh, i. 329
Leinster, Duke of, i. 11
Leith Hill, i. 218, 257, 273, 309
Leonards, St., Forest, i. 303
Leopold, Prince, i. 324
Lethbridge, i. 235, 335, 336; ii. 55
Letter of the People of Kent, i. 401
Leveringsett, i. 60

Lewes, i. 81, 84, 85, 87, 91, 92, 96, 102, 272
Lewis Express, i. 95
Lexington, ii. 212
Libel, prosecution for, ii. 372, 384
Lincoln, ii. 308, 309, 320, 339, 341, 346
Lincoln Cathedral, ii. 340
Lincoln sheep, i. 303
Lindfield, i. 282
Lingard, ii. 241, 242, 243, 244, 245
Liphook, i. 164, 174, 181, 184; ii. 262, 265
Liston, Mr. R., i. 169
Little Neck, i. 25
Little-Shilling project, ii. 158
Littleton, Mr., ii. 359
Liverpool, i. 340, 387, 400; ii. 82, 336
Liverpool, Lord, i. 8, 10, 38, 54, 62, 209, 224, 225, 233, 266; ii. 127, 158
Local Militia, i. 241
Lock or Locky, i. 29, 30
Lockhart, ii. 5
Locust trees, ii. 120, 121, 128, 227, 228, 230, 272, 273
Locust pins for ships; ii. 29, 31
London, i. 1, 40, 81, 82, 83, 156, 159, 160, 161, 206, 244, 245, 268, 271, 331, 377; ii. 3, 5, 74, 97, 181, 187, 226, 246, 247, 332, 367
Londonderry, Lord, ii. 383
London University, i. 368
Long Arm, i. 187
Long, Mr., i. 120, 172
Long Island, i. 1, 2, 25, 110, 112, 218, 219, 403; ii. 29, 30, 137, 323, 357
Long Parish, ii. 4
Longwood, i. 244
Lonsdale, Earl of, i. 256
Loom, Lords of the, i. 220, 230
Lopez, Sir M., i. 163, 167, 189, 190
Losely, ii. 33
Loudon, Mr., i. 32, 110, 118
Louis, St., of France, ii. 150
Louth, ii. 309, 321, 324, 337
Lowther, i. 120, 189; ii. 286
Loyal and Constitutional Association, i. 115

VOL. II.　　　　　　　　　　　　　　2 C

Lucerne, ii., 169
Luddites, i. 337 ; ii. 79, 80
Ludgershall, ii. 49, 50, 58
Luke, Father, i. 86
Lushington, i. 8
Lyddiard, ii. 118
Lymington, ii. 231, 241
Lyndhurst, ii. 192, 221, 223, 227, 230, 231
Lynn, i. 97 ; ii. 300, 301, 308, 313, 314, 315, 316, 332

MABBOTT, Mr., i. 86
Maberley, Mr. John, i. 42, 161 ; ii. 74, 75
Macculloch, i. 368
Machinery and labour, ii. 80
Mackeen, Judge, i. 217
Maddock, Mr., i. 120, 199, 200
Magdalen Hill, i. 244
Maidstone Gazette, i. 17
Maidstone, i. 72, 151, 288, 308, 325; ii. 326, 369
Malmsbury, ii. 119, 120, 129, 131, 136, 137
Malvern Hills, ii. 153
Malthus, Rev., ii. 57, 77, 80, 113, 128, 239, 241
Manchester, i. 214, 220 ; ii. 82, 91, 103, 108, 163, 271, 360
Mangel wurzel, ii. 269
Mansion-houses, ii. 54, 55, 56, 65, 69, 100
Manufacturing interests, i. 148
Margate, i. 40, 319, 321, 322, 325
Market Ilsley, i. 41
Mark Lane, i. 230, 302, 320
Marlborough, i. 1, 18, 20, 164 ; ii. 50, 58, 181
Marlborough Forest, ii. 369
Marriage Act, i. 200
Massena, i. 214
Martello towers, i. 305, 306, 307, 315
Martyr's Worthy, i. 396 ; ii. 4
Mayhew, Mr., i. 255
Mears, i. 240, 242
Mearstam, i. 210
Medstead, i. 372
Medway River, i. 50, 327 ; ii. 326
Men working as horses, i. 91

Meon-Stoke, i. 172
Merchant of Venice, ii. 224
Merrow, i. 114, 116, 331
Merryworth, i. 325, 327, 328
Micheldever, ii. 363
Micheldever Wood, i. 167
Midhurst, i. 121, 227, 271, 368; ii. 17, 18
Mildmay, Lady, i. 48, 49
Militia clothing, ii. 146, 147, 149
Militia law, ii. 207
Militiamen, flogging of, ii. 303, 304
Milston, ii. 54, 55, 56, 60, 64, 66, 68, 69, 72, 74
Mitcham, i. 279
Mitchell, Judge, ii. 29
Modern Athens, ii. 123
Mole River, i. 199, 343
Molyneux, ii. 33
Monasteries, i. 349
Monckton, i. 321
Montague, Lord, ii. 17, 18
Montefiore, Sir Moses, ii. 177
Moor Park, i. 125, 371, 372
Moore, Sir J., i. 213, 238
Morning Chronicle, i. 75, 89, 120, 229, 230, 236, 376, 390, 399 ; ii. 125, 201
Morning Herald, i. 337
Morning Hill, i. 243, 244
Morning Post, i. 120
Morpeth, ii. 374, 379, 385, 386, 387
Morvan Hills, i. 23
Mosborough, ii. 288
Mosquito Cave, i. 25
Mother Ludlam's Hole, i. 371
Musgrave, Sir R., i. 352
Mulhall, ii. 43, 245

NAAS, i. 11
Nadder River, ii. 87
Nailsworth, ii. 141
Nantz, Edict of, i. 352
Napoleon, i. 314, 338, 397 ; ii. 125
Nash, i. 191
National debt, i. 3, 306, 320, 330
National independence, i. 316
National reform, ii. 156
National schools, i. 289, 290
Needham Market, ii. 293, 297
Needles, the, ii. 232
Nelson's Monument, i. 234

Nether Avon, i. 153; ii. 54, 61, 82, 83
Netley Abbey, ii. 248, 252, 253, 254
Newark, ii. 145, 346
New Brunswick, i. 302, 312, 313
Newbury, ii. 57, 213
Newcastle-on-Tyne, ii. 361, 370, 372, 374, 378, 381, 386, 387, 388
New Forest, i. 204; ii. 30, 217, 225, 229, 231, 237, 239, 241, 243, 248, 261
Newgate, i. 351, 352, 355; ii. 303
New Jersey, i. 181, 266
Newnham, i. 326
New Park, ii. 225, 227, 230, 231
Newport, i. 129; ii. 233
New Trespass Act, ii. 102
New York, i. 187, 319; ii. 59, 323, 324, 338
Nicholls, Mr., i. 58, 123
Nicholson, Peg, ii. 90
Night warblers, ii. 330
Norfolk, i. 3
Norfolk petition, ii. 11, 255
Normandy, i. 56
Northawton, i. 16
North Briton, i. 286
North Chapel, ii. 13, 22
North Cray, i. 168
Northern harvest, ii. 362
Northington Down, i. 129, 168
Northleach, i. 39
North, Lord, i. 59
North Riding, ii. 362
North Tyne, i. 166
Northwood, Mr., ii. 277
Norrington, ii. 87
Norton Bovant, ii. 97, 98, 300
Norwich, i. 57, 59, 67, 69, 349; ii. 290, 295, 317, 333
Norwich Cathedral, ii. 317
Nott, Dr., i. 34
Nottingham, i. 111, 337; ii. 289, 346, 296, 316
Nova Scotia, i. 84, 312, 313

OAKS, ii. 253
Ocksey, ii. 133
O'Connel, Daniel, ii. 187
Ogden, ii. 126, 162
Ogle, Sir Charles, i. 372; ii. 4, 5
Oldham, ii. 360, 370

Old Sarum, ii. 212, 229
Orbiston, ii. 116
Orde, ii. 253
Order in Council, ii. 146, 267
Ospringe, i. 326
Ouse, River, ii. 328
Oux, River, ii. 241, 243
Owen, Mr. Robert, i. 278; ii. 116
Oxford, ii. 173

PADDISON, ii. 321
Paine, Tom, i. 61, 62; ii. 157
Painswick, ii. 142
Paisley, ii. 163
Palmer, Mr., i. 24, 26, 29, 31, 38; ii. 122, 143, 146, 151, 169, 182, 264, 346
Palmerston, Lord, i. 215; ii. 84, 201, 203, 222, 239
Palmerston, Vicountess, ii. 226
Paper money, i. 80, 166, 260
Paris, i. 400
Parnell, Sir H., ii. 350
Parsons, i. 249; ii. 5, 256
Partridge, American, i. 266, 366
Patronage, Church, ii. 341
Paul, James and Thomas, i. 210; ii. 325
Paul's, Cathedral of S., ii. 317
Paulet, Sir William, ii. 248, 252, 253
Paupers, i. 346, 349; ii. 209, 284, 285
Peel, Sir Robert, i. 3, 63, 89, 188, 219, 278; ii. 5, 6, 11, 91, 339, 377, 405
Peel's Bill, i. 276, 279; ii. 43, 220
Penal Code, i. 280
Pencoyd, i. 30
Peniston, John, ii. 320
Pennsylvania, i. 287, 210, 217; ii. 325
Penwood, i. 156
Penyard Hill, i. 25, 26, 37; ii. 264
Percival, Mr., i. 222, 305, 311, 314, 318, 320, 323; ii. 55, 150
Peterborough, i. 335; ii. 301, 307, 312, 318, 336
Peterloo Massacre, i. 187, 214; ii. 91, 92, 108
Peter Porcupine, i. 217
Petersfield, i. 1, 164, 174, 175, 178; ii. 1, 813, 223, 262, 265, 272

Peto, ii. 269
Petty, Sir Wm., ii. 226
Petworth, i. 215, 217, 221, 225, 227, 232, 237, 271, 272; ii. 13, 18, 19, 25
Pevensey, i. 81, 87, 313; ii. 366
Pewsey, ii. 56, 60, 62, 73
Philadelphia, i. 67, 86, 299; ii. 59, 325
Pitchcomb, ii. 142.
Pitsparrow, ii. 330
Pitt, William, i. 21, 59, 82, 111, 114, 186, 222, 224, 305, 307, 312, 318, 320, 323; ii. 9, 55, 113, 128, 135, 150, 157
Plaskitt, Mr. Joshua, ii. 322, 323
Ploughs, swing, ii. 94
Plymouth, i. 120, 129, 387; ii. 41
Poaching Act, i. 280; ii. 102, 206, 209
Pollen, Sir John, i. 152; ii. 201, 216
Ponies, New Forest, ii. 239.
Ponsonby, Mr., M.P., i. 120.
Poor Laws, i. 136, 137, 376; ii. 149, 285, 386
"Poor Man's Friend," ii. 215, 220, 269
Poor rates, ii. 149, 251
Pope, the, i. 38; ii. 235, 236, 364, 365
Population, statistics of, i. 160; ii. 129, 240, 245, 386
Porchester, ii. 263
Portal, Mr., i. 48, 394
Portsdown Hill, i. 173, 224, 233, 234, 255, 264, 275, 304, 310, 313, ii. 255, 263
Portsmouth, i. 174, 204, 237, 361; ii. 232, 247, 262, 263
Portsmouth Harbour, i. 4, 8, 51
Portsmouth, Lord, ii. 4
Portsea, i. 51, 52, 174, 319, ii. 263
Potatoes, i. 108; ii. 371, 372, 380, 385
Poulter, Rev. E., i. 135, 172, 247, 248
Power of Imprisonment Bill, ii. 55, 102, 152, 162
Poyntz, Mr., i. 121; ii. 17, 18
Pratt, Judge, i. 286, 288
Preston, ii. 98, 122, 148, 155, 194, 271

Price, Mr., ii. 151, 153, 157, 170, 271
Prince of Saxe Coburg, i. 122.
Privy Council, ii. 147
Public credit, i. 389
Putney, i. 113
Pym, Mr., i. 23

QUAILS, i. 266
Quakers, i. 210, 217, 230, 233, 264, 302, 317, 324, 342; ii. 11, 107, 109, 110, 258, 260
Quebec, ii. 335, 336

RADICALS, i. 198, 307
Radnor, Lord, i. 319; ii. 120
Rag merchants, i. 17
Raleigh, Sir Walter, ii. 62
Ramsbury, ii. 181, 187
Ramsgate, i. 40, 321
Raspberries, ii. 7
Rathbone Place, i. 352, 357
Rawlinson, i. 252, 253, 374; ii. 16
Reading, i. 162, 163, 164, 335; ii. 126
Redbridge, ii. 237, 247, 248, 256
Redburn, i. 103, 105, 106, 108, 109
Redhill, i. 81, 93
Reeves, i. 115
Reformation, History of, i. 376; ii. 15, 17, 239, 253, 292, 305, 311
Reform Bill, i. 123, 127; ii. 126
Register, the, i. 203, 219, 241, 259, 310, 332, 376; ii. 266, 269, 277, 303, 307, 359, 366, 373
Reigate, i. 23, 191, 198, 206, 209, 211, 213, 226, 234, 268, 272, 307, 310, 326, 330, 343, 348, 351, 354, 358, 395; ii. 34, 156, 262, 268, 272
Republicans, i. 116
Revenues, Royal, i. 262
Revolution, French, ii. 350, 352
Revolution Settlement, i. 3
Rhine, i. 306, 315
Ricardo, i. 64, 122; ii. 140, 151, 156, 190, 194
Rich, Sir R., i. 371, 396
Richard II., ii. 99
Richmond, i. 103, 113
Richmond, Duke of, i. 228; ii. 346
Richmond Park, ii. 229

Ridge, Mr., i. 172; ii. 10
Ridley, ii. 377, 378
Ripley, i. 115; ii. 33, 34, 386, 387
Ripon, ii. 362
Ringwood, ii. 241
Robinson, Prosperity, ii. 162, 195, 247
Rochdale, ii. 360, 361
Rochester, i. 49, 50, 289, 327
Rodborough, ii. 141
Roe, ii. 103
Rogate, ii. 13, 15, 16
Rolvenden, i. 285, 296, 297; ii. 274
Roman Camp, ii. 98
Roman Catholic Emancipation, i. 314, 376
Romilly, Sir C., i. 154
Romney Marsh, i. 297, 302, 304, 313, 320, 321, 325; ii. 366
Romney, New, i. 304, 305
Romney, Old, i. 304, 305; ii. 116
Romsey, ii. 4, 221, 222, 225, 231, 256
Ropley Dean, i. 253, 254, 255, 264, 326, 331
Rose, George, i. 225, 244, 249, 251, 373, 374; ii. 216, 222, 241
Ross, i. 24, 29, 37, 282; ii. 182, 310
Rot, sheep, i. 356
Rottendean, i. 88
Rouen, ii. 50
Rowland, ii. 268
Royston, i. 97, 98, 99
Rufus, Wm., i. 228
Rural police, i. 295
Russell, Lord John, i. 163, 167, 189, 368; ii. 253, 312, 313
Russians, ii. 281
Rustic harangue, i. 132
Ryall, ii. 151, 162, 163, 170, 175
Rye, i. 306
Ryland, i. 24

SALISBURY, i. 10, 16, 18, 72, 73, 102, 152, 154; ii. 54, 58, 60, 69, 83, 85, 87, 93, 97, 130, 257, 300, 369
Salisbury Cathedral, ii. 86, 87, 134, 302, 347
Salisbury, Countess of, ii. 17
Salford, ii. 148

Salt hill, ii. 57
Saltmines, i. 320
Salt tax, i. 153, 319, 320, 321
Sandgate, i. 305, 307
Sandhurst, i. 49
Sandwich, i. 317, 319, 322, 325
Sarr, i. 322
Sarum, Old, ii. 3, 61
Saxthorpe, i. 64
Scamblesby, ii. 321
Scarlett, i. 49, 89, 284, 335; ii. 113, 149, 307
Scotch, i. 104
Scotch Reviewers, i. 107
Scot, Mr., i. 256, 322
Scott, i. 288; Sir Wm., ii. 168, 172
Scrips, Mrs., ii. 190
Sebastopol, ii. 281
Sebright, i. 189
Sedgwick, ii. 146
Selborne, i. 179, 185, 224, 247, 256, 261, 331
Selborne, Lord, i. 224
Selsey, Lord, i. 232
Semaphore, i. 268, 271, 361
Serpentine River, ii. 125
Seven-Oaks, i. 71, 72, 82, 309, 330, 331
Severne, River, i. 24; ii. 151, 153, 160, 310, 326, 351
Severn Stoke, ii. 167
Seymours, ii. 248
Shaftesbury, ii. 321
Shakespeare, ii. 179
Shalborne, i. 43
Shalford, i. 198
Sharncut, ii. 130, 131, 132, 133, 194
Sheep, ii. 153, 170, 174, 175
Sheffield, ii. 285, 287, 288
Shepherd's Bush, i. 111
Sheppey, Isle of, i. 54
Sherburne, ii. 183
Sherwood Forest, i. 129
Shields, The, ii. 378, 379, 381, 386
Shrewsbury, ii. 351, 358, 359, 361
Sibsey, ii. 318, 319
Sidmouth, Lord, 49, 67, 80, 186, 218, 328; ii. 5, 150, 162
Sinclair, Lord, i. 185
Singleton, i. 224, 226, 227, 232
Sittingbourne, i. 53, 325

Six Acts, i. 1, 88, 127, 132, 338; ii. 55, 102, 108, 126, 198.
Slaves, emancipation of, i. 385
Small-note Bill, ii. 10, 40, 41, 45, 47, 282
Smith, i. 111, 246, 401; ii. 128
Smith, Asheton, i. 152; ii. 84, 107, 200, 203, 216
Smith, Sidney, ii. 40
Soberton, i. 1, 172; ii. 256, 257
Southampton, i. 72, 173, 204, 246, 253, 254; ii. 3, 223, 224, 231, 237, 240, 243, 246, 247, 248
Southampton Water, i. 378; ii. 243, 246, 247
South Downs, i. 236, 272, 275, 282, 328; ii. 18, 48, 56, 210, 263, 318, 371
South Sea Bubble, i. 12
Spithead, ii. 248, 263
Stanley, Hon. E. G., ii. 53, 156, 162
Stewart, Lord H., i. 169, 367, 368
Stockbridge, i. 152, 392; ii. 4, 221
Stocks, i. 294, 295, 342
Stoke, i. 72; ii. 4, 189
Stonehenge, ii. 3, 88
Straw plaiting, i. 220, 232, 240, 241, 296; ii. 273
Suffield, Lord, i. 59, 60, 335, 383, 385; ii. 195
Sunderland, ii. 381, 384, 385, 386
Sutton, i. 274, 275, 279, 377
Swift, Dean, i. 125, 371
Swindon, i. 20, 164; ii. 119, 181
Swithin, S., i. 212, 216, 224, 234, 262, 267, 273, 324, 375; ii. 86

TANGLEY, ii. 50, 57
Tarrant, i. 1-6
Taunton, ii. 183, 326
Tavistock, ii. 212
Taxes, i. 17; ii. 103, 300, 338, 344, 352
Taylor, i. 189; ii. 111, 156
Tea, duty on, ii. 109, 110
Tees, River, ii. 387
Teme, River, ii. 160
Temple, Sir Wm., i. 125, 373, 396
Tenterden, i. 285, 296, 298, 301, 324, 328

Test Act, ii. 292
Teste, River, i. 48; ii. 4, 10, 56, 221, 222
Teston, i. 328
Tewkesbury, ii. 153, 170, 173, 310
Treaty of Berlin, ii. 281
Treaty of Paris, ii. 281
Thames, the, i. 332; ii. 128, 176
Thetford, ii. 293, 294, 301
Thimble and Cowhide, ii. 187, 188
Thing, the, i. 22, 30, 301; ii. 227, 350, 352
Thompson, Mr., i. 371, 396
Thomson, Poulett, ii. 337
Thornley, ii. 312, 313, 314
Thornton, i. 368
Thursley, i. 174, 177, 180, 186, 216, 262, 268, 274, 359, 369; ii. 13, 19, 24, 26, 28, 31, 223, 261, 267, 268
Thurstan, Abbot, ii. 302
Thurtell, ii. 35
Thwaites, ii. 48, 49, 194
Tidworth, i. 152; ii. 200, 203
Tierney, i. 189
Tilford, i. 124, 330
Times, The, i. 89, 96; ii. 266, 384, 385
Tinkler, i. 395
Tisted, East, i. 255, 256
Titchbourne, i. 170
Titchfield, i. 237, 275; ii. 255, 256
Tithes, i. 133, 144, 223; ii. 87, 97, 113, 165
Todmorden, ii. 361
Tolls, i. 200
Tomline, Bishop, i. 251, 371
Tooke, John Horne, ii. 212
Tooth money, ii. 230
Tooting, i. 206
Torrington, Lord, i. 328
Touche, Robert de la, i. 11
Townhill Common, ii. 246
Traveller, The, i. 89, 96, 97
Trevor and Potatoes, ii. 384, 385
Tring, ii. 272, 274, 276, 279, 281, 284
Trotten, ii. 16, 17
Trowbridge, ii. 79, 105, 116
Truck or Tommy system, ii. 352, 353, 354, 355, 356, 359
Tubb, Mr., i. 152

Index.

Tucky, Mr., ii. 179, 180
Tull, Mr., i. 32, 45, 106, 267; ii. 184
Tunbridge, i. 40, 71, 72, 308, 325, 329, 379; ii. 262, 326
Tunbridge Wells, i. 281, 283, 285
Turkeys, i. 348
Turks, ii. 230, 281
Turner, Jas., ii. 199, 200, 201, 203, 204, 216
Turner's Hill, i. 272, 282
Turnour, ii. 23
Turnpike Acts, i. 200
Tuscany, ii. 273, 275
Tweed, River, ii. 388
Twickenham, i. 113
Twopenny trash, i. 242, 301
Twyford, ii. 16, 17
Tyne Mercury, i. 16
Tyne, River, ii. 375, 376, 379, 386, 387, 388

UCKFIELD, i. 81, 83, 84, 93
Uly, ii. 142
Unitarians, i. 263, 350, 355, 358; ii. 292
United States, ii. 43, 46
Upavon, ii. 62, 73
Upham, i. 242, 243
Uphusband, i. 6, 8, 15, 47, 113, 132, 146, 149, 152, 154, 162; ii. 3, 4, 10, 49, 57, 213, 214, 221
Up Park, ii. 261, 272
Upping-blocks, ii. 176
Uppington, ii. 88
Upsheet, i. 322
Upton Gray, i. 128
Upton Level, ii. 79, 105, 151
Upwaltham, i. 227, 229, 231, 232
Usury, ii. 177, 259
Uxbridge, i. 111

VANSITTART, Right Hon. H., i. 55; ii. 16
Vagrant Act, ii. 106
Verulam, Lord, ii. 117
Vicarages, Parliamentary returns respecting, ii. 129
Victory, The line of battleship, i. 48
Vines, ii. 281
Virginia, ii. 60

Virginia Water, i. 161
Voltaire, i. 19
Vortigern, ii. 179

WADDINGTON, Mr., i. 289
Wages, Agricultural, ii. 68, 250, 251
Waithman, Sheriff, i. 247
Wakefield, ii. 286
Walker, Mr., i. 56
Waller, Mr., i. 53, 325, 326
Walmer, i. 317, 318
Walter, Mr. Jno., ii. 384
Waltham, i. 72
Waltham Chase, ii. 256, 260, 261
Walton Heath, i. 279
Wansdike, i. 15
Ward, i. 120
Ware, i. 97, 98
Warminster, ii. 79, 85, 87, 89, 95, 96, 97, 99, 103, 105, 106, 110, 113, 115, 116, 130, 173, 183, 300
Warner, Mr., ii. 255, 257
Warnford, i. 172
Warwick, ii. 153, 310
Washington, General, i. 317
Waterloo, Battle of, i. 104, 223, 269, 400; ii. 124
Watford, i. 103, 105
Watson, Mr. Joshua, i. 290, 291, 292
Waverley Abbey, i. 124, 371, 396
Wear River, ii. 387
Weavers, ii. 105, 265, 266, 267, 268
Webb Hallites, i. 54, 76, 77, 84, 88, 91
Webster, i. 78
Well, i. 128
Wellington, Duke of, i. 158, 338, 377; ii. 55, 124, 209, 279
Wen, the, i. 52, 57, 71, 81, 92, 97, 103, 176, 180, 206, 209, 215, 228, 236, 245, 255, 261, 273, 279, 283, 295, 308, 321, 330; ii. 34, 66, 67, 82, 83, 123, 129, 161, 165, 180, 183, 272, 297, 331, 334, 347, 349
Wendover, i. 110
West, Mr., ii. 216
Westborough Green, i. 219
Westbourn, i. 232, 233
Westbury, ii. 79, 110, 116
West End, i. 175; ii. 223, 257

408   *Index.*

Westerham, i. 308, 329, 330, 331, 332
Western, Lord, i. 278; ii. 158
Westminster, ii. 212
Westminster Abbey, i. 8, 324; ii. 135
Weston, i. 24, 25, 33, 37, 99; ii. 223, 240, 246, 249, 252, 254, 256, 261, 270, 369
Weston, Mr., i. 115, 184, 203; ii. 33, 158
Westphalia, i. 33
Wetherspoon, Mr., ii. 212
Weybridge, i. 225
Weyhill, i. 15, 118, 132, 150, 151; ii. 49, 193, 194, 198, 199, 215, 257
Wey River, i. 119, 125, 225, 257, 360; ii. 268
Wheat, i. 341, 345; ii. 191, 275
Wherwell, i. 146
Whig oligarchy, i. 36
Whigs, ii. 211, 385
Whitchurch, i. 24, 47, 48, 167, 377, 379, 393, 394, 395, 397, 398; ii. 4
Whitbread, i. 156, 189
Whiteflood, i. 243
Whitehall, i. 224, 301, 316, 332, 333; ii. 105, 127
White, Rev. Gilbert, i. 3, 186, 224, 256, 257, 377
Whitlock, General, i. 213
Whitney, i. 39
Wickliffe, ii. 351
Wilbarton, ii. 332
Wilberforce, i. 189, 284, 287, 299
Wilbraham, i. 316
Wilkes, Judge, i. 286
William the Conqueror, i. 378; ii. 239, 240, 241, 243, 244, 295, 302
Willis, Under-Sheriff, i. 250
Wilmot, ii. 295, 337, 361
Wilson, Sir R., i. 23, 297; ii. 211, 212
Wilton, ii. 145
Wiltshire, ii. 51
Wiltshire, Earl of, ii. 253
Wimmering, i. 234; ii. 263
Winchester, i. 102, 113, 125, 128, 131, 136, 140, 154, 165, 167, 173, 178, 239, 243, 244, 246, 254; ii. 4, 9, 134, 201, 208, 299, 241, 244, 255, 312
Winchester, Bishop of, i. 212

Winchester Cathedral, ii. 302
Winchester, Marquis of, ii. 253
Windham, Mr., i. 82, 369
Windsor, i. 207
Windsor Park, i. 129, 159, 161, 176, 289; ii. 229
Winnall, Mr., i. 31, 32
Winnington, Sir Thos., ii. 160, 162, 173
Winstan, ii. 173
Winterborne Stoke, ii. 88
Winter, Sir Thos., ii. 155
Winterton, Lord, ii. 22, 23, 24
Wisbeach, ii. 301, 308, 312, 313, 314, 326
Wishford, ii. 88
Witchcraft, i. 281
Withers, i. 59
Withington, ii. 173, 176
Witney, ii. 173, 177
Wittersham, ii. 261, 274
Woburn, ii. 312
Wodehouse, Colonel, i. 384
Wodehouse, Mr. Edmund, ii. 12
Wolseley, Sir Chas., ii. 380
Wolsey, Cardinal, ii. 296
Wolverhampton, ii. 351, 352
Wonston, ii. 4
Woodchester, ii. 141
Woodcote, ii. 1
Woodhay, East, ii. 190
Woodhay, West, ii. 190
Woodlands, The, i. 6; ii. 272, 273, 381
Woodman, ii. 182
Wood, Mr. John, ii. 53, 155, 162, 274
Wood, O., ii. 98
Woods and Forests, i. 262; ii. 227
Woodward, i. 86
Wool, ii. 332, 359
Woolmer Forest, i. 175, 179, 181, 261, 262; ii. 29, 30
Wooton Basset, ii. 118, 119
Wooton Rivers, ii. 58, 69
Worcester, ii. 153, 154, 157, 160, 162, 164, 167, 173, 182, 310, 326, 337
Worcester Cathedral, ii. 157
Worth, i. 23, 81, 84, 93, 176, 199, 201, 206, 211, 213, 215, 272, 279, 281, 282; ii. 13, 121
Worthing, i. 40, 360

Wrecklesham, i. 124, 126, 128
Wright, Mrs., i. 280
Wright, Rev., i. 247, 248
Wriothesleys, ii. 253
Wycombe, High, i. 110, 111
Wye River, i. 25; ii. 183
Wykham, i. 383
Wykham, William of, i. 372, 374, 375
Wyly River, ii. 87, 89, 90, 93, 369
Wymondham, ii. 294
Wyndham, Sir Wm., ii. 19, 21
Wynn, Rt. Honble. C., i. 185
Wysihicken, i. 2, 3

YARMOUTH, GREAT, i. 67
Yarmouth, ii. 232, 336
Yelverton, ii. 290
Yeomanry troops, i. 150; ii. 90, 152, 162, 266
Yew trees, i. 129, 257
York, ii. 285, 338
York, Duke of, i. 114, 213
Yorke, i. 288
York Place, i. 49
Yorkshire hills, ii. 362
Yorkshire reformers, i. 335
Young, i. 43, 242; ii. 191

THE END.

Printed by BALLANTYNE, HANSON & Co.
Edinburgh & London

www.ingramcontent.com/pod-product-compliance
Lightning Source LLC
Chambersburg PA
CBHW022115290426
44112CB00008B/682